FROM SUFFRAGE TO A SEAT IN THE HOUSE

From Suffrage to a Seat in the House

The Path to Parliament for New Zealand Women

JENNY COLEMAN

OTAGO UNIVERSITY PRESS
Te Whare Tā o Te Wānanga o Ōtākou

Published by Otago University Press
Te Whare Tā o Te Wānanga o Ōtākou
Level 1, 398 Cumberland Street
Dunedin, New Zealand
university.press@otago.ac.nz
www.otago.ac.nz/press

First published 2020
Copyright © Jenny Coleman
The moral rights of the author have been asserted.

ISBN 978-1-98-859226-8

A catalogue record for this book is available from the National Library of New Zealand. This book is copyright. Except for the purpose of fair review, no part may be stored or transmitted in any form or by any means, electronic or mechanical, including recording or storage in any information retrieval system, without permission in writing from the publishers. No reproduction may be made, whether by photocopying or by any other means, unless a licence has been obtained from the publisher.

Published with the assistance of Creative New Zealand

Editor: Gillian Tewsley
Indexer: Lee Slater

Cover: *Behold! She stands at the door and knocks*. William Blomfield, 1866–1938, H-712-009, Alexander Turnbull Library, Wellington

Printed in China by Asia Pacific Offset.

CONTENTS

- 7 **ACKNOWLEDGEMENTS**
- 8 **ABBREVIATIONS**
- 9 **INTRODUCTION**
  Showing 'my lady' to a seat
- 15 **CHAPTER 1**
  Passionate philosophical parliamentary debates, 1852 to 1893
- 47 **CHAPTER 2**
  The logical conclusion to female franchise, 1894 to 1896
- 79 **CHAPTER 3**
  Serving their political apprenticeship, 1897 to 1910
- 125 **CHAPTER 4**
  The full privilege of citizenship, 1911 to 1919
- 171 **CHAPTER 5**
  Petticoated candidates, 1919 to 1933
- 237 **CHAPTER 6**
  Our first lady member, 1933 to 1935
- 275 **CONCLUSION**
  The 'ungallantly long hesitation'
- 281 Glossary of political terms
- 285 Timeline of significant political events, 1835 to 1935
- 289 **APPENDIX**
  Women members of the New Zealand House of Representatives, 1933 to 2019
- 293 'When the ladies get their rights'
- 297 **NOTES**
- 329 **BIBLIOGRAPHY**
- 335 **INDEX**

ACKNOWLEDGEMENTS

First I would like to thank my academic colleagues for their enthusiastic responses to my 'work in progress' sessions at various Women Writing Away retreats. This book is only a part of what many of them were expecting, so I humbly request their patience as I continue to research and write on women's struggle to achieve a voice in Parliament. I am enormously grateful to the anonymous readers who engaged with several very different manuscripts and whose generous suggestions have resulted in the emergence of this book. It has been an absolute pleasure to work again with Rachel Scott and with Vanessa Manhire and the team at Otago University Press; I could not ask for a more professional and supportive publishing experience. Thanks too to Gillian Tewsley for her invaluable assistance with editing.

I am grateful for the support I have received toward research for this book, particularly during my research sabbatical in 2017, from the Office of the Pro Vice-Chancellor, College of Humanities and Social Sciences at Massey University.

I would like to acknowledge the support I have received from the following institutions: Alexander Turnbull Library; Archives New Zealand; Auckland Libraries Heritage Collection; Canterbury Museum Library; Christchurch City Libraries; Massey University Library; National Library, in particular the Papers Past and Parliamentary Papers online archives; New Zealand Electronic Text Collection; New Zealand Parliament Historical Hansard online archive; Ngā Taonga Sound and Vision; Parliamentary Library, Wellington.

Finally, I would like to thank my partner Mary Nettle for putting up with many months of lost opportunities to play together in the garden or walk in the bush while I retreated to my study to write.

ABBREVIATIONS

AJHR	Appendices to the Journals of the House of Representatives
ATL	Alexander Turnbull Library
JAJLC	Journals and Appendices to the Journals of the Legislative Council of New Zealand
JHR	Journals of the House of Representatives
MHR	Member of the House of Representatives
NCW	National Council of Women
NZPD	New Zealand Parliamentary Debates (Hansard)
WCTU	Women's Christian Temperance Union
YMCA	Young Men's Christian Association
YWCA	Young Women's Christian Association

INTRODUCTION

Showing 'my lady' to a seat

> But everybody that was anybody knew that votes for women meant, rather sooner than later, seats for women, elected with precisely the same wisdom and unwisdom that sent men to parliament. And the only thing any epitomising historian in the far future will note as surprising about New Zealand's conduct in the matter is its ungallantly long hesitation to show 'my lady' to a seat. — MATANGA, 16 September 1933[1]

'I would like to warn honourable members, however, that women are never satisfied unless they have their own way'[2] – so announced Elizabeth McCombs, the first woman elected to the New Zealand Parliament, in her maiden speech on 28 September 1933. Her words encapsulated decades of dissatisfaction and effort on the part of women to achieve full electoral citizenship. During those years there had been patchy support for the cause from male politicians, notably from James Wallis who, in 1878 as a recent convert to the cause of women, announced to his male colleagues in the House, 'I think it would be wise and statesmanlike for us to raise ourselves above prejudice, and declare that in future women shall not suffer from electoral or political disqualification.'[3] But it would be another 15 years before women could vote in general elections, a further 26 years before the Women's Parliamentary Rights Act 1919 was passed, which entitled women to be elected as members of Parliament, and 14 years after that when Elizabeth McCombs proudly took her seat in Parliament. *From Suffrage to a Seat in the House* tells the story of how women achieved the right to stand for parliamentary election and their struggle to take a seat in the New Zealand House of Representatives.

Women's exclusion from Parliament dates from the New Zealand Constitution Act 1852, passed by the British Parliament, under which any person who qualified as an elector also qualified to be elected as a member of the House of Representatives. However, at that time the franchise was restricted to males aged 21 and over who owned property and who were registered to vote. Barring women from Parliament, both as voters and as elected representatives, was a denial of the basic right of women to share the same political rights and privileges as men. The journey to full parliamentary citizenship for women in New Zealand was marked by constant prejudice and debate, slow shifts in public opinion and small hard-won gains. But opportunities to chip away at long-held prejudices arose many times during the nineteenth century in debates on liquor licensing, educational reform and marriage law reform. The spectre of women in Parliament was raised as an anathema during debates on women's franchise, often as a deliberate ploy to undermine support for the franchise. Of the women's suffrage bills presented during the 1880s and early 1890s, four contained clauses that specified women's eligibility for parliamentary election and, of these, two were clauses that explicitly barred women from being eligible to stand for a seat in the House. As Chapter 1, 'Passionate philosophical parliamentary debates, 1852 to 1893' outlines, although the legal right for women to stand for parliamentary election was encompassed in the wider campaign for women's suffrage, it was generally considered a political expediency that could be, and was, sacrificed for the 'greater' goal of the franchise.

Once women's suffrage was achieved, the immediate priority was the upcoming general election and ensuring as many women as possible exercised their right to vote. Murmurings in some quarters of women increasing their political influence through direct representation in Parliament caught the ear of receptive male politicians. Over the next three years Alfred Newman and George Russell each presented bills to the House that aimed to remove women's political disabilities[4] and admit women to Parliament. Women who had been active in the suffrage campaign made use of their extensive networks to garner support for these bills, and many small-scale petitions were sent to Parliament to validate women's demand for greater parliamentary rights. Some Māori women went a step further: they organised a hui and formed their own parliament for Māori women.

When Kate Sheppard, the recognised leader of the women's movement, returned to New Zealand from England, women's efforts to have a more coordinated national political voice culminated in the establishment of the National Council of Women of New Zealand (NCW) in 1896. As the face of the organised women's movement, the National Council of Women embodied a renewed energy and commitment to furthering women's influence and engagement in the political sphere. Chapter 2, 'The logical conclusion to female franchise, 1894 to 1896' discusses the parliamentary debates around the various bills presented during this period in the context of the ongoing activism of women for the right to be admitted to Parliament.

Like the Women's Christian Temperance Union (WCTU), the NCW pursued an ambitious agenda for social and political change across a wide range of issues affecting women and children. However, despite being dubbed the 'Woman's Parliament', the NCW struggled for recognition as the voice of New Zealand women. Their task was made even harder after they lost two of their key supporters in the House, who were reportedly punished for their support for women's admission to Parliament: both Newman and Russell lost their seats in the 1896 general election.

During these years, the NCW was arguably too inward facing: their focus was on educating women within the movement on political matters through publications such as *White Ribbon* and the WCTU pages in *The Prohibitionist*, and at their regular meetings and conventions, rather than attempting to effect change in wider public opinion. Members of the NCW faced persistent charges from politicians that they represented the demands of only a small body of social and political extremists, as well as indifference from many women, including some who were active in the women's movement. They devoted their energies to issues such as repeal of the contagious diseases legislation, raising the age of consent to engage in sexual intercourse, prison reform, and attempting to increase women's participation in civic life by lobbying for women's representation on various boards and in roles such as jurors and justices of the peace. While supporters continued to argue that women's admission to Parliament was the next logical step from the franchise, the bills introduced to the House during this period focused on the removal of women's civic and political disabilities. Chapter 3, 'Serving their political apprenticeship, 1897 to 1910' charts the attempts during these years to pass legislation for women to participate fully in the government of the country.

The push for women's increased participation in civic and political life gained momentum in the years leading up to and during World War One. Debates over the nature and function of the Legislative Council intensified, amid suggestions that women's appointment to the Upper House might be a more appropriate place for them to engage in the workings of government. As women heeded the call to assist with the war effort, new employment opportunities opened up for them – in patriotic societies and in the fields and factories. The Women's National Reserve, launched in August 1915, invited women to register for employment in professional and clerical work, farming, shops, factories and domestic employment.[5] In March 1917 the National Efficiency Board was set up to investigate ways of improving efficiency and productivity during the wartime period, with a specific remit to look at the question of women in the workforce.

As women's civic citizenship increased, so too did support for their full political citizenship. Moves to enact this, however, risked being overtaken by political posturing around parliamentary protocols and principled debates about the constitutional rights and privileges of the respective Houses of Parliament. Chapter 4, 'The full privilege of citizenship, 1911 to 1919' traces these debates that culminated in the passing of the Women's Parliamentary Rights Act 1919.

As with the Electoral Act 1893, which provided for the female franchise, the Women's Parliamentary Rights Act 1919 was passed very close to a general election. Several women's names had already been put forward as candidates, and three women stood for parliamentary election in 1919 – all of them in the province of Auckland. The editor of the Christchurch *Press* commented: 'It seems curious that Canterbury, the New Zealand home of the women's franchise movement, should put forward no women candidates for Parliament, but possibly the local aspirants are waiting to see first how their sisters in the north fare at the hustings.'[6]

For the next four elections the number of women aspirants was, in the words of one commentator, 'extremely, not to say strangely, modest'.[7] Three women stood for election in 1922, one in 1925, five in 1928 and two in the 1931 general election. Chapter 5, 'Petticoated candidates, 1919 to 1933' tells the stories of these early unsuccessful women candidates. In the lead-up to the 1925 general election *NZ Truth* noted that 'petticoated candidates are still regarded by party secretaries as sheer luxuries'.[8] But with each election women became more involved and, by the 1928 general election, women candidates were 'peeling off their written notes with a professional gesture',[9] while others took to the soapbox and spoke on street corners on behalf of candidates, chaired large public meetings, supported male candidates and even embraced the role of heckler.

Views were mixed as to why women did not succeed in these early elections. General prejudice against women was certainly a large component, but apathy on the part of women in general was another reason. Emily Maguire, the unsuccessful Reform candidate for Auckland East at the 1928 election, was openly critical of the many women's associations in Auckland who prided themselves on the fact that they had no connection with politics: some women, she said, seemed to think that the movement for women in Parliament lowered the standard of womanhood and that such views were holding back women's success. Speaking to a meeting of the League of Penwomen shortly after the 1928 election, Maguire railed that, 'until the women of all parties united in some sort of political movement to raise the status of their sex and to give them a better idea of politics there was no hope of any woman going to Parliament in New Zealand'.[10] At the final meeting for that year for the Auckland branch of the NCW, members commented that if women voters had wholeheartedly supported their candidates they would have been elected; some suggested that if women candidates had not allied themselves to party politics, they might have received more support from women voters; and others believed it was simply because the right candidates had not yet stood.

On 2 August 1933, highly respected Labour member for Lyttelton Jim McCombs died suddenly. Seven days later his widow Elizabeth McCombs was confirmed as the Labour candidate for the by-election necessitated by her husband's death. Despite various political manoeuvrings, Elizabeth successfully contested the by-election and made history by becoming the first woman to sit as a member in the New Zealand House of Representatives. Chapter 6, 'Our first lady member, 1933 to 1935' follows her journey on the by-election trail and in Parliament. Her maiden speech, delivered at the low point of the Great Depression, exemplified the political ethos that would underlie her passionate contributions to parliamentary debates throughout her historic but short-lived career as the first woman member to take her seat in the House.

From Suffrage to a Seat in the House draws on many sources. The institutional record of women's struggle for equal political rights and privileges is contained in *New Zealand Parliamentary Debates* (*Hansard*). The parliamentary debates reveal only one side of the story, however. Before the mid-1880s there were a few individual women and men who, privately and publicly, pressed for women's political rights. From the mid-1880s various women's organisations emerged that enabled a concerted and focused effort to effect political equality between men and women. They include the Franchise Department of the WCTU, the various social and political leagues that were established initially in Canterbury, Wellington, Auckland and Whanganui, and the National Council of Women of New Zealand, which became the political voice for New Zealand women for a decade. Along with the papers, minutes, newsletters and conference proceedings of these various organisations, the persistent and prolonged efforts by activist women to achieve political equality are evident in their private correspondence. Newspaper reports, articles and letters to the editor provide further insights and perspectives on campaigns for women to have a voice in Parliament. Together, these sources reveal a determined, if somewhat protracted struggle to achieve a seat in the House.

CHAPTER 1

Passionate philosophical parliamentary debates, 1852 to 1893

All progress is mainly the erosion of prejudice and prepossession. Progress is mainly achieved by developing social sentiment, and if you can appeal to the women of a country such as this, if you can get them into this Chamber and their voice can be heard here, your progress will be more permanent, more rational, and more beneficent than it has been in the past under the regime of men. — HONOURABLE SIR JOHN FINLAY, MHR, 26 September 1919[1]

Towards responsible and representative government

The signing of the Treaty of Waitangi and the proclamation of British sovereignty over all New Zealand in 1840 marked the beginning of Aotearoa New Zealand's long journey from a country in which sovereign power and authority rested with hereditary Māori chiefs and tribes to becoming an independent political democracy. Along the way, New Zealand's government shifted from being a dependency of New South Wales to a separate Crown colony in 1841, a self-governing colony from 1853, a dominion from 1907 and, while it was still part of the British Commonwealth, finally achieving legislative independence from the United Kingdom with the adoption of the Statute of Westminster in 1947. There were many milestones on this journey, such as the passing of the New Zealand Constitution Act in 1852, the beginning of responsible government in 1856, the introduction of Māori electorates in 1867, universal suffrage for men in 1879 and for women in 1893, women's right to stand for Parliament in 1919, and their right to sit in the Legislative Council from 1941.

During the period of colonial government from 1840 to 1854, New Zealand was ruled by a governor who represented Queen Victoria. But the majority of the settler population had experienced the Westminster system of Parliament, which was based on regular elections, politicians representing defined constituencies, political parties competing for power that was attained through gaining a majority in the House, and a Parliament consisting of a speaker, a prime minister overseeing a cabinet, and regulated by rules of procedure. This early period of government aimed to achieve 'responsible government' – a system of government that embodied the principle of parliamentary accountability: the government is formed by appointing ministers who have been elected as members of Parliament, and it remains in power only if it retains the support, or confidence, of the majority of members of the House of Representatives. At times such as the passing of the Budget, this support may be tested through a confidence vote. Ministers are responsible to Parliament both on an individual level through the performance of their portfolios, and collectively in the overall performance of the government.

The New Zealand Constitution Act of 1852 made representative government possible through a General Assembly that comprised the governor and two houses of Parliament. The Upper House, known as the Legislative Council, comprised members nominated by the governor, whereas the Lower House, the House of Representatives, comprised members elected in a general election. The Act provided for six elected provincial governments that were subordinate to the General Assembly, each presided over by a superintendent.

The first general election was held in 1853 and the first elected representative government of New Zealand met in Auckland in 1854. But members of the Executive Council of the governor were permanent appointees rather than elected representatives, and the governor, who was answerable to the Imperial (British) Colonial Office, controlled the Legislative Council, which meant that while this was a representative government, it was not responsible government. Responsible government would require the Executive Council to be appointed from among elected members of the House of Representatives, the governor to act only on the advice of the Executive Council, and the Executive Council to have the confidence of the House.

Responsible government was achieved in 1856 under Premier Henry Sewell when, for the first time, a ministry was responsible to the House of Representatives. While this established the principle of parliamentary accountability, the independence of the provinces meant that the decisions of provincial governments often had more effect on the day-to-day lives of the population than the decisions made by the General Assembly of the central government. Government ministries tended to be based on small cliques, usually of provincial groupings or special interests, and personality clashes were frequent. These groupings comprised unstable alliances that provided a temporary majority, which meant that governments tended to remain in power for only a short duration. Provincial jealousies, coupled with the dominance of the South Island provinces, meant that central government during this provincial period showed little consideration of the interests of the country as a whole. Several premiers of the time characterised it as little more than a 'disgraceful' and 'gigantic scramble' for public money,[2] and historian Keith Sinclair described it as 'a confused competition of cliques which coalesced into so-called "parties", or disintegrated as expedient'.[3]

From the passing of the Constitution Act in 1852 through to the late 1870s when New Zealand's political systems were being established, electoral issues were the subject of frequent and ongoing debate. A series of reforms proposed through numerous bills culminated in the enactment of universal male suffrage in 1879. In the interim, bills had been presented to extend the suffrage to goldminers, freeholders and leaseholders, lodgers and ratepayers. The secret ballot was adopted, changes to the registration of electors and the conduct of elections were enacted, and separate Māori electorates were established. Each of these measures had implications for women's parliamentary rights in terms of female suffrage and the eligibility of women to stand for parliamentary election. Throughout the debates many philosophical questions were raised. Was participation in parliamentary processes a right, a privilege or a trust? Could men adequately represent women's interests or were men and women essentially different with different outlooks and priorities? Was it possible or even desirable for men and women to be considered equal or were women and men best fitted for different spheres of influence? And, rhetoric aside, did women *really* want to participate in parliamentary decision-making?

A right, a privilege or a trust?

Just before the dissolution of Parliament in 1870, Premier William Fox introduced a bill relating to the regulation and conduct of the election of members to the House of Representatives and of superintendents and members of provincial councils. The proposed legislation concerned how these elections would be run, rather than who could vote or who was eligible to stand for election. During the debate it was claimed that the franchise was not a right but a trust; indeed, it was 'a public trust placed in the hands of an individual', and the only 'natural right' of the members of a community was to be well governed.[4] Others insisted that the franchise was a right; but if that were so, it should be extended to every man and every woman, whether they desired to exercise that right or not. If, on the other hand, the franchise was a privilege, it should be extended to women only if there was a demonstrable demand by women that they desired a voice in Parliament. As one member of the House of Representatives put it, 'it would be a disgrace to us in this country, or to any other country, to wait till the women are placed in a position of having asked for a privilege which by right they ought never to have been denied'.[5]

Attempting to avoid this 'vexed question as to whether the franchise was a right or a trust', Edward Stafford, who had been defeated as premier in June 1869, insisted there was a certain amount of trust involved given the franchise was not enjoyed by every adult, but that even if the franchise was a right, it was one which society 'gave' to certain persons.[6] But rights, by definition, are not given; a right is an inherent and irrevocable entitlement. Privileges, on the other hand, are granted, usually as a reward and are often conditional on types of behaviour. A question that frequently arose in the franchise debate was why an ignorant and corrupt man should have the right to vote, and yet that right be denied to an intelligent and educated woman. Underlying this question was a challenge to the basis on which society granted rights and privileges to men and women.

The meaning of the term 'universal suffrage', and whether it even encompassed female suffrage, was raised. There was a glaring discrepancy in the fact that, from 1867, some women in New Zealand had been granted the municipal franchise, which meant women who were ratepayers could vote in local council elections, yet women continued to be excluded from the electoral franchise, which meant they could not vote in public political elections. There was a growing sense of the unfairness of women not having a voice in the decisions that affected their daily lives, particularly those who were property owners and ratepayers.

When it came to issues such as alcohol licensing or representation on school committees, there was broader consensus on the appropriateness of women's right to exercise an active role in decision-making. However, even in these debates it was claimed that women were not interested in the privilege of voting or for a more active role in politics, and that to grant those privileges would bring women into conflict with their husbands.

An important step toward women being able to hold representative positions came in 1876 with the passing of the Municipal Corporations Act. This Act entitled women who owned property and were ratepayers to vote and to stand in local body elections. The number of women who owned property increased after the Married Women's Property Act 1884[7] was passed, and this further highlighted the double standards of electoral rights between men and women. But was there really any need for women to have a say in local or national government, given that their husbands or fathers had legal control over their affairs and could make decisions on their behalf?

Can men represent women's interests?

One of the strongest and most influential advocates in the nineteenth century of the need for women to have legal, social and intellectual independence was English philosopher and politician John Stuart Mill. Mill's *The Subjection of Women*, published in 1869, argued that the legal subordination of women to men was holding back the improvement of society as a whole. This influential book was instrumental in the 'conversion' of many men and women to the cause of women's rights. One convert was surgeon, scholar and politician James Wallis, who emerged during the 1870s as a strong voice in the New Zealand Parliament advocating on behalf of women. Described as 'a man of unusually vigorous character, and possessed of remarkable intellectual powers',[8] Wallis was elected as an Independent candidate to represent Auckland City West in 1877 and held that seat until he was defeated in the 1881 general election. During his first term of office, Parliament was debating a bill to legalise the marriage of a man to his deceased wife's sister.

Wallis considered the bill to be the proverbial 'bad penny' – although it had been 'kicked out' on many occasions there were members of the House who continued to bring it up. Wallis opposed the bill, which he considered 'injurious to the children, injurious to the deceased wife's sister herself, and injurious to the interests of society'. His larger concern, however, was what the bill epitomised in terms of society's attitudes toward, and treatment of women, which went against a growing tide of change. In an impassioned speech to the House he declared that in past legislation women had been treated cruelly, unfairly and unjustly, and that the law still regarded them as 'an inferior and servile class'. Women, he asserted, were still deprived of the rights and privileges that were given to all other human beings. Sensing a mood for change, he spoke of the 'strong social current' that 'something should be done to emancipate women from their present unfair position' and 'be placed in a better legal position than they now occupied'.[9]

Wallis was not alone in thinking that part of the problem was that supporters of the Deceased Wife's Sister Marriage Bill 1877 were legislating 'simply as men' without regard in any possible degree to the feelings of women who had no practical voice in this legislation.[10] Proponents of this view believed that when women had a more practical voice in the election of members to the House, they would have an opportunity to consider candidates' views on such matters and take that into account when they cast their votes. But importantly, some members thought that the House was not justified in legislating on an issue such as the marriage of a man to his deceased wife's sister until women had a substantial voice in the legislation. Colonel George Whitmore, a member of the Legislative Council, went so far as to say that the bill under discussion was 'inopportune and cowardly' because, above all, this was a woman's question.[11] Whitmore maintained that women trusted men to make laws for them but that men had betrayed that trust by introducing a bill for women that men would not introduce for themselves.

In 1869 Mary Ann Müller, an early feminist, asserted that women in New Zealand were 'a wholly unrepresented body of the people'.[12] Writing in secret and under a pseudonym because her husband, who was prominent in civic affairs, held rigid views on the impropriety of women showing an interest in political issues, Müller expressed confidence that supporters of women in Parliament would 'step forth and fight the good fight for those fettered weak ones who can only think and suffer'.[13] One such supporter was Alfred Saunders, who had served in the Nelson Provincial Government before being elected to Parliament. From as early as 1843 he had publicly advocated for the extension of the franchise to women in New Zealand. Saunders had known Müller when she resided in Richmond and suspected she was behind the correspondence in the newspapers under the pseudonym Fémmina but, respecting her wish for anonymity, had used his discretion and had no direct correspondence with her on the matter. In her pamphlet 'An Appeal to the Men of New Zealand', Müller held that the franchise was a natural right that had been denied to women. Her appeal was 'to the common sense of New Zealand men – of New Zealand law-givers'[14] to grant women the right to vote, even though 'its possession would amount to but a fractional power in our government'.[15]

Although many women would not necessarily have shared Müller's view that women were 'wholly unrepresented', throughout the 1870s and 1880s there was, as Wallis had described, a growing tide of public opinion that men's and women's views were sufficiently different for it to be increasingly undesirable and, indeed, impossible for men to adequately and responsibly represent women. The 1870s and 1880s were years of profound social, demographic and political change in New Zealand. Massive immigration led to a doubling in population. Extensive public works schemes resulted in the construction of roads, bridges and public buildings, and the country was opened up with 1100 miles (1770km) of railway and 4000 miles (6440km) of telegraph lines, as well as steamship services. Although these public works were generally considered to have been achieved without waste and mismanagement, some were ill advised and contributed to a public debt of 20 million pounds.

The abolition of the provincial system of government in 1876 and the emergence of strong central government, along with a prolonged economic depression, meant that Parliament was being shaped by new forces. Government retrenchment and foreclosures by banks and mortgage corporations meant that, 'for many, the 1880s was a decade of abject misery and poverty, characterized by low wages and poor working conditions for those with jobs, and unemployment and soup kitchens for those without'.[16] Local concerns and personalities were still important but national issues increasingly took centre stage.[17]

The 1890 general election marked a shift in the political landscape. The long depression and the bitter maritime strike in 1890, in which seamen and watersiders were defeated because longterm unemployment meant labour was easy to acquire, had the effect of uniting small farmers, would-be farmers, farm labourers and the urban working class against the politically dominant pastoralists. This alliance of rural and urban interests, with the support of Independent Labour members of Parliament, resulted in the election of the first Liberal Government, led by John Ballance. Based on a belief that 'the state had a duty to secure the welfare of its less fortunate citizens',[18] the Liberal Government embarked on an ambitious scheme of social and economic legislation that included land reforms, graduated taxation, regulation of work in factories, the introduction of old-age pensions, and legislation to advance the health and education of the nation.

With the suffrage movement in 'full swing',[19] by 1891 even opponents of women's rights conceded that, if it was necessary for women to take an active role in politics to ensure their wants and needs were properly legislated for, they could not allow those wants and needs to be looked after by men: 'She must herself be on the floor of this House in order to give utterance to the wants of women.'[20] But this declaration by Henry Fish, an opponent of women's rights, during the suffrage debates was intended only as a tactical move to influence members of Parliament with moderate views who might concede to women's suffrage but who would not accede to women taking seats in Parliament, and who might therefore be induced to vote against the Female Suffrage Bill under discussion at the time.

The principle of perfect equality

In the various debates on women's participation in public and political life that ensued across the latter half of the nineteenth century, three main trends of opinion emerged: conservative views that opposed any change to women's 'natural' sphere of influence in the domestic home; moderate views that accepted a limited extension of women's influence by way of franchise based on property ownership; and radical views that 'demanded the immediate, total emancipation of the female sex'.[21] In

August 1878 James Wallis ensured that the radical view was thoroughly aired in Parliament by placing several questions to the attorney-general on the parliamentary Order Paper. Wallis asked was it 'lawful in New Zealand, as it is in England, for a man to sell his wife, or to beat her in moderation, or to imprison her in his house; and, if the law here sanctions such doings, to what extent beating (in moderation) and imprisonment can be carried without breaking the law?'[22] In the attorney-general's absence, the minister of justice responded in a jocular and sermonising manner. Circumventing a response, the minister pointed to the parliamentary protocol of only presenting questions that referred to matters of public policy or to measures that were currently before the House.

The following day Wallis's motivation for posing the questions became apparent. In a long speech that elaborated on the ways women were wronged in respect to their employment, education and the marriage contract, he moved a far-reaching resolution: 'That in the opinion of this House, the electoral disabilities of women should be entirely removed, and that the same political rights and privileges be granted to women as to men.'[23] Confident of receiving an impartial and candid hearing from his parliamentary colleagues, even though some might consider his opinions 'heretical' or 'impracticable', Wallis explained that the principle that underlined his motion was 'that the two sexes are equal, and therefore that it is wrong to give one sex rights and privileges which are withheld from the other'.[24]

Along with other supporters of women's rights, Wallis had been greatly encouraged by recent redresses of some of the wrongs against women: female ratepayers in towns had been granted the municipal franchise; in the counties, women had been granted the county franchise and the right to be county councillors; female ratepayers could sit on education boards; and recent laws provided some protection for married women's property. But to Wallis, these measures were piecemeal, and politicians needed to have the courage to put the two sexes on an equal footing. Importantly, his speech systematically presented and countered the usual arguments put forward to deny women equality with men: that women were inferior to men; that the Bible sanctioned the inferiority and subjugation of women to men; the general prejudice that women should not 'interfere' in politics and public affairs; that women were already represented by their husbands; and that women were not interested in politics. Wallis was adamant that 'our rights are irrespective of sex. Our rights belong to us as human beings, and not as men and women'.[25]

To Wallis, the issue was simple: the ideal of a Parliament is that it should reflect the political opinions of the country; 'by excluding women from the public and political sphere we deprive ourselves of the benefit, politically, of half the social forces of the community'.[26] In his speech he drew attention to the large amount of evidence that women were as capable as men in the political sphere, and he pointed out that history had shown that where women had an opportunity to exercise political power they had generally used it with remarkably good sense. In his view, it was now time to declare that in future women would not suffer from electoral or political disqualification. He maintained that class and race prejudices scarcely existed in New Zealand, and neither should sex prejudices.

Parliamentary protocol was used to block the measure. Immediately after Wallis's motion had been seconded, Attorney-General Robert Stout took the floor to protest it was unheard of to bring forward a motion of this nature when there were bills dealing with the subject before the House.[27] In Stout's view, 'affirming any general resolution of this character, can give no value whatever to it'.[28] Instead, the real fight should take place when the two electoral bills currently before the House were discussed.

Wallis was not prepared to withdraw his motion but, having firmly established women's political equality on the agenda, he agreed to adjourn the debate. A parliamentary reporter observed that when he began his speech there were only two ladies present in the gallery, and there were none by the time he had finished. The following week when debate was due to resume, the member for Invercargill Henry Feldwick held that the question Wallis had raised was already prominently before the House by the government's Electoral Bill and it was a serious matter to keep members in attendance longer than necessary 'discussing mere abstract questions' when there was practical business at hand.[29] Feldwick called for a division and Wallis's motion was spectacularly defeated by 44 votes to eight. This use of parliamentary protocol to stifle efforts to achieve parliamentary rights for women, and to treat such issues as cause for derision, were a constant feature in Parliament.

'Person' includes female

In July 1870 when several resolutions were moved to extend the electoral franchise, the member for Mongonui [sic] Thomas Gillies suggested that substituting the word 'person' for 'male' may be a convenient means of getting around concerns about whether the franchise should be entrusted to women. Over the years variations of this semantic tactic re-emerged. The Women's Suffrage Bill 1887 introduced by Sir Julius Vogel, for example, proposed to add 'and female' after the words 'every man' in relevant clauses of the Qualification of Electors Act 1879. If passed, this would have had the effect of extending the electoral franchise to all women, Māori and non-Māori, and it would have meant women were eligible for election to the House of Representatives. Sir Julius Vogel was a known supporter of women's rights who, some years earlier, had commented in a letter to his friend, women's advocate Mary Ann Colclough: 'When one thinks of some of our clever mothers, and our duffers of young brothers of 21, it seems just foolish that the former should have no say in the affairs of the nation.'[30] Around the time he introduced the Women's Suffrage Bill, Vogel was about to embark on writing his novel based on a future world in which women held all of the major political positions.[31]

When introducing the second reading of the Women's Suffrage Bill 1887, Vogel asked the House to consider whether there was any reason why women should be excluded from the exercise of the franchise and from sitting in the Legislature. In his view, if women possessed the franchise and could enjoy the rights of sovereignty, they should be entitled to a share in the general government of the country. To support his argument, he suggested there were issues that came before Parliament on which it would be very useful to have women's input, and he specified 'such measures as those affecting the sanitary condition of the people, education, and so forth' and 'all matters of a social character'.[32]

At the beginning of the parliamentary session in May 1888, a petition organised by Kate Sheppard and signed by the secretary and treasurer of the Franchise Department of the WCTU was sent to Sir John Hall. A former premier with a long background in provincial and central government, Hall was a man of acute intellect, recognised for his enormous capacity for work and as a master in the art of political tactics; 'a more skilful general of the Woman's Franchise Parliamentary forces could not have been found or desired'.³³ Hall was in regular correspondence with Sheppard over many years. The petition in 1888 proposed that when the Electoral Bill came before the House an amendment be made to one of the interpretation clauses to substitute 'person' for 'male'. Hall was asked to present the petition on behalf of the Franchise Department and to move the amendment when the Electoral Bill was being debated. He acceded to both requests.³⁴ The Franchise Department posted a copy of the pamphlet 'Ten Reasons Why the Women of New Zealand Should Vote' to every member of the House of Representatives in the hope of swaying the minority who were not favourable, to sympathise with their project. Unfortunately, the pressure of parliamentary business meant the Electoral Bill was not brought up during that session.

At its fourth annual meeting in February 1889 the WCTU discussed further the implications of the semantics of 'person' and passed the recommendation: 'That, believing that the right of a citizen should not be denied or abridged on account of sex, Convention be urged to appeal to Parliament that in the New Electoral Bill, soon to be brought before our Legislature, the word "person" be understood to include both sexes.'³⁵ As he had promised, Hall moved an amendment to this effect in August 1891 when the Electoral Bill was in committee.³⁶ The following year when the Electoral Bill 1892 was before the House, the Interpretation clause included that '"Person" includes female.' This drew an extended discussion in the national temperance magazine *The Prohibitionist*, in which it was observed there was 'a grim suggestiveness … which will speak volumes to the future historians of the emancipation of women'. The writer pointed to the inference that until that time a woman was not a 'person' in the eyes of the law and, as she was not a person, 'she must necessarily have been a "thing"', and added, 'Now, "things" are possessed and owned, can be taken up and put down, and we shall not be abused on any stretch of imagination when we say that there are still many men who regard woman as a thing created solely for the pleasure of man.'³⁷

The article observed that although the Electoral Bill permitted women a voice in electing law makers, 'it very decidedly debars her from becoming one herself'. Women may have been removed from the list of aliens, rogues, vagabonds and other persons not entitled to vote, but they were explicitly prohibited from being allowed to be elected to the House of Representatives.

The writer added, 'We do not suppose that there is one woman in the Colony desirous of a seat in the General Assembly; but we scarcely see the necessity of expressly prohibiting women from being nominated.' She closed her article with the remark, 'To have become "persons" is a great step. The translation from "things" to rulers might have been too much.'[38]

'Woman's Parliament is her home'

The use of 'person' rather than 'male' was central to the Electoral Bill that had been introduced in August 1878 by Stout. The government-sponsored bill consolidated a wide range of measures around who was eligible to vote and how they could exercise that vote, and granted every person enrolled on a ratepayers roll the right to vote in the election of members for the House of Representatives and the right to stand for election to the House of Representatives. Stout was fully aware of the significance of the latter provision. To his knowledge, no bill had ever been introduced to any Parliament that gave privileges as wide as those proposed here: any woman who was a ratepayer would be entitled to be placed on the general electoral roll and to be elected as a member of the House. But for many who opposed the bill, the provisions for women were secondary to the real issue at hand, which was the extent to which Parliament was prepared to legislate for universal male suffrage. In the words of one member, 'a taste of female suffrage' was intended simply as some sort of compensation for the restriction of manhood suffrage and was, effectively, 'a kind of by-play while the main performance is going on'. This member believed that 'Nature ordained that women should not take part in public life' and considered it would be a 'social calamity' to politicise women. He asserted that 'Woman's Parliament is her home, and it is within that sphere that her function lies for making laws for our peace, order, and good government.' He argued that if woman was transferred from the domestic sphere to the political sphere, she would be spoiled for both: 'A woman who becomes a member of the Legislature would be, I think, the wrong person in the wrong place, just as much as any one of us would be if called upon to take charge of nurseries, or to try to imitate those womanly charms and refinements which civilize and ennoble mankind, and which woman, domestic, not political woman, is alone able to exercise.'[39]

During parliamentary debates members often asserted that it would be impossible for women to discharge the duties of the House without sacrificing their home duties. In the words of one member, 'I will not call upon women to do work which Nature did not intend them to do; and until we have considerably reformed the proceedings in this House it would be absurd and cruel to ask women to take part in these duties.'[40] The member for Eastern Maori, James Carroll, was opposed to women's suffrage: he believed it would have the effect of making women unwomanly. He espoused the conservative view of many of his colleagues: he would not encourage women's presence in the House but he did not think they could withhold that right if women were granted the primary step of the franchise. He admitted to being 'one of those who think that the fitting and proper place for woman to exercise her functions is round the hearth, is within the domestic circle, bringing up her family, in the household ... But I think if you put women out of their place ... if we allow them to exercise the privileges and functions of men, they will lose their charm, they will lose that modesty which surrounds them, they will lose that surrounding of womanliness which endears them to our minds.'[41] This view was based on the premise that not only were men and women essentially different, but the proper functioning of society necessitated the preservation of separate spheres – metaphorically and physically – for men and women.

The House is his castle

The counterpart to woman's Parliament being her home was that Parliament had always been a privileged male space and men were not prepared to envisage it as otherwise. For many, this manifested as a refusal to take the prospect of women's parliamentary rights seriously. Aware of this when he moved the second reading of his Women's Suffrage Bill in 1887, Vogel admonished those members who were so sceptical that they refused to view women's parliamentary rights as a legitimate and serious question; he charged some of his colleagues with having gone so far as to supply themselves with 'books of anecdote and facetiousness' in order to air them during the debates.[42] But even some members who were supportive of women's franchise made light of the added prospect of women being admitted to the House. One member suggested that one of the main reasons for not admitting women to the House was because men should not stand on equal terms with them. He described the scenario of the first lady elected to Parliament rising to address the House, and his male colleagues being so intoxicated on the occasion that 'if she were to talk the greatest twaddle that has ever been talked in this House' they would agree with her every word and vote with her without hesitation.[43]

One member who opposed female suffrage, let alone the admission of women to Parliament, admitted to being 'astonished and startled' at how little notice the House seemed to take of the logical consequence of granting women the vote. While professing alarm, he could not take seriously the prospect of a man contesting an election with his wife; he claimed that instead of coming to the House to legislate, men would be left at home to look after the babies and, 'instead of carrying Bills through the Legislature, would be engaged in carrying their little "Bills" about the nursery'.[44] For this member, women taking a seat on a Roads Board was one thing but the presence of women on the electoral roll of this House 'would be productive of mischief, and not of good'. He believed it was not natural, that women did not have the physical fortitude, that they would be susceptible to the coercion of men, and that it could not be expected they would ever 'take a position in the front rank'.[45] Others were more open to the prospect and treated it as an experiment of sorts. One suggested: 'Why should we not try the experiment? We are trying all sorts of experiments – experiments in steam, in telegraphy, in what not. The whole of our life is one great experiment, and it only depends upon how you work it out whether it is a success or not. Let us try this experiment.'[46] But the women Henry Manders had canvassed in his Wakatipu constituency were opposed to being represented by one of their own sex on the municipal or county councils, let alone in the House of Representatives. Confident in the workings of parliamentary procedure, Manders stated, 'I do not think the warmest advocates of women's rights would have them take seats in this House, and that, no doubt, is a point which will require amendment in Committee.'[47]

Those who could not accept women's full involvement in parliamentary processes could often muster no real arguments of substance to support their position. One member who argued strongly that all women should be extended the electoral franchise, insisted equally as strongly, 'The logical outcome of my argument would be that they should have seats in this

House. I object to it. If there were no other argument against it, I would use the argument that it would be inconvenient. That is a sufficient argument.'[48] Some asserted that women would be a distraction, particularly if they were beautiful ladies; and one member asked, 'But what is to become of the unmarried men of this House, who are to be handed over to the tender mercies of a party composed of unmarried women? Talk about pressure, log-rolling, and asking for roads and bridges! If ten or fifteen good-looking ladies were elected to the House by large constituencies, and adopted the plan of putting pressure upon the Government or upon private members of the House, political purity would disappear.'[49] Another claimed that honourable members would be so distracted by the presence of ladies in the House they would not pay so much attention to the affairs of the colony, and he facetiously suggested that, 'If the honourable gentleman in charge of this Bill would introduce a clause providing that only plain women should be allowed to come into the House, I think the source of danger would be removed; but if any beautiful ladies were sent to this House I am quite sure they would lead astray the tender hearts of some honourable gentlemen, particularly the elder members of the House.'[50]

One member was prepared to support the ratepayers' franchise but was not ready to admit that, because a woman occupied the highest position in the British Empire, this meant it would be appropriate to have female members in the House of Representatives – 'not that they would not conduct themselves wisely, decorously, and well, but their agreeable presence would, I fear, prolong the sessions greatly'.[51] But others suggested the opposite, that 'if we had women here we should get through our business much more quickly, we should act in a more refined manner' and 'behave ourselves better in the lobbies'.[52]

In 1879, recently elected member for Hokitika, Liberal politician Richard Seddon said that although he was very fond of the ladies, he was not prepared to give them the electoral franchise: 'The ladies are all very well in their place.' He expected arguments on their behalf to be made by bachelors and men married to strong-minded women, but thought 'All domestic felicity would be destroyed, once the ladies commenced to dabble in politics.'[53] Another member said that although he had a very high appreciation of the 'fair sex', he thought they would be 'altogether out of their place at the polling-booths, and also in this House'.[54] Others drew attention to the fact that there were times when the gallery needed to be cleared due to the nature of the discussions in the House; women might become members of the House and even become judges but, in hearing cases that men deemed not suitable for women's ears, 'the influence for good they now exercise would be weakened, perhaps lost, by their taking man's coarser work upon themselves'.[55] But as one member pointed out, why uphold women's refining influence on the one hand, yet deny them the opportunity to exercise that influence where it was most needed?

Temperance advocate and veteran politician Alfred Saunders regularly corresponded with Kate Sheppard on the progress of the various suffrage and electoral bills. Saunders was a strong and influential speaker in the House. Although he was an Independent, his political sympathies were closely aligned to Liberal philosophies, yet he was equivocal on the prospect of women sitting in Parliament. He thought if women sat in the House in an equal position with men, male politicians would not be able to discharge their duty to their constituents as they would not be able to bow to their female colleagues as was expected between men and women in the usual order of social etiquette. He did, however, think that if women were to be given the electoral franchise for a period, Parliament may find it desirable to have an Upper House comprised of women 'to revise our proceedings'.[56]

Thomas Tanner, the Independent member for Waipawa, had been thinking about the practicalities of women in Parliament. He believed women's presence would have a civilising influence on the debates and would check the manner and the content of male members' discourses but, he said, 'if you got a lady on the Government side and another on the Opposition side I think the debate might assume a very interesting but at the same time a very alarming character'.[57] Tanner did not elaborate on the 'alarming character' of the imagined debate but his comments were followed by claims and counterclaims of women's capacity or incapacity to sit as members. One member who admitted to having 'not a very heavy weighted brain' said he understood it was an acknowledged fact that a woman had, on average, five ounces less brain than a man; had she had five ounces more than a man she may have been some use in Parliament.[58] His comments were typical of the flippant nature with which many men in Parliament approached issues of women's influence in the House.

Henry Fish called it 'a species of insanity to talk of ladies being admitted to this Parliament to guide the destinies of the country', and he talked up how men would be helpless but to insinuate themselves to please women in the debating chamber.[59] To prove his point that it would be 'absolutely ridiculous' to have women members, he suggested women might even bring young babies into the House and then need to pass them to their male colleagues to nurse while they spoke.[60]

As these debates resurfaced, some members in the House became more entrenched in their views while others were increasingly prepared to give serious consideration to extending women's participation in the political sphere. One of the strongest speeches in favour of women entering Parliament came from the member for the City of Dunedin, Richard Oliver, who in 1879, along with Premier John Hall and Colonial Treasurer Harry Atkinson, expressed strong views as to 'making the House the real reflex of the opinions of the community – a representative body in the truest sense'.[61] Oliver, who had first-hand experience of the actions of public women in England, was sure that 'this House would lose nothing by the presence among them of half a dozen of these women'. He did not think that women were likely to become members of the House if they were granted full suffrage but, if they did, at the least the tone of the debates would be elevated.

The principle of the franchise

By the time Hall introduced the Female Suffrage Bill 1890 he considered it politically expedient not to specify in the wording of the bill women's eligibility to sit in Parliament. The operative clause stated, 'For all purposes connected with and having reference to the right of voting in the election of members of the House of Representatives, words in Acts providing for the representation of the people importing the masculine gender shall include women.'[62] Hall played this as a master tactic because the principle of the franchise, as it had operated until that point, was that a person who may exercise the electoral franchise was eligible for election to Parliament. When introducing the bill, he was silent on that point; he spoke instead of his personal belief 'that woman is entitled to be placed on a perfect equality with man', but said that, as the House was in the closing days of the session, in the interests of expediting the bill he was prepared to take the 'half loaf' approach and settle for the electoral franchise.[63] In the debate that ensued, only Saunders referred to the issue of women being elected as representatives by saying he had 'far too much faith in the thorough good sense of women' to believe they would soon agitate for seats in Parliament on being granted the franchise.[64] But Thomas Tanner felt compelled to point out that without some restriction of the franchise to the power of voting alone, giving women the franchise would put them in the position, if they desired it, of being able to become a candidate and of being elected to the House of Representatives.

Not all members assumed that the principle of female franchise extended to the right of women to sit in Parliament. James Carroll expressed the view that if it was considered right for women to vote at a general election, that right would be limited to voting and not extended to women representing themselves in the House of Representatives. But he declared a total disinterest in the Female Suffrage Bill 1891 because it did not propose to extend the franchise to the women he represented as the member for Eastern Maori. His primary concern in the debate was that, 'if it is fair, if it is right, for the women of the European race to exercise the franchise at the general elections of this colony, I claim also that it is perfectly right and perfectly just that the same privilege should be enjoyed by the Native ladies – by the women of the soil, by the children of the country'.[65]

Until women demonstrate they want this

A constantly reiterated claim was that there was no clear evidence that women desired the level of political participation proposed in the various electoral and suffrage bills. Indeed, it was often asserted the opposite was true: women trusted their male representatives to make decisions in their interests; women were content to fulfil their roles in the domestic sphere; and, even if the laws did allow women to vote and stand for election, they would not be inclined to exercise these privileges. It was conceded that there were a few women who desired a role in politics, but they were considered a minority and were not representative of women in general.

In 1869 when Mary Müller was arguing for women to be granted the franchise, her assumption was that, if granted, it would be based on property ownership, as was male franchise at the time. By her reasoning, not many women would meet the criteria and, of those who did, not many would choose to exercise the right. She did not see that at that time there was any demand on the part of women for a greater role in the political affairs of the colony: 'As to the *bête noir* of women sitting in Parliament with men, rely upon it there is scarcely a woman in New Zealand who would desire or consent to do so. It is a bugbear, an absurdly exaggerated view of a new notion taken by men whose intellect must be as weak as it is intolerant.'[66] But Müller did signal that although women might not be likely to call any great female convention or form a society for the promotion of female suffrage, women's interest in taking part in the government of their adopted land 'will grow apace, enlarging the scope of their ideas, and in time changing entirely the habit of their thoughts'.[67] Contingent on men giving women scope, the next steps were for women to harden their minds by the principles of reason and 'make good strides in the noble race for knowledge – knowledge of all kinds tending to the welfare of the community, and some knowledge of and share in the Government of our country'.[68] Müller shared the correspondence between herself and John Stuart Mill about her pamphlet with Kate Sheppard, and told her how she had been encouraged by Mill in her work towards recognition of women's rights to full citizenship.[69]

Several weeks before the publication of Müller's pamphlet, her contemporary Mary Ann Colclough wrote an article under the pseudonym Polly Plum, 'What have women to do with politics?' In the article she admitted that although it was a matter of common fairness for women to achieve the franchise, she was not particularly anxious that votes for women be allowed. Married women, in her view, did not need an active share in politics because they could generally influence their husbands. But she saw no reason why women who were engaged in the world as householders and taxpayers, and therefore liable to seizure for debt, should not be able to share an opinion along with all the other privileges accorded to men in such positions. She strongly avowed that, 'the argument that women are quite unfit for politics is nonsense', and insisted that 'Some of the best and most able sovereigns the world has known were women.'[70]

Colclough had read Fémmina's pamphlet and agreed that it was 'an injustice, and really a relic of barbarism' to withhold the right to vote from what she referred to as 'self-helpful women', but said she would be sorry to see the day when women occupied the position of men and 'men ceased to show us the chivalrous devotion, the protecting courtesy, that real manly men feel bound to accord to women as the weaker vessel. I shouldn't feel at all compensated for such a change by being allowed to be myself a lawyer, a doctor, or even a member of Parliament. I don't want to be any one of these things, and I don't believe any true woman does.'[71] By the time Colclough took to the public platform for the first time to lecture on women's rights in June 1871, she expressed a more radical view. She maintained that the vote should be extended to all married women and that the drunken behaviour exhibited by many men at elections was a bitter satire on men's boasted superiority. By 1873, she confidently announced she believed the time would come when women would be eligible to fill any office in the church or state.

For some men and women, however, opinion on women's participation in political affairs was much slower to change. Speaking at the annual soirée of the Dunedin YWCA in 1880, the president of the Dunedin YMCA, Mr John Aitken Connell, said he 'considered that the modern attempt to put women in Parliament had a degrading tendency', and he thought only 'a very small proportion of the women of the Colony desired to be politicians'.[72] The most vociferous voice in Parliament promulgating the view that women did not want a voice in Parliament continued to be Henry Fish. When the Women's Suffrage Bill 1890 was before the House he admitted that there were a few earnest women who were doing a considerable amount of good work through organisations such as the women's Christian associations and Good Templars, but he absolutely denied there was any desire on the part of women for the privilege of the franchise.[73] Even with evidence to the contrary, as in 1871 when a petition signed by 1140 men and women in favour of women being eligible to vote in relation to liquor licensing was presented, or when women stood for election on school committees, opponents continued to assert that until it was clear that women collectively desired full electoral rights, there was no point in Parliament even discussing proposed legislation.

Some activist women had definitely heard the message: at the annual meeting of the WCTU in February 1891 members were advised not to place much confidence in members of Parliament who declared themselves in support of women's suffrage, as many of them had said they would not support the measure until a majority of women asked for it. The WCTU noted an inherent double standard: men's political education, for the most part, did not begin until after the privilege of citizenship had been extended to them, and they had not seen any good reason proffered as to why women should be any different.[74]

The scene was set for women to demonstrate once and for all that they desired, and demanded, equal political rights. Various women's organisations had already begun to mobilise. 'Hints to the Franchise Superintendents of the Women's Christian Temperance Union' included contributing articles in reply to any reports in daily newspapers on women's franchise; influencing literary or debating societies to discuss the question; and asking parliamentary representatives and other influential people who were in support of electoral reform to present public addresses.[75] In Whanganui a public meeting for women interested in women's franchise resulted in a committee being formed to organise signatures for a petition to both houses of Parliament asking for the franchise to be extended to women. Fish's assertions prompted women in Otago to organise petitions; one in Balclutha collected 83 signatures, and another was signed by all but two of the women living in the Catlins district. It was reported in the local newspaper that the petitions were prepared and signed 'without any suggestion or assistance from the other and more privileged sex' and that 'Even Mr Fish must now be convinced that they do wish to be placed on the same footing as men so far as political rights are concerned, and having taken definite action in the matter they mean to gain their point.'[76]

Small-scale local petitions, however, were not sufficient proof for the likes of Fish, and in late January 1891 he requested that the premier formally canvass the opinions of women over the age of 21 through a 'plébiscite' to accompany the upcoming census. The registrar-general advised that this would not be feasible: it would add considerable cost in taking the census, would be difficult to arrange as enumerators had already been employed under contract, and would pose logistical difficulties because of the large bundles of papers necessary. Importantly, too, it would set a precedent that could motivate other lobby groups such as those advocating Bible-in-schools or temperance. Not prepared to let the matter rest, when the Female Suffrage Bill was before the House in August 1891, Fish repeatedly questioned the veracity of signatures on a petition presented by Hall that had been signed by 9000 adult women – at that point the largest petition ever laid before Parliament. But Fish had another tactic up his sleeve. He had already placed several amendments to the bill on the Order Paper with the intention of delaying, if not scuttling the legislation. One amendment proposed that every woman who was registered as an elector should be qualified to have a seat in the House.[77] This proposed amendment put Hall in the awkward position of needing to explain: 'That is not asked for by women. I do not think it is expedient at present. That is not the question before us at present. Let us confine ourselves to the question before us.'[78] In the to and fro that followed, Fish insisted that the only reason he proposed the amendment was on legal advice that it was necessary to make the bill legal.

Fish was not alone in attempting to seek a clearer mandate for such a major constitutional change as women being eligible to take a seat in Parliament. James Carroll asked his colleagues, 'Why should we here – seventy-four of us – in this House, who have not been returned by the people on this question – this question was not fought out at all last election … why should we, immediately we get here, attempt to grapple with and deal with a matter altogether foreign to anything that occurred during the elections … I think it is not fair to the women of the country that we should arrogate to ourselves the intelligence we profess to have of what their real feelings are on the matter. We do not know.'[79]

Some members voiced contradictory thoughts on women's desire to sit in Parliament. Liberal member for Wallace, James Mackintosh, for example, did not think women would ever seek to take part in 'the turmoil of Parliament' even if granted that privilege, and they would continue to vote for male candidates even if women became eligible for parliamentary election. But he believed that women would get accustomed to the idea of sitting in Parliament and that 'many of them would be able to take part in the proceedings of this House quite as well as we can'.[80] However, as Richard Taylor, Independent member for Sydenham pointed out, the presence of so many women in Parliament's galleries when the various franchise and electoral bills were under discussion was evidence that they did take an active interest in the proceedings of the House. Moreover, if the premier (Ballance) was 'honest, fair and true when he talks about the women of the colony having the same voice in the government of the colony as the men, he will in a few days, or months, allow the ladies to go, at any rate, to the Upper House'[81] where they would have the opportunity to veto or amend legislation passing from the House of Representatives. Taylor added, 'I trust the Premier will not take offence when I tell him I am afraid he is not sincere in respect of this subject, because the logical result of granting to women the franchise must be that every woman who has the right to vote should have the right to offer herself as a candidate for election to Parliament, and a right to ask the Government to introduce women into the Upper Chamber of this colony'.[82] Taylor took exception to Hall's claim that women did not want the right of election to Parliament; he personally knew of 10 or 12 women across the country who were anxiously waiting for the opportunity to be nominated for appointment to the Legislative Council, and he advised the premier to avail himself of the chance to nominate two or three of them to that Chamber.

The Female Suffrage Bill 1891, having passed a second reading in the House with a majority of 25 votes, proceeded to committee – where there was an immediate move to use the spectre of women holding seats in Parliament to stifle the bill's passage into law. This came in the form of an amendment moved by anti-prohibitionist Liberal member for Taieri, Walter Carncross, who had voted against the second reading of the bill. His amendment read: 'Every woman registered as an elector shall be qualified to be elected a member of the House of Representatives for any electoral district.'[83] Thus, by an 'exceedingly adroit move' by 'a strange combination of enemies to the franchise and friends who were sticklers for logical legislation',[84] this had the calculated effect of encouraging those who did not support the bill to vote for the amendment. The amendment passed by a majority of six votes and, with Carncross readily admitting his intention was to kill the bill in the Legislative Council, it passed its third reading and proceeded to the Upper House. At the request of Hall, James Fulton read a telegram received the previous day from Kate Sheppard addressed to the Speaker of the Legislative Council, which stated: 'On behalf of the ten thousand women who petitioned the Council, permit me to urge that honourable Councillors will not deny our request because of alterations made in the Women's Suffrage Bill by its enemies in the Lower House.'[85]

Introducing the bill in the Legislative Council, Fulton, husband of the Dominion president of the WCTU Catherine Fulton (née Valpy), said there was apparently cause for alarm in the minds of some people that if women were granted electoral rights they would go further and claim the right to a seat in the House of Representatives. To those 'tremblers', he offered the advice of Lady Harberton[86] that no one could enter Parliament until they were elected, and that no woman could be elected until she offered herself for election. Fulton added, 'Women do not ask for political rights in order that they may govern; they ask for it in order that they may not be misgoverned.'[87] Others were not so sure. One member said anyone who had been following events over recent years knew there was no doubt that the result of the franchise would be the appearance of women in Parliament, and another suggested that Fulton was 'almost childish'[88] in suggesting women would not offer themselves for seats in Parliament. Another member thought granting the franchise might be an effective means of postponing the day when women would take seats in either house. Some held that if the bill was passed in its present version, in all fairness women should be admitted to both houses, whereas others said this part of the proposed legislation had never been fully debated and the only benefit to be derived for the Legislative Council to pass the second reading would be to ensure the bill returned to the Lower House for this clause to be debated in a more considered fashion. As in the Lower House, there were members who freely admitted they had not treated the bill as a serious measure and had used the opportunity to describe farcical scenarios of women sitting alongside men in both chambers. Although it was evident, only one member suggested on the record that the bill had been sent to the Legislative Council 'for the express purpose of casting on us the odium of rejecting it'.[89] Unsurprisingly, the division on the second reading of the bill in the Upper House was lost and the bill was deferred for six months.

Political expediencies

When the bill remerged on the Order Paper as the Women's Suffrage Bill 1892, sponsored by Sir John Hall, the clause granting women the right to sit in Parliament had been omitted. As the government had resolved to support the inclusion of the female franchise in the Electoral Bill, Hall considered it expedient to support the government measure and the Women's Suffrage Bill 1892 did not progress beyond the first reading in the House. In moving the second reading of the Electoral Bill 1892 on 1

July, Premier John Ballance explained, 'We have left out what might be considered a part of woman's franchise – namely, that they should become members of this House,'[90] and he noted that, while that provision had been carried in the previous session of Parliament, it was not carried by the friends of the measure. Although he professed his personal support for women entering Parliament, Ballance considered it better 'to postpone this debatable question until another and more convenient season'.[91] Even with the 'distraction' of women's admission to Parliament gone, granting the female franchise remained a point of contention as the Electoral Bill was debated; in the words of one member of the House, 'The Bill includes a good many amendments which are very desirable … but … to include in this general Bill the special subject of the female suffrage is to imperil the passing of some of those important amendments'.[92] The following week a petition signed by 18,407 women calling for Parliament to grant the vote to women was presented to the Legislative Council. After some questioning whether the petition complied with the Standing Orders, the petition was accepted but no direct action was taken.

Māori women, likewise, were deploying strategic tactics and demanding a voice in Te Kotahitanga. Modelled on the New Zealand Parliament, Te Kotahitanga or the Maori Parliament, which met for the first time in 1892, was composed of an Upper House of 50 elected chiefs and a Lower House of 96 selected men. Meri Te Tai Mangakahia, who was descended from Te Rarawa chiefs and was married to the elected premier of Te Kotahitanga, and Akenehi Tomoana, who was married to the speaker of Te Kotahitanga, had formed a committee as a forum for Māori women to engage in political debate. On 18 May 1893, with Tomoana's support, Meri Te Tai Mangakahia presented a motion to the Lower House of Te Kotahitanga which read:

E whakamoemiti atu ana ahau kinga honore mem e noho nei, kia ora koutou katoa, ko te take I motini atu ai ahan, kit e Tumuaki Honore, me nga mema honore, ka mahia he ture e tenei whare kia whakamana nga wahine kit e pooti mema mo ratou kit e Paremata Maori.

[I exult the honourable members of this gathering. Greetings. The reason I move this motion before the principal member and all honourable members is so that a law may emerge from this Parliament allowing women to vote and women to be accepted as members of the Parliament.][93]

After her address, Tomoana suggested they wait until the men had secured recognition for Te Kotahitanga before they discussed the issue of Māori women's participation in the Maori Parliament.

Unlike the motion presented to the Lower House of Te Kotahitanga, neither the Women's Suffrage Bill 1893 prepared by Hall nor the Electoral Bill 1893 introduced by the Liberal Government provided for women to be elected as members of Parliament. The interpretation section of the Electoral Bill was carefully worded to include women's suffrage but to exclude women from being eligible to sit in Parliament: 'person' included female but 'candidate' meant any man who had been nominated as a candidate for a seat in the House of Representatives. At the end of August 1893, by which time the Electoral Bill had passed its second reading in the Legislative Council and had proceeded to committee, an amendment to have the word 'man' replaced by 'person' was proposed. If passed, this would have meant that women would have been eligible to sit in the House.[94] But, as with Carncross's amendment in 1891, this amendment was proposed by a member who had openly opposed women's suffrage, and was intended as a hostile measure to provide grounds for rejection of the bill. A division on this amendment was taken and was lost by a majority of only three. After various political manoeuvrings and last-minute attempts to scuttle women's suffrage, the Electoral Bill 1893 was passed and on 19 September 1893 it gained the assent of the governor and passed into law.

The passing of the Electoral Act 1893 marked a watershed in world history as New Zealand became the first nation in the world to grant the electoral franchise to women. In announcing the governor's assent to the Electoral Bill, Premier Richard Seddon drew attention to the short amount of time between the close of the parliamentary session and the date the electoral rolls would close for the upcoming general election – a mere six weeks – and declared, 'if we are to have a real live women's vote something extra will have to be done to get them on the rolls'.[95] With an additional 130,000 voters, more electoral forms, polling booths and clerical assistants would be required. Government officials organised for extra polling booths while politicians debated the best means to ensure as many women as possible from all regions, social classes and political persuasions could be enrolled to vote and cast their vote. They debated how best to prevent touting for women's votes and bogus voting. Meanwhile, women around the country mobilised into action.

An all-out campaign followed to ensure as many women as possible were enrolled so they could exercise their hard-won rights. Various branches of the Women's Franchise League and temperance societies held meetings and provided electoral forms to facilitate women registering on the electoral rolls. Work parties were organised to canvass on a house-to-house basis.[96] Women were urged to form ward committees and to poll candidates on their views on issues of interest. A meeting of 200 women in Gisborne resulted in the formation of the Free Association of Women Electors to support male candidates of good and honest character who were independent of all political parties. Determined to show themselves worthy of the dignity bestowed on them through the electoral franchise, women encouraged each other to not be apathetic, to inform themselves on political issues and questions of legislation and, above all, to remember their friends and allies in Parliament on election day.

Amid the reflections on the great achievement of the female franchise and the imminent task of securing women's registration on the polls, there was great confidence that women's vote would be used to ensure abler men were elected to Parliament. Little reference was made to the fact that while women were now able to vote for their parliamentary representatives, they were still not eligible to stand for election themselves. When this issue was raised it was usually by someone who was against women standing for election. Many throughout the country would have shared the view expressed by Reverend Mr Watkin at a public meeting at Feilding School on 27 September 1893: that while it was fitting that women should have a voice in the election of representatives, he would not like to see women in Parliament.[97] Others, though, disagreed. In a letter to the editor of the Dunedin *Evening Star*, 'Male Voter' wrote, 'Undoubtedly we shall in a few years see women in Parliament. It is the logical conclusion to female franchise. Would it not be well if meanwhile some preparation were made in that direction. We should have women on our Charitable Aid Board, our Hospital Board, and indeed represented on all our local institutions. They would thus be useful and in training as future members.'[98] This writer considered it a pity that women had not served on these boards as there were questions that continually cropped up that women could deal with and for which their sex 'would be a positive advantage'. He suggested, given women's interest in educational questions, they would be of 'great service' on high school and primary school committees.[99]

Some women who had not been strong supporters of the campaign for female suffrage now contemplated, if not embraced, the prospect of women extending their influence within the walls of Parliament. One woman was moved to write to the newspapers to say that, although she was still not entirely sure that granting women the franchise was the right action, she did not see any reason why some women should not devote their lives to politics. To her mind, 'The woman who was most attentive to her home duties would make the best politician.'[100]

With the eyes of the world on them, the women of New Zealand flocked to the polling booths on 28 November 1893. Once again, opponents of women's suffrage had been proven wrong as proportionally more of the adult female population voted than their male counterparts.[101] The day after the general election, New Zealand again made international headlines by electing the first female mayor in the British Empire. 'Lady mayor' Elizabeth Yates was to become the most talked about woman in 1894, although not always for the right reasons.[102]

After the general election in November 1893, Kate Sheppard resigned her presidency of the Christchurch WCTU and as editor of the WCTU page of *The Prohibitionist*, as well as her position as convenor of the economics section of the Canterbury Women's Institute, and went on extended leave to England. Although there appeared to be a brief hiatus in women's political activity, important work was occurring behind the scenes. Some of the women's franchise leagues renamed themselves women's political leagues to signal their commitment to a wider range of women's issues, including economic independence for women, equal pay, reform of the laws relating to marriage, divorce and the custody of children, and social issues such as assisting illegitimate children and eliminating prostitution.

A priority was educating women to become politically aware, and to this end new organisations were formed. In Auckland, as well as the Auckland Women's Political League and the Auckland Women's Democratic Union, the Women's Liberal League was founded to support the Liberal Government. Margaret Sievwright established the Gisborne Women's Political Association, and in Wellington the Women's Social and Political League was founded under the patronage of Louisa Seddon, wife of Premier Richard Seddon. In 1895 Anna Stout, wife of Chief Justice Robert Stout, established the rival Southern Cross Society in Wellington, which was dedicated to the study of economic and political principles and legislation before Parliament and to advocating reforms that would benefit women. Although both organisations were focused on political issues and parliamentary proceedings, the Southern Cross Society did not support women sitting in Parliament. Christchurch women were well served with the Canterbury Women's Institute, the Canterbury Social and Political League and the Canterbury Political Association. In 1895 the Dunedin Women's Franchise League with Marion Hatton as president published a manifesto and, in Wellington, Marianne Tasker established the Women's Democratic Union. While some of these organisations were relatively short-lived, they were testimony to a renewed energy for organised political activity.

The debates culminating in the passing of women's suffrage had been marked by political posturing, entrenched conservatism, scaremongering, mock chivalry and facile ridicule. Opponents of women's participation in political life had played the prospect of petticoats in Parliament like a political football, and many viewed the achievement of women's suffrage as the final whistle. But, as time would show, it would prove to be a game of two halves.

*

Why were women not granted the right to sit in Parliament at the same time as they were granted the right to vote in 1893? The prospect of women sitting in Parliament was a constant feature of debates on electoral bills in relation to women's suffrage and in the various women's franchise bills presented to the House between 1880 and 1893. For some, the right to vote and the right to sit in Parliament went hand in hand, as was the case for men, but for others the spectre of women in Parliament was raised as a political ploy to deter those with moderate views from voting in favour of women's suffrage. Throughout these debates, there was no consensus on whether women's full parliamentary citizenship was a right or a privilege. When James Wallis moved in 1878 that Parliament recognise the principle of perfect equality and that the same political rights and privileges be granted to women as to men, he was met with charges of wasting time on 'mere abstract questions' when there was serious parliamentary business at hand.[103] This prolonged unwillingness to admit women's shared humanity and to recognise that human rights belonged to all human beings regardless of sex went hand in hand with a general refusal to take women's demands seriously. The pages of *Hansard* and the reports from parliamentary press reporters are replete with examples of how issues of direct concern to women were constantly treated with ridicule, derision and facile humour and, when they did become the focus of debate, were treated as light amusement and a welcome distraction from the 'real' business of Parliament.

Premier Ballance's attempts to defer passing female suffrage came from his belief that women were, in a political sense, uneducated.[104] Premier Seddon followed a different strategy: he decided to support women's suffrage and rely on the Legislative Council to block the passage of the legislation. It is evident in the official parliamentary record as well as in newspaper reports that many, including Seddon, voted for women's franchise not from any conviction that women should be granted the vote, but with an eye on political capital at the upcoming general election. Despite Seddon's statement that it might be considered part of the franchise, the legal right for women to be elected to the New Zealand House of Representatives was a political expediency that was sacrificed for the 'greater' goal of achieving the electoral franchise. The debates on women's suffrage had demonstrated there were double standards around men and women's participation in politics. Some prejudices against women's participation in the political sphere had been eroded with the granting of the franchise, but there remained a widespread belief, even among women, that the 'experiment' of women's suffrage would fail; that most women would not choose to exercise their right to the franchise, but would be content to remain largely within the parliament of their own homes.

CHAPTER 2

The logical conclusion to female franchise, 1894 to 1896

If you say they are not represented at the present time, if you say we cannot represent the wants and wishes of the softer sex as we now represent them in this House, then why should we restrict them to the exercise of the vote? Why not open the doors of this Chamber to the fairer sex? Why not allow them to take part in our deliberations and to take part in our divisions on matters affecting their own interests. Surely that is fair argument. Why should we halt halfway? — JAMES CARROLL, MHR, 24 August 1891[1]

The achievement of the electoral franchise meant that women now had a direct voice in the election of members to Parliament. They would soon learn, however, that although they had assisted individual men in being elected to the House, this did not guarantee that those men would actively represent their interests: male politicians tended to become more responsive to women's political demands around election time. But New Zealand politics was changing. The enfranchisement of women was part of an emerging electoral democracy in New Zealand that would have a big impact on women's struggle to achieve full parliamentary citizenship.

The rise of Liberalism

The 1890 general election heralded this new era in New Zealand politics. Cleavages between radicals and conservatives that had been developing for several years, along with the formation of political associations such as the National Liberal Association, the Political and Financial Reform Association and the Canterbury Electors' Association were evidence of the emergence of nascent political parties. The first Liberal Ministry won 40 of the 78 seats in the House of Representatives and took office under Premier John Ballance on 24 January 1891, marking the beginning of the longest period for any political party[2] in New Zealand to remain in government.

A defining feature of the Liberal Government was its emphasis on populist attitudes and social legislation. The 1890 general election was an important marker of electoral democracy in New Zealand: the system of plural voting[3] was abolished, as was the 'old order' of governments being formed on the basis of political personalities, in what has been described as 'the era of "the best man"'.[4] This was particularly evident in the composition of the Ballance Ministry, which was made up entirely of former Opposition members of Parliament whose politics could be characterised as centralist rather than representing provincialist blocs. Although they were somewhat lacking in experience, all had proven themselves to be loyal supporters of moderate conservatism under the ministry of Premier Harry Atkinson in the years leading up to the election.

A feature of the early years of the Ballance Ministry was its adherence to the notion of slow progress towards policy goals. Democracy dictated the pace, and that entailed educating public opinion. One of Ballance's notable achievements during his short ministry[5] was to effect a ruling by the Colonial Office in relation to the obligations of the governor to accept the advice of government ministers on appointments to the Legislative Council. This decision was critical to securing the passage of Liberal legislation in both houses of Parliament, and it was seen as an encouraging development for those who thought the Upper House a more suitable political atmosphere for women. The emergence of a more united body of Liberal members in the House of Representatives contrasted with the 'motley assortment' that comprised the Opposition in Parliament before the 1893 general election, to the extent that there was no confidence that opponents of the government would be capable of forming a stable administration with a coherent set of policies.[6] As expected, and assisted by women's votes, the Liberal Ministry under Premier Richard Seddon was reformed following the 1893 election with an increased majority.

A fundamental principle of Liberalism as expressed in the New Zealand political context during this period was the need to advance the interests of the whole community. This manifested as being opposed to placing any section of the community in a special or privileged position or, conversely, in an inferior or disadvantaged position. This principle, which had been evident in the debates around women's suffrage, went hand in hand with the belief that reform should proceed only as far as public opinion would allow at any given time. Both principles were to be used by politicians to deny there was sufficient support for women's admission to the House of Representatives, and by supporters of increased political citizenship for women.

During the early years of the Liberal Ministry under Seddon, as Parliament was feeling its way into new processes of party government, the government was discovering the extent to which it could depend on members for support for legislation. Over time, various mechanisms and principles would be developed around the use of caucus, the amount of legislation placed before Parliament, and the level of independence from members that could be tolerated without undermining the effectiveness of the government. Throughout this process, party discipline developed into a problem for Seddon: aggressive and antagonistic factions of so-called loyalists and independents abused each other in increasingly violent terms, questioning the other's liberal credentials and accusing each other of either blind obedience to the government line or disloyalty to Liberalism.[7] But the culture of Parliament was changing in other ways. It was still a place for debate, argument, the expression of public opinion and political ideas, but the tenor and content of parliamentary debates were impacted by changes to the Standing Orders in 1894 that placed time limits on speeches so legislation could pass more efficiently, and by individual members becoming increasingly subordinate to the party they represented and accountable to the voters who had elected them to represent party interests. Often treated as a welcome distraction from these internal politics and the 'real' business of the House, various bills promoting women's admission to Parliament during the second term of the Liberal Government between 1894 and 1896 became fodder for parliamentary posturing.

Parliamentary Disabilities of Women Abolition Bill 1894

In June 1894, eight days before the new Parliament was due to sit, the idea of women meeting for a few hours each week to read and discuss *Hansard* was mooted in a letter to the *Evening Post*.[8] Within days a Women's Political Club was formed in Wellington. On the eve of the opening of Parliament, the president and secretary of the club hand-delivered a letter to Alfred Newman, which petitioned to have the bill for the admission of women to Parliament reopened. Members of the Women's Political Club were confident that the majority of the women of New Zealand were 'as anxious to obtain the privilege of legislating for their country as many of the present members of the House are for the obstruction of it'.[9] As had been the case with the female franchise, they did not look to the successful passage of the bill as an end in itself, but as a means to an end. Their most urgent priority was 'the principle of equality that will give to women the right to command the same value for the same amount of labour as performed by man'. Until women were admitted to Parliament, they argued, the value of women's labour would continue to be viewed as less than that of men, and they were confident that 'if time and serious attention be given to this great principle of industrial reform by the members of the House ... their nobleness of character and common sense will force them, in common justice to humanity, to remove the disabilities which now encircle us on account of sex'.[10] The secretary of the Women's Political Club wrote to Kate Sheppard requesting her assistance in organising a petition signed by women in Christchurch 'for our freedom'. Convinced that 'if the women ask, the bill will pass',[11] after their experiences with the passing of women's suffrage legislation they admitted their resignation to the prospect that it may not eventuate in the current session of Parliament.

There were great expectations on the part of women voters that the government they helped to elect would be more receptive to women's issues. A report from the special parliamentary correspondent, however, suggested otherwise. Parliament had been in session for only a couple of weeks, but already it had been observed that, 'whenever anything is mentioned in connection with women, there is, all round, laughter, with jeering and ribald remarks, which are audible in the Press gallery, and presumably are also heard in the ladies gallery'.[12] Laughter had greeted Newman's notice of a bill to admit women to Parliament, and Independent Liberal member Benjamin Harris had been interrupted 'by frequent remarks meant to be humorous' when he quoted from a letter received from a member of the WCTU. There had been 'a similar outburst of mirth' when Independent Liberal member George Russell gave notice of a question whether the government would legislate to permit women being appointed justices of the peace. Members who indulged in such 'ill-timed merriment' were not confined to any section of the House. The parliamentary reporter concluded: 'Evidently the House is determined that it shall not be known as the Women's Parliament; but surely it is not necessary for it to emphasise its virility by taking up the vulgar attitude of contemptuous ridicule which its actions seem to imply'.[13]

The following month Newman introduced the Parliamentary Disabilities of Women Abolition Bill, which proposed to admit women to both the House of Representatives and the Legislative Council. The strategy of the bill was straightforward: minor changes in wording were proposed to the Legislative Council Act 1891 and the Electoral Act 1893 – substituting 'person' for 'man'; and omitting the word 'man' and deeming 'person' to include women. These wording changes would have the combined effect of women being eligible for election to the Lower House and appointment to the Upper House.

When introducing the bill, Newman reminded members that when they were dealing with the women's franchise late in the previous session, several members who were in favour of women being eligible to stand for parliamentary election had voted against that principle to ensure that the passing of the Women's Franchise Bill was not hampered by this additional demand. Now it was time to put right the issue of women's admission to Parliament. He expressed confidence that the bill did not call for much discussion; he believed it was 'quite impossible for the House much longer to deny [women] the right to equal political privileges in all respects with the men'.[14]

Despite his assurance that there was nothing new, revolutionary or radical in the bill, one member gasped audibly when Newman explained that he had added a clause stating that, if a Māori woman wished to enter either house of Parliament, she would be free from any disability to do so. In response to the member's reaction, Newman insisted: 'Seeing that Maori women are also electors in the Colony of New Zealand, it would be simply monstrous to say that, if white women are allowed to become candidates for Parliament, Maori women should not be allowed to do so.'[15]

As it was a private member's bill, there was no obligation on the part of the government to provide a lead on the matter. Moreover, with the next general election a long way off there was no urgency to even address the issue. But the government's silence on the bill, along with the empty benches, prompted criticism of the government by Opposition members. The elected leader of the Conservative Opposition, Captain William Russell, accused the government of 'abrogating their functions almost entirely' and insisted that any bill that proposed changing the constitution of the colony should at least be subject to '"rough and tumble" debate'.[16] There was a debate of sorts with various members rising in turn to express their support or opposition. Those who expressed support drew attention to the measure being the logical extension of the right to vote and to women successfully proving themselves capable of taking part in public affairs through their work on education boards and school committees. One Opposition member accused government politicians of selfishly using women 'as stepping-stones in order that they may enter Parliament' only to then deny them eligibility for a seat in either house.[17] Independent Liberal member William Reeves, who held several ministerial posts at the time, pointed out that even though one would not suppose for a minute that the mass of women were qualified for parliamentary duties, the same was so for men. But, he added, there were 'exceptionally able, exceptionally energetic, and exceptionally forcible women' and some of them may like to take a seat in Parliament or at least have the opportunity and, at the end of the day, it would be up to the electors to decide whether they would like to be represented by these women or not. In line with Liberal philosophy, Reeves was 'perfectly prepared to trust the people' but was prepared to wait until there was a mandate for the next government in the matter. He was confident that: 'lady electors will have a "say" in the matter, and I think they will look very rigidly and narrowly at the qualifications of any female candidate who may come before them, and will not be specially disposed to return them to this House simply because they are women. They will vote after asking themselves whether the lady candidate is likely to represent them specially well. If they decide she is, I say allow her to come here.'[18]

Those opposed to the measure believed it was premature, and insisted on the need to be fully certain that women wanted this right. William Russell had voted in favour of women's franchise but considered it an entirely different matter that women be allowed to take a seat in the parliamentary chamber. He took umbrage at Newman's claim that as a colony, New Zealanders took pride in 'being in the van of legislation'. In a speech that was as much opposed to the Liberal Government's policies as to the particular bill under debate, he described the current move toward progressive legislation as 'a vulgar craze' and bemoaned the fact that, 'We are constantly told that the eyes of the whole world are centred on this colony, and that the social legislation which is now being carried on here causes the world to watch us with unwonted interest, and that all the world is standing either amazed or aghast at our proceedings.'[19] He considered it nonsense and 'an utter absurdity' to 'imagine that we, a small colony in a remote part of the world, are the centre of interest to the remainder of the civilised world'. He advised caution, insisting that 'if we travel ahead any faster, and try to set the example to the world of putting women into Parliament, we shall merely earn the contemptuous smiles of the world'.[20]

Russell believed that if Parliament affirmed the principle that women were, in all respects, the equals of men, and allowed them to take their seats in the Chamber, they should be required to serve as volunteers in the army and undertake the same duties and responsibilities in the defence of the country. He questioned whether it was in the interests of the colony that Māori women be admitted to the House of Representatives; he invited any 'reasonable' person to explain how this could be the case, and asked whether it was 'desirable that the legislation of this country should be affected by the admission of Maori women?'[21] This drew responses from several Māori members, including Hōne Heke Ngāpua. Ngāpua's granduncle was Hōne Heke, the Ngāpuhi rangatira who had led the opposition to the government to draw attention to their broken promises after the signing of Te Tiriti o Waitangi. Ngāpua shared his granduncle's commitment to Māori independence and was emerging as a strong advocate and influential member of Te Kotahitanga. Committed to furthering this agenda, Ngāpua, aged in his early twenties, had been elected as the Northern Maori member for the House of Representatives in the general election the previous year. Despite professing that Māori women had every right to a seat in the House, he was not prepared to support the bill until it was certain women wanted this right.²²

William (Bill) Massey, the member for Waitemata who was emerging as a leader in the Conservative Opposition, had been asked during the 1893 election campaign whether he would support women's admission to both houses of Parliament. His response had been consistent: as soon as women showed they were keen to take part in the legislative duties of the colony he would support the measure. But he noted that women were silent on this point: 'We have received no petitions, and, except on the part of one or two agitators, we have heard of no resolutions on the subject.'²³ Others who had not been questioned on their position during the election campaign took that as evidence that women did not want this privilege. Even Alfred Saunders agreed that this was not a priority for women: 'The ladies are not in a hurry, and are satisfied with what they have at present; and I think we should move very cautiously in matters of this kind.'²⁴ He saw no necessity for women to be in Parliament, although he admitted there would come a time when women's services could be employed in many other ways, and he pointed to the possibility of having a second chamber composed of ladies.²⁵ Only one member reported having canvassed the women in his constituency on the issue. Ngāpua, who had earlier not supported the bill, had sent telegrams to various parts of his Northern Maori electorate, and although the responses from women were mixed, they were sufficient for him to have decided to vote in favour of the bill.

In his speech of reply, Newman conceded that no one could hope that a measure of the kind proposed could go through the House all at once; as with female franchise, 'The public, and even Parliament, have to be educated … slowly in this direction.'²⁶ He felt sure that if the bill was not successful there would be a steady movement outside the walls of Parliament to carry out the reform.²⁷ The ensuing division was an even split of ayes and noes, leaving the casting vote to the speaker to determine whether the bill would proceed to a second reading. Voting with 'great pleasure' in favour of a second reading, the speaker explained, 'I think the women of New Zealand behaved so well at the general election in the exercise of the privilege that was conferred upon them by the last Parliament, in returning this House, that I feel it my duty to give my casting-vote in favour of conferring on them the higher honour of their being henceforth privileged to take seats in this

House whenever any constituency of New Zealand shall elect a woman as a member of the New Zealand Parliament.'²⁸

The speaker's sentiments were not shared by the government. The following week when the bill was due to proceed to the committee stage, Newman reminded the House that the Minister of Education (William Reeves) had stated that if the bill proceeded to a second reading the government would consider supporting it. This drew a response from Premier Seddon that, in the absence of the minister, the government thought it would be unfair to interfere lest they do injury to the women of the colony, and he would therefore leave it to Dr Newman to deal with. Tantamount to an invitation to not take the bill seriously, the premier's comments set the tone for the ensuing debate and bolstered those who had voted against the second reading to stifle the passage of the bill. One opponent suggested Newman should be satisfied the bill had proceeded as far as it had, and added it was regretful that notions of sitting in Parliament had been put into women's heads. Independent Liberal Alexander Hogg resorted to unabashed buffoonery, asking members to 'reflect for a moment on the splendid impression it would make upon that House if they had a good assortment of young ladies, dressed in the highest style of fashion, occupying the benches here and there, like flowers in a vegetable-garden, mingled with the turnips and the carrots and potatoes';²⁹ singling out the two most prominent supporters of women's admission to Parliament, Hogg, whose opinions were said to 'have the quality of matching the changing colour of his political environment',³⁰ invited his colleagues to 'imagine a beautiful blond sitting alongside the honourable member for Wellington Suburbs [Alfred Newman], and enlivening him with her conversation while a debate was going on' and 'a young lady, who had just got beyond her teens, sitting alongside their venerable friend the honourable member for Riverton [sic],³¹ and making to him somewhat delicate although perfectly legitimate proposals'.³²

After an hour and a half of personal attacks on Newman's motivations for sponsoring the bill and assertions that women had no interest in the measure, the Independent Liberal member for Riccarton George Russell expressed his dismay at the way Parliament had disgraced itself that evening. He considered the tone of the discussion 'distinctly discreditable' and thought it inappropriate to treat such a serious issue as burlesque.³³

In Russell's view, Newman was largely to blame; his inability to resist the temptation of making a speech to the full galleries opened the way for further debate which, after the supper break, had descended into farce. Not recorded in *Hansard* was a facetious proposal to amend the title of the bill to read 'The Women's Parliamentary Abilities Bill'.[34] Amid the chaos, the bill proceeded to committee but by then it was well after midnight and a motion to further consider the bill that afternoon was lost by nine votes.

In reporting the previous evening's debates, various newspapers that had a reputation for being generally hostile to the Liberal Government lent tacit support to the unprofessionalism of many in the House. Members' behaviour was excused as 'not very elaborate foolery',[35] although it was noted that the premier 'did not cut a dignified appearance'.[36] The *New Zealand Times* was an exception: it ran a damning account of the previous evening's session, which it described as 'the most degrading in the history of our Parliament':

> *For absolute moral cowardice, the conduct of the majority cannot be beaten. For lack of dignity, for want of courtesy, for boorish folly, nothing worse could be conceived. And this is the House which prides itself as being in the van of political progress, poses as an example to the universe, boasts of the lead it gives in all things of importance to the future of the race. But bad as the exhibition was, it was quite in keeping with the history of women's suffrage in New Zealand.*[37]

The *Auckland Star* cautioned that when the time was right for women to be admitted to Parliament, women would not forget the names of those members who treated the subject with ridicule. After only one general election, the female vote was recognised as too important a factor to be trifled with. Women, too, were quick to remind the public and politicians of this fact. In the words of one female correspondent in a letter to the editor, 'Surely, those funny members must have forgotten for the time, not only their own dignity, and what their constituencies have a right to expect from them, but as well the existence of "Hansard" and reporters! Either this, or else they have no desire to ever be returned again, unless, indeed, they imagine themselves secure, without the women's votes, for which, however, they manifested, before the election, some little solicitude.'[38]

Women's Political Rights Bill 1894

On the same day as the Parliamentary Disabilities of Women Abolition Bill 1894 was being debated for the first time, George Russell had given notice of a bill that, if it became law, would allow women to be appointed to every and any office in the state. The bill contained one operative clause: 'From and after the passing of this Act, a woman may be appointed or elected to any public office or position to which a man may be appointed or elected, any law or statute to the contrary notwithstanding.'[39] Given the debacle that scuttled the Parliamentary Disabilities of Women Abolition Bill the night before, the timing of the second reading of the Women's Political Rights Bill did not bode well. As one parliamentary reporter noted, it was 'local bills' day[40] and none of the measures on the Order Paper promised much in the way of either amusement or instruction.

Introducing the bill to a sparsely populated and 'singularly inattentive'[41] House, Russell explained that the bill affirmed the principle that sex should not bar from public office persons who were otherwise fit for office. He stated that, by women having called into existence this Parliament through their votes, 'the law has thus recognised woman's potential as a lawmaker'.[42] In his view it was idle to say that New Zealand was merely experimenting with women in politics, and he questioned why women's share in making and administering the law should be confined to the potential function they could exercise by electing members to the Chamber. He saw no logical ground for opposition to the bill and proceeded to address each of the three main objections, namely, that women did not want to be members of Parliament, that women had not asked for this right, and that it was not expedient for women to sit in the House.

Russell freely admitted that before the Liberal Party had accepted women's suffrage he was not in favour of that measure, but he had bowed to the leaders of the party. But the 1893 general election had opened his eyes to the fact that women possessed 'a keen appreciation of politics as they affect the home, the family, and social questions'.[43] Experience had taught him that, just as there were men whose abilities and intellect fitted them for the service of their country, so, too, were there women who possessed 'in a remarkable degree the same qualities'.[44] He referred to the stock argument that woman's sphere was in the home and acknowledged that this was so for the average woman, just as the factory, the shop, the farm, or the office was the accepted sphere of the average man. However, in a clever twist that pandered to the egos of his colleagues in the Chamber, he added, 'But when we deal with public offices and appointments we deal neither with the average man nor with the average woman. Our system of government has been designed to select those men who are not average men, but those who, by experience, ability, sagacity, or public spirit, or all combined, stand out as representative men.'[45]

Russell's speech was interrupted by a member who accused him of breaching parliamentary protocol by reading his speech. With the assurance that he was only referring to his voluminous notes to save time and to discuss the question in a different light to the way it was discussed the previous evening, Russell affirmed the commonly held view that even if the bill passed, it would likely be years before women entered Parliament and even longer before they would sit in the courts as judges. But, he insisted, 'the removal of the barrier of sex will widen their sphere. It will throw backwards their horizon.' Most women would be content to deal with 'the anxieties and toils of a home life', but to some, and an increasing number over the years, this measure would 'provide the possibility of a career which, stimulated by a noble ambition, will react beneficially on the womanhood of New Zealand'.[46] There was a long silence after Russell moved the second reading of the bill; no one rose to speak and the motion was securely defeated by 41 votes to 19.

According to the editor of the *New Zealand Times* the events in the debating chamber on the evening Newman's bill was discussed were a repeat of the suffrage debates the previous year. Just as the majority of those who finally voted for women's suffrage cared nothing of the principle or even condescended to think about the principle, the majority of those who supposedly supported women's entry into Parliament were interested only in securing political capital for themselves. Most were afraid to say they opposed the bill, and feigned enthusiastic support. But the editor of the *New Zealand Times* predicted that, in time, they would be caught in their own net of false pretences and the result would be 'that women will get into Parliament, and every coward who has shilly-shallied openly, and offered obstruction in secret, will pose as a woman's champion consistent from the first'.[47] For these politicians, expediency had overrun principles and it was now up to women to seize the moment, take up their pens, present petitions and demonstrate that they did want the right to sit in Parliament. He stated frankly that men would grant whatever women demanded, 'not because the demand will be just or proper, but because it carries votes'.[48]

Women did take up their pens, but it was a far cry from the monstrous petitions in the lead-up to women's suffrage. Kate Lunday organised a petition 'That the bill for admission of women to Parliament be passed', which gained only 220 signatures.[49] As with the suffrage issue, however, there was no unified voice within the various women's organisations on the need for women to sit in Parliament. The Dunedin branch of the WCTU had discussed Newman's bill and passed a resolution disapproving of it. This action came as a surprise to Kate Sheppard, among others, given that the women in Dunedin had worked harder than many other regions to secure the franchise. An article in *The Prohibitionist* titled 'Hugging our chains' commented that the fact that the women in the Dunedin branch had opposed the logical outcome of the franchise suggested they had discussed the bill more than they had considered it. The writer held that, 'The disability of women to sit in Parliament is one of many shackles on the freedom of women. It was imposed for selfish reasons, and Dr Newman's bill is a chivalrous attempt to remove it. It matters little whether we would like to sit in Parliament or not ... every woman should be as free as every man to work out her own destiny.'[50] The article suggested that had a Frances Willard[51] been sitting in the Upper House during the recent debate on the Divorce Bill, there would likely not have been councillors contending that men should be able to divorce an unfaithful wife yet deny women legal escape from an unfaithful husband. The writer hoped that the women in Dunedin would come to the realisation they had acted in haste by taking 'a retrograde step', and suggested that perhaps they were exhausted from their vigorous efforts to obtain the franchise and this had temporarily dulled their senses.[52] The charge prompted Marion Hatton, president of the Dunedin Women's Franchise League, to respond: 'I am by no means an advocate of a Women's Parliament, believing that, so long as good men can be found, who will shape the laws of our colony in harmony with equity and common sense, there will be no need for our sex to do anything further than help to return such men to the House of Representatives.'[53]

Hatton's position on women in Parliament did not stop others expressing differing views. At the annual public meeting of the Dunedin

Women's Franchise League, held in the City Hall on 22 August 1894, Mrs Hislop, a member of the league executive, spoke of the beneficial effect of women's influence in the last parliamentary elections and urged that that influence needed to be carried into Parliament. She encouraged mothers and daughters to study politics and follow parliamentary proceedings in their local newspapers; and by such study, she argued, women would be more fitted to take their place as intelligent companions to their husbands and brothers. Mrs Hislop was followed by Mrs Elizabeth Yates who, amid loud prolonged cheers and the waving of handkerchiefs, was introduced as 'the only lady mayor in the British Empire'. Greeted with laughter when she pointed out that politicians were so conservative in making very small concessions, Yates thought it very one-sided that when they granted the franchise to women, they said women could elect men but not come to Parliament themselves. Acknowledging that their president held a different view, she urged the women of the league to agitate until seats in Parliament were open to them. The Reverend W. Saunders then said he was in accord with Mrs Yates' hope that women would yet be in Parliament, on education boards and on other public bodies. Likewise, Mark Cohen, editor of the *Star*, acknowledged that while he and the executive of the league had agreed to differ, his counsel was that women prepare themselves by a study of public questions for the time when the logical outcome of the franchise – the taking of a seat in Parliament – would be reached.[54]

Despite various petitions, neither bill progressed beyond the early stages: the Women's Political Rights Bill did not pass its second reading and the Parliamentary Disabilities of Women Abolition Bill was voted down in committee.

A new year heralded new forums for women to discuss their views. On 9 February 1895 *Daybreak*, a weekly periodical 'Written by women for women about women',[55] was launched in Wellington. However, the inaugural issue explained that the journal did not support women's admission to Parliament; its principal aim was 'to ventilate the evils and grievances that exist in our midst, and to let not only the men in Wellington, but New Zealand, know that we do not intend to overstep the power we have received in having the franchise granted us by forgetting our sex and appearing in places where we shall be not only the laughing stock of the ill-natured, but (what is far worse) merit the contempt of the wise and true'.[56]

Meanwhile, Māori women were rallying. At a hui held at Te Hauke near Hastings in January 1895 to mark the passing of chief Hone Nea Nea and to discuss matters of interest to Māori, several Māori women raised the issue of equal rights. They noted that for years the work done by their husbands had not been sufficient and that women needed to act. They pointed out that under the Treaty of Waitangi Māori and Pākehā were treated alike, but that Māori had not been well served: 'Their men had been following up the root of the grape vine, and did not know what fruit it would bring forth. While the men had done nothing for themselves, the bush and root had passed into the hands of the Europeans. They were going down every day, losing their lands and their *mana*.'[57] They could no longer count on their men. They decided to try and form some rules and regulations by which they and their lands might be protected. Two of their members in the House – Hōne Heke representing Northern Māori and Wī Pere representing Eastern Māori – were expected to speak at the hui, but in the meantime the women decided to form a committee to address all matters related to the sale or disposal of land they owned and to withdraw all land from sale. Seven resolutions – all relating to land issues – were passed at the hui, which was reported as a session of the Maori Women's Parliament.[58] Chairwoman Makera Mihi Waota noted in drawing the hui to a close that, after many years, 'men's endeavors [sic] to carry out our interests have failed' and that the women had decided to form their own parliament. She added, 'Our lands are slipping away from us every day into the hands of the Government, and therefore we must protect ourselves. Should we not succeed we will find ourselves like shags on a sandbank spreading our wings to the wind.'[59] The resolutions passed were reported widely in newspapers across the country and prompted one person to suggest what a noble example they had set for their Pākehā sisterhood. Accusing her Pākehā sisters of sitting 'idle and dumb', Priscilla Peahen, in a letter to the editor, denounced the fact that there had not been one serious proposal to admit women to the House of Representatives, 'much less to constitute an Uppermost House of Women to revise without appeal the legislation of incompetent and self-interested men'. She rallied the sisterhood with the cry, 'Sisters to arms! Let us be up and doing. Never let it be said that we have been surpassed by our Maori fellow countrywomen.'[60]

Admission of Women to Parliament Bill 1895

In anticipation of Dr Newman reintroducing legislation to the House, women's groups across the country collected signatures to petition the government for the removal of women's political disabilities. But once again, although they represented a geographical spread of individuals and women's groups, the total number of petitioners was far from impressive. Member of the Legislative Council William Jennings presented four separate petitions with a combined total of 790 signatures from men and women, 'For the introduction of a bill to declare absolute equality to be the law of the land for men and women'.[61] His colleague Charles Johnston presented a petition with the same wording with three signatures organised by Amey Daldy on behalf of the Auckland Women's Franchise League. Charles Button, Conservative member of the House of Representatives for Auckland, presented a petition with 19 signatures from the Auckland Women's Political League, 'That the disabilities that prevent women becoming members of Parliament be removed',[62] and Alfred Newman presented a petition with three signatures from the Auckland Women's Political League, 'That women be admitted to Parliament, and that laws be made equal for men and women'[63] as well as one with the same wording with three signatures from the Napier WCTU.[64] The Malvern Women's Institute petition, 'In favour of women having equal rights with men'[65] with two signatures, was presented by George Russell, and the Independent member for the City of Christchurch George Smith presented a petition with two signatures on behalf of the Canterbury WCTU, 'For revision of the laws of the colony so far as they affect the women of New Zealand'.[66] James Carroll, Liberal member for Waiapu, presented a petition with 324 signatures on behalf of E. Townley and others, 'That the disabilities which prevent women from becoming members of Parliament be removed'.[67]

On 21 June the Admission of Women to Parliament Bill 1895 moved by Newman had a first reading. In all respects other than its title, which had been changed to provide clarity on the intention of the legislation, Newman's bill was the same as that presented the previous year. If the assessment of political feeling by the editor of the *Otago Daily Times* was correct, there seemed little hope that the bill would be successful. Demeaning it as a 'little bill to admit women to the General Assembly', the editor suggested Dr Newman should have been content that his efforts the previous year had passed a second reading, given the House had no intention of passing the bill at that time; indeed, 'the subject was played with and the second reading passed half in joke, half in cowardice'. The editor was not alone in thinking it was too soon to take this step; he went on, 'It will be time enough to talk of further developments when the results of that great step [the franchise] have been conclusively displayed.' However, his anticipation of 'a sterner and more sensible attitude' being reflected in the parliamentary debate would prove overly optimistic.[68]

The following month when Newman introduced the second reading of the bill, he confidently reported that nearly all the women's political leagues across the country had passed resolutions in favour of women's admission to Parliament. In the period since the equivalent bill was last presented to the House, laws had been passed in both the State of Colorado and in South Australia giving women the right to sit in parliament; three women were now sitting in the state legislature in Colorado, and Newman had recently been informed that two women were seeking seats in South Australia. With a slight exaggeration he asserted that 'all over the world the question was being agitated as to whether women should have seats or not in Parliament, and in almost every case it was agreed that they should have that right'.[69] As he had done the previous year, Walter Carncross seconded the motion and, although he admitted he would not admire the spectacle of any female friend of his appearing as a candidate, it was only fitting that having granted them suffrage they should 'go the full length' and allow women the right to be elected members of the House.[70] He issued a mild warning that if he saw any members who had supported women's suffrage now voting against this bill, the charge would be fairly brought against them that it was 'pure selfishness on their part that made them support woman suffrage'.[71]

The debate that ensued over the next two hours was largely a repeat of the charade that had taken place the previous year. Opponents of women's admission to Parliament referred to the bill as 'perfectly ridiculous',[72] 'altogether unnecessary',[73] a 'fad', and a subject 'scarcely worth debating'.[74] Newman came under repeated personal attack; he was charged with being none the wiser since his last attempt to introduce the legislation, and accused of working up the various women's organisations to 'fever-heat'[75] by bringing out his hobby-horse for another ride. One member suggested Newman had introduced his 'stock Bill' to gain 'a little cheap popularity', and noted that Newman was a 'leading light' among the various ladies' organisations around Wellington and was under 'a very deep obligation to the ladies for the present position he occupied as a member of that House'.[76] The Liberal member for Buller, Roderick McKenzie, contended it 'might be properly called a parliamentary "side-show", brought forward by the honourable member for Wellington Suburbs for the special entertainment of the galleries', and noted that many of Newman's constituents were present and it was likely he was putting on a serious show of trying to get the measure passed 'so as to enlist their sympathies on his behalf during the next election'.[77]

Opponents repeated the well-worn lines that women were not qualified to sit in Parliament, that they would not be any better off if they had women representatives and that women were, in fact, better represented in the House than men because members of Parliament voted on almost every occasion as their wives, sisters and aunts told them and bachelors voted as their sweethearts told them. Some claimed that women were too influenced by their hearts and sentiments; government required one to be guided by 'firmness and sound conclusions' and if women were brought into the House 'their sentiments and feelings would bring on a weak administration of the law'.[78] Others were more blatant: they stated simply that they had got along very well without women in Parliament and there was no great or urgent need to change that.

During the debate several members referred to the class of womanhood that would likely attempt to enter Parliament. One member said if the bill passed, 'it would only be the masculine sort of women who would avail themselves of it, as the better class of womanhood always held itself aloof from active politics'.[79] But another member turned the tables on his parliamentary colleagues and asked, 'Were the seventy best men in the colony in that House?', and added that the answer was self-evident.[80]

The short-lived mayoralty of Elizabeth Yates featured in the debates. Opponents of the bill attempted to use the fact that Yates' failure to be re-elected as mayor of Onehunga after only one year in office was indicative of women not being fit for political office. This prompted the member for Wanganui to stand to Yates' defence, claiming there had been many reasons why the lady mayor's term had not been a success and it did not follow that there were not other women who could occupy the position with more satisfaction to the constituents. There was a great deal of truth in these comments. Elizabeth Yates had faced a 'hard core' of opposition to her election: four councillors and the town clerk resigned immediately on her appointment, her meetings were constantly disrupted, and several councillors mounted an orchestrated policy of opposition to her initiatives. Yates' 'tactless, dictatorial manner and partial disregard for established rules of procedure'[81] exacerbated criticism of her leadership and term of office as mayor, and it came as no great surprise that she was defeated at the polls in November 1894. But the member for the City of Dunedin was particularly scathing; he said that if they had a lady of the calibre of the late mayor of Onehunga in the House it would do more injury than good to the women of New Zealand. His comment prompted another member to say such remarks were quite out of place given the lady mayor had served her term of office and had now retired back into private life. After all, there were plenty of politicians who were not re-elected to Parliament and Mrs Yates' case did not mean women should never have the opportunity of being appointed to that position in the future.

After little more than half an hour the debate started to regress into what Newman later referred to as 'ludicrous statements and the same absurd and ridiculous arguments' heard during the debates on women's suffrage.[82] Some spoke of men having to do the chivalrous thing and retire in favour of a woman candidate standing in the same electorate. Another (unmarried) member suggested if a lady stood for the electorate he represented, he would be willing to share transport and hold their meetings at the same venue on the same evening, purely in the interests of saving expenses. There was the usual recourse, veiled in light sexual innuendo, to difficulties associated with women's presence in the Chamber, such as it being awkward if a lady member asked for a 'pair' in voting or if approached by a whip for a private or confidential discussion. Constant references were made to members' marital status, insinuating that it was mainly those members who were henpecked who supported the measure, as well as eligible bachelors who may have something to gain from the presence of ladies in the Chamber.

Only a couple of members voiced genuine protest over the 'jocular flippancy and covert disparagement' that had been levelled against half the electors in the colony.[83] The member for Avon railed that 'any true man, possessing the dignity of true manhood, must have been pained at what he had listened to during the last hour' and felt that 'some expression of resentment ought to be recorded against the tone rather than the substance of some of the speeches which had been uttered'.[84] Others were unapologetic: the 'distinct jocularity' that had marked most of the speeches was 'perhaps the very best way to deal with a Bill of this kind at the present juncture', and 'there was no doubt that when a measure of an objectionable kind came before the House sarcasm was the most effective weapon to deploy against it'.[85]

The flippant and disparaging comments were interspersed with attempts by supporters to establish that the various petitions presented to the House demonstrated women did want an equal position with men in contesting parliamentary elections and, even if women as a rule would not seek to contest elections, it was a matter of common justice they be given the opportunity. They stressed that passing this bill did not actually give women a seat in the House; women would still need to stand for election and be elected by a majority of voters so, ultimately, it was electors who would decide if any individual female candidate was suitable for the position. As Liberal member Major William Steward argued, logically, 'one should permit to the people the choice of their representatives in the widest sense, and if the people chose to elect a lady he did not know why they should not be permitted to do so';[86] the essential question was, 'whether or not they had a right to set up the barrier of sex in connection with the representation of the country, seeing that that barrier had been removed in regard to the voting of members of the House'.[87] For those who took this position, it did not matter whether one or two or the majority of women claimed this right; the House had no right to deny them. The insistence on both sexes observing laws that were exclusively framed by one sex was seen as an anomaly that was illogical and, even if the bill was to be lost that night, supporters were certain it would pass at some stage.[88]

Some members professed support for the bill while at the same time betraying their opposition to women in the House. Few addressed the fact that in every case, the entry of women to Parliament would be at the expense of a man gaining or retaining a seat. The member for Timaru declared that, 'honourable members knew that there were some ladies of very brilliant intellect in their constituencies, who, if they had this right to sit in the House, would oppose those honourable gentlemen at the next election.'[89] But the dominant voices were those that thanked Newman for putting the House 'in a good-humoured and jocular mood before serious business began',[90] and, rather than complain of the waste of time, welcomed the subject as 'an oasis in the dreary desert of parliamentary debate'.[91]

In his reply, Newman insisted this was not a fad. From the time he was a medical student in London and long before he thought of entering politics, he believed women should be allowed to enter the medical profession. He had never doubted that women ought to have the same rights as men and he could see no reason why his parliamentary colleagues should make this a joke or treat it with flippancy in the same way as they had treated attempts by supporters of the female franchise. He was certain that sooner or later what was proposed in this measure would be granted, 'notwithstanding the fallacious arguments and feeble jokes that were urged against the Bill'.[92] Following his reply a division was taken and the motion to pass the second reading was lost by a majority of nine votes.

The male bastion of Parliament was not the only place where the prospect of women in Parliament was treated as a form of entertainment. Back in April 1893 the ladies of St Andrews Church in Wellington performed a play titled 'The Women's Parliament' as part of a concert entertainment,[93] and in July 1895 St Mary's School in New Plymouth opened its winter night entertainment series with the production of a scene from 'The Women's Parliament of New Zealand House of Representatives 1910', in which 26 ladies took part in a debate on the motion for the re-enfranchisement of men.[94] A preview of the entertainment said the most amusing item was a musical medley by a ladies' orchestra 'which is screamingly funny, and beggars description'.[95] The entertainment did not disappoint: the large schoolroom was crowded to excess and 'uproarious laughter' constantly interrupted the performers on the stage furnished to represent the House as they followed parliamentary protocol in the second reading of a government bill, presenting humorous and sensible arguments.[96]

Removal of Women's Disabilities Bill 1895

With the Admission of Women to Parliament Bill defeated, attention shifted to the Removal of Women's Disabilities Bill 1895 sponsored by George Russell, which had its first reading on 12 July 1895. Russell's bill had also had a change in title, as well as an extended preamble that read: 'Whereas women are now possessed of equal voting powers with men, and it is desirable that equal opportunity should be given to them to serve the country in offices in which they are competent to fill.'[97] The wording in the single operative clause was almost identical to the Women's Political Rights Bill that Russell had presented the previous year; the only change was the addition of a woman being nominated as well as appointed or elected to any public office or position.

The bill was discussed at a meeting of the executive of the Dunedin Women's Franchise League on 25 July and a resolution was carried unanimously: 'That while this Executive would urge upon the Government to give every facility for the passage of Mr G.W. Russell's Removal of Women's Disabilities Bill … they would prefer not urging the claims of women to seats in the House until the members of the present Parliament have had the opportunity of proving whether they are prepared to do full justice to our sex'.[98] Again, the timing of the bill was inopportune as the Seddon Ministry struggled with sensitivities around lack of discipline in the House and the pressure of so many bills on the order table. After languishing for nearly three months, on 2 October 1895 the Removal of Women's Disabilities Bill, along with 30 other bills, was discharged without debate. A 'brief lament to the slaughtered parliamentary innocents' appeared in the *Otago Daily Times*, which mentioned the Removal of Women's Disabilities Bill as one of several that was 'no great loss' and had been 'righteously and mercifully removed from the world where they might have done much mischief'.[99]

The National Council of Women of New Zealand

Early in 1896, Kate Sheppard returned from England, where she had networked extensively with the leaders of the British women's movement and had been in constant demand speaking at meetings. Louisa Blake, one of the founders of the Canterbury Women's Institute, wrote to welcome her home. It was not that women had stood still during her absence, Blake said, but that her presence inspired them as nothing else could. Blake's ambition was, 'that women go to the "House" and that you should be our Member'.[100]

A highlight of Sheppard's trip to England was her meeting with Eva McLaren, the foreign corresponding secretary of the International Council of Women. Formed in 1888, the council was an umbrella organisation representing 53 women's organisations from Canada, Denmark, Finland, France, India, Ireland, Norway, the United Kingdom and the United States of America. McLaren encouraged Sheppard to form a National Council of Women in New Zealand, and this confirmed the thinking of other women activists in New Zealand. During Sheppard's absence the Dunedin branch of the Women's Franchise League and the Canterbury Women's Institute had already discussed forming some type of federation of women's organisations, and the Canterbury Women's Institute had sent invitations to kindred societies throughout the country 'to cooperate ... in matters which shall tend to national progress'.[101] The response was the formation of a federation of the Canterbury Women's Institute with the Auckland, Gisborne and Wanganui Women's Political Leagues and the Dunedin Women's Franchise League. At the annual meeting of the Canterbury Women's Institute on 8 February 1896 it was resolved to organise a convention of women representatives of various organisations, 'to consider the advisability of future united action on important matters'.[102]

The convention was held across six days in the Canterbury Provincial Chambers in Christchurch and attended by representatives from 11 societies. The first item on the agenda was whether to form a national federation of women's organisations. After several presentations and discussions, members voted unanimously that the convention would resolve itself into the National Council of Women of New Zealand. On the final afternoon George Russell, in his capacity as member of the House of Representatives for Riccarton, spoke on the 'Political Disabilities of Women', after which Amey Daldy, the delegate for the Auckland Women's Political League, moved the resolution 'That all disabilities be removed which at present hinder women from sitting as members of either House of the Legislature, or from being elected or appointed to any public office or position in the colony which men may hold, and with regard to all powers, rights, duties and privileges of citizens, to declare absolute equality to be the law of the land for both men and women.'[103] The wording of the resolution encapsulated principles expressed by supporters of women's full equal citizenship in the resolutions and legislation that had been put before Parliament over the last two decades. That the resolution was carried unanimously affirmed that the admission of women to Parliament was to be an important part of the platform of the National Council of Women.

Possibly influenced by their experiences in the suffrage campaign, many of the prominent women in the NCW and its component organisations believed that change would be a gradual rather than radical achievement. It was continually emphasised that women needed to develop their understanding of political institutions to ensure that they were qualified to hold political office. To this end, the programme for the Christchurch convention included sessions on party government, referenda, and reform of the Upper House. A vast range of topics was discussed, many concerning the need for legislative reform in areas such as the regulation of 'sweating industries',[104] setting a minimum wage, review of marriage and divorce laws, a woman's right to a share of her husband's earnings, support for the unemployed, old age pensions, reform in the treatment of criminals, women serving on juries, immigration, reform of the police force, repeal of the contagious diseases legislation, and raising the age of consent. There were calls for women to be eligible for seats on all local bodies that administered charitable aid funds, and renewed calls for women to have a seat on school committees, education boards, and hospital and charitable aid boards.

On the face of it, that the women attendees at the convention believed 'in the calm conviction that in fifty minutes by the clock they were capable of introducing, discussing, forming an opinion, and passing resolutions upon a problem'[105] could suggest a political naivety, but in fact many of the women present had been discussing these issues in their respective organisations long before the convention took place. The ambitious programme of the convention was indicative of renewed energy and commitment to extending women's influence and engagement in the political sphere. Throughout the suffrage campaign it had been repeated that the franchise was a means to an end. Likewise, in the debate over women's admission to Parliament over the intervening two years one message was very clear: until women presented a concerted voice demanding the right to sit in Parliament, many sitting members would not lend their support to the measure. The formation of the NCW was a next step in women's political organising beyond the petitions with two or three signatures or even 200 or 300 signatures. As a nationwide umbrella organisation, the NCW was a representative voice for women in New Zealand. The challenge would be to convince members of Parliament that this was so.

'The Charter of the Independence of Women'

Within the first week of the opening of the new session of Parliament in June 1896, both Newman and Russell signalled their intention to reintroduce their respective bills for the admission of women to Parliament and the removal of women's disabilities. With the second general election in which women would be a voting force due later that year, the press impugned the motives of politicians who were deemed to be touting for the female vote. An Otago newspaper commented, 'The advent of lovely woman, into politics, is causing many New Zealand politicians to coquette with fancy legislation in the hope of winning the smiles and votes of the fair sex, at the next election. Appropriately enough, Dr *New*man, M.H.R. is a strong advocate of the new woman.'[106]

Newspaper editors predicted that the Lower House would, as an electioneering measure, likely pass the Removal of Women's Disabilities Bill but that it would be scuttled in the Upper House. On 25 June, Russell had the opportunity to move the second reading of the bill. In doing so he explained that while women's conduct at the 1893 general election completely justified their being granted the franchise, the franchise was not their goal; the franchise was simply 'the means of enabling them to exercise their power in connection with the government of the country'.[107] The intention of the current bill was to remove the disabilities under which women stood, namely, being debarred from becoming members of the legal profession, members of the House of Representatives, nominated to positions in the Legislative Council, and serving on juries. Alongside these legal disabilities were others that had arisen from custom and practice, such as holding office as justices of the peace and thereby being shut out from being official visitors to the gaols and lunatic asylums, and being shut out from the civil service except in offices of a minor character such as typists, telephonists and secretaries.

George Russell's argument was straightforward. Behind each of these disabilities was what he referred to as 'the sex distinction'.[108] Granting women the franchise had effectively exploded this distinction and made woman man's equal politically. It was, therefore, a logical outcome of the franchise that public offices should be open to women in the same way as they were open to men. He suggested the bill might be thought of as

'The Charter of the Independence of Women' because with a single stroke of the pen it swept away their legal disabilities. The bill dealt with the broad principle by affirming that every qualified voter would be entitled to offer themselves as a candidate 'for the suffrages of the people'.[109] When it came to the question of whether it was desirable that women take seats in Parliament, that would remain a question for the constituencies to decide. Drawing attention to the fact that at present there was no restriction as to the character, race or ability of any man who may choose to offer himself as a candidate for the suffrages of the people, and that the present laws allowed a 'naturalised Chinaman' to offer himself as a candidate and, if elected, to take a seat in the House, Russell asked, 'can we refuse to women, on the ground of sex-distinction, that right we offer to the naturalised Chinaman?'[110] Anticipating the suggestion that women were not in favour of this proposal, Russell stated that at every representative gathering of women during the year, resolutions had been passed in favour of the bill. He referred to the convention in Christchurch, the way the women present had conducted their business, the interest shown in the affairs of the colony, and the resolutions passed as further evidence of women's support for the measure.

James Allen, the Conservative member for Bruce, called for some expression of opinion on the bill from the ministers before the debate progressed. In his opinion, the bill went 'a great deal too far' and, while the enfranchisement of women was a step in the direction of this bill, it should be 'a very gradual development'.[111] To his mind it was a question of expedience, but his argument betrayed an underlying racial and cultural prejudice. He referred to the views of unnamed advanced writers who believed that evolution would lead to increased competition between men. If this was true, before long all men would be placed socially and politically on the same plane. This was not a very encouraging prospect for men and boys and became even more grim if women were then added, thereby doubling the competition. So, to Allen, the question was less what are we going to do with our women than what are we going to do with our men and boys?

In his speech in support of the bill, Alfred Newman accused the government of underhand politics. He drew attention to the fact that while the ministry seemed not to be prepared to move in the direction proposed by this bill, they had been diligent of late in lending support to women who were regarded as leaders of political thought. These women were members of Liberal associations and supporters of the government, and the support was by way of political scholarships to their male relatives in the form of appointments as inspectors of lunatic asylums. According to Newman, the government was encouraging women who had male relatives in the civil service to come forward at public meetings to propose and second votes in favour of the government's actions. He suggested that, in time, these women would likely be rewarded through promotions of their husbands and brothers.

Aside from Newman's snide criticisms of the government, the tone of the debate was refreshingly courteous and dignified. Several members referred to the recent convention in Christchurch and women's increased efforts to educate themselves politically. Speakers stressed that passing this legislation would not result in any radical changes: once their political disabilities were removed women could take pride in educating themselves for positions they would have a right to occupy, and which they would gradually assume. As one member stated, 'members of Parliament have to be elected, and Judges have to be selected, and merit has to be developed before any results will be achieved'.[112]

In his reply, Russell said he was heartened that the levity that usually accompanied discussions in Parliament regarding the position and claims of women was conspicuous by its absence. In his closing comments he suggested that one result from women being placed in positions to deal with public matters would be more attention to questions of special importance and interest to women. His list was remarkably like the range of issues discussed at the recent convention: the treatment of the insane in asylums, the treatment of criminals including juvenile criminals, prostitution, illegitimacy, the supply of food to children and to the poor, state doctors and old age pensions. Russell's optimism was boosted when the motion to read the bill a second time passed by a majority of four votes and the Removal of Women's Disabilities Bill 1896 proceeded to committee.

Newspaper reports of the positive reception of the bill observed that while this may be indicative of a general growth of public support for conferring on women all the privileges men held, it was more likely that members voted with the upcoming general election in mind. What was significant was that, in the voting, government ministers were divided, with three now for and two against the bill. It was significant that party discipline was at a point that threatened to split the Liberal Party. The Independent Liberals had never been more independent than at this point and there had been increased talk of the possibility of a more definite grouping of what Russell referred to as 'the advanced section of the Liberal party', himself included.[113] Reports were circulating about the imminent formation of a Radical Party with the aim of securing the balance of power in the House by defeating Premier Seddon at the general election. Although he refused to talk publicly on the matter, Russell was implicated as the originator of this new political grouping. Attempts to formally secure a leader – dubbed in the press 'the sensation of the hour' – were aborted and Russell and his supporters were looked on 'as fair butts for bantering ridicule', but the attempt to formalise this grouping served to demonstrate that there was sufficient support for a nucleus of an Independent party 'as a "stand-by", in the event of political confusion arising at the general election'.[114] The publicity received over Russell's extra-parliamentary discussions did nothing to increase parliamentary support for his bill, and the optimism engendered by the smooth passage of the bill through its second reading to committee proved ill guided. In committee, Independent Liberal member for Clutha Thomas Mackenzie, the 'arch representative of the conservative and country political outlook'[115] who had not supported the second reading of the bill, moved that the chairman leave the chair, thereby ensuring the vote was won by a majority of six which, in the words of one reporter, effectively 'slaughtered' the bill.[116] In a Parliament prone to 'periodical fits ... of retaliatory obstruction',[117] tactical gameplaying by opponents of women's increased political participation had again been deployed to stifle passage of the legislation.

Admission of Women to Parliament Bill 1896

As was the case when Russell introduced his bill for a second reading the preceding week, Newman was able to confidently report, when introducing the Admission of Women to Parliament Bill for a second reading, that in the recess he had received letters from individual women and from women's political societies strongly urging the measure be passed. He noted the resolution passed in favour of the measure by the NCW, and once again he referred to women's achievements in South Australia and in Colorado, as well as the bill recently introduced in the English House of Commons that proposed to grant suffrage to women and to allow them to sit in Parliament.

Identifying himself as 'a convert to this Bill', the Independent Liberal member for Ashburton John McLachlan typified the posturing of some members motivated by securing women's votes at the upcoming election. Having the previous year described the bill as 'scarcely worth debating', McLachlan now professed support in a speech replete with contradictions. He did not think there was any probability that large numbers of women would be elected to the House; the women would themselves raise enough objection to any of their sex coming here and they would not vote for female representatives. He deplored the prospect of any of his lady friends coming into the House as it was not a fit place for a woman, indeed, 'it is not her proper sphere', but this did not mean women should be barred from the House. There were many physical difficulties in the way of women being in Parliament and it would be 'exceedingly inconvenient for married women especially to be in Parliament' as they would not always be able to attend when Parliament was in session and therefore their constituents would be disenfranchised. McLachlan ended his speech in bluster: 'But, notwithstanding these difficulties, I shall vote with the honourable member, and will not stand in the way of a woman exercising a right which is already granted to men. I should be sorry to see women come into Parliament, but if they wish to come they have a right to come, and, if their sisters wish to see them here, let them come.'[118]

Thomas Mackenzie refuted the claim made by an earlier member that women were demanding this measure; he insisted that 'a few unsettled women are making a fuss who in no way represent our best women, nor yet the majority of women, in New Zealand'.[119] He believed the measure was being thrust upon them in the same manner as the franchise had been thrust upon them when they did not want it. He claimed that 'some of the most absurd resolutions that have ever been proposed in New Zealand were carried by the women at that conference', including restricting a man to bequeathing no more than five per cent of his property to charity, and allowing one half of a man's wages to be set aside 'if his wife elects to be a mother of children, or to look after her home'.[120]

Premier Seddon was another who had purportedly shifted in his opinion, although he reminded the House that, while he had opposed women's franchise some years back, at that time he had said that when the franchise was granted to women it would be logical to support their admission to Parliament. He pointed out women's progress over recent years, and noted that women had proven themselves the equal of their male competitors in both the medical profession 'where nerve and application is wanted', and in the legal profession 'where study and quickness is wanted, and a quick grasp of a position, and the sifting and taking of evidence'.[121] Women had gained the highest educational positions available in universities, and they could no longer be claimed to be an 'inferior creation'.[122] He declared he was ready to trust women and was confident that, if the opportunity arose and women did gain election, they would do justice to those who had sent them to the House.

Seddon's change of view appears to have placed him in opposition to his wife's views: the previous evening William Collins, the Independent Liberal member for the City of Christchurch, received warm applause for speaking strongly against the admission of women to Parliament at a meeting of the Women's Social and Political League in Wellington chaired by Louisa Seddon. But addressing the House, Seddon roundly countered claims that the atmosphere of Parliament would not be to women's taste. He knew of nothing 'in this Chamber, or in the lobbies, or the library, or anywhere in connection with the parliamentary benches and its surroundings, that would be uncongenial to woman'. He was adamant 'a woman could be here without any harm to herself', and he rejected the mock modesty of those who suggested there may be matters that arose in debates for which women would be out of place; instead he insisted, 'there is nothing that comes before Parliament, or matters that require our consideration and attention, in which she is not capable of taking her part'.[123]

Always the clever and astute politician, Seddon followed these speeches with an attempt to talk up a rivalry between Newman and Russell, and the latter rose to the bait. Seddon had suggested the House was being 'double-banked' with two concurrent measures to effect the admission of women to Parliament and that this 'double-barrelled process' was unduly pressing on members. He thought it was unkind of Russell to 'jump the claim' on Newman, who had been consistent in bringing the measure forward for so many years. When Russell interrupted to say this was the third year he had brought the issue before the House, Seddon responded with, 'Why, before the honourable gentleman was born the honourable member for the Suburbs was introducing a Bill removing disability from women,'[124] to which Russell retorted, 'I defeated him twelve or fourteen years ago.'[125] Having made his point, Seddon let the matter rest, but it opened the way for other members to focus on personality politics.

There was no doubt that the upcoming election influenced the tone of the debate. Some members professed to being new converts. In the words of serial opponent to the bill William Earnshaw, the Independent Liberal member for the City of Dunedin who had wrested the seat from Henry Fish at the previous election, 'There is a lot of cant and nonsense talked on this question about the admission of women to Parliament; and it is all done purely for the purpose of capturing votes at the coming elections. There is not the slightest doubt of that.'[126] Earnshaw disputed the representativeness of the resolutions made at the recent women's convention: he asserted they were simply the individual views of the individual women attending the convention; the women in attendance had not been deputed from the different organisations on the questions discussed let alone on the constitution of the National Council of Women of New Zealand. His claim that the most politically active women in the country were those in the electorate he represented provoked interjections to the contrary from the members for Auckland and Christchurch, which only led to accusations that those members were trying to stall the bill through constant interruptions to his speech.

To his credit, Russell challenged some of the claims made by his colleagues. First, the women's convention met to deliberate on issues, and, as part of that process, they passed a number of resolutions; had they attended simply to record votes already taken by their respective organisations there would have been no need to meet. Second, it was unworthy of the premier to create an impression of rivalry between himself and the member for Wellington Suburbs; no such rivalry existed, and each had been supportive of the measures the other had brought before the House. Finally, if the premier now felt so strongly that women should be admitted to Parliament, he should take it up as a matter of government policy. It did not make political sense when a great social revolution of this kind was taking place in the country for the premier to support a private member and yet be unwilling to take that same stand in leading the country, particularly as he had a very large part of the Liberal Party behind him. In his closing comments, Newman reiterated that 'Notwithstanding all the fanfaronade' in the speeches, the women of the colony had undoubtedly voiced their desire to have a seat in the Chamber 'and their desire that all the restrictions which prevent them from entering this Chamber should be promptly and effectually removed'.[127] But those opposed to the measure held the day and the motion for the second reading of the bill was lost by a single vote.

As the general election approached and candidates on the campaign trail touted for women's votes, sitting members were reminded of their record on the bills that had been presented during the current session on the removal of women's political disabilities and women's admission to Parliament. Some candidates who conveniently misremembered how they had voted were reminded through the letters to the editor columns of the daily newspapers. Printing these was at the discretion of the editor and their individual political leanings came into play on occasion. The editor of the *Temuka Leader* was a case in point: noting a second letter from the same correspondent on the issue of women's admission to Parliament, the editor commented, 'Surely you cannot expect the whole paper taken up with this paltry subject'.[128]

During the closing debates on Newman's Admission of Women to Parliament Bill 1896, somewhat prophetically, the Independent Liberal member for the newly created electorate of Waimea–Sounds, Charles Mills, stated: 'I believe that if the majority of women wish for the entry into Parliament it will come in the course of years, because they have the early education of their children, and, as they grow up imbued with the mother's sentiments of wishing women to come into this House, the probability is that they will eventually reach this Chamber whenever they earnestly wish to do so.'[129] His words reflected the prevalent opinion that women were not ready for this step and that they did not really desire admission to Parliament. Male politicians and women activists alike believed that women needed to become more educated, develop their understanding of political processes and gain experience in other civic roles before they would be ready to take a seat in the House.

CHAPTER 3

Serving their political apprenticeship, 1897 to 1910

They have valuable political rights; they are now serving their political apprenticeship, and when the time comes that they ought to occupy a position in this House ... the men of New Zealand will have sufficient gallantry to let them assume their proper position. — ALEXANDER HOGG, MHR, 29 JULY 1898[1]

The 1896 general election was a victory for the Liberal Party and a second term for the Seddon Ministry, albeit with a lesser majority and a greater Conservative presence in Parliament. The orderliness of proceedings was again credited to women's attendance at the polls. But the election came at a high cost for the cause of women's admission to Parliament: the three most consistent allies of women in the House – Alfred Saunders, Alfred Newman and George Russell – had all been defeated in their electorates. Another ally emerged in the person of Thomas Edward (Tommy) Taylor, the newly elected Independent prohibitionist member for Christchurch City. Taylor was a forceful orator in Parliament, 'capable of filling the House as soon as word spread that he was on his feet',[2] but his reputation as a strong critic of Seddon's leadership, style of government, and dominance over party and Parliament would prove to be not conducive to winning support from his parliamentary colleagues for the two bills for the removal of women's disabilities he presented during this parliamentary term.

A national council of men

The editor of the *New Zealand Times*, reflecting on election day and on women's involvement in politics in the previous three years since gaining the electoral franchise, said he believed that women were now participating fully by organising, speaking and in committee and meeting work, to the extent that their appearance in the political arena was no longer a novelty.[3] But in her presidential address to the NCW conference in Christchurch in April 1897, Kate Sheppard argued that far greater involvement by women in politics was necessary at local and national level. She spoke of a national council of men which assembled every year in Wellington for several months, for which every member was granted a free railway pass and received a salary sufficient to maintain him during the year. This national council of men deliberated and legislated on matters of general interest as well as on matters of special interest to women and children. Women were excluded from taking part in this council and, at times, even from listening to the discussion. Sheppard maintained that, by necessity, the subjects discussed by men were likely to be only from a man's point of view, and this had been evident in the indignities imposed on women by the contagious diseases legislation, and in the arguments used to defend the inequality of divorce laws. To Sheppard, this was sufficient justification for 'a National Council which largely represents the thinking and working women of the colony' and, as she pointed out, cost the country nothing. But this was only a temporary solution and she trusted 'the day is not far distant when men will no longer exclude women from their deliberations, when legislation will no longer be one-sided, and when the necessity of Men's Councils and Women's Councils, as such, will be swept away'.[4] She contrasted the unfairness of New Zealand law with the law that applied to 'our sister colony of South Australia', in which women could be elected to Parliament.[5]

These comments by Sheppard suggest that the executive of the NCW at least, if not the wider council membership – dubbed the 'Woman's Parliament' by politicians, the press and the public – understood themselves to be a counter-balance to Parliament in all but legislative powers. But it would prove a long struggle to convince politicians, the press and the public that the NCW had genuine credibility as the voice of women in the colony, particularly regarding the call for women's rightful entry into all areas of civic and parliamentary decision-making.

A paper on 'The disabilities of women' presented by Amey Daldy offers insights into what shaped the thinking of members of the NCW at the time. A staunch Congregationalist and founding member of the Auckland branch of the WCTU, Daldy had a keen sense of tailoring her arguments to her audience. Back in 1892 when she was speaking at a public meeting in Auckland to gauge support for forming a branch of the Women's Franchise League, she said that while women wanted the vote they did not want to take a seat in Parliament. Later she admitted to former premier Sir George Grey that she had made this claim only because she did not want to frighten the public.[6] In her paper to the NCW convention she identified five causes that had led to women's disabilities: women's constitution, heredity, education, misconstrued Scripture, and laws. Explaining what she meant by women's constitution, she said there were times when women were incapacitated from taking a share in public life and this had probably led to women being interested only in domestic concerns. To illustrate her argument she drew on the writings of eighteenth-century English philosopher and women's advocate Mary Wollstonecraft, who said it was 'natural' for women to focus on their outward appearance when men talked about business, politics or literature because women had no business, had not turned their thoughts to the political world, and had not had the opportunity to cultivate a taste for literature. In referring to heredity, Daldy did not mean genetic heredity, but the great influence a mother had over her children. The essence of her argument was that all these causes of women's disabilities were social and a product of the times. History, however, had proven that women did have the ability to take an active and intelligent part in every sphere on an equal basis with men. The key was for women to develop their own fitness, ability and willingness: 'We need to arouse in woman a reasonable degree of self-respect, and to remove from man that feeling engendered by prejudice and training.'[7] She described women as being 'in the chrysalis state, hardly knowing our own capabilities, yet feeling we could accomplish something if only we were free, free as the other sex'.[8]

Motivated by the need for a political ally in the House, in September 1897 Kate Sheppard wrote to journalist and lawyer Patrick O'Regan, the radical Liberal member for Buller, to ask if he would take charge of the bill to abolish women's political disabilities. It was perhaps an indication of the lack of supporters in the House that led her to approach O'Regan, a young, relatively inexperienced politician who was on record for not supporting the recent measures introduced by his former colleagues Newman and Russell. Although O'Regan had voted for the Removal of Women's Disabilities Bill the previous year, he had voted against each of the bills that would have admitted women to Parliament presented since he was elected to the House at the 1893 general election. On the only occasion he had spoken on this issue he admitted he 'almost owed his election to the support of the ladies',[9] but had opposed the measure on three grounds: he did not believe women had the physical strength or stamina required for an election campaign or for the duties of a member; he believed that if ladies were admitted to the House they might lose their charms; and he claimed that women had not expressed a desire for the measure. His response to Sheppard was unequivocal: he regretted he was unable to accede to her request because he was opposed to women sitting in Parliament, but he had the good grace to add that he was 'none the less sensible of the good intentions actuating the organisation you so ably represent'.[10]

The suggestion made by men and women alike that women would become unwomanly if they sat in Parliament was the subject of an article in the *White Ribbon* titled 'Women's disabilities'. The writer observed that the mere idea of women taking a seat in Parliament seemed to these people 'a picture of utter unwomanliness, and arouses their deepest indignation'. The article questioned why it should be considered such an anomaly for women to sit alongside men in the Parliament passing laws for the relief of the needy, the care and education of children and the welfare of the people; and why, if members of the House of Representatives were, as their title designated, honourable men, there would be any need to fear that women's modesty would be harmed by being associated with them: if they were not all honourable men, they should not be allowed in the House. The writer pointed out that it was not actually unusual for women to be in Parliament – early every morning women would be in the House with pads and brushes cleaning up the dust and litter of the Legislative Chambers as well as the tobacco ash and spittoons at Bellamy's – and stated, 'If this work does not injure the dignity of womanhood (and we hear no outcry against it), would it be degrading to occupy one of the cushioned seats and speak as to the wants and wishes of the people?'[11]

In the first week of the new session of Parliament in September 1897, in her capacity as president of the NCW, Kate Sheppard wrote to Premier Seddon requesting that the government introduce a bill for the removal of the civil and political disabilities of women.[12] She was aware the present session was likely to be a very busy one and suggested that even if the bill did not become law, 'good would be done by having the subject discussed and ventilated'.[13] Backtracking on the position he had stated in the House the previous year, Seddon replied he was not in a position to agree to introduce the bill, but he assured her that while he personally favoured the disabilities being removed that prevented women from taking places on local bodies, he did not think it was time yet for women to be elected as members of the General Assembly.[14]

Sheppard corresponded with Tommy Taylor, who advised that O'Regan was 'a good fellow but not very forceful' and she should approach someone who was in sympathy with the bill; he suggested Sir Robert Stout or, if she could gain no other supporter, he would gladly assist himself. But he advised her that there was not the slightest chance of any private member's bill being passed in the current session unless it was connected with harbour or local finance.[15] Former premier Stout was known for his progressive political philosophy and his formidable debating skill. But since he had been ousted by Seddon as successor to John Ballance in 1893, largely because he was too closely associated with the radical prohibitionist lobby, Stout was becoming increasingly disillusioned with Seddon's style of government and with the way party politics were developing. Taylor had discussed Sheppard's request with Stout, who agreed there was not even a remote chance of the Disabilities Bill becoming law this session or even reaching a debate, although he thought there was usefulness in proposing it be included on the Order Paper and agreed to attend to that. Stout suggested that if there was any chance that Seddon might introduce the bill in the next session it would be advisable to wait, although he suggested to Taylor that any measure the premier agreed to introduce would likely fall far short of Sheppard's ideal.[16]

The Parliament of 1897–99 was dominated by personality politics, and Taylor was central to this. He, like Russell in the previous session, was part of the 'left wing', comprised of dissident Liberals who would not be drawn into

Seddon's ranks and who sought to galvanise the government to more radical action, in line with what they considered to be true Liberalism. Taylor's main grievance with Seddon was because of Seddon's anti-prohibitionist stance which, for someone such as Taylor who had come to national prominence through his activities as a prohibitionist, placed Seddon squarely in the camp of the enemy. But having developed a reputation in Parliament for carrying his personal campaigns to excess and frightening away potential allies, Taylor's erratic conduct had the effect of further fragmenting the disorganised opposition to Seddon's government. With Seddon determined to organise the Liberal Party in Parliament, by the end of 1897 he was regularly calling meetings of his caucus to establish a better rapport with his party and to reign in support for government measures. The Independents, encouraged by Tommy Taylor, began holding their own caucus as a signal to Parliament that they were neither subservient to the government line nor did they consider themselves members of the Opposition.

Both inside and outside Parliament there was a growing acceptance that while women would, one day, achieve the right to take a seat in the House, it may be some time away. In a letter to Sheppard in February 1898, Sir John Hall said that while the claim for women's political emancipation was 'absolutely just & reasonable that it *must* prevail', he may not live to see it, but he was confident that Sheppard would.[17] Sheppard acknowledged that the legislative record for 1897 was disappointing; in her analysis, 'The various measures of reform for which we have hoped have been sacrificed mainly to prejudice and party strife.' This led her to question whether in fact the present system of party government was not a 'huge mistake ... most detrimental to the interests of the people'.[18]

After the disappointments of the previous year, it was more than symbolic that the venue for the annual convention of the NCW in April 1898 was Bellamy's in Parliament Buildings. In her president's address Sheppard said she was delighted to accept the hospitality of their Wellington friends. As she put it, 'the advent of women in Bellamy's may be looked on as prophetic; a shadow of that coming time when women shall no longer be forbidden to act as representatives of the people'.[19] Once again the council confirmed its resolve: 'That in the opinion of this Council the time has come when all disabilities which at present hinder women from sitting as members in either House of the Legislature, or from being elected or appointed to any public office or position in the colony, should be removed, and that with regard to all powers, rights, and duties of citizens, absolute equality be the law of the land.'[20] Another whose resolve was indomitable was Mary Müller, who had been corresponding with Sheppard since women's suffrage was won: writing in pencil because of her rheumatic hand, she told Sheppard, 'I am a very old woman now (70) but my desire for the complete emancipation of my sex is my dearest earthly prayer.'[21]

Removal of Women's Disabilities Bill 1898

One week after the beginning of the parliamentary session of 1898, the Opposition proposed a motion of no confidence in the Seddon Government. Although the motion did not succeed, the margin of six votes provided little comfort for the government, who were put on notice that they could not rely on what one parliamentary reporter described as 'the free and easy go-as-you-please of the past, experienced by having so large a majority'.[22] The 'left wing' and 'independent' reaction against the Seddon Government was abating and Tommy Taylor, along with the Conservative member for Pātea, George Hutchison, were treated simply as 'erratic loners'.[23]

Whether Sheppard was aware of Taylor's increasingly ostracised position in Parliament or not, she was dependent on him to advocate on behalf of women. Taylor remained good to his word and agreed to sponsor the Removal of Women's Disabilities Bill as a private member's bill. The operative clause of the bill read, 'After the passing of this Act a woman may be nominated, appointed, or elected to any public office or position to which a man may be appointed or elected, any law or statute to the contrary notwithstanding.'[24] Introducing the bill in July 1898, Taylor pointed out that the population of the colony was almost equally divided, with 376,969 males and 337,175 females. He then proceeded on a somewhat dubious line of argument, asserting that there could be no doubt that women had a superior claim in connection with any public position on the basis that there were significantly fewer females than males in prisons and lunatic asylums. Anticipating the argument that women were too emotional to be in Parliament, he made the curious and provocative claim: 'there are as many men in the colony mentally incapable of occupying positions in this House as women'.[25] He suggested that if the morality of the sexes was tested, 'you will find that on that score, as on nearly every other point, the men come out second best'.[26] Like many of his colleagues, Taylor believed it quite unlikely that many women would offer themselves for nomination to the House, and he suggested perhaps only as many as 12 women would do so in the next five years. He remarked on the dignity with which the suffrage campaign had been pursued under Mrs Kate Sheppard's leadership, and noted there were some exceptionally able women with wide knowledge of public affairs whose aid in legislation would be invaluable. He countered the anticipated argument that women did not have the powers of endurance to occupy seats in the House with: 'They are the nurses of the world, and their powers of endurance are beyond dispute.'[27] In moving the second reading of the bill, Taylor hoped it would pass 'to the credit of the Parliament and to the intense satisfaction of many thoughtful women'.[28]

Taylor came under some criticism for depreciating men in order to elevate women in his speech. But the real issue, as one of his parliamentary colleagues observed, was that anything anyone might say in the debate that was to proceed had already been said fifty times over and any new speech was new only inasmuch as it was 'a rearrangement of words and phrases in repeating the same sentiments'.[29] Another member referred obliquely to the 'mournful consequences' that had befallen those individual men who had brought the measure before the House on previous occasions. 'What did the women do to these reformers in the last general election?' he asked. 'I refer to Dr Newman and Mr Riccarton Russell. What did the women do for these distinguished champions? Why, Sir, they extinguished them. They killed them off.'[30]

Three positions that had emerged over recent years predominated in the ensuing debate: it was not yet the right time for women to be admitted to Parliament; women had not demonstrated a strong consistent demand for the measure; and the measure should pass, and it should be left to the electors to decide when it was appropriate for women to be elected to seats in the House. All three positions had merit, yet there was still no consensus within the NCW. This was evident in the report on activities of the council from 1896 to 1899, prepared by Kate Sheppard and Margaret Sievwright in their respective capacities as president and secretary and presented by the New Zealand delegate Beatrice Webb to the International Council of Women in London in July 1899. English socialist economist Beatrice Webb was not a supporter of the cause of women's suffrage; however, she and her husband Sidney Webb had been critical of Seddon during a visit to New Zealand the previous year, and Beatrice Webb made reference in her diary to 'the petty unscrupulousness and vulgarity of his parliamentary tactics and administrative action'.[31] The report to the International Council of Women noted that, although the resolution for the removal of all women's disabilities had been unanimously carried at the last National Council of Women of New Zealand meeting, 'We wish it to be clearly understood that the above opinions [in the report] do not necessarily represent the unanimous vote of our Council members, but the majority vote.[32]

The debate on the Removal of Women's Disabilities Bill 1898 was marked by political posturing, with some members professing support for women's rights yet rehearsing the gambit of arguments for why they should not be admitted to Parliament. Some called for a referendum, others drew on the language of justice and rights, and others drew attention to trust in the people being the fundamental doctrine of Liberalism. Described by one reporter as a 'piece of misplaced indulgence',[33] the consensus of the debate was in favour of a second reading of the bill, which passed without division. Although passing a second reading would generally be taken as a positive sign, as former member for Riccarton George Russell wrote in a letter to the Christchurch *Star*, the bill was 'by no means out of the wood'; many of those who had allowed the second reading to pass would be 'only too glad to see it killed in committee'. Experience had told him 'the supineness of friends is a far greater danger to progressive legislation than the open hostility of declared foes'.[34] Russell's advice of caution proved correct: three weeks out from the close of the parliamentary session, the Removal of Women's Disabilities Bill was one of 39 bills discharged.

Removal of Women's Disabilities Bill 1899

Early in the parliamentary session the following year Tommy Taylor again presented the Removal of Women's Disabilities Bill to the House. Only one member spoke to the bill and even that was on the pretext that it would be discourteous to the honourable member for Christchurch City if the bill passed a second reading without at least a few criticisms of it. Again it was stressed that support for this measure did not necessarily require members to express any opinion on whether or not women should take their seats in the House as that was a question for 'the free and independent electors of this colony'.[35] The bill subsequently passed its second reading by a majority of eight votes but again it sat for weeks on the Order Paper.

With the general election three and a half weeks away,[36] on 12 October Seddon indicated 'with a facetious wink'[37] that the parliamentary session would end the following week. Earlier that day a caucus had relegated about a hundred bills to be discharged, but it was reported that the demand by 'one of Tom Taylor's protegés' for a division on the Removal of Women's Disabilities Bill was upheld. It was clear from both the tone and the content of the newspaper report that, despite the upcoming general election, there was little political will to support the measure. Various members in turn dodged 'the invidious honour' of being tellers against the bill, to the point that Taylor suggested that the premier should take the job himself. It was reported that 'the majority of the horrid males ungallantly voted for the continuance of the disabilities of the sex, and to the slaughter went the little Bill'.[38]

Over the 1897–99 period there was a growing belief that if the Seddon Government was replaced it would be by a more distinctly radical ministry, but as long as the current government was prepared to keep in touch with 'the expanding Liberal sentiment of the country'[39] they would likely be returned. The 1899 general election proved this correct. The outcome marked the acceptance of the majority for the programme and policies of the Liberal Government under Premier Seddon, which was returned with 51 of the 70 seats in the House and was starting to take on 'an air of permanence'.[40] The election was a mixed result in terms of allies for women's admission to Parliament. Newman was unsuccessful in contesting the Wellington Suburbs seat, but Russell regained the Riccarton seat by a single vote, while Taylor lost his Christchurch City seat to Independent Liberal Harry Ell, who espoused the causes of prohibition and women's rights.

As Taylor had done during the previous session of Parliament, Russell soon re-established himself in the role of radical critic of the government. In Russell's case, however, he proved to be little more than a nuisance to Seddon and the government; and, as was the case with Taylor, being continually offside with the majority of the House compromised his capacity to be an influential advocate for the cause of women.

Following the 1899 election, despite its strong majority in the House, political allegiances in the Liberal Government were very fluid. Seddon's practice of using caucus to impose uniformity on Liberal members had proven less effective during the previous term of office and he turned to the practice of receiving deputations from members and, when necessary, changing policy in response to pressures from various factions in the party. In a move that engendered considerable unease among government members, the Opposition decided to terminate its formal existence by not electing a parliamentary leader. As distinctions between Liberal and Conservative blurred and seemed to make less sense, debates ensued about the usefulness of the Liberal label, particularly as many were now referring to themselves as 'old Liberals', 'new Liberals' and 'true Liberals' without necessarily having an interest in a progressive agenda for reform.

George Russell had consistently been at the centre of debates on the real meaning of Liberalism. In a Budget debate in 1895 he had stated that the Liberal party had been elected 'to undertake the settlement of social problems' and that its policy must be progressive. In his view, Liberalism could not '"stand at ease", for the moment it falls back or ceases to move forward to meet the changing aspirations and needs of the people it will cease to grow, and the end cannot be far away'.[41] Amid concerns that the era of Liberalism might be coming to an end, Russell continued to speak out against the demise of 'true' Liberalism and the increasingly populist agenda of Seddon. There remained a wide divergence of opinion within the Liberal Party and this was evident during debate on the single bill to remove women's political disabilities presented during the Parliament of 1900 to 1902.

Removal of Women's Disabilities Bill 1900

Six years after he first introduced a similar bill, on 27 June 1900 in front of a packed Ladies' Gallery George Russell moved to bring in the Removal of Women's Disabilities Bill 1900. From the onset there were signals that the bill would be opposed but that it would provide light relief on the part of some members of the House. In a blatant attempt to stifle the bill before any opportunity for debate, George Fisher, the Independent Liberal member for Wellington City – considered troublesome because of his ambition to advance himself by unsettling the government – called for a division. His tactic failed spectacularly, and the division passed by a majority of 52 votes.

Russell's introductory comments when moving the second reading the following day were perfunctory, in acknowledgement that the House was in 'a distinctly business frame of mind'.[42] Recognised as 'one of the characters of the House'[43] on account of his comic nature, unconventional style of attire[44] and his propensity to end his speeches with lines of verse, Edward Smith, the Independent Liberal member for Taranaki, drew attention to the participation of women in the Liberal Federation, which had been formed before the last general election. Having supported the bill on every occasion it had been brought before the House, to Smith's mind, women's involvement in the Liberal Federation and their now routine work on committees and school boards sealed any doubt that they should be given equal parliamentary rights. When a fellow member interjected by calling out 'Mrs Yates', Smith expressed his regret that the former mayor of Onehunga had not been given fair play and had been subjected to ridicule. Characteristically, he ended his speech with a rallying verse:

> Arrayed beneath the stainless light,
> Shoulder to shoulder sternly true,
> In the cause of common right,
> There is noble work to do.
> Then, awake ye dull lethargic crew,
> Dash down oppression's iron wall,
> And claim, in voice as thunder loud,
> A fair equality for all.[45]

The following speaker attempted to move an adjournment of the debate in the interests of returning home early that night, but he was ignored. The usual array of supporters and detractors arose in turn to reiterate the well-worn arguments. Some were more colourful in their comments. George Fisher, who had attempted to scuttle the bill by calling a division before its first reading, called the bill a 'travesty'; 'the whole thing is too suggestive of feeding-bottles and perambulators,' he said.[46] Feigning a more ominous note, he added, 'This is no mere plaything; there is danger in it,' and he accused the House of 'trifling with the question of putting members of Parliament into petticoats'. He them recounted a potted history of the legislation of the House regarding the female franchise, starting with the days of Dr James Wallis in the Parliament of 1877 and tracing through the various efforts by Sir Julius Vogel, Sir John Hall and John Ballance, noting that such proposals 'seem to bud with greater profusion as these politicians approach their days of senility'. He accused each of trying to outdo the other, until Sir Richard Seddon came on the scene and, by employing processes of 'a very questionable character',[47] outstripped all his previous competitors and got the franchise passed. According to Fisher, the female suffrage would not have passed had it been subject to a ballot rather than open voting; the men who voted for it had not the courage of their convictions and were afraid to give open expression to their real beliefs on the subject. As he drew his long tirade to a close, Fisher asked Parliament to not make itself ridiculous in the eyes of the people by taking another 'idiotic step'. He referred to 'the evil consequences of having passed the female-franchise vote' and, to discredit Premier Seddon, he repeated his point about the discreditable means by which the female franchise was secured. His recommendation was to send the bill 'to the limbo of oblivion, where it ought ever to remain'.[48] Despite this extended appeal for conservatism to rule the day, or possibly because of, the bill passed its second reading by a majority of nine votes.

There were some who persisted in scaremongering on the 'type' of women who sought the removal of women's civil and political disabilities. The editor of the *Auckland Star* was one: he claimed that the passage of the bill would open the way for 'a class of aggressive females who, thirsting for publicity, would be constantly pushing themselves forward into positions for which they are in no sense fitted' and this would bring both women and the offices to which they aspired into ridicule.[49] Nevertheless, the bill had proceeded to committee, where *Hansard* records that there was a challenge to the short title and some proposed amendments, and a division was taken to report the progress to the House.

The parliamentary reporter's account of what occurred in committee presents quite a different picture. In committee the bill was burlesqued, ridiculed, strongly opposed and stalled. Jackson Palmer, an Independent Liberal member who maintained his independent distance from government, and who had attempted to adjourn the earlier debate in the House, led the charge, sounded 'a note of war'[50] by calling for a division against the adoption of the short title of the bill. This was followed by ridicule from Captain William Russell to the effect that if the bill passed women might be appointed to Mr Seddon's Horse – a recently formed mounted infantry corps. Despite complaints about the ribaldry with which the matter was being treated, another member made a naïve expression of surprise to a colleague's consistent opposition to the bill, given he had a reputation for being a notorious lady-killer.

Right-wing Independent Liberal John McLachlan, known as 'a very rough diamond'[51] who 'presented almost a caricature of the Seddon type of shrewd political dealing disguised under crude sociability',[52] continued the theme of ridicule by moving to insert words in the bill that would reduce the operative clause to entitling women to be nominated, appointed or elected to any public office in the army, and he added that he would be willing to throw the navy and the volunteers open to the ladies as well. Jackson Palmer and John McLachlan continued to undermine the bill: the former declared that the introduction of the bill and the discussion of women's disabilities in the House were an insult to the sex; and the latter declared he had never met a respectable woman who truly desired to see the bill passed, 'and those who did want it were not the most desirable women and mothers, but belonged to the National Women's Council and kindred political organisations'.[53] Blame for the debacle in the House was laid squarely on the shoulders of George Russell; had he not moved the bill, women would not have been exposed to insult.

No one intervened in the House to bring the debate to order. After an adjournment for supper, Roderick McKenzie moved unsuccessfully to report the progress as a tactic to close down discussion, but several members continued to speak until Seddon, recognising there was no chance of the bill proceeding, intervened and submitted to the inevitable by agreeing to progress being reported, but did so in a manner that made light of the situation. In the parliamentary reporter's opinion, the whole proceedings had been a farce and members were simply playing to the galleries. At 12.20am the motion to report progress was carried by 10 votes.

The flippant and facetious tone of the debate was reported widely in newspapers throughout the country. There were, however, more signs of changing views: one newspaper reported that if the question was considered from an equity point of view, there could be no doubt that women had as much right to sit in Parliament as men; demanding that privilege might upset our preconceived ideas of what a woman ought to be, but, 'if she put in a claim to the title we cannot in justice deny it to her'. The writer insisted that the old command 'woman obey your husband' had become obsolete 'through the gradual action of emancipation, and man's claim to consider himself lord of creation is only a fiction founded on the reality of bygone ages'.[54]

Regardless of the views of newspaper reporters, it was clear there were few genuine supporters of the measure in the House, although many were prepared to feign support in order to stay on side with the ladies and rely on the Legislative Council to reject the measure. But this was an increasingly risky tactic. It had been claimed that the Upper House had passed the female franchise only to teach a lesson to those in the Lower House who courted popularity. Stonewalling the current bill in committee may have been prompted by fear that the Legislative Council might act on the same principle as in the case of the female franchise and pass the bill. But there was a much more mundane reason for stonewalling the current bill in committee. The Address in Reply debate had been much shorter than anticipated and this had left members unprepared to commence the priority business of the House. Extended debate on the Removal of Women's Disabilities Bill was, in the words of one newspaper editor, a convenient way of 'whiling away an evening in which there was little else to do'.[55] By the time debate on the second clause of the bill resumed in committee the following week it was well after midnight, and when a division was called for the chairman to leave the chair, the ensuing majority vote sealed the bill's fate.

The claim persisted that, apart from 'a comparatively small body of political and social extremists',[56] the women of the colony had made no demand for the concession. There was a long way to go to convince politicians, political reporters and newspaper editors that the NCW was truly representative of the views of most women across the country. The editor of the *Evening Star* asked: 'It is true that the Women's "National" Council demand the concession of the right to sit in Parliament, but do the Council represent the women of New Zealand in this matter any more surely than on the question of Imperial patriotism?'[57] Accusing George Russell and his supporters of 'merely posing as champions of an unreal grievance', the editor believed the House of Representatives had done well to put the bill to one side, although he added that he was supportive of the growing tendency for competent women to be employed in social and public activities. He was convinced: 'It is not in Parliament that women's tact and tenderness and practical knowledge would be most valuable, but those qualities are being utilised in many places, with admirable effect, in less ambitious forms of public life.'[58]

Although there was no concerted effort to solicit signatures to demonstrate beyond doubt that the demand for the removal of women's civil and political disabilities was widespread and insistent, there were some petitions organised over the next few years, and organisers were heartened early in 1901 when many branches of the WCTU lent their support to distributing a petition. Instead, the approach was a slow and gradual education of women on political matters and an equally slow and gradual increase in the numbers of women participating in public affairs. The *White Ribbon* continued to be an important organ for disseminating information about women's political activities and about legislation of interest to women and contributed greatly to women's understanding of political processes. There was steady and ongoing interest in the issue of women's admission to Parliament, as was evident from requests to the *White Ribbon* for details of women's disabilities and the text of the bills before Parliament, reprints of various papers on the issue, and comment on topical news reports.

News of the death of Queen Victoria on 22 January 1901 cast a shadow over the new year. As tributes flowed and attention was drawn to her long and successful reign, inevitably connections were made with women's demands for political equality. An unnamed woman from St Albans in Christchurch wrote to the *Press* of 'the most intense, painstaking, and active interest' the queen took in all political matters, and went on to say: 'no one will venture to assert that it ever, in the very slightest degree, detracted from her womanly qualities, or made her a less loving wife, devoted mother, or impaired her ability to discharge the domestic relations and obligations of her life'. That three of England's four queens had 'most brilliant reigns' was, to her mind, sufficient argument for removing all civil and political disabilities from women; and she issued a challenge to 'those men who are so dreadfully afraid that if we were possessed of equal civil and political rights with themselves we should at once lose all the womanly qualities which adorn us': the late queen had 'proved that the most womanly woman can actively and constantly take part in the Government and politics of her country and still retain in their most lustrous perfection all the womanly graces and qualities which are our chiefest possession',[59] and a most fitting tribute to the memory of the late queen, the writer suggested, would be the passing of the bill in the next session of Parliament for the removal of all civil and political disabilities from the women of this colony.

Among those women working toward this end there was a growing intolerance of women's general apathy in relation to achieving full political rights. In response to an article on 'The indifference of women' published in the *Woman's Journal*,[60] the *White Ribbon* noted that some truths in the article applied equally to women in this country. New Zealand women had been enfranchised for more than seven years, and it was reasonable to expect that the removal of all artificial disabilities would have followed; however, 'There are women even in our Union who are as apathetic and indifferent to the removal of disabilities which hamper the usefulness of women as are the women referred to in the article which we quote.'[61] This indifference was to be found among women who had profited by the struggles of the early pioneers of the emancipation movement, and the extract from the *Woman's Journal* article was dedicated 'to these, and to all others where the cap may fit'.[62]

The charge of indifference was not fully warranted. The annual reports and conference programmes for the WCTU and the NCW confirm that women were politically active on a wide range of issues. At the WCTU annual convention held in Palmerston North in March 1902, for example, as well as a resolution for the removal of women's disabilities and that absolute equality be the law of the land, resolutions were passed on the repeal of the contagious diseases legislation, provision of protection for young people, the appointment of women as visiting justices to prisons, and the provision of accommodation for those suffering from venereal disease who voluntarily presented themselves for treatment. The programme of meetings for the NCW convention held in Napier in May was even more extensive, with sessions devoted to temperance, the duty of the state to children, contagious diseases legislation, prison reform, old age pensions, political reform, equal pay for equal work, the ethics of wage earning, education, internationalism, peace and arbitration, economic independence, as well as the removal of the civil and political disabilities of women. In March 1902 the Wanganui Women's League hosted an animated discussion on the Women's Disabilities

Bill which resulted in a resolve to unite with women in other towns across the country to present a 'monster petition' to Parliament urging the immediate removal of all disabilities.⁶³ The Progressive Liberal Association reaffirmed its commitment to the removal of women's disabilities; and the issue of women's electoral equality with men was starting to be raised in relation to religious organisations.

The 1902 NCW conference turned out to be the last time most of the key executive members met. While the scope of women's activities undertaken by these women's organisations indicated different political priorities, it exacerbated divisions within the organisations, and a dissipation of energy and focus on the issue of women's admission to Parliament. In addition, there was a growing awareness that the Liberal Government was becoming 'too remote to be immediately influenced by an expression of popular opinion' and this led to a sense of the people being 'compelled to express their views in an indirect and unsatisfactory manner'.⁶⁴ Calls for the abolition of the Legislative Council and for the introduction of referenda were increasing, too. But behind the scenes the stalwarts were still hard at work. Margaret Sievwright had been lobbying the Liberal member for Mataura, Robert McNab, to introduce a disabilities bill. McNab had consistently supported previous bills on the abolition of women's disabilities, including the Divorce Bill in 1896. On his advice the scope of the proposed bill was scaled down to focus solely on the right of women to sit in Parliament. A petition had been circulating for some time and, at the insistence of the secretary of the NCW, Christina Henderson, a deputation to Seddon was arranged to discuss the disabilities referred to in the petition. Seddon showed little sympathy for their requests and his response was patronising and dismissive: he asserted women's physical inferiority to men and their primary roles as wives and mothers, and paid lip-service to raising their appeals with his fellow politicians.

Although no bills to remove women's disabilities or to admit women to Parliament were presented to the House for several years, these issues, and how the urgency of these measures might be impressed on government, arose frequently. For example, the potential for women's increased participation in civic life emerged during debate on the Hospitals and Charitable Aid Boards Election Bill 1901. Several members raised the issue of the desirability for women to be elected to these boards. The bill proposed direct election by ratepayers, rather than boards being elected from local bodies. One suggestion – which could have set a precedent that would have worked in women's interests – was that the bill could state that anyone who was eligible to vote would be eligible for election to these boards. George Russell took the view that under the proposed measure, because of the enlarged franchise there would be less probability of women being elected than under the present system. Given his previous promotion of the removal of all women's disabilities, some were astonished at the position taken by Russell. When elections arose, very few women had shown inclination to occupy seats on these boards and it was expected that extending the franchise regarding hospital and charitable aid boards would enable many women to vote on this question and it might encourage more women to stand and more women to vote for female candidates.

In March 1902 Sievwright, as president of the NCW, had warned women at a meeting in Hawera of the danger of relapse, 'of women taking possession of the half-way house, or of satisfying their hunger on the proverbial half-loaf'.[65] Referring to the remaining disabilities of women as 'a drag on their normal evolution', she challenged Seddon's claim that women did not want the removal of women's disabilities. She asked, 'What woman in New Zealand does not want to be free to live her own life – to earn not only dry bread to keep body and soul together, but a living wage; that is, money, the means of procuring what will raise her, mentally, morally, and physically, from a human slave to that of a legitimate child of the race.' She asserted that every New Zealand woman was aware, or ought to be, that the removal of women's disabilities did not simply mean economic independence, but 'the accession of responsibility and power' and the 'right to do right' which, she claimed, was 'the birthright of all, irrespective of sex'.[66]

Sievwright urged every woman in the electorate to regard it as her duty to sign the petition that was circulating and to thereby silence Mr Seddon or any other member of 'the People's Chamber in New Zealand' from claiming women did not want this measure. She acknowledged that the passage of the Removal of Women's Disabilities Bill would not achieve everything, 'but it would go a long way towards the restitution of justice'.[67] A few months later in her presidential address to the annual meeting of the NCW on the first day of the council's conference in Napier, Sievwright acknowledged that a great deal of work needed to be done; few people seemed to understand the meaning of the movement and 'the comic element is not wanting in the naïve way in which some ... ridicule our proposals'.[68] She countered accusations that the council wanted to turn women into men and that they were one-sided, and emphasised instead that they wanted 'to increase the truly feminine – in the home, in the market place, in the Civil Service, and in the forum' and that reports of proceedings of the council in its six years of operation spoke clearly of the council's efforts towards 'the restoration of a fairly balanced, truly dual life for *both* sexes, for the abolition of all privilege and protection, and for the inauguration of a reign of justice and brotherly interdependence'.[69] The annual report noted that the movement for the removal of women's civil and political disabilities needed to be pursued with greater vigour during the coming year on account of the bill to that effect being dropped in the last parliamentary session. Sievwright again reminded women, as a matter of duty to their sisters, to sign and promote the petition that was currently in circulation.[70]

Sievwright, in her paper on 'The removal of the civil and political disabilities of women' presented at the annual conference in May 1902, outlined the improvements for women after the removal of some disabilities, such as admission to universities, entry into various professions and the suffrage, and she called for every position to be open to women. Highlighting the importance of women's economic independence from men, she said, 'if we wish to live in an ethical world, the only safety lies in woman's absolute independence'.[71] She again took Seddon to task for stating that women did not want the removal of their disabilities; while there may be a few women who, through sheer ignorance, said they did not want it and some who dared not admit they wanted it, it was simply untrue to claim that most women did not want it. She insisted that the government, in the administration of its power, should make use of 'the fullest wisdom of the whole people ... Not until then shall we have seen true democracy; not until then shall we indeed have a government of the people, by the people, and for the people.'[72]

Mrs H. Hill, Napier delegate for the WCTU, emphasised in her paper on 'Men's rights and women's claims' that women were asking to be admitted as co-equals with men 'into the consideration of all those questions of a public character which go to the making of a wise and progressive nation'.[73] The franchise was a significant step, but women's rights were still unfairly limited. She argued that including women in the consideration of public affairs was needed to ensure not only that the interests of women would receive more attention but that they would receive more rational attention than could be given by men.

Kate Sheppard's paper to the 1902 conference focused on 'Reform in government'. Like Sievwright, she took as her focus the principle of government of the people, by the people, for the people, and presented her views on the changing shape of politics over the previous decade. She maintained that under the present methods the people had almost no voice apart from electing representatives every three years. The issue for her, she said, was not that politicians were far below average, but that the system of government was 'dangerously inimical to the maintenance of a higher political morality'.[74] Her main concern was that the party system of government tied members to work with a party and to agree to, or at least not oppose whatever the leader of that party did, even if that meant sacrificing the interests of the people. Putting aside the much debated question of whether the Legislative Council was a desirable institution, she observed that it was almost entirely composed of men who had been chosen not because they had served the people well in the past, nor because they were wise or experienced or of judicial mind, but simply and solely because they had been useful to the party, or had served the private interest of the private politician in whose hands the gift of place, for the moment at least, rested. This, she added, had the effect that most of the gentlemen in the Upper House were not likely to possess 'a very exalted idea of their responsibility to the people'.[75]

Although no monster petition eventuated, women activists kept the issue of the removal of women's disabilities in the minds of members of both houses of Parliament. On 22 August 1902 a petition with 71 signatures was presented to the Legislative Council and another with 67 signatures was presented to the House of Representatives.[76] But even some of the men who had been supporters of women taking their seats in Parliament were having second thoughts. During the debate on the Electoral Bill 1902, Russell commented that one point he considered 'somewhat anomalous' was that under the Legislative Council Act 1891 it was within the power of the governor to summons such persons as he thought fit, yet the legislation currently before the House was reinforcing the status quo that a candidate for the House of Representatives must be a man. Despite this observation, he stated he would not argue in favour of women being admitted to the Lower House as he had done on previous occasions for he had come to the conclusion that, 'although strictly logical, it was in advance of the times' and he did not intend to introduce the bill to remove women's disabilities 'until public opinion has risen to a greater height in connection with this matter'.[77] He suggested that if the government wanted to experiment in this regard, they could take advantage of their own legislation currently under debate and admit a few ladies to the Upper House.

Given that the newspapers were always quick to print articles and letters that opposed the movement for women's civil and political equality, it is curious that Russell's about-turn on advocating women's admission to Parliament scarcely raised a mention. But the backlash was just around the corner, and was to come from within the women's movement. On the anniversary of the granting of women's suffrage the *New Zealand Times* published a damning article by Mrs Emily Nicol, who had been connected with most of the women's leagues in Auckland and Wellington as well as the NCW. Nicol welcomed the temporary abandonment of Russell's Removal of Women's Disabilities Bill as a prelude to its final dismissal: she believed that any further legislation for women's rights would have 'a cruelly disastrous effect upon the community, to say nothing of our sex'.[78] In her view, the NCW had proved a 'dire failure' since it was and always had been run 'by a small clique of women who have dominated everyone and everything'. She doubted that the council, supposedly the mouthpiece of the women of New Zealand, was even the voice of a score of political women, let alone leagues, because so many leagues had seceded or become defunct because of the injustice meted out. She accused those who held positions on the council of having courted publicity and enjoyed sundry trips around the country on council business. She referred to women being 'politically bought and sold, like so many cattle in the market' at election times, and condemned the allocation of a portion of the ladies' gallery in the House to so-called lady reporters who were no more than a public nuisance: they did little or no reporting and their hysterical laughter made it impossible to listen to the debates. To her mind, the petitions presented to the House in favour of Mr Russell's bill were not worth the paper they were written on, 'the most fallacious reasonings being given to induce non-thinking women to sign'. Reporting on Mrs Nicol's 'candid statement', the editor of the *Hastings Standard* suggested that Mrs Nicol displayed the inconsistency that stultified the progress of the women's movement.[79]

It was not the first time Nicol had been at the forefront of public criticism of the NCW. Several years earlier she had taken Amey Daldy to task for her response to a newspaper report that had made implicit criticisms of the NCW conventions. The report had contained excerpts from a sermon which suggested that instead of older women filling younger women's ears with tales of the monotony of the home and the drudgery of housework, they should teach them the importance of home life and of women's duties in the domestic sphere.[80] Reading this, Daldy had felt compelled to 'vindicate the position of the Women's National Council'. In a letter to the editor she asked how many older women the minister had heard 'propounding the heresy he charges them with', whether they were women of the National Council, whether he had attended any of their meetings or exchanged ideas with any of them.[81] Nicol took umbrage at Daldy's lengthy response and suggested that 'Social Purity women' should use their efforts to try to instil in the minds of men and young women 'the priceless value of that natural law – love'. Nicol admitted she had in the past been a strong advocate of women's rights, but she confessed to having seen the error of her ways: she now held that 'if love and mutual confidence reigned supreme to-day, we would hear little more about women's rights'.[82]

Decline of the National Council of Women

Public criticisms aside, with no strong allies in Parliament and smaller attendances at its annual conventions, the NCW was in a period of decline. Despite this, there was still discussion of the removal of women's disabilities outside of the various women's gatherings, the parliamentary debating chamber and the columns of the newspapers. Various groups, from the Norsewood Social Club to the Christ Church Club Debating Society in Whanganui, rehearsed the various positions for and against women's admission to Parliament. The issue also featured in the electioneering during the lead-up to the general election in November 1902. The Canterbury Women's Institute prepared a series of questions for members to ask of their local candidates that included whether they were in favour of an elected ministry within government, the use of referenda, men and women serving on all local boards, and the removal of all women's civil and political disabilities.[83]

The 1902 general election was noteworthy in that there was no clear Opposition party; instead, 'Independent Oppositionists' and Independent Liberals presented 'ambiguous and frustratingly ill-defined alternatives to government candidates'.[84] In some electorates several Liberal candidates contested the same seat while in others, where the sitting government candidate was not opposed, the prohibition lobby put forward candidates to ensure the local liquor licensing liquor poll was held.[85] Seddon's electioneering tactics consisted largely of scaremongering about the consequences of a government defeat and the prospect of returning to depression if those who opposed government policies were elected. As a sign of the Liberal Government's attempt to redefine their relationship with the growing labour lobby, a Liberal–Labour Federation promoted by Seddon had been formed prior to the 1899 general election. Although it was intended as a body to assist in preparing the Liberal Party election platform and in the selection of candidates, its platform for the 1902 election was 'extremely vague and bland'.[86]

Two issues faced the Liberal Party in the lead up to the 1902 election: the risk of voter apathy and a surplus of Liberal candidates. Voter registration was low, and the absence of an organised Opposition coupled with the Liberal Party having successfully contested the past four elections led to a risk of complacency on the part of voters to cast their ballot to ensure the return of the Seddon Government. There was the risk of vote splitting, as some electorates were contested by multiple government supporters. Seddon used his influence to give official party support to Liberal candidates who had demonstrated loyalty to the government and, in the case of dissidents such as George Russell, even went as far as endorsing the Oppositionist candidate. Seddon's concerns proved unfounded. There was no downturn in voter turnout and the Liberal Party was returned for a fifth term, gaining an additional four seats as well as winning three of the six new seats.[87] Seddon's tactics had successfully unseated Russell, although his nemesis Tommy Taylor was re-elected to the Christchurch City seat.

By 1903, although the decline in the membership of the NCW and many of its member organisations was evident, there were women across the country keeping the issue of the removal of women's disabilities alive. The *White Ribbon*'s large advertisement on the final page of each issue, which read 'Are you working to get signatures to the petition for the Removal of Women's Disabilities?', encouraged women to demonstrate their collective demand for greater involvement in all aspects of civil and political life. In July a petition from A.M. Aitken and 77 others was presented to the House of Representatives, followed by three more the following month, from Annie Gordon and 59 others, G.M. Aitken and 71 others, and from Grace Fox with 406 signatures from women in Gisborne.[88] A petition was sent to the Legislative Council from Ella Nolan of Gisborne with 404 signatures.[89]

At the WCTU convention in Dunedin in March a decision was made to focus on just a few measures. In her paper on 'The disabilities of women', Kate Sheppard acknowledged that women had made some gains, but they had been made 'fitfully, grudgingly, and partially'[90] and no legislators had been bold enough to assert that women were as valuable to the state as men were, that they have equal intelligence and equal probity and should, therefore, have equal rights and privileges with men. She thought it a 'curious instance of a reversion to the primitive and barbaric idea of the subjection of women'[91] that in order to ensure the franchise was passed 10 years earlier it was expressly stated that women were not to be treated equally with male electors but were to be debarred from Parliament. She went so far as to say that 'By barring women from Parliament in defiance of their logical rights as electors, our legislators are either most fantastically chivalrous, or most barbarically tyrannous. In either case they are out of tune with the spirit of civilisation and Christianity.'[92] Sheppard maintained that it was not only women who suffered by not having representatives of their own sex to watch and take part in legislation; the whole community was seriously affected by what she referred to as 'our mono-sexual system of representation' wherein half of the electors were excluded from direct representation, resulting in legislation being as lopsided as the system of election.[93]

While Sheppard's paper stimulated strong discussion, there was still a wide range of views among the membership of the WCTU on the desirability of women taking seats in Parliament. One member spoke of the absurdity of a young man aged 21 being eligible for Parliament while his mother was excluded, and suggested annual deputations for the next three years to urge the removal of women's civil and political disabilities. But even that suggestion betrayed a lack of confidence that the measure would eventuate soon. Despite the difference in viewpoints, after discussion on Sheppard's paper, six resolutions were passed:

(1) 'That in a free community the laws should be in the direction of giving each of its members equality of opportunity;' (2) 'That, in the best interests of the State, every human being should be free to enter upon such duties and honourable occupations as may be suited to his or her natural or acquired capacity, that only by such freedom can the State obtain the fullest economic and social value of its citizens;' (3) 'That the legal restraints now placed upon women exclusively imply a sense of inferiority, and are dishonouring to the womanhood of the community;' (4) 'That the removal of the civil and political disabilities of women is a logical sequence to the extension of the franchise to them;' (5) 'That the legal recognition of the economic equality of married women is desirable for the attainment of justice and for the furtherance of a truer marriage relationship;' (6) 'That the time has come when all disabilities which at present hinder women from sitting as members of either House of Legislature or from being elected or appointed to any public office or position in the colony should be removed, and that with regard to all powers, rights, and duties of citizens absolute equality should be the law of the land.'[94]

Several major newspapers followed the conference proceedings. In a long editorial titled 'Women and politics' the *Southland Times* suggested that 'though our women's rights pleaders are not representative of their sex, their claims may be significant of future developments'. The editor considered the extension of the franchise was 'the thin end of the wedge' and the admission of women to both houses of Parliament was only a matter of time. But he contended that women, by being more emotional, less logical and narrower in their outlook than men, would 'render legislation more impulsive and capricious' and, judging by the resolutions of the WCTU and other female societies, they would be constantly making new laws 'to obviate some evil or injustice'.[95]

An editorial in the *Lyttelton Times* suggested that women had taken it for granted that Parliament would, of its own motion, proceed to the logical step of removing women's civil and political disabilities. Although the editor believed that the real test was not whether women desired equality of opportunity but whether it was right that they should have it, he noted that Parliament had only begrudgingly made some concessions to this end. In his opinion, 'If the leaders of the emancipation movement took it into their heads to organise public opinion, and especially the opinion of women, on the question, instead of contenting themselves with addressing gatherings of already-converted societies, the issue would not long be in doubt.'[96] But this seemed increasingly unlikely. Nearly all available funds of the legal and parliamentary department in all the WCTUs throughout the country had been exhausted in the 'no licence' campaign;[97] little attention had been given to the usual parliamentary work and none of the reforms put forward by the unions had been carried in the last session of Parliament.

Despite this lack of success, there was growing appreciation that it was in politicians' interests to pay more attention to women's demands. A report presented to Parliament on the impact over the last four elections of women being granted the electoral franchise noted that the proportion of men exercising the franchise had increased and that women's interest in politics had been sustained. The difference of 3–4 percent fewer women than men casting their votes was attributed to 'the irremovable disabilities of the gentle sex', namely, that women were often tied to their homes and those in remote country districts could not be expected to tramp long distances to the polls.[98]

Electoral Act Amendment Act 1903

After much lobbying Robert McNab, the Independent Liberal member for Mataura, was secured as an advocate for women's political equality in the House. McNab had said that he was keen to see women placed on the same footing as men in political matters. In the first week of Parliament he introduced two bills: the Juries Act Amendment Bill 1903 which provided for women to sit on juries for crimes committed by women, and the Electoral Act Amendment Bill (No. 1) 1903 which, by substituting the word 'person' for 'man' in section 99 of the Electoral Act 1902, provided for women to qualify as candidates for parliamentary election.

With these bills before Parliament, various women's groups mobilised. They organised petitions and the NCW arranged for a deputation to the premier that consisted of Margaret Sievwright, Lily Atkinson and Jessie

Williamson (president, vice president and secretary respectively of the NCW), Kate Sheppard, Stella Allan (née Henderson) and Fanny Cole (representing the WCTU), accompanied by three Independent Liberal members of the House of Representatives – Tommy Taylor (Christchurch), Harry Bedford (Dunedin) and George Laurenson (Lyttelton). Sievwright opened the interview with Seddon on the morning of 1 August 1903 by reminding the premier that in the period since he had been congratulated, through an honorary degree from the oldest of English universities, for being the first premier in all Her Majesty's dominions to grant the suffrage to women, federated Australia and almost all its states had enacted this right – and on the same conditions as men. She noted that as Mrs Sheppard, who had done a large share of the work of securing the attention of legislators and of organising the petitions, was on the eve of her departure for England, it would be fitting for the premier to now provide them with some guarantee that the remaining 'half a loaf' would be conceded.

Kate Sheppard spoke of woman's anomalous position in being represented in Parliament yet unable to represent herself. She drew attention to the fact that 'any naturalised negro or Chinaman was eligible to take his seat in Parliament, but the most refined and cultured woman could not so serve her country even if a whole constituency desired she should do so'.[99] Removal of women's disabilities was only one of a wide range of issues the delegation raised. They drew to the premier's attention the need to address married women's inability to form a business partnership without their husband's assent, women being appointed as visiting justices to gaols, the need for mixed juries on cases of offences against women and children, repeal of the Contagious Diseases Act, direct election by the people of hospital and charitable aid boards, women's appointment to the Upper House, equal pay for equal work particularly in relation to the salaries of school teachers, as well as amendments to the Factories Acts so that women were able to work the same hours and earn the same wages as men.

The various newspapers around the country that reported on the deputation provided interesting commentary on the proceedings. A detailed report in the *New Zealand Herald* suggested that Premier Seddon had taken amusement in baiting the delegates. Seddon's advice was for the women to educate members of Parliament to favour the admission of women to Parliament. He felt bound to say that the admission of women to Parliament had not been a burning question at the last election; that what women would do when they got to Parliament would depend on the women who got there; and that some would be quite equal to some of the men on some subjects. Seddon engaged with the women on the range of subjects they raised; at times he was interrupted with a chorus of dissent, and on several occasions Jessie Williamson did not hold back her disgust at his comments.[100]

Under the title 'The shrieking sisterhood', an editorial in the *Mataura Ensign* complimented Premier Seddon for his tact and diplomacy in the face of the 'estimable ladies whose powers of oratory and possibilities of eloquence have been cultivated to the highest pitch by Women's Conferences and similar assemblies'.[101] An editorial in the *Hastings Standard* made light of the deputation: it commented that the premier's 'long experience in the gentle art of fencing with deputations' had served him well when 'a large and strenuous deputation of "female women" bearded the lion in his den, and waited up on the Premier demanding to have their sexes [sic] grievances redressed'. The editor added that had Seddon either received the ladies seriously or displayed any open hostility to their claims, 'the advocates of woman's rights in this colony might have flattered themselves the cause was on the eve of another advancement along the path of progress towards the attainment of their ideals, and the conquest of the tyrant man'. According to this editor, the premier was neither hostile nor serious.[102] The *Feilding Star* was even more scathing: it claimed the women's councils were composed of 'gossips with a morbid desire for notoriety, who discuss unsavoury subjects and debate the decrease in the birth rate, instead of attending to the birth rate themselves', and that 'These gossips elect those of their number who are most expert in dodging home duties to the National Council, under the extraordinary delusion that it represents the views of the women of New Zealand.'[103]

Although the editor of the *Hastings Standard* had reported that the outcome of the deputation was far from satisfactory, a report in the *White Ribbon* from the delegates' point of view deemed the deputation satisfactory even though the premier's style had proven 'fatal to their objectives'.[104] There was banal acceptance of the premier resorting to debating women's 'natural' disability of physical inferiority and 'the lame old phrase that the women had not asked' for the removal of their disabilities. Nevertheless, Sheppard remained optimistic: at least the issue had been ventilated throughout the country, even if some of that was in the form of ridicule. She had come to accept that ridicule, followed by active opposition, were necessary stages though which every reform must pass.[105]

There were positive signs that some of the key messages promulgated by the NCW were being heard by the premier and other politicians. During debate on the Barmaids Abolition Bill, which sought to prevent the employment of barmaids, Seddon, who considered the bill overly restrictive and a ploy on the part of the prohibition lobby, made reference to the NCW delegation having lobbied him more generally on equal rights and equal pay and having pressed home the point that 'physically, mentally, and in every way you like to apply the test, women are equal to the lords of the creation'.[106] Like Seddon, Liberal member for Napier Alfred Fraser took offence that the bill implied that all barmaids were immoral. Describing himself as 'a social reformer and woman's friend', Fraser argued that the bill was inconsistent with the 'clamour' about the removal of women's disabilities by way of deputations, lectures, meetings and 'paper-writings' because it accentuated the barriers that divided men and women in all occupations and all walks of life.[107]

Because some key members of the executive were unavailable and others had health problems, the NCW convention in New Plymouth in September 1903 was held much later than usual and was a shadow of former conventions. Only six societies were represented and only two evening sessions were open to the public. Noteworthy absences were Kate Sheppard, who was overseas, and Amey Daldy, whose husband was gravely ill. The local newspaper gave positive coverage of the convention, and claimed that the meeting of the 'Women's Parliament' was a matter of considerable interest. Unlike most of his contemporaries, the editor of the *Taranaki Daily News* hailed the National Council of Women as being fully representative of the women of New Zealand, truly national in character, and a reliable indicator of the thoughts and aspirations of women regarding their disabilities. He added that their affiliation to the International Council gave it a wider and more important significance than a merely local council would have.[108] This assessment of the importance and representativeness of the NCW was not a commonly held view. Despite this, the annual gatherings had over the years been reported widely in the newspapers and were followed with interest by politicians and those with an interest in social reform, and in this respect the annual conventions had served an important influential and educative function.

The New Plymouth convention was not particularly successful. The weather did not oblige and Sievwright described the audiences as 'miserable'.[109] There was a sameness about the speeches and papers presented, suggesting a series of position statements rather than topics for discussion and debate. One Wellington weekly newspaper gave hollow praise to the way members dealt expeditiously with all matters brought before them. The full and frank appraisal of the diminished effectiveness of the organisation offered by the *New Zealand Mail* rang a note of truth: the executive of the council was by now so familiar with the questions submitted for consideration that there was virtually no need for debate, and the reporter for the *New Zealand Mail* questioned whether it was even worth the expense and trouble of a convention; compared to its early years when the council's proceedings were the subject of leading newspaper articles and editorials, 'their influence now in forming public opinion is a vanishing quantity. It is now realised that the women of the Council have ceased to be a power in the community.'[110] The *New Zealand Mail* was not alone in this view. An article in the conservative weekly *Free Lance* suggested it was not fair to call the 'councillors' the 'shrieking sisterhood' because, even if they did raise their voices a trifle hysterically, they did not hurt, and their following was small.[111] Even Sievwright conceded that, 'The novelty of the Council is over and it will take a long pull, a strong pull, a stoney pull and a pull-together to ride the storms of the next ten years. Nor are storms perhaps the worst we have to fear – the apathy and cheerful indifference of the great majority is distinctly benumbing.'[112]

Women's admission to Parliament received very little attention in the NCW's discussions, in the newspaper reports and in the parliamentary debates. In a debate on the Referendum Bill in November 1903, Seddon referred to measures being set back by both the houses of the Legislature because they were raised at a time when public opinion was not ripe or when the representatives of the people were not as advanced as some might wish. In such cases, Seddon suggested, 'the thing to do is to go on steadfastly, holding on, never losing ground, and in the meantime educate the people'.[113] The question of the removal of women's disabilities was one example of a matter that had not been dealt with 'calmly and dispassionately'. His deputation earlier in the year from the NCW had left him unsure as to whether they were in accord as to what they wished to be granted. Nevertheless, he pointed to this being one of the questions agitating the minds of the women in the colony and that it needed to be resolved whether women should be given equal opportunities.

Earlier in the 1903 session of Parliament Seddon had informed members that the government did not propose to ask the House to follow the usual practice, referred to as the 'slaughter of the innocents', of striking bills from the Order Paper; instead, bills would be 'put to sleep'. It was an important distinction: bills that were slaughtered could not be revived, whereas bills that were put to sleep would appear again on the Order Paper in the next session of Parliament. As the parliamentary session drew to a close in November, both the Juries Act Amendment Bill 1903 and the Electoral Act Amendment Bill (No. 1) 1903 were put to sleep.

'Wanted – A Woman's Party'

Women's admission to Parliament was not discussed at the WCTU convention in Blenheim in March 1904 or in Whanganui in March 1905, although on each occasion they passed their now standard resolution about the removal of all women's disabilities and the enacting of women's absolute equality with men.[114] There were no conventions of the NCW held over these years and the passing of stalwart Margaret Sievwright in March 1905 signalled a further decline in the organisation.

In recent years Kate Sheppard and others in the WCTU had expressed strong opinions against the party system of politics. However, in November 1904 an argument was put forward for 'a definite, determined sound' from women in the form of a Woman's Party as a means to counter the indifference of politicians to calls for an end to women's disabilities. The call came from Lucy Smith, who had recently taken up the editorship of the WCTU page in *The Prohibitionist* and who had been instrumental in establishing the *White Ribbon*. Unlike most of the women activists at the time, Smith was in paid employment, performing office duties and proofreading in a family printing business. Poor health, work commitments and a quiet disposition contributed to her taking a behind-the-scenes role in the women's movement, but this did not detract from her being 'a strong feminist, progressive thinker, and courageous reformer who cared deeply about social issues and ... prepared to espouse unpopular viewpoints'.[115] In her article 'Wanted – A Woman's Party', she issued a challenge to women to organise themselves. She affirmed that women were still labouring under many disabilities and were subject to grave injustices. She believed the reason for politicians' indifference to petitions and protests was that women were not sufficiently organised: 'There is no definite, determined sound coming from the whole of our women. We ask for measures but our own confidence is not strong as it would be were protest and petition certainly backed by the solid vote of the women of the colony.'[116] Smith called for women to make up their minds to overcome apathy, to ignore minor differences of opinion, and to demand, in a united voice, for their righteous claims to receive attention.

No united voice emerged, although there were some actions that indicated that the goal of women achieving full parliamentary representation was still on the agenda. In June 1905 the Canterbury Women's Institute asked the NCW to communicate with the Young New Zealand Party to ascertain whether it supported the removal of women's political disabilities, on the belief that women ought not to support any party that refused women full rights as citizens. For several years there had been sporadic rumours of the formation of a Young New Zealand Party comprised of New Zealand-born members intent on providing a strong patriotic alternative opposition to the Seddon Government through the promotion of progressive self-reliant policies. No formal party existed, but there was a loose grouping of members within the House who spoke occasionally under this banner and who were motivated by the desire for 'pure and honest administration'.[117]

Electoral Bill 1905

There was a glimmer of hope for progressing women's admission to Parliament in August 1905. The Legal and Parliamentary Department of the WCTU had circulated information on a subsection in the Electoral Bill[118] that rendered nomination papers for women candidates invalid. This subsection had been a new inclusion in the Electoral Act 1902 which, like the previous Electoral Act 1893, specified that only males were eligible to be nominated. Many branches of the WCTU had subsequently adopted resolutions protesting the clause as undemocratic. On their behalf, Tommy Taylor moved an amendment to the Electoral Bill to strike out the subsection.

Despite these resolutions, the majority of members present at a meeting of the WCTU in September 1905 declared themselves in favour of the clause, and this prompted Lucy Smith to question 'on what grounds these ladies have their objection to feminine candidates'. To her mind, there was no substance to the stock arguments against women's admission to Parliament, which she described as 'airy fancies, dissolving as soon as touched'.[119] In an article in the *White Ribbon* she asked, if the parliamentary arena was considered too unsavoury for the entry of women, what was it about male politicians that they felt they would not be able to mind their manners when in the company of ladies? After all, men and women worked side by side in many other circumstances, such as in church life and in social life, as well as in professional, business and workroom activities. Like many women's advocates, she had tired of the double standards inherent in arguments against women's admission to Parliament. Women neglecting their homes was, in her words, 'another bogie sometimes trotted out' and yet there was never any proposal to send any or all women to Parliament irrespective of the electors' wishes. She asked whether electors inquired whether a male candidate's business concerns justified his giving up so many months of the year to parliamentary duties, or whether they asked if he had sons who required the constant care of a father's eye and hand, or even whether his wife could, unaided, 'pilot the family boat', and then give or withhold their vote accordingly?[120]

In the debating chamber no ministers replied to Tommy Taylor's motion to amend the Electoral Bill, and there was practically no discussion on the motion, although it was reported that Sir Joseph Ward caused an uproar when he said that 'for the purposes of the electoral law "male embraces female"'.[121] Taylor's amendment was lost by 48 votes to 23.[122] There was no flurry of discussion in the newspapers apart from an article in the *Lyttelton Times* that drew attention to the 'masculine and illogical prejudice against the recognition of the full political rights of women' that still influenced the House.[123]

Members of the executive of the NCW continued to discuss the removal of women's disabilities. In September 1905, Miss McKay delivered a paper on the 'Wills and won'ts of feminine citizenship', which focused on what women would do when they entered Parliament and when they stood on an equitable economic footing with men. Speakers at functions to celebrate the anniversary of women's suffrage spoke of the need to further women's political rights. At an 'At Home' in Christchurch attended by 150 people, resolutions were unanimously carried that recognised the earlier contributions of Sir John Hall and Alfred Saunders and urged the removal of all disabilities preventing women sitting as members of the House of Representatives or being elected to any public office. Their failure to even mention the contribution of John Ballance drew some criticism from Samuel Saunders, editor of the *Lyttelton Times*, in an article titled 'A forgetful generation'.[124] Writing to correct the record, Kate Sheppard agreed there was a forgetful generation consisting of those women 'who calmly profit by the efforts of pioneer women, but absolutely hold aloof from those who are to-day working for further reforms'.[125]

It was not the first time Sheppard had criticised women who were content with what they personally had gained from the efforts of women's advocates. She received some sympathy for her views from Saunders, who acknowledged that the burden of agitating for further rights had been left to a few enthusiasts who had been subjected to abuse and ridicule over the years. Son of Alfred Saunders, Samuel Saunders was known for his progressive Liberal editorial stance. He, too, was of the opinion that if there was 'a semblance of organisation in the electorates' and the removal of all civil and political disabilities became their concerted aim, and if this demand was presented clearly and emphatically to candidates in the upcoming general election, Parliament would be compelled to grant women their full rights as citizens.[126] Even if women's remaining disabilities were swept away tomorrow, he suggested, it would be unlikely that a woman would be elected to the House for at least a decade, but the fact that women may not pine after a parliamentary career was no reason they should be denied the opportunity to pursue a parliamentary career. He encouraged women to remember, when they took to the polls in a few months' time, those who had opposed the removal of their disabilities.[127]

Women did remember those who paid lip-service to women's political equality: they challenged them at electioneering rallies and wrote to the newspapers naming those who unabashedly courted women's votes. The

Canterbury Women's Institute wrote to all parliamentary candidates asking whether they were in support of the popular election of all public boards and the removal of all women's disabilities. Likewise, the Christchurch branch of the WCTU sent questions to all candidates for the five local electorate seats and held a special meeting to read and discuss the responses.[128] The candidates' responses were reported in the *Lyttelton Times*, along with resolutions passed by the Canterbury Women's Institute, which exposed the premier's incorrect claims of legislation passed in favour of married women's rights. Some candidates held women-only meetings, and the fact that many stated publicly their view on the removal of women's disabilities was evidence that the issue was squarely in the minds of candidates and the female voting public. It was obvious that women had established themselves as a serious voting force, but there was still a strong view, even among those who publicly supported the removal of women's disabilities, that women's admission to Parliament was the least important of women's current demands.

The 1905 general election was notable for two breakaway factions in the form of the New Liberal Party (which included Tommy Taylor) and the Independent Political Labour League, both of which mounted opposition to Seddon's policies. Although neither gained any real ground, it was indicative of shifting allegiances and, in the case of the Independent Political Labour League, a step toward an independent working-class political party. The Liberal Government was re-elected for a sixth term with a substantial majority in the House, holding 58 of the 80 seats. But with Russell and Taylor unsuccessful in contesting seats, once again women struggled to find advocates in Parliament.

By now it was clear that the momentum for achieving women's right to sit in Parliament had dissipated. The view expressed by the editor of the *New Zealand Mail* that 'Short of the right to occupy a seat in Parliament women in this colony are on a practically equal legal footing with men' was widely held.[129] There had been no rush in South Australia for women to stand for parliamentary election and it was conceded that it would probably be years before male and female electors in New Zealand reconciled themselves to parliamentary representation by a woman. The ranks of the pioneers of the NCW were sorely depleted. In the past two years, Margaret Bullock, Annie Schnackenberg, Marion Hatton and Margaret Sievwright had passed away. Kate Sheppard was recovering from a serious breakdown, Christina Henderson had resigned, and Amey Daldy had been incapacitated by a severe stroke.

In April 1906, at what would prove to be the last the meeting of the executive of the NCW for many years, resolutions were made for presentation at the meeting of the executive of the International Council of Women in Paris in June. Among these was the statement: 'The executive believes in the election of women with men to all public boards and councils, from the Charitable Aid Board and Hospital Boards to the Parliament of the colony. Unfortunately there is a clause in our Electoral Act which denies to women the right to be nominated for a seat in Parliament. The executive is also of opinion that women should take their places on juries in equal numbers with men.'[130] Lacking any sense of urgency, the tone and wording of the resolution conveyed a sense of resignation and acceptance of the status quo.

After the sudden death in office of Richard Seddon in June 1906, a new ministry was formed under Sir Joseph Ward. In October the honorary secretary to the NCW forwarded a letter to the prime minister[131] congratulating him on the progressive policy outlined by the new government but expressing surprise and disappointment that no reference was made in the government's programme to the necessity to rectify the many civil and political disabilities under which women had so long laboured. It was noted that the justice of this reform had been repeatedly urged on the Legislature by women's societies over many years and the time had come when they might reasonably expect 'a practical recognition of our claims'.[132] This was followed with a list of some of the more pressing disabilities that women desired to see removed, the first of which was that women were allowed no direct voice in framing the laws by which they were governed.

Having determined that Robert McNab, Liberal member for Mataura, who held two ministerial posts, was the most likely sponsor in the new Parliament for presenting legislation on behalf of women to the House, a deputation of women met with him when he passed through Christchurch in March 1907. McNab was reported as 'sympathetic without being unduly encouraging'.[133] As the issue of removing women's remaining civil disabilities had not yet been considered by Cabinet, McNab was not able to provide any positive assurance. But with the cause having been at a standstill for the last couple of years, there was some reason for optimism. Prime Minister Ward and three other Cabinet ministers were known to have some sympathy. McNab had supported previous bills for the admission of women to Parliament; George Fowlds had always been a warm supporter of women's rights; and John Millar was known for his democratic principles.

In a fitting tribute to the late Sir John Hall, an address titled 'Should women, on account of their sex, be subject to legal restrictions not shared by men?' was presented as part of a series of educational meetings inaugurated by the WCTU. The focus of the address was how New Zealand had forfeited its leading position in women's political citizenship. In many of the American states women now had full political equality with men, women were eligible to sit in the Parliament of the Australian Commonwealth, and at the last general election Finland had returned 19 women to Parliament. After some discussion and questions, the following resolution was passed unanimously:

> *That, in the opinion of this meeting, citizenship should be free, and should neither be restricted by disabilities nor favoured by privileges on account of sex; that the present restrictions placed upon women's liberty by legal enactment are injurious to the community as a whole and that they hinder women from much usefulness, as well as being out of touch with the progressive spirit of the times. This meeting therefore asks the present Government to introduce effective legislation in order that such civil and political disabilities should be removed.*[134]

The tone of the resolution differed from the resolution that had been reaffirmed each year by the NCW at its annual conventions. This was an important difference. For some months the eyes of the press had been on the 'bizarre methods of the English suffragettes', with frequent reports of their campaign for female suffrage.[135] In contrast, the WCTU was one of the few organisations engaged in social reform work that was exempt from bitter criticism; instead they received public praise for their material common sense and for having religious sanction in their favour. By this time, the WCTU was almost the only organisation left pleading for the removal of women's political disabilities. Many of the women's organisations that had emerged in the previous two decades of political activity had fallen away. The fact that the WCTU had continued and flourished was attributed to having a deeper grounding than mere politics and having clear aims beyond the immediate amendment of acts of Parliament. It was suggested that members of Parliament would benefit from occasionally referring to the resolutions carried periodically by the WCTU and thereby correct their own ideas of political righteousness.[136] Although the government showed no intention of introducing legislation for the removal of women's disabilities, there was an opportunity to lobby for women's admission to the Legislative Council.

Legislative Council Election Bill 1907

In July 1907 the Liberal Government introduced a bill that sought to make changes to the present system of appointment of members to the Upper House. During the debate, four positions emerged: maintenance of the status quo, whereby members were appointed for a term of seven years; election of members by the Upper and Lower Houses; retention of the Upper House but election of members on a broader basis than the House of Representatives; and abolition of the Upper House. The Liberal member for Hutt, Thomas Wilford, was one who believed that reform of the Legislative Council was needed but thought it very unlikely that even if the bill proceeded through the various readings in the House of Representatives it would be passed by the Upper House. When the bill did pass a second reading in the Lower House, Wilford took the opportunity to propose an amendment in committee which would have had the effect that women would be eligible for nomination and election to the Legislative Council.[137]

Over the years members of both houses of Parliament had expressed support for women to be appointed to the Upper House although – as with support for women's admission to the Lower House – it was not always genuine. There is reason to question Wilford's motives. Twelve years after proposing this amendment he claimed that his reasons for doing so were twofold: first, he believed that women being eligible for nomination to the Upper House would be a step towards recognition of the fact that they were able to do parliamentary work; and second, it was a more civilised and appropriate role for women to play in parliamentary proceedings – they would not have to 'battle through a strenuous election' and in the 'calm serenity' of the Upper Chamber they could prove they were capable of carrying on parliamentary work effectively and to an excellent standard.[138] Politicians, newspaper editors and political commentators had expressed similar reasons many times over previous decades. However, Wilford's recollection of what motivated his actions is at odds with sentiments he expressed on the campaign trail at the 1911 general election. When asked whether he was in favour of removing women's disabilities, instead of responding courteously he treated the question as a joke and, in a derogatory manner, suggested that women may be more at home having a seat in the Upper House. His offhand manner prompted an elector to write to their local newspaper to accuse Wilford of using the ladies to secure his return to Parliament by having a lady at his side during the election campaign, explicitly to attract women's votes.[139]

Wilford's amendment passed by a comfortable majority of 11 votes and the bill proceeded to a third reading. However, there had been several amendments made in committee and members were divided on progressing the bill. Significantly, Prime Minister Joseph Ward indicated that while he had voted for the amendment for women to be eligible for election to the Upper House because he considered it 'a proper thing to do',[140] he had voted against the second reading of the bill and intended to vote against the third reading because he opposed the principles of the bill. Despite having been a supporter of women's franchise long before he had been a member of Parliament, and despite agreeing that logically it was difficult to deny women the right to nomination to a seat in the Lower House, he had always been opposed to women being elected to the Lower House; he believed 'there are many things that stand in the way of their mixing in the turmoil of politics that such a proceeding would necessitate'.[141] The bill passed the third reading and proceeded to the Legislative Council where it did not pass its first reading on a voice vote.

Once again there was criticism of the way the debates had proceeded. An article in the *White Ribbon* titled 'Not good for man to be alone' commented that the 'derisive spirit' of some of the speeches showed that in some electorates the interests of women were in 'unfriendly, and to put it mildly, ungentlemanly hands', and that the mere presence of women in Parliament 'would of course prevent such exhibitions on the part of unmanly representatives'.[142] The time had come for women to turn the tables, to cast the burden of proof on the other side, as exhibitions of ill-breeding on the part of certain legislators were a 'striking commentary on the unfitness of man to rule alone'.[143] The article signalled a change in tone and message: motherhood needed to have a direct voice not only in the kitchen, the nursery and the sickroom, but also in the schoolroom, the workroom, the hospitals, the asylums and the gaols. This writer believed it was 'futile to complain of injustice and inequality ... when those specially charged with the moral welfare of the race are barred from exercising their national functions'. Rather than ask why women should have a seat in Parliament, we should ask, 'why should she not?' because 'obtaining a direct voice in framing and administering the laws under which man, woman and child have alike to live' was a '"religious" duty'.[144]

Calls for a change in tactics were well warranted, particularly as the political landscape was also changing. The spectrum of Liberal–Labour politics was very broad, encompassing 'left-wing', 'right-wing', prohibitionist, anti-prohibitionist and labour factions. Although the Conservative Opposition under Bill Massey was soundly beaten in the 1905 election, it was gaining ground and there had been significant growth in the establishment and organisation of political reform leagues. A general decline in Liberal Party support, their gradual loss of rural and country town seats over recent elections, a shift to a labour-aligned vote in city electorates, and the Opposition tactic of ensuring at least one Reform or anti-government candidate stood in each electorate meant the Liberal Government could not rest on its laurels. Amid Opposition demands for administrative reforms, Ward approached the election campaign in 1908 on a platform of having what he referred to as 'a rest from legislation'.[145] Despite its superior organisation, the Opposition still did not have a strong message that resonated sufficiently with voters and the Liberal Government under Ward was re-elected, but with a reduced majority.

Since achieving the right to elect members of Parliament, women advocating for their full citizenship rights recognised the need to understand the workings of parliamentary procedure. For the most part their political strategies had been to use small-scale petitions and deputations to demonstrate their demands and to identify and lobby individual supporters in Parliament to present bills on issues relevant to women and children. These tactics had met with success. At the WCTU convention in 1911, members took pleasure in listing legislation that had been passed since women had been enfranchised 'for the moral and social betterment of the people'.[146] The achievements were impressive: employment opportunities and protections for women had been enacted, including the appointment of police matrons in gaols and police stations, regulation of Servants' Registry Offices, the Shop Assistants' Act which safeguarded the interests and health of shop girls, recognition of the principle of equal pay for equal work in the Factory Act, women now being admitted to the practice of law, technical schools giving equality of opportunity to both sexes, and women who were ratepayers being able to vote and be elected to hospital and charitable aid boards. There were many legislative advances to protect the rights of women and children, too, such as the regulation of paid childcare under the Infant Life Protection Act, acts to regulate the adoption of children, amendments to the Industrial Schools Act, achieving an equal standard of morality in the Divorce Act, legislation enabling women to receive compensation for slander, recognition of the principle of economic partnership of husband and wife in the Municipal Franchise and Old Age Pensions acts, legal provision for married women on separation or if their husband died without providing for them or their children, the provision of old age pensions, and repeal of the Contagious Diseases Act. Yet on the issue of women achieving full citizenship rights through being eligible for election to the House of Representatives, members of the WCTU had met with repeated failure. A change in tactics was needed, but, more importantly, there needed to be a change in public perception and political will.

The WCTU was now placing greater emphasis on women's responsibilities as citizens, which they expressed in terms of the need for women to avail themselves of the opportunity to serve – on school committees, education boards, hospital and charitable aid boards, licensing committees, or borough and city councils. The WCTU emphasised women's responsibility to help others to develop a civic consciousness. Doors had been opened to women and they now had to make use of those positions and opportunities as a training ground for the more responsible position of legislator.

This shift in focus was evident in the subjects discussed at the annual WCTU conventions. The union continued to reassert the resolution for the removal of women's civil and political disabilities, but the focus had shifted to other forms of disability. A session at the 1908 WCTU convention was devoted to the disabilities of married women, and the following year

Kate Sheppard read a paper on 'Some points on the question of women's disabilities, with special emphasis on those connected with the guardianship of children'.[147] With the NCW in abatement it was time to reflect on why the struggle for women to be admitted to Parliament had not succeeded. In her presidential report to the Canterbury Women's Institute in 1908, Rose Atkinson questioned how many more elections would pass before women had the opportunity to vote for one of their own. This, she determined, would be decided 'mainly by the energy, or lack of energy, displayed by the women's associations and other agencies making for political progress'. She considered it scandalous that their representatives in Wellington made women 'the butt of the ribald jokes and ill-timed merriment'[148] whenever a measure for their fuller enfranchisement came before the House, and she renewed the call for women to remember when casting their votes those who sympathised with the cause of justice and those who demeaned themselves to insult women who had placed them in a position of trust and power.

Some called for a new strategy. Rather than repeat the demand for the removal of women's civil *and* political disabilities, the editor of the *Lyttelton Times* suggested that members of the WCTU might be advised to concern themselves for the present with the removal of women's political disabilities. He explained: 'Politicians who want to keep women out of Parliament may object to their having an equal voice in the disposition of their husbands' estates, and those who want to leave the men in the undisputed charge of the children may demur at women being given public appointments.'[149] But if women restricted their demands to political rights only, their request would not only be simpler, it would more likely be met with a direct answer. Acknowledging that prejudices took a long time to break down, the editor firmly believed that opinion was mounting as to the gross injustice of denying women the opportunity to sit in Parliament, even if it was unlikely that once that right was secured any would be returned in the near future.

Aside from resolutions at women's meetings, however, little was being done to pursue this aim. Reports of the increasing militancy of parts of the suffrage movement in Britain and of recent successes by political women in Australia led some journalists to reflect on the relatively passive tactics of New Zealand women to effect an extension of their political rights. A writer for the 'Woman's World' column in the *Press* suggested New Zealand women needed to be more loyal to themselves rather than be influenced by the interests of their husbands and brothers and divided by the competing claims for their votes.[150] This call did not go unheeded. By mid-1909 the Women's Political League resolved to make changes to the rules and aims of the organisation and that its chief aim would be the removal of women's disabilities. One of the changes was to institute monthly meetings, and at the first of these a paper on 'The disabilities of women' would be presented. This was met with parody in the periodical press. The Auckland pictorial weekly magazine the *Observer* published a cartoon of a 'Forlorn brute' left nursing the baby for three hours while his wife attended a Women's Political League meeting, with a caption that asked, 'What about the disabilities of men?', and another depicted women and their male supporters lining up on the shoulder of the premier to gain his ear.[151] The Women's Social and Political League in Wellington favoured a more direct approach: it hosted a 'welcome home social' for Sir Joseph and Lady Ward on their return from attending the Imperial Naval Conference in London. In their welcome address league members said that 'the defence of our hearths and homes is essentially a woman's question' and they impressed on Ward their understanding of the importance of New Zealand's role in the defence of the Empire.[152]

But scaremongering and resistance continued. A newspaper article commenting on the agitation for the franchise in England claimed that since women in New Zealand had been granted the suffrage, divorces had increased by nearly 300 percent, although it did qualify this somewhat by stating that during this period legislation had been passed that made divorces 'fairly easy'. The writer suggested that even if women were permitted to enter the legal profession, they would not be better off because women's general disability was one of incapacity; and he added, 'For much the same reason, politics offer no career to a woman, and the demand to be allowed to sit in Parliament would, even if conceded, be of little use to feminine aspirants for political notoriety. Few women want to be legislators, and, judging by the results of municipal and school committee elections, where there is no disability, fewer still can secure election.'[153]

Others were more generous and viewed women's ability to work together toward a common goal as indicative of their suitability to engage more fully in the political sphere. One example was a newspaper report on the proceedings of the recently formed Society for the Promotion of the Health of Women and Children. The report noted the promptness with which resolutions were carried and recorded, the fixed attention of the meeting on the questions under consideration, and the way everyone worked in unity to progress the work of the conference, and contrasted this with 'the carefully-edited reports of the councils of men' published in the daily newspapers in which 'every board (of men) has its obstructionist – the man who is pining for a fight' and where differences of opinion result in 'strife and clash of tongues'.[154]

In June 1910 a meeting of the Parliamentary Debating Society discussed a petition: 'That the time has come when the disabilities under which women are now placed with respect to entrance into Parliament should cease'. Most members present spoke against the petition. Obviously there was still work to do to establish the principle that women's eligibility to sit in Parliament was the logical conclusion to female franchise.[155]

CHAPTER 4

The full privilege of citizenship, 1911 to 1919

Why, then, should [women] not possess the full privilege of citizenship, and be given an opportunity of taking part in the actual framing of the laws of the country? — EDITOR, Wairarapa Age, 3 July 1911[1]

The election of a Liberal government in 1890 had marked the beginning of a party political system in New Zealand. The successive re-election of the Liberal Government contributed to a growing dissatisfaction and disillusionment with the party system. By the early 1900s, party politics were developing in ways that would provide fresh opportunities and challenges for women's efforts to achieve the full privilege of citizenship.

A new era of party politics

The 1908 election was notable on several counts. Prime Minister Ward's decision to campaign on a platform of taking a rest from the ambitious legislative programme that had characterised previous Liberal governments met with criticism from both within and outside the party. The introduction of a second ballot system was controversial, too.[2] Underlying this was the prime minister's acceptance of the inevitability of factions and a wide diversity of opinion in the Liberal Party. One effect of the new electoral system was a 'Liberal free-for-all on the first ballot', on the basis that if the Liberal vote was split there was the safety net of the second ballot to ensure the Liberal Party retained the seat. But a surprise of the election was the number of Labour candidates contesting city and some provincial seats. This was indicative of the growing unrest within, and organisation of the labour movement. In the general election, just over a quarter of the 80 electorate seats went to a second ballot and, while most of these confirmed the result of the first ballot, eight seats reversed the order of the two leading candidates. There was also a tendency for Labour votes to be transferred to Liberal candidates.[3]

Ward was re-elected at the 1908 general election, with a reduced majority in the House. After the election he engaged in a controversial restructuring of his Cabinet that left many Liberal members dissatisfied. Inevitably, his administration of government was constantly compared to that of his predecessor Seddon and, with frequent and lengthy trips abroad and preoccupation with imperial policy, there was a growing sense of the prime minister's detachment from the life of the Liberal Party, and concern about the future prospects of the Liberal Government. Ward's response was increasingly to resort to scaremongering tactics of what might happen if the Opposition leader William Massey formed a government with the Reform Party and managed to capture the growing body of disillusioned Liberal members.

The long lead-in to the 1911 election was further indication of this changing political climate. For several terms under the Liberal Government the various factions within the Liberal Party had become stronger and more vocal against a backdrop of no strong organised Opposition. The Liberal–Labour Federation formed by Seddon had broken down and, outside Parliament, trade unionists were feeling more and more isolated from the government. Inside Parliament there was growing dissatisfaction with the prime minister's lack of consultation with Cabinet on major issues of policy, and there were rumours of Ward's impending resignation. An increasingly organised Opposition under Bill Massey, adept at exploiting the rifts within the Liberal ranks, was engaging in aggressive party politics, and it gained momentum when, in 1909, it transformed into the Reform Party. The advent of the Reform Party was welcomed by some as a sign of a 'real' Opposition and an opportunity for a revival of 'true' Liberalism and 'true' democracy, but, as many political commentators at the time observed, in reality there was very little difference between the Reform Party's platform and that of the government; rather, 'the Opposition accepted the permanency of the basic reforms brought about by the Liberals in the 1890s and presented itself not as a radically different, conservative party but as an alternative and "better" Liberal party.[4] These shifts in political allegiances were particularly evident during the 1911 election campaign, and prompted leaders within the women's movement to urge women to support only those candidates who pledged support to women's causes.

The outcome of the 1911 general election marked the end of the domination of the Liberal Party. But the formation of the government was a protracted and acrimonious process. After the first ballot, the Reform Party held 25 seats, the Liberal Party held 20, and one seat was held by an Independent. This meant the election outcome would be decided on the results of the 30 electorates that necessitated a second ballot. In the week between the first and second ballots there was a flurry of activity, talk of recounts and absentee votes, competition for securing election meeting venues and various charges of cowardly and underhand tactics by candidates.[5] In order to secure the passage of the Second Ballot Bill in 1908, under protest about the freedom of the press the prime minister had been forced to withdraw the controversial 'gag clause' which would have prevented press commentary between the first and second ballots. As a result, newspaper editors had free rein to publish claim and counterclaim of party leaders and candidates vying for the voters' second ballots. Both major party leaders expressed confidence in the final ballot while hurling charges of unfair politics against their opponents. Massey accused journalistic supporters of the government of 'trying to explain away the fact that the Ward Ministry is engaged in a life and death struggle', and claimed 'the people of New Zealand are heartily tired of the spurious Liberalism, the sham democracy, and the improper and extravagant methods of the present Administration'.[6] Ward, while he talked up the common interests of Liberal and Labour as the two progressive parties, made a counterclaim that his party 'had to contend against most unfair and most unscrupulous tactics' and that Reform had resorted to every possible means to discredit the Liberal Party.[7]

The possibility of a change in government sparked renewed interest in women voters. One writer to the newspaper warned women not to be taken in by the 'sugar-plum' promises of the Reform Party and to 'Refuse to be patronised by these representatives of the wealthy'; 'Opposition ladies drive to your door in motorcars, and are very amiable to their "good friends"; they will even motor you to the polling booth, children and all, but will they recognise you when they meet you next week?'[8] The *Dominion* carried an article on some 'curious revelations' about women's attitudes towards elections; it reported that many women did not follow 'blindly the lead given by the men of their families' and sometimes voted 'in complete opposition to the candidates supported by the husband or the father'. The writer claimed that women had taken 'the broader and more patriotic view' and voted for the candidate who met their convictions, whereas men were influenced by friendships and alliances and tended to vote for the man and not the party.[9] The veracity of these claims about women and men's voting behaviour was dubious, and it is likely the pro-Reform article, which appeared in the 'Woman's World' column, was simply courting women's votes by encouraging women to vote on specific issues and independently of their male relations.

The second ballot resulted in the government holding 35 seats, the Opposition 37 and Labour holding four seats. Although the election for the four Māori electorates would not be held for several days, it was assumed that they would go to the government and, in the event of the government resigning, they would likely support the party in power. Of the four Labour seats, two had indicated they would vote against the government on a no-confidence motion. In any case, there was consensus that the tenure of the Ward Ministry was 'exceedingly precarious'.[10]

With uncertainty over whether the government had a majority in the House, Prime Minister Ward embarked on a series of consultations and signalled to the governor-general his intention to not meet the House until June 1912. When the governor-general challenged the constitutional impropriety of this, Ward, faced with the prospect of a constitutional crisis, announced that Parliament would resume on 15 February 1912. At the opening of Parliament, after the speech from the throne, Massey as leader of the Opposition moved the traditional motion of no confidence which began the Address in Reply debate. During this debate, Ward announced that if the government won the division on the no confidence motion, he would retire. The division was tied at 39 votes for and 39 votes against, which meant the speaker was obliged to cast the deciding vote in favour of the status quo and the Liberal Government survived. At the end of

February, Parliament was prorogued to meet again in June. In the interim, Thomas Mackenzie was elected as the new Liberal leader and formed a new Cabinet. There was little confidence that the Mackenzie Ministry, comprised of a 'miscellaneous assortment of factions and independent-minded members',[11] would provide any political stability. This proved correct. Parliament reassembled at the beginning of July and a vote of no confidence moved by Bill Massey was carried 41 votes to 33. Mackenzie tendered his resignation to the governor-general and Massey was called to form a government. By the time Parliament resumed in early August, Reform could command an overall majority in the House.[12]

The formation of the Reform Ministry under Bill Massey was more than simply a change in government. The Liberal Government had been in office for a generation, and its progressive legislation had enacted the belief that the state had a duty to promote the welfare of the less privileged members of society. During its 21 years in office, it had passed humanitarian and social welfare legislation that had been promoted by women for many years, most notably female suffrage and the introduction of old age pensions. It had improved labour and employment conditions through a range of factory acts that regulated hours of work, factory working conditions, wages, sweated labour and the exploitation of child labour, and had passed the Industrial Conciliation and Arbitration Act 1894, which marked New Zealand as a pioneer in labour relations. The defeat of the Liberal Government was indicative of changing patterns of political support that had been emerging for some years. Conservative voters had been increasingly attracted to Reform's pledge to permit leasehold land to be turned into freehold land, and the urban working class were increasingly attracted to the policies of the precursors of the Labour Party.[13] As New Zealand moved toward a three-party system, the diversity of women's political priorities became more evident as women aligned with party political platforms.

The National Association and the political reform leagues from which the Reform Party had emerged had attempted to include women in their organisations as part of their efforts to form a broad-based party. From the mid-1890s women were organising alongside men, and had set up women's branches of the political reform leagues, which they used to promote their goal of greater political representation. When the Opposition formally adopted the name Reform Party in 1909, the first women's section of the Political Reform League was established in the Wellington branch. Combining political organisation with education, their meetings included papers and discussion on women sitting in Parliament and party government, as well as on issues such as compulsory military training, women's work, and present-day children.[14]

Women's differing political allegiances were evident in moves both to resist and to align themselves with political party organisations. After a by-election in Christchurch North in August 1911, for example, the ladies' committee for the Reform candidate decided to form a women's Political Reform League in Christchurch. The speaker at the inaugural meeting was Octavia Newman, president of the Wellington Women's League and wife of Alfred Newman, who had stood as a Reform candidate at the 1911 general election. Octavia Newman used her speech to urge women to work together to remove the Liberal Government from office. The following year there was a split in the Canterbury Women's Social and Political League when the president proposed a merger with the Women's Political Reform League.[15]

The WCTU remained apolitical, while continuing to advocate for women's political rights. At its annual convention in March 1911 the union passed the resolution: 'This meeting is of opinion that as men and women have equality of franchise they can rightly demand full civil and political rights, those rights to ensure economic equality.'[16] Despite criticism in the newspapers for repeatedly passing resolutions, members of the WCTU were confident of the influence their resolutions would have on proceedings in Parliament when bills concerning women were debated. While they talked up 'the great importance of right legislation',[17] their principal work was educational, and for several years the issue of women having a direct voice in passing legislation was only sporadically aired at women's conventions, in newspaper editorials and articles and, very occasionally, in parliamentary debates.

An editorial published in July 1911 questioned how long it would be before all women's political disabilities were removed. Women were now entering fully into professional and business life; they had demonstrated their intelligent interest in political affairs and, since being granted the suffrage, had 'infused new animation into electoral proceedings'.[18] The article stated that claims of women not being physically fit to endure the strenuous work of a parliamentary session were easily refuted. That women were physically capable of demanding professions such as school teaching was evidence enough that they were capable of performing the functions of legislators. But more importantly, the editor asserted that reform was overdue in ways parliamentary business was conducted and that all-night sittings, in particular, should be abolished to ensure legislation was not rushed through in the early hours of the morning 'when members are fagged in brain and worn-out in body'.[19]

John Paul, the member of the Legislative Council from Otago, advanced strong reasons for women to be admitted as members of Parliament in an address to the WCTU convention in Dunedin in 1912. He urged the audience of over 200 women to make more use of the political rights they already had by being represented in greater numbers on hospital and charitable aid boards, and to put more pressure on members of Parliament, particularly before elections, if they were serious about achieving the removal of women's political disabilities.[20] An article in the *White Ribbon* gave a similar message about women's responsibilities as citizens: the writer, while they praised those friends of the women's cause who were loyally striving to break down the barrier of women being 'debarred from the doors of Parliament', suggested that perhaps it was just as well that the extension of women's rights in this regard should not proceed too easily and rapidly. The article urged women to take up the various positions already available to them in civic life 'that will afford splendid training for the more responsible position of legislator'.[21]

Women were heeding this advice: in April 1913, in a milestone in women's political representation, Auckland lawyer Ellen Melville became the first woman to be elected to the Auckland City Council – a position she held for 33 years. Born in 1882 at Tokatoka south of Dargaville, Melville was educated at first by her mother, a former schoolteacher and governess, and then at the small local school, before she won a Junior District Scholarship to attend Auckland College and Grammar School. Three years later she passed her matriculation and her Solicitors' General Knowledge Examination and received early legal training in Auckland before formally studying law at Auckland University College night classes. In December 1906 she became the second New Zealand woman to be admitted to the bar and establish a sole practice.[22] Her passion was the advancement of women and, as she was financially secure, she devoted a great deal of her time outside her law practice to encouraging women to stand for public office, leading by example when encouraged to stand for the Auckland City Council.

Ellen Melville's commitment to women's public citizenship was shared by Rosetta Baume, the well educated and somewhat flamboyant American widow of barrister and former Liberal member of the House of Representatives Frederick Baume. Rosetta Baume's experience of women's civic leagues in America had convinced her of how influential women could be in public life. The previous year she had discussed with Melville and other like-minded women the idea of forming a women's civic league in Auckland, and in March 1914 they called a meeting to put this in place. Several speakers addressed the large gathering of women, including feminist journalist and novelist Edith Searle Grossman, who spoke on the work of women's local government boards and municipal parties in England. Florence Keller, a Seventh-day Adventist and noted social reformer, feminist and prohibitionist, pointed out numerous ways in which the women of Auckland could make a contribution to improving the city. In outlining the aims and objects of the proposed Auckland Civic League, Ellen Melville stressed that while it did not aspire to be absolutely non-political, it did intend to be non-party. She spoke of the 'very wide field for women in the betterment of the welfare of the community', and emphasised that the league would aim at 'cooperation, and not antagonism, with men to secure better conditions of life in the city and in interesting not only women, but also men, in all sections of civic and community life'.[23]

The establishment of the Auckland Civic League was emblematic of a new focus in women's political organisation. Early meetings revealed a commitment to action in the form of networking with leading Auckland citizens and nominating women candidates for election to school committees. Special interest committees were formed, including a tree planting committee and a scenery conservation committee to agitate against the destruction of Auckland's volcanic cones. Early successes included: three members of the league elected to the committee of the recently established Town Planning Association; seven women elected to school committees; a petition to Parliament from the education committee for women to be included on the National Council of Education; and a women's restroom was established in the central city on the recommendation of a delegation from the league to the Auckland City Council Works Committee.[24]

The advent of world war

A crowd of about 10,000 gathered outside Parliament in the afternoon of Wednesday 5 August 1914 to hear Governor Liverpool read a message from King George expressing his appreciation of the Dominion's loyalty, after which it was announced that the British Government had declared war on Germany. Many in the crowd were visibly affected by the gravity of the announcement. Prime Minister Bill Massey then addressed those gathered: he reinforced the sentiments expressed by the King that the Empire 'stand together, calm, united, resolute, trusting in God', and he called on the country to willingly 'do our duty' individually and collectively and to make whatever sacrifices were required to protect our country and assist the Empire; his advice was 'to keep cool' and 'stand fast'. Leader of the Opposition Sir Joseph Ward assured the crowds that 'People in all parts of the Empire, at this grave juncture, will stand united, with undoubted courage and inflexible determination' and that the motto 'For King and Country' 'would be fervently breathed by the loyal people of this Dominion, as it will be throughout our widely scattered Empire'.[25]

Immediately on confirmation that war had broken out, Minister of Internal Affairs Francis Bell moved that a New Zealand Expeditionary Force be mobilised. Two days after the declaration of war, Annette, Lady Liverpool addressed the women of New Zealand from her residence at Government House in Wellington. She appealed for their assistance with providing 'any necessaries which may be required' for the citizen army being mobilised, and suggested that small committees of ladies form in every centre to set up a fund to receive contributions in money and in kind. Her list of contributions followed the suggestions made by the commandant of the New Zealand Forces: 'underclothing, flannel shirts, socks, hold-alls (containing knife, fork and spoon), housewives[26] (to contain needles and buttons, etc.), or contributions of materials to make these, such as flannel, knitting wool and knitting needles, American cloth, binding thread and buttons'.[27] Within days women's patriotic associations and guilds were formed in Auckland, Wellington, Canterbury and Otago and women across the country contributed through their local patriotic committees to the Lady Liverpool Fund.

News of the outbreak of war coincided with debate in Parliament on the Budget. Traditionally this was an opportunity for the Opposition to attack government spending, and Ward obliged in leading what was condemned in the newspapers as a regrettable melodramatic display, given the circumstances facing the country. The editor of the *Dominion* reflected widespread opinion when he said this was not a time for party bickering or seeking advantages on party lines, but a time for all members of Parliament to unite to keep the administration of the country running smoothly.[28] There were calls for unity of purpose from inside Parliament as well, including from Prime Minister Massey, who said, 'We may have our party differences, and we may indulge in party warfare, but when a crisis comes along such as we are experiencing at present it is not a question of what is best for the party, but it is a question of what is best for the Empire as a whole.' He expressed his confidence that along with the people, the government and the Parliament 'will do their duty calmly and quietly, but firmly and determinedly'.[29]

Legislative Council Bill 1914

Both the Liberal and the Reform parties had contested the 1911 general election on a platform to reform the Legislative Council to make it an elected body rather than an appointed body. After several unsuccessful attempts, in 1914 the Reform Government introduced a Legislative Council Bill proposing an electoral process with fixed terms of office. Over the years there had been many suggestions that women may be more suited to take a seat in the Legislative Council rather than in the House of Representatives, and supporters of women's parliamentary rights saw this bill as an opportunity to make some gains towards women's full political citizenship. In support of this, during the committee stage of debate of the bill in the Lower House, Alfred Newman proposed an amendment to remove a subclause that specified that any person who may be elected a member to the House of Representatives – but no other – was eligible to be elected a member of the Legislative Council. This motion was successful, as was Newman's subsequent motion to insert a subclause that specified that any person registered as an elector may be elected to the Legislative Council. The combined effect of these two amendments would be that, if the bill was enacted, women would be eligible to be elected to the Legislative Council.

During the debate on the third reading of the Legislative Council Bill in the Lower House, the Liberal member for Riccarton, George Witty, challenged the prime minister on his government's claim to be democratic and yet not being prepared to grant women the right to sit in the House of Representatives. Massey's response set the scene for another round of arguments for and against women's admission to Parliament: he asked whether the House was a fit place for a woman, and Kitty replied that if a woman were sitting in the House now, 'every man would be on his p's and q's, and we should not hear the snoring that some members are indulging in now'. Witty's position was based on the logic of rights: if a woman had a right to vote she had equally a right to occupy a seat in the House if elected by the people. He referred to women's role as mothers, and his words carried a particular resonance given the current calls for maternal patriotism in time of war. Witty said that women were thinkers as well as mothers and they had to think not only of their own lives but of the future of their children, and that a mother thinks for her children far more than a father does. He concluded with 'it would be only the good women who would come here – the women who everybody respected'.[30]

The passage of the bill was complicated by various amendments and a printing oversight which meant the revised copy of the bill still specified that only a male person could be nominated for the Legislative Council even though the House had given the right for either men or women to be nominated. Although the prime minister gave his assurance that the error would be corrected when the bill was returned to the Legislative Council for a third reading, the Legislative Council did not agree to the amendments and, with both Houses in disagreement, the bill went to Conference. The position subsequently adopted by the managers on behalf of the Legislative Council was somewhat convoluted: first, the question of women sitting in Parliament was a question for Parliament; and second, the question was whether women should sit in Parliament and not whether women should sit in one or other of the houses of Parliament. Moreover, the question had to be decided by Parliament and therefore by a bill which, according to parliamentary procedure, would need the assent of the Legislative Council. The managers also stated that once such a bill had been agreed by Parliament and passed by both houses of Parliament, women would be eligible to sit in both the Upper and the Lower House.[31]

The amendments proposed by the managers stimulated debate among members of the Legislative Council, ranging from those who considered it 'most unfair' for the House 'to spring upon the Council such an important alteration in the Constitution'[32] to those who considered the alteration should have been introduced by the government and not 'in a kind of side-wind' by a private member's amendment.[33] The motivation for the amendments was questioned; one member stated that inserting the clause in the bill 'was in keeping with a custom they all deplored – that of shoving things into Bills at the end of the session, particularly on the eve of an election, more for propaganda work than anything else'.[34]

Several members of the Legislative Council spoke out strongly in support of women's admission to Parliament. The question of the removal of women's political disabilities, they said, needed to be addressed sooner or later by the council. One member argued that if it had been the case that women were not permitted to become doctors or to take a leading part in many other professions, something might be said for keeping women in the sphere allotted to them a hundred years ago; but society had changed and women had proved themselves in their intellectual capacity to be the equal of men.[35] Another member agreed that women sitting in Parliament was the logical sequence to the franchise, and said he thought it would be beneficial to have highly educated women in the Legislature 'assisting in the government of the country'. In an oblique reference to Ellen Melville, he noted that 'There was a lady lawyer on the City Council at Auckland, and that she was an acquisition was generally agreed.'[36] Other members expressed concern that such a significant constitutional measure did not have the mandate of the people, and some suggested that the issue of women's admission to the Legislative Council should be canvassed at the next general election and then supported by the government of the day. Despite these concerns, the Report of the Managers of the Conference was agreed to by the Legislative Council and proceeded to the Lower House for discussion.

In moving that the report be agreed to by the House of Representatives, the prime minister noted that this was 'a distinct advance' and 'a very powerful lever' for those who favoured the admission of women to both Houses of Parliament.[37] But Ward cautioned that a contingency clause would not be binding on the Upper House and, as the legislation had a specific clause deferring its operation for 12 months, whichever party was returned in the upcoming general election would have the power to review it.[38]

Liberal member for Avon George Russell was more concerned with whether anyone had ever heard of 'conditional legislation of this kind' being placed on the statute book and considered it 'absurd' to think the Upper House might be bound to accept and pass such legislation in the future.[39] Likewise, Newman considered the clause to be 'of no use whatever to the women's cause' but still hoped the bill would be passed because, with an elected Upper House, women could exercise their franchise and take into account the views of candidates on this issue.[40] As several members pointed out, debate on the clause relating to women's admission to Parliament had tended to obscure the fact that the original bill was to establish the principle of an elective Legislative Council. Several members mentioned that when the Bill had been in committee, 39 members of the House had voted for and 16 against women being admitted to the House, and this effectively affirmed the principle that women should have a right to stand for Parliament whether or not they chose to do so.

Legislature Amendment Bill (No. 2) 1914

Earlier in the year there had been mention of another possibility of legislation to admit women to Parliament. During debate on the Factories Amendment Bill in July 1914 there had been an element of scaremongering to the effect that factory owners would have no option but to close their factories if they were required by legislation to place women woollen workers on the same footing as those in other factories. Arguing for justice for the women workers of New Zealand, the Social Democrat Party member for Grey, Paddy Webb, suggested that women should 'raise a rebellion against the Parliament that deprives them of their rights' and that it would do well to have a few suffragettes in the House. He hoped that 'when the member for Lyttelton moves his Bill to admit women to Parliament every well-wisher of womanhood will support that Bill, and so give women the right to come into the House and take their part in this honourable Assembly'.[41]

The Social Democratic Party member for Lyttelton, Jim McCombs, had a Legislature Amendment Bill drawn up with the express object of conferring full political rights on women electors by removing the disqualification that forbade nomination of a woman as a candidate. But while his private member's bill sat on the Order Paper, in October 1914 the government's second Legislature Amendment Bill came up for debate, necessitating a change of tactics on McCombs' part. The basis of McCombs' argument was that the object in women having been given the franchise was for women to gain direct representation in the House. However, the Legislature Act explicitly stated that the nomination paper of a woman as a candidate would be absolutely void and rejected without question by the returning officer, so the amendment he proposed involved omitting the word 'male' from one section, substituting the word 'person' for 'man' in another section, and repealing a subsection.

In the debate that ensued several members made lewd comments when it was stated that women were perfectly well qualified to represent their interests in the House and that 'women could hold their end up'.[42] Jim McCombs took offence at this innocent statement being wilfully misinterpreted at the expense of women, and at the fact that the disgraceful hilarity that had accompanied the speech was not on public record in *Hansard*. He subsequently accused the government of 'hypocrisy and cant' in relation to extending the franchise to admit women to Parliament, and he listed the various countries and states that had enacted full electoral privileges for women by way of direct representation. McCombs had received hundreds of letters from women and women's societies throughout the country in support of his measure. He assured his parliamentary colleagues that he did not think women were anxious to come to the House as representatives of the people, 'but they do want the stigma removed – the stigma which arises from their being classified with the criminals, the paupers, and others who are not allowed to be nominated as candidates for election to this House'. He closed his speech by admonishing Parliament that it would be no use for any member, including the prime minister, to campaign at the upcoming election on the basis of having voted for women to be elected to the Legislative Council when they knew full well that the Legislative Council would not pass that measure. What did matter was that they had an opportunity to give women the right to sit in this House, and 'if they could have got away from cant and humbug they could have shown they were really sincere in the matter by voting for this amendment this evening, but they have failed to do so'.[43]

Undeterred, when the bill was in committee Jim McCombs again tried to move an amendment that would have conferred on women direct representation in both houses of the Legislature, but the proposed new clause was ruled out of order by the chairman of the committee on the basis that an amendment previously dealt with cannot again be moved in the same session. In a tactical manoeuvre, McCombs moved to report progress on the bill in order to take the speaker's opinion on the chairman's ruling. In challenging the subsequent ruling of the speaker, he contended that Parliament had not yet been asked to vote on the proposition that women should or should not be admitted to Parliament, and he expressed his regret that there were members 'who wish to dodge a vote on this question'.[44] Once again he was not successful and the speaker's opinion prevailed.

War time contingencies

Bill Massey's leadership style was like Seddon's: he 'ruled largely through personal authority and political acumen',[45] dominated Parliament and Cabinet, and tended to announce his decisions to Cabinet rather than form them through a consultative process. Much of the domestic legislation passed in the Reform Government's first few years in office continued in the Liberal tradition, but a notable difference was their anti-trade union stance. This was implicated in the success of the two Social Democratic Union candidates, Paddy Webb and Jim McCombs, in the by-elections in 1913, necessitated by the death in office of two Liberal members. The acrimonious general election campaign in 1914 was dominated by Massey's aggressive anti-unionism as he talked up the dangers of 'revolutionary socialists' dictating policy if Liberal were re-elected under Ward.

As with the 1911 general election, the outcome of the 1914 election held on 10 and 11 December was controversial and protracted. With a return to the single ballot system, on the night of the election for the European seats there appeared to be a hung Parliament. Reform had won 38 seats, Liberal had won 30, and Labour had won eight. It was expected that two more seats would be aligned with the government after polling for the four Māori electorates the following day. But errors in counting were quickly identified and after many days of recounting a by-election was ordered. By early February it was determined that the Reform Government had a majority of two seats. But the close results of several seats and continued allegations of irregularities led to a record number of petitions and, in early May 1915, the results for a further two seats were declared null and void, and each needed to be decided on a by-election. By the time the election result was finalised at the end of June 1915, the Reform Government held 41 of the 80 seats.

The special circumstances of war necessitated special political arrangements. After months of political infighting, against a backdrop of daily newspaper reports of shifting battlefronts, mounting war casualties and manpower issues, on 4 August 1915, one year to the day when war was declared, Prime Minister Bill Massey and Opposition Leader Sir Joseph Ward announced their agreement, in the interests of wartime unity, to the formation of a coalition national government comprised of five Cabinet members from each of the Reform and Liberal parties. The coalition government would remain in power for four years, and the general election due in 1917 would be delayed until 1919. During this period, the government was largely managed through ministerial decree rather than parliamentary resolution.[46]

It was inevitable that political priorities would change while New Zealand was at war, but being a country at war also exposed further divisions in women's political views. The manifesto for the New Zealand branch of the Women's International League for Peace and Freedom, published in August 1916, stated that the league would work for 'the development of the ideals underlying modern democracy in the interests of Constructive Peace' and for 'the emancipation of women and the protection of their interests'.[47] These league members were ardent pacifists, but other women viewed pacificism as inimical to their patriotic duty. Some members of the WCTU took offence at efforts by Ettie Rout to prevent venereal disease among the troops. At a time when calls to fulfil one's patriotic duty adorned every shop window and newspaper stand, the issue of conscription proved extremely divisive. This was evident among Māori in the Waikato, where anti-conscriptionists led by Te Puea Herangi angered those Māori who considered war service a way to demonstrate and uphold their equality as citizens.[48] Patriotism took many forms. While women were exhorted to not begrudge sending their sons to fight for King and country, many Māori women experienced a heightened sense of disenfranchisement: not only had much of their land been taken from them, Māori men were excluded when conscription was first introduced in 1916. Old wounds were reopened when Māori men were needed to serve overseas. Māori members of Parliament welcomed Māori serving on an equal footing with Pākehā troops, but some Māori refused conscription and engaged in defiant acts of civil disobedience.[49]

The advent of war opened up opportunities for women to engage in active citizenship and accelerated women's entry into wider fields of employment. Women's contributions to the war effort – in paid work such as clerical workers in public service departments, replacing male workers in factories and on farms, in voluntary patriotic work and serving overseas as nurses or in the New Zealand Medical Corps – lent a new dimension to women's roles and responsibilities as citizens.

Patriotic activities were prominent in many women's organisations and served to unite women in the common cause of providing relief for those serving overseas and for their families struggling without them. In May 1915 Governor Liverpool held a public meeting to appeal for funds for equipment for a hospital ship for wounded New Zealand soldiers. Speaking at the meeting in her capacity as president of the Auckland Civic League, Ellen Melville spoke on behalf of a large number of the women of Auckland, but she might as well have been speaking on behalf of women throughout the country when she said there was scarcely a woman in Auckland whose heart was not in the Dardanelles at the present time. She welcomed the governor's scheme for providing 'a further and more intimate opportunity of contributing to the welfare of the Empire in its time of need'.[50]

The Auckland Civic League's activities were typical of many organisations at the time. The league contributed to efforts coordinated by the Auckland Patriotic Committee, such as a special collection of garments for the Auckland contingent of the Expeditionary Forces as part of the Lady Liverpool Fund, and offering the league organisation to assist in any way. They formed a Civic League Patriotic Guild to care for the wives and dependents of members of the Expeditionary Force, and a Civic League Sunshine Guild to bring sunshine into the homes of wives of soldiers and sailors by visiting them several times a week to assist those who were overworked and distressed. They organised bridge parties to support the Red Cross Fund, and hosted parties for children whose fathers were away at war.

Women's engagement in the war effort renewed the call for them to be afforded the full privileges of citizenship. Each year on the anniversary of women's suffrage, articles reflecting on the gains made and on what still needed to be achieved since women had attained the franchise were printed in the major newspapers and in periodicals associated with the women's movement. On the twenty-first anniversary of women's franchise in 1914, the mood was celebratory;[51] by the following year it was acknowledged that the best way to effect real change was for women to be allowed to become candidates for parliamentary election. An article in the *White Ribbon* asserted, 'When we have women in the Legislature of the land, they cannot be kept out of the Jury, the Police Force, the Magistracy and the Bench.' The writer, undeterred by the fact that although women in Australia had the right to be nominated for Parliament no woman had yet been elected, stated, 'We only want women to have the right to come before the electors. If rejected by the electors, we will not grumble; we'll only set to work to educate the electors.'[52]

The formation of the New Zealand Labour Party in 1916 provided new opportunities for women to be involved in party political processes. Women on the political left, including Emily Gibson, who had called for unionisation of domestic servants in 1899; feminist social worker Elizabeth McCombs; daughter of Alfred Saunders and staunch socialist Sarah Page; her close friend, founder of the Canterbury Women's Institute and first national secretary of the NCW Ada Wells; and temperance worker Elizabeth Taylor, had been involved in the New Zealand Housewives' Union formed in 1912, which focused on consumer issues such as living costs, cooperative buying, childcare and education,[53] as well as in political organisations such as the United Federation of Labour and the Social Democratic Party, which were predecessors of the New Zealand Labour Party. McCombs and Sarah Snow, who succeeded Elizabeth Taylor as president of the New Zealand Housewives' Union, were elected to the first national executive of the Labour Party in 1916. The Labour Party gradually affiliated the housewives' unions and other radical women's organisations such as the Auckland Women's Political League and, over time, these were incorporated into women's branches.

Sarah Snow was an important voice in promoting women's representation in the labour movement and for feminist concerns to be included on the agenda of the labour movement. As one of several women delegates at the 1918 Labour Party conference, she was unsuccessful in her bid to ensure that when affiliated organisations had both male and female members and more than one delegate on the local Labour Representation Committee, one delegate must be female. However, she was influential in the Labour Party adopting a clause in the party platform that was reminiscent of the long-held NCW resolution, calling for 'perfect equality between the sexes in every department of public life'.[54]

Women were increasingly entering local body politics. The local body elections in 1917 were notable for the number of women returned, and among them was Ada Wells, who became the first woman elected to the Christchurch City Council. These achievements fuelled the determination for women to again press for the right to be elected to Parliament. At a public meeting held during the WCTU convention in Auckland in May 1917, Melville moved a resolution that, 'whereas women have, during the present war, proved their capacity to fill every position to which they have been appointed, and whereas the right to elect logically carries with it the right to be elected, this meeting earnestly urges the Government to take without delay steps to remove the obstacles in the way of women entering Parliament; and also to clear the way to their serving as Magistrates, Justices of the Peace, and Jurors'.[55] Melville recounted the attempts over recent years by Alfred Newman and Jim McCombs to enact women's eligibility for parliamentary election. She concluded by referring to the speaker's belief that if the women of the Dominion organised and put a definite request before Parliament it would likely be passed without much opposition.

Support for women entering Parliament was gaining momentum but there was still a vocal conservative element. Some politicians were equivocal about women being employed in the place of men who were serving in the war. The member for Dunedin Central, Charles Statham, balked at women entering business life and receiving the same wages as men, and delaying marriage because of their working lives. 'Women have a great influence in the community without actively dabbling in politics,' he asserted, and he saw no need for women to aspire to 'doing exactly as the men do, and wanting to get into Parliament, and that sort of thing'.[56]

Celebrations of the end of the war in November 1918 were muted, as many communities throughout New Zealand were gripped by the influenza pandemic. Over a two-month period more than 8500 New Zealanders died, most of them aged between 20 and 40, and many children were left without parents – particularly among Māori where the death rate was four and a half times that of non-Māori. Around 18,000 New Zealanders died during or as a result of World War One, and this coupled with the death toll of the influenza pandemic triggered debate on issues ranging from declining Pākehā birth rates, promoting and rewarding motherhood, improving children's health, and providing adequate hygiene and housing. Women took an active role in these debates and drew on accepted understandings of their roles and responsibilities as mothers of the Dominion to argue for extended citizenship rights on this basis.

In February 1918, more than 85 years after the first petition calling for women's suffrage was presented to the British Parliament,[57] the Representation of the People Act was passed, which allowed women in Britain over the age of 30 (and men over the age of 21) to vote. Nine months later, the Parliamentary Qualification of Women Act was passed, which entitled women to stand for election in the British House of Commons. It had been a drawn-out and divisive campaign and, even though women in Britain did not have the suffrage on the same basis as women in New Zealand,[58] there was a sense that New Zealand needed to catch up with Britain in terms of women's eligibility for parliamentary election. However, rather than pursuing a dedicated bill to remove women's political disabilities, the issue was again caught up in convoluted debates around the respective rights and privileges of the two houses of Parliament.

Legislative Council Amendment Bill 1918

At the request of various women's groups, in November 1918 Jim McCombs asked the prime minister if the government this session would introduce legislation to confer full political rights on women electors. In doing so he drew attention to the fact that the British Government had recently made women electors eligible to sit in the House of Commons. In reply, the prime minister said the matter would be referred to Cabinet in due course and the House would be informed of the Cabinet's decision.[59] This lack of commitment on the part of the Reform Government firmed McCombs' resolve to again try to introduce a private member's bill to amend the Legislative Council Act to allow women to be elected to the Upper House.

In the meantime, the government's Legislative Council Amendment Bill was back on the Order Paper. The Legislative Council Act passed in 1914 had been due to come into operation on 1 January 1916. When the National Cabinet was formed in 1915, one of the conditions made by the Liberal Party under the leadership of Ward had been that the legislation would not come into force during the period of the coalition government. With the recent cessation of the war, the Act needed to be revisited to realign the termination of the appointments of members of the Legislative Council and to arrange for election of members to the council. During debate on the legislation, McCombs signalled his intention to again move an amendment when the bill proceeded to committee to the effect that women should be eligible for election to the Upper House. But the prime minister interjected to say it would be wrong to take that action in committee.

Having been 'jockeyed out' of an opportunity to introduce his private member's bill by both Massey and Ward, McCombs called attention to the many resolutions carried at women's conventions and conferences about the urgent necessity for women's parliamentary representation: 'These women feel that they are not enjoying their full rights of citizenship until their electoral privileges are made exactly the same – identical with the electoral privileges enjoyed by men electors.' He presented the full text of a resolution recently passed by the Lyttelton branch of the WCTU which outlined women's arguments for admission to Parliament. The first principle in their resolution was 'That the general, social, economic, and moral aspects of government affect women equally with men.'[60] They then detailed the functions of government that had a special interest for mothers and for other women – those associated with hygiene, social purity, neglected children, guardianship of children, orphanages, education, and so on.

The main argument presented in the resolution was that when women were granted the suffrage in 1893, Parliament denied them the full benefit of the franchise by denying them the right to represent an electorate, a right enjoyed by every male elector regardless of their nationality. In doing so, Parliament deprived the electorates of the right of a free choice of representative, and this went against the modern trend of democratic government, which was towards giving 'the freest and fullest right to every citizen'. Because there had been no women in Parliament to represent women's demands, the government of the day had been able to ignore or refuse women's repeated requests for women justices of the peace, women jurors, women police, the equal co-guardianship of children, equal pay for equal work, raising the age of consent, better protection of young women and children, and other reforms. The resolution therefore requested 'That the Government be asked whether it will cause such an alteration in the law as to give electorates the right to elect a woman representative to Parliament.'[61]

As McCombs pointed out, both the Reform and the Liberal parties had enthusiastic women supporters who worked hard to see their parties returned to the House. In this respect, the right for women to sit in Parliament was not a party matter; it was a matter of justice. Newman framed the issue as a well-deserved right and a matter of justice. He said that women had proven themselves worthy of this honour during the war and the recent influenza epidemic; that they had a right to sit in Parliament, and to continue to bar them from the House and the Legislative Council 'is exceedingly archaic, old-fashioned, and out of date'.[62] The Independent Labour member for Grey Lynn, John Payne, agreed and asserted that 'the last vestige of argument has been taken away against such an innovation being carried out'. The fact that women were more in touch than men with society's moral and social problems was reason enough for them to 'take a share in the councils of the nation'.[63]

As he had signalled, McCombs moved several new clauses omitting the word 'male' and substituting 'man' with 'person', and his motion was carried by a majority of four votes. Bill Massey attempted to raise a point of order that the amendment was foreign to the present bill, but this was overruled by the speaker. Immediately the amended bill was reported to the Legislative Council the attorney-general, Sir Francis Bell, moved that the council disagree with the amendments to allow women to be elected to both houses on the basis that the amendments were 'rubbish'.[64] The prime minister did not elaborate on his objections to the amendments. Sir William Hall-Jones who, while maintaining an Independent stance, had always been a supporter of Liberal politics, drew attention to the work of various women, including the wife of the prime minister, who 'had spared neither time nor money in doing what she could' during the war and who had 'risked her life in helping those who needed help' during the influenza epidemic. He held that 'the women of New Zealand had proved themselves sound Imperialists – more so on the average, perhaps, than the men' and he believed that 'in either House their advice, especially in social matters and questions relating to home life, would be of great advantage to the country'.[65] But Hall-Jones was in the minority and the motion that the council disagree with the amendments made by the House of Representatives was carried by 26 votes to three.

Trade unionist John Paul, who had been appointed to the Legislative Council by Sir Joseph Ward in 1907 and who had publicly advocated for women's admission to Parliament for many years, was not prepared to let the matter rest. When the attorney-general reported on the reasons for disagreeing with the amendments, Paul reiterated his position that 'if it was good enough for the House of Commons to agree to legislation which permitted women to sit in the House of Commons it ought to be good enough for New Zealand'. He questioned what had changed the opinion of fellow members of the Legislative Council who, four years earlier, had been perfectly prepared for women to be eligible for election to the council as soon as they were permitted to sit in the House of Representatives. He maintained that a great deal had changed in the 25 years since women had gained the franchise and the time for argument had now passed. Many other countries had extended the franchise to women and this had included the right for women to sit in Parliament. There was no reason for the Legislative Council to put itself 'in the objectionable position of retarding a reform which ... would prove beneficial in every way'.[66] Paul's sincerity was matched by the insincerity shown by other members of the Legislative Council: one member suggested that if women were to enter both houses, perhaps they should be over the age of 50 for the Lower House and under the age of 30 for the Upper House.[67]

To ensure members of the Legislative Council were fully appraised of women's views on the admission of women to Parliament, the following day Nellie Coad, who had been elected to the government's advisory Council of Education, led a deputation of women to meet with the attorney-general. Coad pointed out that the fact that the speaker of the House of Representatives had ruled the clause in order only for it to be rejected by the Legislative Council on a technicality created an impression among women that the Legislative Council was evading the question. Not only were women playing an increasing role in society, their services were indispensable in a national crisis. There were many issues that would be dealt with more efficiently if women were in Parliament, and women were particularly interested in housing and town planning, and in regulations that dealt with the conditions of women's work. She was quick to counter the charge that many women did not desire seats in Parliament; she said this was also true of men but had never been used as a reason to deny them the right. Women had proven they had the ability and, as there was no moral right to exclude them from Parliament, there should be no legal right. Other members of the delegation raised additional arguments. Children's author Edith Howes asserted that women who were engaged in the education of children were convinced that women's point of view needed to be considered, and Miss Nicholls who spoke on behalf of university women, pointed to the way universities had demonstrated the benefits of cooperation between men and women.[68]

Sir Francis Bell responded by insisting that it was not that the Legislative Council opposed the principle of women sitting in Parliament, but they objected to the irregular and unconstitutional manner in which the amendment had been introduced.[69] When the bill was sent back to the Lower House, the prime minister asked that members rescind the amendments made to give women the right to become members of the Legislative Council. He contended that, 'It is a great policy question, and an amendment of that sort is really an amendment of some of the most important legislation that we have on the statute-book today.' He was prepared to accept the principle, but he wanted it done 'in a proper and regular manner'.[70] Massey gave his word that an opportunity to thoroughly consider the proposal would be given in the next session. When asked if he was prepared to go as far as bringing down the current bill if members did not agree to his request to rescind the amendments, after some prevarication he admitted he could do so. In supporting Massey's proposal, Ward said he too was not prepared to follow the member for Lyttelton in this matter; he accused McCombs of being someone who, 'as a rule, is out to advertise himself – who is prepared upon any occasion, however important it may otherwise be, to introduce an element of discord in connection with any proposal of importance contained in a Bill brought down by the Government'.[71]

Rising to speak in his own defence, McCombs drew attention to the flippant remarks made about the women of New Zealand by members of the House. He accused the prime minister of 'subterfuge' and of pursuing an 'extraordinary course' in what he believed to be 'the first time on record in the history of the legislation of New Zealand when the Prime Minister has not requested even one Conference on a question of disagreement with the Upper House', and he ventured to say, 'it is the Prime Minister who is pursuing the irregular course on this occasion'.[72] He went so far as to accuse the government of wishing to win popularity by appearing the next year to be the author of the reform that had in fact already been approved by the House of Representatives. Accusations and counter-accusations of breaches of protocol followed until McCombs was silenced by the speaker from responding to claims that he had not given any prior notice of his intention to propose the initial amendments. The division to not insist on the amendments was carried by a majority of 11 votes.

Reinstatement of the National Council of Women

From the onset of the war, constant appeals to women's maternal citizenship – which cast the duties of motherhood as a service of fundamental importance to the state – demonstrated how critical women's involvement was to the collective war effort. New Zealand women here and overseas showed no hesitation in heeding the call to serve. Their service did not end when armistice was declared, either: women took on vital roles in the influenza pandemic, and they were the ones who carried the burden of healthcare for wounded and traumatised veterans who suffered from physical and psychological conditions, often for years to come.

Leaders in the women's movement brought a political analysis to women's experiences of and contributions to the war. For decades women had been arguing for increased engagement in all aspects of civic life and for widening the sphere of employment opportunities. The necessities of war afforded them these opportunities. However, although the war facilitated their greater involvement in the paid and unpaid workforce, it did not transform women's work in New Zealand, and many women returned, not necessarily of their own accord, into their pre-war roles. The war had drawn attention to 'the pitfalls of a social model based on male "breadwinners"'[73] and had made it clear to leaders of the women's movement that women's continued lack of a direct voice in Parliament was hindering their ability to contribute to legislation that would serve all sectors of society.

In November 1916 it was reported that 'a movement is on foot [sic] to found a National Council of Women of New Zealand'.[74] The impetus to revive the National Council of Women came from women from different parts of New Zealand and was led by Kate Sheppard, Christina Henderson and Jessie Mackay, who networked with prominent women in other main centres. Although the main aim of the new council was still 'to unite all organised societies of women for mutual counsel and co-operation, and in the attainment of justice and freedom for women, and all that makes for the good of humanity' as it had been when the council was originally established in 1896, affiliation to the council was to be open to societies of women and men who were in sympathy with the national policy of the council. The council would be organised 'in the interest of no one propaganda' and it would have no power over constituent societies 'beyond that of suggestion and sympathy'. Importantly, too, the council aimed to encourage the formation of associations of women engaged in the trades and professions as well as in social and political work where no such associations existed.[75]

There were important continuities and differences between the earlier NCW and the new council, which began in April 1918. The constitution of the new council was based on branch representation, which enabled a New Zealand-wide network that could confidently claim to be more genuinely representative of the voice of New Zealand women. By the first annual meeting there were local councils in Auckland, Hamilton, Gisborne, Whanganui, Wellington, Christchurch and Dunedin, with efforts in tow to establish councils in Napier, Palmerston North, Timaru and Invercargill. There were about 40 women's societies acting in cooperation with the council, which assured a substantial voice for the organised women's movement. This structure meant that, in the interests of democracy, consultation processes were often slow and resulted in either deadlock or compromise. In effect, the radicalism of the earlier council was 'tempered by democracy'.[76]

Women's Parliamentary Rights Bill 1919

Early in 1919 Kate Sheppard wrote to Sir William Hall-Jones to thank him for his comments in the Legislative Council in support of women's admission to Parliament, and for his subsequent confirmation of his support in a letter to her. Hall-Jones had suggested organising a petition to both houses but, as a petition was already in circulation regarding licensing legislation, Sheppard undertook to discuss the matter with the executive of the NCW before making a commitment. Recent comments by both Massey and Ward in the House in support of women's admission to Parliament had given her cause for optimism that if they held their next convention in Wellington during the parliamentary session and formed a strong deputation to government to present their claims, they would be met with a supportive hearing.[77]

On 6 August 1919 a deputation representing the Auckland branch of the National Council of Women met with Deputy Prime Minister Sir Joseph Ward to discuss women's eligibility to sit in Parliament. At the meeting Ellen Melville pointed out that women should be eligible to ensure they could take an active share in sorting out the serious legislative problems of postwar reconstruction the country faced. Other members of the deputation presented further arguments in favour of women's parliamentary rights and Ward gave his assurance he would do everything in his power to pass legislation to this effect.[78] The Women's Parliamentary Rights Bill had its first reading in the House of Representatives on 29 August 1919. Promoted by the government, the bill had only one operative clause: 'A woman shall not be disqualified by sex or marriage from being appointed or elected as a member of the Legislative Council or of the House of Representatives, or from sitting or voting as a member of either House of Parliament, anything to the contrary in the Legislative Act, 1908, or in any other Act notwithstanding.'[79]

The first annual conference of the new NCW held in Wellington in early September signalled a changing of the guard. In May, Sheppard had forwarded her letter of resignation effective from the eve of the annual general meeting held at the conference. She did not attend the conference but had arranged for her president's address to be printed as a broadsheet with copies sent to all members of the Legislative Council. In setting out an agenda for the NCW for the next decade, she noted that the admission of women to Parliament remained the question of outstanding importance in the 1919 plan of work. Her message was clear: 'any community which deliberately excludes women from its government is lacking in a true perception of the functions of government'.[80]

Sheppard was optimistic that even the pressure of only a few women in Parliament would make a difference on issues such as mothers having a legal right to guardianship of their children. Years of requests, resolutions and petitions to Parliament on this issue had come to nothing, and this led her to conclude, 'Justice to mothers was not in the game of party politics.'[81] Other reforms in the legal status of married women were urgently required, in particular economic equality and provision for a motherhood endowment to assist with the costs of bearing and raising children. More general reforms were needed, too, such as the appointment of women as police officers, justices of the peace and jurors, equal pay for equal work, especially in the teaching profession to ensure greater equality for female teachers with their male counterparts in respect of salaries, as well as opportunities for promotion and the appointment of women school inspectors.

In her closing comments Sheppard expressed her support for changes to the electoral laws to allow for proportional representation which would ensure that the number of seats a party held in Parliament would be determined by the proportion of votes that party received. The need for this was self-evident: 'We cannot claim to be a self-governing people while half (and in the present Parliament more than half) of the electors are unrepresented.' The prime minister was reportedly introducing a proportional representation bill that applied to urban constituencies, but Sheppard insisted: 'We should see to it that every honest opinion held by a substantial number of people should be voiced in our Parliament: and that can only be done by Proportional Representation applied to every part of the Dominion.'[82]

Melville read Sheppard's address in her capacity as chairwoman for the conference. Single-minded in focus, Melville was adamant that the one and only aim of the NCW should be to educate and motivate women to realise their civic responsibilities. She bemoaned the comparative lack of progress of women in New Zealand, which she attributed to the wasted years when the NCW had been in recess and to women's general apathy about taking responsibility for their duties as citizens. She believed women and men were fundamentally different in the way they viewed the world as well as in their political opinions; women's interests could not, therefore, be effectively represented by male politicians.[83]

Sheppard, in her address, said it was 'illogical and unfair' that the prohibition against women sitting in Parliament had persisted so many years after women had been granted the electoral franchise, and that 'the frequent efforts for justice that had been made by earnest women and chivalrous men have been met by indifference and a scarcely-veiled hostility'.[84] To the editor of the *Dominion* this was an unfair and unbalanced appraisal. He insisted that the only reason women had been denied the right to sit in Parliament was because they had not demanded this right.[85] His view was supported by the prime minister. In moving the second reading of the Women's Parliamentary Rights Bill 1919 on 26 September, Massey reminded the House of the events that had occurred when the bill had been presented in the previous parliamentary session and of his promise to bring a bill to this effect. Stating that 'The principle of the Bill is really the outcome of granting the parliamentary franchise to the women of this country,' he claimed that at that time and in the 25 intervening years, 'there was no demand that the women of New Zealand should have the right to become candidates and members of either House of Parliament'.[86]

According to Massey's rewriting of the historical record, the fact that the franchise had been widened in Britain and women there had recently gained the right to be elected to the House of Commons had called attention to the laws in New Zealand, 'and created a certain demand that women in New Zealand should be placed in the same position as the women of England so far as parliamentary rights were concerned'. He added, 'I have always taken up the position that as soon as the women asked for this right they were entitled to it.' He acknowledged there were women who would make very good members of Parliament in either of the two houses and, when prompted, agreed they would make good Cabinet ministers. Asked if women would also be suitable as prime minister, he responded, 'Certainly. If the lady has the requisite ability, and has the confidence of the electors and Parliament, why not? I believe the coming into the House of a number of able women, who are given the opportunity of taking part in public affairs, would have a very steadying influence upon members, especially in the matter of all-night sittings.'[87]

Joseph Ward as leader of the Opposition concurred with the prime minister's rendering of history, and asserted that when the right of women's suffrage was recognised in New Zealand, 'there was no attempt of any sort or kind made by women to have the logical sequence to that legislation put on the statute-book to admit women to Parliament'. He went on to claim he did not know 'of any agitation of any importance in connection with [women's admission to Parliament] among the women in New Zealand since they have had the right to vote'.[88] In Ward's view, the important shift was the work women had performed during the war, which 'warranted their recognition to the fullest extent, and their having equal rights with men to stand for the House of Representatives'. Expressing his 'hearty and cordial support' for the bill, he added, 'It is, in the altered circumstances of the world, the right thing to do.'[89] Ward could personally name women who 'could speak on public questions, and hold their own in debate, with the best of us in the matter of logical reasoning and fine language, or of putting their views before the public', and expressed his hope that during his time in Parliament he might see some women occupying seats in the House.[90]

Sheppard had raised the issue of what Ward referred to as 'the altered circumstances of the world' in her final president's address to the NCW. She noted that, during the war years, people had gained 'truer and clearer perceptions of truth and justice, of rights and of duties'; they had 'realised that the peer and the peasant, the male and the female, are fashioned out of one common clay', and a general understanding had developed 'that the accident of birth or the incidence of sex cannot be allowed to bar the right of each human being to self-development'.[91] The upheaval of war had broken up old prejudices and women were welcomed into professions and industries that had previously been deemed the sphere of men. Women's desire for a change in their political status was now worldwide; all 26 countries where national councils of women had been established were working to remove the remaining political disabilities of women. At the Peace Conference at Paris that began in January 1919, the League of Nations had agreed that all positions connected with the league would be open equally to men and women. The United States of America had passed the federal amendment that prohibited the denial of the right to vote based on sex; more than half of the states had passed female suffrage, and a woman from the State of Montana had been elected to congress. Women in Austria, Canada, Denmark, Finland, Germany, Holland, Norway, Poland and Sweden had the right to vote and to stand for parliamentary election. The French senate narrowly rejected a motion to grant these rights to women, but their chamber of deputies had overwhelmingly voted in favour of women's franchise with eligibility for all elected bodies by 344 votes to

97. In Australia women had the franchise and in four states they were also eligible to stand for parliamentary election. All these developments were evidence of 'the strong desire among the representations of the world's most powerful nations to deal even-handed justice', and had fuelled Sheppard's conviction that 'the one-sided laws which operate against women and the welfare of the family will not be repealed until we have women representatives in Parliament'.[92]

Although Labour Party members of Parliament were supportive of the proposed legislation, they challenged the government's reasons for moving it. The chairman of the party, Harry Holland, took a principled stance: he rejected the claim that women should have a right to take part in the law-making of New Zealand or any other country in recognition of their contribution to the war effort; rather, he believed, women should be entitled to stand for parliamentary election because they were citizens and because laws expressed, or should express, the collective morality of the nation. Holland had great faith in women's ability to influence the proceedings of the House for good, whichever political party they represented. Unable to resist a dig at the current administration, he suggested that if Parliament consisted wholly of women and they managed to bungle every law they handled, 'they still could not make a worse job of it than this Parliament of men has made'.[93]

Peter Fraser, secretary of the Labour Party and member for Wellington Central, said the Labour Party was particularly glad that women were at last being given this opportunity and looked forward to them being in Parliament before too long. If the success of women Labour candidates in local body elections was indicative, the party anticipated there would be a strong representation of women on the Labour benches who understood working-class conditions because they belonged to that class. He added, 'the Labour party stands for no sex privileges – either for men or for women – and would oppose ... any effort to make special provisions for women representatives'. This stance was in line with the claims women made for themselves, 'not as women, or as members of a sex, but as human beings'. What mattered for working people was that if they voted for a woman it was because 'she is a broad-minded, a progressive, and a radical candidate'.[94]

Other members looked forward to women's empathy with the young, the weak and the unfortunate finding a voice in legislation. Jim McCombs expressed concern that New Zealand's reputation as a world leader in women's parliamentary franchise had long been overshadowed by the failure to confer full electoral rights, and this placed New Zealand firmly behind a growing list of nations and states in Australia, Canada and the United States of America. Other countries such as Denmark boasted full electoral rights for women as well as proportional representation, with nine women sitting in the two houses of Parliament. Finland had 19 women members of Parliament, and Norway, Sweden and Iceland had one female member of Parliament each. Thirty-eight women had recently been elected to the national assembly under the new Constitution of Germany, and there were seven women in the Austrian Parliament. In other countries such as Hungary women had full eligibility to stand for parliamentary election.

Vigor Brown, the Liberal member for Napier, felt that the measure was 'in the right direction' but spoke of the practical impossibilities for women with family responsibilities to attend to parliamentary duties, especially with the late sittings on Thursday evenings. He believed it would be almost impossible for a woman who had a family, even if it were possible to accommodate them close to Parliament Buildings, but even before they were elected, he thought women seeking election would create difficulties for male candidates on the hustings having to speak nicely about their rivals.[95]

Even though the legislation was still being debated, some members hazarded a guess at the likely numbers of women in Parliament in the next session. It had not gone unnoticed that 15 female candidates had stood in the general election in Britain in 1918 and only one had been elected.[96] Two Auckland women were preparing to stand for the upcoming New Zealand general election, and the member for Eden suggested six or seven or even as many as 22 women might stand. Not all members were as confident that there would be a tide of women flowing into the debating chamber after the election. Robert Wright, the Independent Reform member for Wellington Suburbs and County District, thought 'the conservative element in human nature' would mean women would not be elected for some time.[97] Convinced that women should have representation in the House immediately, he proposed that four new seats be allocated exclusively to women, with two seats assigned to each of the North and South islands. In time, he believed, more women would be elected but this arrangement would at least secure enough women elected from the first available opportunity. Wright's proposal sparked a barrage of questions: where would these women be seated? Would it be allowed for the wife of a sitting member to be elected? Refuting the charge that his proposal was a vote-catching measure, Wright further proposed that the government take steps to ensure that women were represented in the Legislative Council; he suggested it would be 'a graceful act' for the government to nominate one or two of the prominent women of New Zealand as a sign that they were 'genuinely anxious for reform'.[98]

Politicians expressed great hopes for women's influence in the Chamber: women would not tolerate the insincerity and inefficiency that existed in parliamentary affairs; the 'asperities and acrimony of party warfare'[99] would be softened by the presence of women; the party system itself may even be doomed; and there would likely be an end to all-night sittings. One member admitted there had been social subjects that male members had, to date, been either unable or unwilling to address and that women would take these up. Women would 'deal fearlessly with the marriage laws' and 'handle the marriage question as men have never handled it; they will be opposed to anything that will perpetuate hereditary disease or insanity; they will oppose firmly and absolutely the bringing into the world of children that are crippled and deformed, if they can do so by legislation; and in various other ways by the display of intelligence and caution they will bring about a vast improvement in our social life'.[100]

Others anticipated a range of changes that would be necessitated by the presence of women in the House. McCombs noted wryly that, as there was a nicely furnished room set aside for the wives of the members of Parliament, when married women were elected there would need to be a room set aside for their husbands. Another member drew attention to the various ways the forms and rules of the House had been built up on the assumption that there was some great and impassable barrier between the sexes: 'Everywhere one goes inside the Parliamentary Buildings – and it strikes a new member more forcibly than the members who have been accustomed and hardened to it – there are notices up "No ladies must be admitted here", "Members only", and so on. We find in almost every portion of the House the sex line is drawn. Now, that line will have to go. In some ways the effects may be quite serious.'[101] For the most part, the regulations that pervaded Parliament Buildings were considered absurd and obsolete. It was not simply a matter of removing signage that warned women off the premises of Bellamy's; the public galleries needed to be open to women, and there would be no need for separate women's galleries.

With support on both sides of Parliament there appeared to be consensus, at least among those in the debating chamber on 26 September 1919, that the Women's Parliamentary Rights Bill would be passed. But as Alfred Newman – who had moved seven years earlier to admit women to Parliament – pointed out, the bill still needed to be supported by the Legislative Council and they were a 'pretty conservative' lot who had 'poleaxed this question of women's political rights on other occasions'.[102] Newman's reserve was warranted. The first reading of the bill in the Upper House was deferred on a technicality: one of the privileges of both Houses of Parliament under the Legislature Act 1908 was that any proposed change to the constitution of either House must originate in the House whose constitution would be affected. Having originated in the Lower House, the bill was a breach of the privileges of members of the Upper House. Recognising that this was a difficult technical question, the speaker referred the matter to a committee to investigate. Following advice, the speaker ruled that insofar as the bill referred to the Legislative Council, it was an infringement on the privileges of the council, and that that portion of the bill should not be accepted.

During debate in the Legislative Council on the second reading of the bill, similar issues of parliamentary protocol were raised. Thomas MacGibbon submitted that a bill that, by the speaker's ruling, was decided to be 'irregular and an infringement on the privileges of this Council should not have been brought up for consideration again'.[103] But he was deemed to be traversing the ruling of the speaker and was therefore out of order. Prefacing his comments with the assurance that he had no intention of traversing the speaker's ruling, lawyer John MacGregor, who was known for his mastery of constitutional principles, proposed to move an amendment to the motion submitted earlier by the attorney-general: 'That this Bill be laid aside on the ground that its introduction in the other House was an infringement of one of the most important privileges of this House, inasmuch as it purports to alter its constitution.'[104] The speaker was not prepared to accept this amendment as it was in contradiction to his ruling and therefore needed to be dealt with in a constitutional manner. Another member reiterated the argument that the government did not have a mandate from the people for such a significant constitutional change, but this was countered by the attorney-general, who reminded members that the women's franchise had been passed with no mandate from the people at the end of the third session of a Parliament that expired in 1893, and that was for a far greater change as it doubled the constituency of voters, whereas the current measure was 'merely a widening of the choice of the electors'.[105]

The bill proceeded to committee where, in line with the speaker's earlier ruling, the second clause was amended to read,: 'A woman shall not be disqualified by sex or marriage from being elected as a member of the House of Representatives, or from sitting or voting as a member *thereof*, anything to the contrary in the Legislature Act, 1908, or in any other Act notwithstanding.'[106] Following the speaker's direction that the amendment proposed by MacGregor needed to be dealt with in a constitutional manner, before the third reading of the bill in the Legislative Council MacGregor moved to discharge from the Order Paper the motion he had earlier given notice to. This cleared the way for the final procedural hurdle of the third reading of the bill. In moving this third reading, the attorney-general confirmed that as the bill now stood there was no interference with the privileges of the Legislative Council, and he recommended that members should agree to the bill, regardless of their private opinions on the question of women sitting in Parliament.

Again, debate over constitutional issues threatened to stifle the passage of the bill. Anxious not to let this happen, John Paul spoke of the necessity for Legislative Council members to remember that they were, or ought to be, the servants of the general public. As he explained, both houses had supported the bill being passed into law and yet they had created an impasse of sorts that could wreck the bill. To his mind, this was an example of 'just where the parliamentary machine fails to register the opinions of the people' and was the reason some great constitutional writers expressed fears as to the future of parliament: 'unless Parliament is a more workable machine, and registers the opinions and desires of the people more readily than it appears to be able to do in some cases, then Parliament is not going to keep the hold on the affections of the people that it ought to have'.[107] He urged the immediate introduction of legislation to give the absolute right to women to sit in the Legislative Council. As far as Paul was concerned, the prime minister had given his promises to deputations in various parts of the country that he would introduce legislation to this effect and it needed to be unequivocal that, whether by nomination or election, women should be eligible to sit in the Legislative Council.

But still the insistence that there was no demand for the measure was voiced. Liberal member William Earnshaw contended, 'public opinion is absolutely dormant on the matter ... There has been no demand anywhere that women should have seats in the Parliament of this country. It is not a live political question.'[108] Tureiti Te Heuheu Tukino, fifth paramount chief of Ngāti Tuwharetoa and a strong advocate for Māori equality and rangatiratanga, put forward a case that, if the bill was passed, provision should be made to exclude Māori women from being eligible to sit in Parliament in either house on the basis that it would be against Māori custom. He claimed, 'It has been the custom of our people from the time of their ancestors down to the present day that the male should on all occasions and under all conditions be the leader, and be the channel through which the affairs of the people should be cared for; that he should think out what is best for the people and for the protection of the people. The male has always been the master mind.'[109] Despite these arguments, the amended bill comfortably passed its third reading with a majority of 16 votes and was sent to the House of Representatives with a request for their concurrence with the decision of the Legislative Council.

On receiving the bill in the House, Prime Minister Massey immediately moved that the amendments made by the Legislative Council which would mean that women could not be appointed to the Upper House be not agreed to. Jim McCombs congratulated the prime minister for keeping his promise to the women of this country to do his best to secure for them full parliamentary rights. The prime minister's motion was agreed and, in line with parliamentary procedure, he then moved that a committee be appointed, consisting of Newman and McCombs as well as himself, to draw up reasons to show why the amendments made by the Legislative Council should be disagreed with. This was a straightforward task as the only real objection was that the amendments proposed by the Legislative Council would, if passed into law, create the serious anomaly of women having the right to be elected to the House of Representatives but not to sit in the Legislative Council.[110]

Once again there was an impasse: unless either house gave way, the bill would be killed. In a game of political football, the attorney-general moved that the Upper House insist on its amendments. Only one member put up an argument for the council to not insist on the amendments. In George Jones' opinion, there was a 'big majority' in the council who 'would deem it a privilege to vote that women should be included in their ranks' and they should not be diverted from their duty in this regard because of the ruling that, in this case, there had been a breach of parliamentary protocol. But the attorney-general stood behind his duty as leader of the Legislative Council to uphold its privileges as defined by the speaker. He had no doubt that if the House of Representatives sent another bill dealing with the constitution of the house in a manner that did not infringe the privileges of the council, the council would pass it. His motion that the council insisted on its amendments in the Women's Parliamentary Rights Bill was agreed to by a majority of 13 votes. With their reasons for this action drawn up and agreed to, the bill was again sent to the Lower House.[111]

The Lower House asked for a conference and the three members who had drawn up the reasons for disagreement earlier – Newman, McCombs and Massey – were appointed managers. On the basis that, 'The constitutional rights of this House are involved; the privilege question has been definitely challenged,' McCombs took the position that the question of privilege took precedence over the question of the right of women to sit in the Legislative Council. Once again demonstrating his detailed understanding of the Constitution Act 1852 and its application to parliamentary protocol, he elaborated the need for the House to 'be jealous of its constitutional rights in a matter of this kind' and the dangers of precedents being set for infringements of those rights by the Upper House. He clarified that in relation to the current issue, 'we are dealing with a broad question of women's parliamentary rights – not the question of the right of women to sit in the Upper House, but the broad question of granting full parliamentary privileges to the women of the Dominion; and in giving that broad privilege we have to give them the right of appointment in the Upper House.'[112]

McCombs had done his homework. The bill that had imposed the disability on women electors in New Zealand denying them the right to be elected to the House of Representatives or appointed to the Legislative Council had originated in the House of Representatives on 11 August

1893 and, having passed, was transmitted to the Legislative Council for its concurrence. This meant, 'The disability which we are now seeking to remove was actually imposed by a Bill originating in this House, and it seems the height of absurdity for the other Chamber to say to the House that originated the Bill which imposed the disability that that House shall not originate a clause removing the disability.'[113] This triggered a philosophical discussion on the nature and historical origins of parliamentary privilege and a request from former leader of the Legislative Council and now member of the House of Representatives for Hawke's Bay, Sir John Finlay, that 'the Prime Minister ... insist that this method of raising a question of privilege to reject legislation coming from this House, and backed by the great mass of the people, is not going to be encouraged'.[114] The Liberal member for Wairau Richard McCallum expressed an opposing view and considered the action taken by the Legislative Council was justifiable. Protesting the waste of time taken on this issue, he believed the substantial point of difference was the vast difference between appointing and electing. He suggested the House 'gracefully retire from the position taken up, and alter the Bill by striking out the words "appointed or", so that ladies may only be elected by the constituents to either branch of the Legislature'. This action would mean that until the Legislative Council was made elective there would be no right to appoint women to the Upper House unless the Upper House chose to do so.[115]

Ward was more circumspect: he said that if members of the House stood firm on the rights of the House of Representatives, women would not attain any parliamentary rights at all this session. He was fully prepared to give women full parliamentary rights for both branches of the Legislature but he did not want to see the proposal that women might be candidates for the House of Representatives at the coming election killed by members continuing to take up the attitude of insisting on their rights as against the Upper House upholding what they advanced as their privileges.[116]

As other members entered the debate the central issues became very clear. In the words of one member, 'The whole thing comes down to this: the right of a Chamber which is not an elected body attempting to clip the wings of a Chamber which is an elected body.'[117] Harry Holland took a similar view: he was not overly concerned about the right of women to be given seats in the Legislative Council because it was unlikely that any woman representing the labour movement would be appointed to the council under the present system of government. For him, the central issue was 'whether the will of the people is to prevail – whether what is undoubtedly the will of an overwhelming majority of both the men and women of New Zealand shall be given effect to – or whether a handful of very estimable gentlemen who are wholly unrepresentative shall be permitted to say that because their privileges are at stake the will of the people shall not be allowed to prevail'. He told his parliamentary colleagues: 'We all know – whether we belong to the Government side of the House, to the Liberal Opposition, or to the Labour Opposition – that there is no serious opposition whatever [sic] to women having a right to sit in Parliament, and consequently there is no necessity to extensively discuss that at this stage of the proceedings.'[118]

In turn, members questioned the right of the Upper House to dictate proceedings, the possible basis on which they might deny women a seat on the Legislature, and the basis of their assumed authority. Various arguments for women's right to represent the people in Parliament were put forward and the few voices that agreed with the position of the Legislative Council and those who questioned the claimed widespread support for women to sit in Parliament were drowned out in passionate monologues on the nature of rights and privileges. As the debates drew to a close, the Labour member for Wellington Central Peter Fraser expressed his hope that 'nothing will take place between the two Houses that will jeopardize the right of women to enter this House and sit as elected representatives of the people'.[119]

Both houses agreed to a conference on the matter, but the managers representing each house failed to reach agreement in that conference. On reporting this outcome to the House, the prime minister proposed to go with 'the lesser evil'[120] and agree to the amendment made by the Legislative Council. But he informed the House that he had arranged with a colleague in the Legislative Council for a bill to originate in the council to replace the clause that had been struck out, thereby ensuring that women would not be disqualified by sex or marriage from being appointed or elected to the Legislative Council, and that this was achieved in a manner that did not affect the privileges of the council. While there were members who did not agree on giving way on the question of privilege, others agreed this was the only best course of action and welcomed a later opportunity to debate more fully the future of the Upper House.

Women's Parliamentary Rights (No. 2) Bill 1919

As arranged, the Attorney-General Sir Francis Bell introduced a Women's Parliamentary Rights Bill to amend the law with respect to the capacity of women to be appointed to the Legislative Council. The operative clause in the bill read: 'A woman shall not be disqualified by sex or marriage from being appointed to being a member of the Legislative Council, or from sitting or voting as a member thereof, anything to the contrary in the Legislature Act, 1908, or in any other Act notwithstanding.'[121] In moving the second reading of the bill on 23 October 1919, Bell said that although 'This bill may be ... the logical sequence to the admission of women to the right of election to the House ... it is not a necessary sequence.'[122] These words signalled to members of the Legislative Council to not feel compelled to vote for the measure. In following an orthodox course in his judicial analysis of the bill, it was evident Bell's heart was not in the measure. He pointed out that as soon as Parliament rose, the Legislative Council Act would be proclaimed and in one year would become the law of the land. That meant a unique interim period of one year in which men could still be appointed but not elected to the Legislative Council, and women could be elected but not appointed to the Legislative Council.

There were still influential voices speaking against the bill. Although he had been an 'ardent supporter' of women's suffrage 15 years earlier, Henry Michel, who had been appointed the previous year to the Legislative Council by the Reform Government, indicated his intention to vote against the bill because he was not satisfied there was enough demand on the part of the women of New Zealand for this additional change. In support of this claim he said that in the 15 years since women had the ability to be elected as mayors or councillors of cities and boroughs, there had been only one woman elected to the position of mayor. He thought it reasonable to suppose that if women really desired to enter into 'the turmoil of national politics' they would have shown more of a desire first to serve at the local government level.[123] As other 'proofs' of women's lack of desire to sit in

Parliament he claimed that women did not seek the services of lady doctors or lady lawyers and that in the last elections in Britain no women succeeded in winning a seat in the House of Commons.[124]

Long-serving member of the Legislative Council George Jones spoke against the bill, claiming that as the present Parliament had existed for nearly six years instead of three, it effectively had no mandate from the people. He suggested that the only thing to be gained by allowing the government to proceed with this bill was that the government would use its power of appointment for electioneering purposes. Determined to not 'attempt to find some reason in some out-of-the-way corner of my intellect why I should oppose this measure', as some of his colleagues appeared to have done, Jones considered that all the objections that had been raised could equally apply to any measure brought before Parliament, and he expressed his impatience that the topic was being treated with levity by fellow members.[125] Te Heuheu Tukino was also irritated by the bill and repeated his view that the issue should be taken to the country to decide. He believed most women would vote against women entering Parliament, and he reiterated that Māori women had emphatically stated to him that they did not wish to enter Parliament and he believed the male voters of the country held this same view.

As the debates continued, most members stated their opposition to the bill, and this was confirmed when a division was taken and the motion to read the bill for a second time was defeated by a majority of 10 votes. This meant that on 29 October 1919 the original bill was passed, with the one operative clause: 'A woman shall not be disqualified by sex or marriage from being elected as a member of the House of Representatives, or from sitting or voting as a member thereof, anything to the contrary in the Legislative Act, 1908, or in any other Act notwithstanding.'

This should have been a cause for celebration at women finally having secured the right to be elected to the House of Representatives. Instead, the newspaper reports were scathing on the fiasco that had resulted in women still being barred from the Legislative Council. The editor of the *New Zealand Times* commented on the extraordinary ease and subtlety of the Massey Government in contriving to 'humbug the people' in relation to the bill. He considered 'the whole episode is an illuminating example of political duplicity and hypocrisy cleverly stage-managed for political purposes'.[126] Some newspapers had denounced the Legislative Council for closing its doors to women, but as the editor of the *New Zealand Times* observed, the Legislative Council had done nothing of the kind and was the first chamber to concede to women the right to election. Moreover, the council had not recently questioned the right of women to offer themselves for any elected position, either in Parliament or elsewhere, and had been almost unanimous in conceding to women the right to enter the House of Representatives. The editor was adamant that it was purely for electioneering purposes that the government was now posing as the champion of the political rights of women.[127]

Ellen Melville, when interviewed as president of the NCW, said she did not think the Legislative Council's decision was of much practical importance although it was 'inconsistent and creates an absurd anomaly'. It made no sense that the law would make it possible for a woman to become a minister of the Crown or even prime minister and yet not be able to sit in the Legislative Council. In her view, while the Legislative Council was 'very jealous of its privileges ... the public generally care little about them'.[128] What mattered was that the government intended to proclaim the Act when Parliament rose. Women were interested in reform of the Upper House, and she doubted many women would wish to become members of it as it was now constituted. But, she suggested, this might change once women's admission to the House of Representatives had been secured.

*

Why did it take so long for women to achieve the right to stand for parliamentary election and why was this legislation finally enacted in 1919? Following the enactment of women's suffrage there was a sense of politicians and the country in general basking in the achievement of being the first country in the world to grant women the right to vote. But with an additional 130,000 voters, they soon realised that women's votes mattered. This did not bring about any noticeable change in the behaviour of politicians for most of the parliamentary term, but it did come into play during debates on bills promoting the removal of women's political disabilities, and in the lead-up to general elections when members postured on the campaign trail. But many women believed it was too early for women to be granted full parliamentary honours. The Wellington Social and Political League and Lady Stout of the Southern Cross Society, for example, echoed Ballance's view that women's education in politics was still in its infancy, and on that basis they did not support women's admission to Parliament.

As was the case for women's suffrage, political rivalries between individuals and parties and ongoing debates on the rights and privileges of the respective houses of Parliament were central to the long hesitation in passing legislation for women to be admitted to Parliament. The increasingly diverse agendas of groups within the wider women's movement was another important factor. As the records of the WCTU and NCW show, there was a consistent demand from women for the right to sit in Parliament, but it could not be claimed to be a strong demand representing the views of most women in the country. Even within the organised women's movement opinions were divided, and other issues took priority. The comprehensive programme of social legislation of the Liberal Government resonated with the comprehensive agendas for change that featured at the annual conventions of the WCTU and the NCW. Women in the organisations represented by the NCW continued to be politically active on a wide range of issues and, while women's admission to Parliament remained a priority, this was not at the expense of concerted efforts to achieve change in other areas of social legislation.

During the period when Parliament was dominated by personality politics and when party politics emerged as the dominant force in Parliament, women depended on allies in the House to introduce and support measures on their behalf. After women had achieved suffrage, the men who were prepared to introduce bills for women's full political citizenship – Alfred Newman, George Russell and Tommy Taylor – were all outspoken critics of government policy, and this, coupled with general prejudice against women's admission to Parliament, militated support for the measures those members introduced for removal of women's civil and political disabilities.

Women tended to rehearse their arguments for full civic and political participation within like-minded forums such as WCTU and NCW meetings and conferences and in the pages of the *White Ribbon* and *The Prohibitionist*. Extracts from their papers, along with their resolutions and detailed records of their meetings, were reprinted in the columns of most of the major daily newspapers, effectively gaining a much wider audience. But the claim that women had not sufficiently demonstrated that they wanted to sit in Parliament was loud and persistent. To some extent, the strategies employed in the campaign for women's suffrage affected the politicians' expectations of what constituted evidence of a demand from women. Petitions were presented over the years, but none was anywhere near the scale of the suffrage petitions of 1892 and 1893. Instead, small scale petitions, some with only a handful of signatures, were presented and were generally discounted as representing the views of an insignificant number of women. As well, most of the strategies women employed to influence male politicians were on an individual level – delegations to the premier and prime minister; personal letters to politicians from individual women and representatives of women's groups; resolutions made at women's conferences and communicated to individual politicians – and this meant those recipients could choose not to speak up in Parliament on women's behalf if they considered it politically expedient.

Both inside and outside the Houses of Parliament, proponents of women's full political citizenship consistently exposed the lack of substance and the often illogical nature of the litany of 'arguments' against women's admission to Parliament. Whether it was women's supposed physical or intellectual inferiority, threats to social etiquette, or practical considerations such as the lack of parliamentary facilities for women, counter-arguments failed to convince those with the power to change the law. Even as women's increased participation in public and civic life proved these arguments outdated, entrenched conservatism continued to hold sway. Long-held prejudices were slowly chipped away through legislative gains such as increased citizenship rights for married women, and in local and municipal politics. Despite this, an underlying sexual double standard persisted whereby it was assumed that men, by virtue of being men, were capable of fully participating in public decision-making roles, whereas women had to collectively demonstrate their capability through a long apprenticeship in active decision-making by serving on school boards and local committees.

The exigencies of war and the influenza pandemic opened up opportunities and expectations of women's active citizenship. Calls for women to actively engage as patriotic citizens were based on an awareness that women's paid and voluntary work needed to be harnessed toward the war effort for the sake of the country and the empire. Arguments based on an extension of women's roles as mothers of the future generation and as moral guardians took on new meaning and significance, and as women heeded the call to demonstrate active citizenship it became increasingly difficult – and politically naïve – to not recognise their competence and the essential nature of their contribution. As Kate Sheppard rightly observed, 'the altered circumstances of the world' had enabled 'truer and clearer perceptions of truth and justice, of rights and duties'.[129] But even when it had been acknowledged by both houses of Parliament that women should be granted the right to stand for parliamentary election, rivalries between the Lower and Upper House threatened to stifle the passage of the legislation. The final debates that resulted in the passing of the Women's Parliamentary Rights Bill 1919 were a convoluted masterclass in parliamentary protocol, to such an extent that the passing of the legislation was almost obscured in the process.

CHAPTER 5

Petticoated candidates, 1919 to 1933

I hope that at the coming election those women who are capable and able will come forward and offer themselves, and that thus women will begin – for a beginning must be made, even though failure is met with at the outset – to aspire to places in this Chamber. — THOMAS WILFORD, MHR, 26 SEPTEMBER 1919

Members must not run away with the idea that because a woman stands for election to this House, therefore all the women in the electorate are going to vote for her. — ROBERT WRIGHT, MHR, 26 September 1919[1]

As the collective shell-shock of World War One and the influenza pandemic subsided, a renewed focus and energy emerged in the women's movement and in politics more generally. The recently reconvened National Council of Women had a youthful line-up of women: only two of the 10 delegates present at the first annual general meeting in September 1919 had served on the executive of the previous council. Symbolic of this change of guard was the absence of Kate Sheppard, whose resignation as president marked the end of her three decades of leadership of the women's movement in New Zealand. Equally symbolic was that Ellen Melville took the chair; subsequently elected dominion president of the NCW, she was later described as 'one of the most significant women of the twentieth century in the struggle for women's rights'.[2] It had taken 26 years since gaining the right to vote for women in New Zealand to achieve the complementary right to sit in parliament; but now that they were finally eligible to stand for parliamentary election, they faced other forms of electoral disability – how to convince and empower women to come forward as candidates, how to convince the political party hierarchy to endorse their candidatures, and how to convince male and female voters to cast a vote for them. Each of these steps was to prove a challenge, with obstacles around every corner.

There was renewed focus, energy and challenges in the political sphere in the immediate postwar period, too. The success of Labour candidates at the five by-elections held during 1918 put the Reform Government on notice that the policies of the Reform–Liberal coalition had been unpopular in many working-class communities. In 1919 radical socialist and editor of the *Maoriland Worker* newspaper Harry Holland[3] became the parliamentary leader of the Labour Party. Holland's dogmatism and lack of willingness to compromise made him a formidable politician in Parliament and on the campaign trail. In November 1918 the Reform Party caucus had carried a resolution to merge with Liberal but this had been rejected by Liberal leader Joseph Ward. Tensions arose within the Liberal Party when Ward, while he was overseas in May 1919, announced he would leave the coalition government.

With three political parties contesting the election set for December, the pattern of New Zealand politics was changing. The wartime coalition between the Reform Party and the Liberal Party had been replaced by a second Reform Government Ministry led by Bill Massey. Fierce rivalry developed between the Liberals and the Labour Party in the lead-up to the general election: the latter was convinced that the radical policies announced by Ward were deliberately aimed at Labour voters. With little middle room between Reform and the Liberals, Labour subsequently launched its campaign in defiant opposition to the Liberals. Key issues that emerged in the election campaign were rising inflation, rapidly increasing land prices, union militancy and levels of payment to soldiers.

1919 general election: 'They should not be discouraged'

In anticipation of the Women's Parliamentary Bill 1919 being passed, as early as October 1919 two 'certain lady candidates'[4] were being freely named in the newspapers: Rosetta Baume (who campaigned under her married name, Mrs F.E. Baume) and Ellen Melville. In early November, the candidature of outspoken advocate for the working people Aileen Cooke (who campaigned under the name Mrs Lindsay Cooke) was announced. All three women were colourful figures, and each came with a solid foundation of political activism. Baume was involved in a wide range of civic activities, particularly in the field of education. She had the distinction of being the first woman elected to the Auckland Education Board, had served on the board of governors of Auckland Grammar School and Elam School of Art, was a member of the Workers' Educational Association and honorary secretary of the Auckland Association for the Advancement of Education. She was involved in a number of women's groups including the Society for the Protection of Women and Children, the Auckland Women's Club, and was honorary secretary of the Auckland Women's Patriotic League. The previous year, during the influenza pandemic, she was president of the Auckland centre for the Women's National Reserve of New Zealand.[5] She was vice-president of the NCW and a committee member of the Auckland Women's Club (later known as the Auckland Lyceum Club), inaugurated by Melville to provide a forum for 'women interested in social, public and artistic affairs'.[6]

Melville herself, as well as running her independent legal firm, was instrumental in forming the YWCA Women's Club in Auckland and reviving the NCW in 1917 and had been a member of the Auckland City Council for six and a half years.

Aileen Cooke had a background in unionism and workers' rights. Born in Ireland in the early 1860s, she worked as a domestic servant and nurse before marrying Frederick Garmson, a carpenter from Australia. She was active in shearers' unions in Australia and New Zealand, and claimed to have been involved with the maritime strike in 1890 and the Broken Hill miners' strike in 1892 in Australia. Described as 'an articulate and forceful speaker with a command of the gritty language of shearers', her early advocacy for workers gained her some notoriety in the press.[7] Over time she became more involved in political activism around women's issues. She was instrumental in the New Zealand Workers' Union endorsing the organisation of women into trade unions, and she attempted, unsuccessfully, to establish a domestic workers' union. She was secretary of the women's section of the Canterbury Liberal Association and served on the committee of the Canterbury Women's Institute. By the late 1890s she had publicly declared her disillusionment with working within organisations.[8]

Rosetta Baume consented to her nomination as an Independent Liberal candidate for the Parnell electorate in response to a large deputation of women and three petitions from representative women of Auckland. As the media was quick to point out, she had parliamentary tradition in her family: her late husband had been a member of the House of Representatives, as had her cousin by marriage, former minister and current member for Auckland East, Arthur Myers. During her campaign Baume emphasised her Liberal leanings and her belief that the Liberal Party was responsible for a great deal of New Zealand's progress. But she was keen to reserve her right to make decisions as an individual on any matter that concerned the welfare of the people and for this reason she chose to stand as an Independent Liberal. She was on record as being 'utterly opposed to the official Labour Party, or to any party which could support a "go-slow" policy, or by its actions ally itself with revolutionary Labour, whose pernicious doctrines had already wrought such havoc in the world'.[9] When pressed, she admitted she was a friend of moderate Labour and, to her knowledge, she was the only woman in Australasia who had ever taken a case to the Arbitration Court on behalf of a women's union of workers.[10] On any matter affecting the welfare of the people she stated she would always place country before party, but for ordinary purposes and for no confidence motions she intended to unfailingly support the Liberal Party.

As with Baume, Melville's decision to contest the Grey Lynn seat was in response to requests from women in the electorate. The press pointed to her experience on the Auckland City Council and her success at the polls in every municipal election she had contested as holding her in good stead for her challenge to the Grey Lynn seat. She had a reputation as a hard worker on committees and was 'in every sense of the term a womanly woman'.[11] Her brother Ronald Melville was the *New Zealand Herald* representative in the parliamentary press gallery. In standing as a Progressive Reform candidate,[12] Melville not only had the endorsement of a political party but, unlike the other two women candidates, campaigned on a party platform. The significance of the backing of the government for her candidature received comment in the local press as something few would have dared to predict five or 10 years ago and for which there was no precedent in the political annals of the British Empire.[13] But Melville insisted that, for her, people came before party politics. She was reported as saying that party was not the main thing and that the party that put its own interests first should not have the confidence of the people.[14]

The newspapers, in announcing Mrs Lindsay Cooke's candidature, noted that while she was almost a stranger to most Thames voters, she had been closely associated with politics for the last 30 years. By her own description she had always been an 'advanced Liberal' and a Labour leader and organiser.[15] Unlike Baume, Cooke would not be drawn on motions of no confidence. Her decisions, she stated, would be on a case by case basis: if it was a beneficial measure she would vote for it and against a no-confidence motion; if she considered the measure against the interests of the Dominion she would vote against it and in support of a no-confidence motion. She stood as an Independent on the Returned Soldiers' platform as endorsed by the Auckland Returned Soldiers' Association, which was based on 'the spirit of goodwill, unity, honesty, and constructiveness ... as the vital principle of immediate future progress and the national health and welfare'.[16]

Baume and Melville wasted no time in arranging meetings of supporters to form a strong women's committee to assist with their campaigns. The Women's Citizen's Association sent a hearty message of congratulations on coming forward as candidates and a sincere hope that they would both be voted in.[17] Cooke did not have the backing of any particular women's groups and she financed her campaign entirely from her own pocket. She stood on behalf of women as a matter of principle and was prepared to stand down and support any other women candidate should they come forward. But she apparently made the curious statement that the electors would make an awful mistake if they did not vote for her and they would only realise this mistake if and when they elected another woman.[18] As with the other two women candidates, as Cooke's campaign progressed, her advertisements stated that ladies were specially invited to her meetings.

Each of the three women candidates attracted large audiences and made strong impressions at their opening campaign meetings. The Parnell Picture Theatre was packed for Baume's meeting and over a hundred latecomers were turned away by the police. Baume stated from the outset that she did not intend to indulge in any destructive criticism. There were practically no interruptions during her speech and she was frequently greeted with applause; afterwards she was swamped with questions which she answered freely. It was reported that 'every question was answered with a spirit and decision, and an occasional touch of humour, that evoked applause, and frequently laughter at the discomfiture of the questioner'. The questions ranged from 'inquiries as to the imposition of old maids' and bachelors' taxes to State banks and the duty on tea', and Baume had 'a ready answer for all'.[19] As her campaign progressed, the media commented that 'her inherited spirit of American "hustle" must serve her in good stead in an election campaign'.[20]

Melville was greeted warmly when she entered the packed Empress Theatre for the opening of her election campaign. There was loud applause as she stood to speak, and the audience was generally courteous, responsive and sympathetic, although there was an element of antagonism from a small group of extremist Labour supporters near the end of the meeting. Her address covered a wide range of subjects, and each received a careful and logical (though sometimes brief) exposition. There were many questions from the audience and she responded to every question 'with a promptness and ready wit that brought forth loud applause'. There was, however, a 'clamour of a number of dissentient voices' when a vote of thanks and confidence was passed at the close of the meeting.[21]

Cooke's opening campaign meeting was one of the largest political meetings ever held in Thames. It was widely reported in the newspapers that she spoke 'trenchantly'[22] and was given a cordial hearing, and that she described herself as 'the mother of the Arbitration Act',[23] having been associated with then minister of labour, William Pember Reeves, at the time of its inception in 1894. Aside from that, no detail on the substance of her speech was printed. Not everyone was impressed with Cooke's campaign performance, let alone her political acumen; notably, Ruby Watson from the Women's International League gave her a thorough drubbing in a lengthy and detailed letter to the editor of the *Thames Star* in which she expressed her surprise and disgust at some of the sentiments put forward at Cooke's opening campaign meeting. Watson found Cooke's claimed authoritative stance on matters on which she was clearly ignorant offensive; she felt that Cooke spoke rather too long on her own family history, betrayed her superficial knowledge on issues of land economics and her ignorance of diplomatic history, used objectionable metaphors for topics of considerable gravity and did not provide straight answers to any of the

Reverend James Wallis
The Cyclopedia of New Zealand, Auckland Provincial Council, 1902, New Zealand Electronic Text Collection

Alfred Saunders
PAColl-1022-1, Alexander Turnbull Library, Wellington

George Warren Russell
35mm-00093-c-F, Alexander Turnbull Library, Wellington

Alfred Kingcome Newman
35mm-00107-c-F, Alexander Turnbull Library, Wellington

Thomas Edward Taylor
S.P. Andrew Ltd, Portrait negatives, 1/1-014939-G, Alexander Turnbull Library, Wellington

James McCombs
PAColl-3861-29-14, Alexander Turnbull Library, Wellington

Kate Wilson Sheppard
1/2-C-09028-F, Alexander Turnbull Library, Wellington

Ellen Melville
1/2-118138-F, Alexander Turnbull Library, Wellington

Rosetta Baume
PAColl-0785 C-016164-1/2, Alexander Turnbull Library, Wellington

Aileen Cooke
AWNS-19191127-37-1, Auckland Libraries Heritage Collections

Annie Herbert
Heritage Photographs Collection, CCL-06-36-1, Christchurch City Libraries

Elizabeth McCombs
1/2-150372-F, Alexander Turnbull Library, Wellington

Annie McVicar
PAColl-5482-009, Alexander Turnbull Library, Wellington

Emily Maguire
New Zealand Herald, 4 August 1928, p. 8

Margaret Young
Evening Post, 6 November 1928, p. 10

'THE QUEEN CITY. Here's luck to you ladies, go in and win!'
Free Lance, 3 December 1919, p. 13

'Parliament as Dr Newman would like to see it.'
William Blomfield, 1866–1938, H-713-121, Alexander Turnbull Library, Wellington

'A PEEP INTO THE FUTURE. The Honourable the LEADERESS of the Opposition has a few words with the HONOURABLE the PRIME MINISTER.'
Free Lance, 8 October 1919, p. 13

'MRS BAUME to MISS MELVILLE – After all dear, there's no place like home for a woman. We can always get elected to this house without opposition.' *Free Lance*, 23 December 1919, p. 13, Alexander Turnbull Library, Wellington

'ALL PERFECT LADIES. New Zealand's first undoubted woman member of Parliament. Mrs McCombs is described at the opening of Parliament as having worn a tailored suit of brown heather mixture, with a light blouse with turn-down collar and jabot. She wore no hat.'
Auckland Star, 23 September 1933, p. 10

Next page: Auckland candidates for the Reform Party, November 1928.
New Zealand Herald, 8 November 1928, p. 5.

REFORM PARTY

AUCKLAND PROVINCIAL CANDIDATES of the

VOTE FOR Conscient Ordered Administra Tried— Efficient— Secure.

AUCKLAND SUBURBS ELECTORATE

"Gunson for Progress"

SIR JAMES GUNSON
Official Government Candidate

EDEN ELECTORATE

I have had the honour to represent the districts for nine years, and will again contest the Eden Electorate in the Reform Interests.

I STAND FOR:
Equal opportunities for all.
Special privileges to none.
Sane Legislation.
A policy without frills.
No promises that cannot be fulfilled.
An appeal to women's intelligence to vote for practical measures, not impractical theories.

VIVIAN H. POTTER, M.P.
OFFICIAL REFORM CANDIDATE

PARNELL ELECTORATE.

Vote for Dickson, who has represented Parnell for 17 years.

Mr. Dickson has been the Chief Government Whip for the past 9 years, and Chairman of the Railway Committee for five years, and he is a past Chairman of the Labour Bills Committee.

Mr. Dickson has also had wide experience on Public Bodies, including Member of the Remuera Road Board for 15 years, 5 years of which he was Chairman. Member of the Auckland City Council, Auckland Drainage Board, and of the Auckland Hospital Board, and is now a Member of the Manukau County Council.

He has been connected with Friendly Societies for 40 years.

Mr. Dickson is acknowledged to be the most popular and hardest working Member in the House.

Vote Dickson and Reform

It's time we had Women Parliament.

ELECTO ROSKI
Suppo
Miss E
Melv

OFFICIAL REFORM CANDI FOR ROSKILL.

A trained business woman, a thoroughly experienced in public

MRS. MAGUIRE
THE CANDIDATE.
AUCKLAND EAST ELECTORATE.

MRS. MAGUIRE stands for reduction in the cost of living, and improved conditions of life for the worker. Is in sympathy with women's movements and would support any legislation to give all New Zealand children equal opportunities in matters affecting health and education.

She is keenly interested in land settlement, and believes in agriculture, and intensive cultivation as a remedy for unemployment.

She stands for equal opportunities for men and women in all walks of life, and above everything for the rising generation in matters affecting health and education.

MEN OF AUCKLAND EAST!
Vote for MRS. MAGUIRE
She has your children's interests at heart.

Electors of AUCKLAND WEST, Vote for
FRANK ADEANE
OFFICIAL REFORM CANDIDATE,
because he stands for:
PEACE — Both Industrial and National.
PROGRESS — By Sound and Sane Government.
PROSPERITY — By fostering trade within the Empire.
EQUALITY—Equal opportunities for all—irrespective of rank or creed.
PROHIBITION — By the will of the people—on a bare majority issue.
DAYLIGHT SAVING— As a measure of National Economy, and in the interests of the health of the Nation.
BIBLE IN SCHOOLS—The basis of Civilisation and the Text Book of Christianity—to be read, but not expounded.
INFANT WELFARE—Increased State Aid for the Plunket Society and the St. Helens Hospitals. (The new baby is the best immigrant to "assist.")
REDUCED TAXATION—More particularly by means of reduced Customs duties on the everyday needs of the people.

MANUKAU ELECTORATE
BERTRAM BUNN
GOVERNMENT CANDIDATE
OF THE PEOPLE AND FOR THE PEOPLE.

In the early part of his career he was a practical farmer, bringing into productivity a block of land from its native state.

Of recent years he has been engaged in commercial pursuits, and by his integrity, has gained the respect of the business men of the Auckland District. He is a New Zealander born, and has the interests of his country at heart. A man with strong convictions, he is confident of the country's future.

A CLEAN-FIGHTING DIGGER,
VOTE FOR HIM

Electors of WAITEMA

Has Mr. He failed you? H record is one both he and h tuents are proud. He ha put the interest Electorate first. ected to Parlia 1911, he has seat continuous since. Stand by who stood by y your transport was threatened o

VOTE HARR
INDEPENDENT REFORM CANDIDA TRIED AND TRUSTED.

TO THE ELECTORS OF AUCKLAND CENTRAL ELECTORATE.
MR. F. J. LYSNAR
OFFICIAL NOMINEE.

Mr. Lysnar is a brother of Mr. W. D. Lysnar, the retiring member for Gisborne, and was born in the electorate to which he is now offering his services.

He has resided for the past two years in Parnell, but spent the greater part of his life in Gisborne, where he was a wellknown sheepfarmer and public man, serving extensively as member and chairman on the Cook County Council and Gisborne Harbour Board; also had a service of 16 years on the Gisborne Public Hospital Board.

He was for 14 years a member of the Gisborne High School Board, and is a life-member of the Gisborne Racing Club. Mr. Lysnar has sheep farming interests at Waiouru. He unsuccessfully contested the Bay of Plenty seat against the Hon. K. S. Williams upon the death of the Hon. W. D. S. Macdonald.

P. B. FITZHERBERT

OFFICIAL REFORM CANDIDATE for
GREY LYNN.
Double War Service.
Good Record of Public Bodies' Service.
A Fighter.
A Caustic Critic.
A Constructive Politician.

Knows the requirements and aspirations of Grey Lynn Electors and is the best man to achieve them.

Your confidence in P. B. Fitzherbert at the ballot box will be justified.

A. M. SAMUEL
M.P.,
OFFICIAL REFORM CANDIDATE FOR THAMES.

New Zealand born.
Will represent Thames electors with the same conscientious care which has earned him the gratitude of the electors of the old Ohinemuri Electorate.

He stands for sound, progressive legislation, for the benefit of all sections of this important constituency.

Vote SAMUEL for SECURITY

ROTORUA ELECTORS
Vote for HOCKI
WHO SUPPORTS A GOVERNMENT THAT FOR THE MAINTENANCE OF THE UNITY o BRITISH EMPIRE.

For the defence Empire.
For strong, p prudent finan
For closer sett practical linea
For the co-ord our various b education.
For the impro the health o people.
For assistance directions, to primary and industries effe
For a wider scheme, fede for invalides.
For the care o tate and me ficient childr less.
For equal opportunity to all to work out their own For a safe, sound, and responsible Government.

FRANKLIN ELECTORS!
THE ISSUE IS IN YOUR HANDS! SUPPORT
J. N. MASSEY
THE PROGRESSIVE CANDIDATE

MASSEY is a young, virile man, possessing common sense, ability and integrity, which he uses with sound judgment.

MASSEY'S hands are free. He believes in independence and will use his vote on his judgment and his conscience dictate.

MASSEY is a practical farmer. He knows the farmers' needs and his aim is to secure more sustenance for the rural community, particularly the struggling farmer.

MASSEY STANDS FOR
Trade within the Empire, with preference to Britain.
Easing of Burden of Land Taxation imposed for benefit of the People.
Less Party in Parliament and More Business in Less Time.
Legislation for all the People—not for any particular section—that forgetting that the Progress of the Dominion rests upon the Prosperity of the Farm.

Support Your Own and the Country's Interests and Return
J. N. MASSEY

WAIKATO ELECTORATE.
MR. D. S. REID
Reform Candidate for Waikato

Mr. Reid has had a wide public experience, which, with his three years' service as a member of Parliament, qualifies him for a renewal of the Electors' confidence in him.

He has served on Public Bodies for 10 years, as Chairman of the Waipa County Council and the Tokiroamua Road Board Committee. He has been a member of the No. 2 Highways Board and the Central Power Board.

Mr. Reid discounts the report of electorate who declare that the country is on the verge of ruin, and that unemployment is seriously lowering the standard of living.

Mr. Reid advocates the construction of the Tanga Railway, as it will give employment to many, and, if the right style of settler is encouraged, increase prosperity to the country.

Mr. D. S. Reid.

ON THE MERIT OF ITS ACHIEVEMENT IN THE PAST, AND THE HOPE ITS PRUDENT AND HUMANE POLICY HOLDS FOR THE FUTURE, MR. REID UNHESITATINGLY SUPPORTS THE REFORM PARTY.

RAGLAN ELECTORATE
Mr. Walter Seavill, Reform Candidate for Raglan, stands for MODERATE PROTECTIVE TARIFFS.

He believes that New Zealand is financially sound, and advocates the return to the income basis of taxation for all sections of the community, and favours a prudent and helpful Land Policy.

Extract from a report of Mr. Seavill's Address at Glenmassey, which appeared in the New Zealand Herald, Saturday, November 3:—"I have been in the country 36 years, and the Reform Party still impresses me as being the best."

Mr. Walter SEAVILL
REFORM CANDIDATE

MARSDEN ELECTORA

Vote for Jones and own Interests. Jackson Constitu tents. He has done The man that has supported the Reform pa the Militia through the building, providing roads and communication the farming people, keeping the farming people in farming; and on unemployment is N he has done good w In vote for Macinde The Member for the N to ensure a continu tion of his good work hope that he will be r on the primary produ industries effectively For the case of te tate and me ficient chil less.

You want a man who carries in in watching your interests.

VOTE FOR JON

questions posed. The full letter, which took the space of an entire newspaper column, was published 'by arrangement' on the front page of the *Thames Star*, ensuring maximum readership.[24] The following day another letter critical of Cooke's wholesale stance against prohibition and conscientious objectors was published, and the *Waihi Daily Telegraph* reported that she had told her audience at another campaign meeting that she intended to stand for the borough council and 'shake up the City Fathers'.[25] Her self-attributed credentials as a long-serving Labour leader and organiser were questioned, given her demonstrated 'rather shaky' knowledge of the history of the party over the period she claimed to have been an active supporter.[26] Rumours soon circulated that Cooke was not serious in her candidature and this prompted her to take out a front-page advertisement in the *Thames Star*: 'The rumour is in circulation that I am only having a "joke" with the electors of Thames and that I have no intention of going to the poll. I wish to give that report a straightout denial. I will, God willing, contest the election against allcomers and as an Advanced Independent Liberal. AILEEN M. (LINDSAY) COOKE, Junction Hotel, Thames.'[27]

Rumours circulated early in Melville's campaign that she was running as part of the Protestant Political Association, a recently formed grouping with the motto 'Equal rights for all and special privileges for none', who opposed the level of political influence and government funding received by the Roman Catholic Federation.[28] Founded by the Reverend Howard L. Elliott, the Protestant Political Association targeted Joseph Ward because he was an influential Catholic, along with the liquor trade and the rising Labour Party, which Elliott viewed as comprised of atheists, Roman Catholics and revolutionaries. The association actively supported Massey and Reform candidates in the 1919, 1922 and 1925 elections.[29] Melville strongly refuted the idea that she had backing from the association: 'I wish to state publicly that this rumour is absolutely false. I have never been to any of the PPA meetings, and although friends of mine belong to the association, I am not connected with it in any way. I do not think the question of religion should come into politics at all. The question of politics is one for the people as a whole, that of religion one for the individual.'[30] At a later campaign meeting when she was asked directly about the Protestant Political Association she dealt with the question in a relaxed manner and with a touch of humour: she was a Scotch Presbyterian, she said, and she hoped she would have the support of the PPA as well as every other political association in the electorate. She emphatically denied another rumour that she was being 'run' by the liquor lobby: she had always stood for prohibition and did not support state control of alcohol under any circumstances; it was her strong conviction that many of the social problems pressing heavily on the country would disappear if the liquor trade was abolished.

During their campaigns Baume and Melville emphasised the necessity of women's viewpoint being taken into consideration in matters of legislation. Baume said that in this age of specialists, with so much legislation connected in some way to the home, women's viewpoint was essential as the nation rebuilt the social and industrial system after the wreckage of war. Women could no longer lead sheltered lives and ignore the difficulties some of their sisters were facing. Those who had the time, training and experience were required in wider fields of community service, and women and men needed to cooperate in the duties of citizenship on a common platform of the welfare of the state.

Melville was adamant from the outset that she was not presenting herself as a candidate to gain a sympathy vote because she was a woman. Her decision to stand was based on a firm conviction that women, as citizens, were needed to assist in every aspect of social and political life. There was nothing strident about the way she expressed her feminist perspectives. She stated that 'there was ample room for some women to take their places in the House and help in the country's constructive social work'. The *Auckland Star* reported that 'she gently scoffed at the idea of the creation of a sex-war' and that there was danger of women 'attempting to dominate the country',[31] and her comment that she did not think there was any danger that the House would be overrun by women was greeted with laughter. There were many social questions that would benefit women's viewpoint, but women needed to be prepared to undertake their full responsibilities as legislators 'with the requisite knowledge and training to deal with all questions that might come before the House'.[32]

The strongest plank of Baume's political platform was the advancement of the welfare of women, children and the home. For her, social and economic reconstruction was the burning question of the age and with that objective women were justified in assuming their place in the political world. The issues she brought to the campaign were of great importance to everyone.

She was strongly in favour of the state providing support to mothers ('the endowment of motherhood'), improved conditions and facilities in schools, dedicated special schools and homes for 'backward and defective children', establishment of training colleges for domestic service, the establishment of a child welfare department to supplement the Plunket Nurse Society, free maternity homes and state nurseries, increases in widows' and old age pensions, better roads and railways and cheap hydroelectric power to encourage people to reside in outlying districts and thereby relieve the housing problem in urban centres, and sound immigration policies. She was in favour of introducing a state bank to bring about financial stability but did not support an increase in the honorarium paid to members of the House of Representatives.

In line with Reform Party policy, Melville stressed that the main problems New Zealand faced were the result of the depletion of manpower, decreased production and delayed domestic legislation. Changes and advances to the education system were essential. In her view what was needed was 'not merely a system that taught children to read and write, but one which would teach the citizens of tomorrow how to think clearly and independently on matters of vital importance'.[33] Education should continue to be free, secular and compulsory, with more emphasis on the 'free'. Specific advancements included the establishment of a special branch of the Government Printing Department that could provide the bulk of schoolbooks to education boards for free distribution through school committees.

The welfare of returned soldiers featured strongly in Melville's platform. A priority was to get as many able-bodied men as possible onto the land but, rather than settle them on land already under cultivation, this was an opportunity to open more land with community settlements funded by generous state assistance to establish homes and improve cultivation. This would increase production, contribute to a reduction in the cost of living, and take some pressure off a housing shortage in the cities. Extending suburban rail networks would facilitate growth beyond town centres, particularly in Auckland. The Reform Party platform considered that the government should substantially fund the building and maintenance of main roads but that local bodies should be responsible for other roads. Melville also campaigned on the development of hydroelectric power, systematic and controlled immigration, extension of district nursing services, the motherhood endowment, and an increase in widows' pensions.

Campaigning on a Reform ticket did not prevent Melville from speaking on other issues that had been on the agenda of the WCTU and the NCW for years. These included the need to appoint a practical woman member to the permanent board of trade, raising the age of consent to 18, the establishment of women police and emphasising their role in attending places of entertainment to provide advice and assistance to young people who might be out of control, and state assistance to mothers while their children were young. To alleviate the shortage in domestic help, she suggested setting up training hostels where young women could learn domestic skills and earn a state certificate and recognised social status in their vocation. In response to concerns about the morals of military training camps she suggested a version of 'hostess houses' where women were in charge and the young men could receive visits from their mothers, sisters and girlfriends, thereby introducing something approaching home life.[34]

Of the three candidates, Baume was most popular with the press and had the most media coverage. The *Observer* reported, 'Mrs F.E. Baume, the accomplished lady, who is "out" for the Parnell seat, is creating quite a favourable impression, and as she is a highly-cultured woman, with very definite ideas about the necessity of women in public life, and is able to express them with convincing coherence, she will probably poll very well. She has the great gift of earnestness.'[35] Melville, as her campaign progressed, received consistently good audiences at her rallies and increasingly positive press reports of her 'thorough grasp of social, economic and political problems', 'the lucid manner in which she explained her views'[36] and her ability to respond to often complex and awkward questions. It was noted: 'She did not try to fence or dodge any query, and showed an excellent knowledge of public questions.'[37]

Views were mixed on the prospects of the women candidates. The general tone of the media coverage was more of curiosity as to how well they would poll rather than any sense they would come near to winning an electorate seat or pose a real threat to any of the leading contenders, given the prevailing level of prejudice against women sitting in Parliament. At most, Rosetta Baume might split the progressive vote, which would benefit the Reform candidate. On a pre-election flying tour around the country, Bill Massey talked up a win for Miss Melville; referring to the recent election of the first woman to the British House of Commons, he said: 'I expect to see the first lady elected to the New Zealand Parliament at the forthcoming election in the person of Miss Melville, a lady solicitor who is contesting the Grey Lynn seat as a Reform candidate,' and he added with a laugh, 'Miss Melville is getting a great hearing, especially from the men.'[38] There was no real expectation that Aileen Cooke would win many votes and, with no party backing, she had to take out a whole column on the front page of the *Thames Star* to advertise her political platform.[39] There was minimal reporting of her meetings during the campaign, apart from a detailed report of her final election meeting two days before polling day. In response to a report in the *New Zealand Herald* that she was standing as an 'Oppositionist' candidate, she took out a front-page advertisement in the *Thames Star* to make it clear she was standing as 'an Independent Liberal owing no allegiance to any party leader'.[40]

There were some interesting political messages to be taken from the results of the general election. Although their share of the overall vote declined, winning 47 of the 80 seats gave the re-elected Reform Government an increased majority. Labour, having contested three times as many seats as in the previous general election, achieved its largest presence up to that time in Parliament, winning eight of the 54 seats it contested. The greatest number of casualties went to the Liberal Party, which won only 19 seats, 15 fewer than in the 1914 election. Losses included the Awarua seat, previously held by Sir Joseph Ward, which went to the Reform candidate. Ward's defeat was taken as a sign that his political career was over. Massey referred to the Liberal Party as part of New Zealand's 'dead past',[41] and the editor of the *Press* said that whether or not Ward managed to be re-elected at some time in the future, it would be 'idle to pretend that he is any longer a useful force in the public life of the Dominion'.[42]

Ellen Melville, with 2660 votes, polled only 481 votes behind the winning Independent Labour candidate Fred Bartram, and 255 votes more than former Cabinet member and supporter of women's rights George Fowlds. Rosetta Baume fared less well than anticipated: she polled in third place with 1026 votes, 1261 votes behind the Labour candidate and 4680 votes behind the winning Reform incumbent James Samuel Dickson. Aileen Cooke won only 72 of the 5734 total votes cast in the Thames electorate. At least she did not suffer the ignominy of polling last: the Independent Labour candidate gained only 56 votes. The media commented that it was 'rather ungallant of the electors of New Zealand' that Baume and Cooke were among the 23 candidates who forfeited their 10-pound deposits as they polled less than one fourth of the votes received by the successful candidate.[43]

The post-election commentary on the standings of the three women candidates was gentle. The *Press* reported that 'Fate and the electors were unkind' to all three candidates and that Miss Melville's defeat was particularly regrettable as she had proven herself 'a candidate of unusual promise'.[44] The overall evaluation was positive: there was no doubt as to the earnestness and sincerity of the women candidates who, for the most part, were well received. The editor of the *Press* suggested that the unsuccessful candidates should not be discouraged because they were pioneers. The recent experience of their sisters in Britain was cited as encouragement, as the first woman to take her place in the House of Commons did so less than 12 months after 16 women candidates had been defeated at the general election. The editor predicted that 'Possibly before the new Parliament of New Zealand has run its course, certainly before many years have passed, women will sit in our Legislature, and will justify their election.'[45]

Immediately after the election, Melville was 'unusually busy' making up lost time with her work as president of the NCW.[46] She was in demand as a speaker to women's groups on the importance of active citizenship[47] as the revived NCW became more firmly established over the next few years. By the 1921 conference there were 59 affiliated organisations, and the council had affiliated with the International Council of Women. Although the National Council of Women was to play an important role in politicising New Zealand women, it still struggled to have any great influence on parliamentary proceedings. At the 1921 conference in Wellington the secretary, Hilda Northcroft, complained that only one of 17 resolutions sent to government departments after the last conference had received formal acknowledgment.[48] The most important issue in recent years had been women gaining the right to sit in Parliament, but it was a matter of regret that women had not at the same time become eligible for the Legislative Council despite the 'strenuous efforts' to this end by executive members of the NCW. As had been the case a decade earlier, remits were passed at the 1921 conference to urge the government to pass legislation providing for the employment of women police, the appointment of women justices of the peace, and the removal of the disqualification of women as jurors.[49]

An issue that had divided women's groups for several years gained prominence in 1922 when the government announced an inquiry into the high prevalence of venereal disease and its causes, including promiscuity.[50] Promoting social purity (sexual chastity and faithfulness) had been the focus of women involved in the WCTU since its formation in the mid-1880s. Kate Sheppard had broached 'the delicate but serious subject of social disease' in her president's address to the NCW in 1919; venereal diseases, she said, were 'probably the greatest menace to the public health' that existed.[51] The focus at the time was on the health of soldiers and whether notification of venereal disease should be mandatory. By the time the official inquiry into venereal diseases in New Zealand was launched in 1922, the focus was on the sexual behaviours of young women as evidenced in births that occurred out of wedlock or within the first seven months of marriage. The committee of inquiry was ordered to report on the prevalence and causes of venereal disease. Despite the lack of reliable statistical data, the committee took an alarmist view in its report, based on the premise that venereal disease was a major and escalating health problem, and framed its recommendations within a critique of the moral failings of contemporary society.[52]

The alleged prevalence of sexual promiscuity was attributed to a range of factors such as changing social conditions, moral laxity among young people – in particular girls, the weakening of parental control, delayed marriage, overcrowding in urban housing, the effects of alcohol, lack of sexual education, and the influence of the cinema. To combat the problem the committee of inquiry stressed the need for greater moral self-control and better education in sexual hygiene. Recognising that many parents were reluctant to provide this education, the report recommended that teachers be trained to answer questions on sexual hygiene and that 'school medical officers or other qualified practitioners should give occasional "talks" to the elder boys and girls'.[53] Other recommendations focused on extending the hours of venereal disease clinics, providing women doctors in women's clinics, introducing female health patrols, and requiring a sworn declaration before the registrar before marriage as to the presence or absence of communicable and mental disease.

The concluding remarks in the report mentioned the relatively high incidence of venereal disease among 'mental and physical defectives'.[54]

Stopping short of making claims regarding the proportion of 'defectives' who were the direct product of venereal diseases, the committee observed that 'there is clear evidence that a tendency to lead dissolute lives is especially noticeable in the females belonging to this unfortunate class' and it was suggested 'some method of dealing with mental defectives – by segregation or otherwise – must be found as part of the problem of dealing with venereal disease'.[55] The committee met with individual women as well as representatives of various women's organisations, including the Women's International and Political League, the women's branch of the Social Hygiene Society, the Society for the Protection of Women and Children, the Women Prisoners' Welfare Society, the Young Women's Christian Association and the NCW. The issues raised in the inquiry were discussed at WCTU meetings and influenced the questions women asked of candidates in the 1922 general election.

1922 general election: 'That time is not yet'

The long shadow of the war impacted the 1922 general election. Rampant postwar inflation coupled with record overseas prices and high land values had led to an economic collapse in 1921, resulting in sharp falls in export prices, growing unemployment, and many newly settled farmers facing bankruptcy. Despite a request from representatives of the Federation of Drapers and Clothiers to bring the election date forward to the end of November so it wouldn't interfere with Christmas trade, the election was set for 7 December, with the Māori election the previous day.[56]

At their annual conference held in August 1922, the NCW reaffirmed the non-party and non-sectarian nature of their organisation. Their list of very specific questions for candidates gives an indication of their priorities:

> 1. Are you in favour of married mothers having equal rights and responsibilities in regard to their children with the fathers?
>
> 2. Are you in favour of the removal of all sex disqualifications in the appointments to the Public Service?
>
> 3. Are you in favour of extending the principle of payment of prisoners so as to include all men committed to gaol for failure to obey maintenance orders?

4. Are you in favour of women J.P.s?

5. Are you in favour of women police to work in the interests of women and children?

6. Are you in favour of the establishment of an institution intermediate between a mental hospital and a gaol for delinquents of sub-normal tendencies?[57]

Three women were to contest the election. Early in August 1922 Mrs Ann E. (Annie) Herbert, a well-known and popular social worker who had been working with the unemployed, announced she would be standing as an Independent candidate in the Avon electorate. A deputation had presented her with a petition signed by 1610 electors in the Avon electorate asking her to consent to be nominated as an Independent candidate for the seat, based mainly on her experience on the Canterbury Hospital Board. Those who collected signatures spoke of the considerable amount of goodwill toward her candidature and the cordial reception they had received, and added that there were more signatures still to be submitted. Unsure whether she could fulfil parliamentary duties and continue to attend to her social work commitments, Herbert did not immediately consent to the nomination, but when the number of signatures reached 2000, with the assurance of practical assistance from a 60-strong committee of supporters, she assented and her campaign began in earnest.

Ellen Melville chose to stand for the Roskill seat but, on this occasion, the Reform Party did not endorse her candidature. Supporters suggested she stand as an Independent in protest at being overlooked by the party hierarchy, but she did not think that being badly treated was sufficient reason for her to change her politics and cease to support the party.

Annie McVicar consented to stand as an Independent Reform candidate for the Wellington East seat after a petition asking her to do so was circulated by women in the electorate. She had always supported and worked for Alfred Newman and it was well known that she had refused to accede to requests to contest the seat he had held until it was known that he was definitely retiring. Simultaneous with the announcement of Newman's retirement was the announcement that Thomas Forsyth had been adopted as the official Reform candidate, and it was at that point that a group started a petition to persuade Annie McVicar to stand. Her chances of success were deemed not good and there was criticism that by standing she might even contribute to the Reform Party losing the seat. Aware of these concerns, she made it clear from the outset that although standing as an Independent she would vote for the government on a motion of no confidence.

The calibre of all three women candidates was very high. Described as 'a woman of strong and attractive personality', Annie Herbert was an ardent prohibitionist and a conscientious worker in the field of women's health. In 1919 she was elected to the North Canterbury Hospital and Charitable Aid Board, and she worked on the Benevolent Committee of the Hospital Board. In that work she had encountered many distressing cases of families in need and – with the board's assistance limited to provisions and rent – she had co-founded a Social Welfare Guild which, through its various committees, provided a range of services including visiting sick and needy people, providing clothing, raising funds and arranging musical entertainment programmes, as well as lobbying politicians.[58] Her suitability as a member of Parliament was strongly endorsed by prominent citizens who had petitioned her to stand for election; she had never spoken ill of her political opponents, and was 'a thoroughly honest, and thoroughly capable and practical representative'.[59] In her campaign advertising she said she was 'The kind of woman we need in Parliament – straight, practical, sincere, versed in ordinary politics since girlhood' and that she was 'specially experienced in Social Needs through faithful service on Hospital Board, Social Welfare Guild, Technical College, Prison Gate Mission, Social Hygiene, Etc.'[60]

Scottish-born Annie McVicar was a trained nurse who had immigrated to New Zealand in 1901. Her first husband died in the Auckland Mental Hospital in 1906 and later that year she married Alexander McVicar, a widower with three children. From the time of her second marriage she became actively engaged in social and educational work in Wellington and was a member of the New Zealand Society for the Protection of Women and Children and the Plunket Society, and was vice-president of the Wellington women's branch of the New Zealand Political Reform League. In 1919 she was elected to the Miramar Borough Council and in 1921 she was the first woman to be elected to the Wellington City Council.

The campaign platforms of the women candidates reflected the concerns and priorities of the women's organisations and the policies promoted by the major parties. Herbert focused on the need for financial security for women, whether they were widows, wives of men who were invalids or disabled, or married to defaulting husbands. She also campaigned on more effective treatment of degenerate sexual offenders of both sexes, provisions for wayward girls and those suffering from venereal diseases, prison reform, provision of better and more affordable housing, and encouragement for children to attend secondary school. In expressing her commitment to progressive legislation, she was in general support with Liberal policies such as government assistance for secondary industries, increased public works to provide employment, afforestation schemes, and re-evaluation of the land assigned to returned soldiers. Health policies were her primary interest and during her campaign she discussed the false economy of recent government measures to cut funding at the expense of public health. She assured voters she was physically fit for the responsibilities as a member in the House, and habitually worked for up to 15 hours a day.[61]

A feature of Herbert's campaign was her ability to keep audiences spellbound by the poignant real-life examples she drew on to insist that current legislation was not adequate to address the needs of the community. She spoke of how philanthropists, lawyers, doctors and social workers came up against flaws in the current legislation that prevented them from dealing adequately with sickness, poverty, ignorance and weakness, and how this resulted in an unnecessary drain on taxpayers' pockets and waste of human lives. She insisted that 'This waste of money and human treasure would never cease until good men and good women collaborated and cooperated in Parliament,' and added, 'We know how disadvantageous is the rearing of a family by one parent only, so likewise the national family were suffering by being administered to by fathers only. There must be some of the mothers too if we would have real progress. Men and women see different sides of a question. To get the whole we must have their combined vision.'[62]

There was no substantive media coverage of either McVicar's or Melville's election campaign, aside from a mention of McVicar's work during the influenza pandemic and reports that she was 'quite a good platform speaker' who dealt mainly with social issues.[63] Both she and Melville were publicly criticised for standing as Independent Reform candidates and risking splitting the vote to the detriment of the government.

Herbert's decision to contest the Avon seat meant she would be standing against incumbent Labour member Dan Sullivan, Reform candidate Colonel Loach 'of Gallipoli fame', and former Liberal member George Russell, who had helped bring the legislation for the removal of women's civil and political disabilities before the House. The contest for the Avon electorate was tipped to be one of the most interesting of the election, and all four candidates had a strong following.[64] Sullivan had won the seat in 1919 with a majority of 1648 votes over the incumbent Russell, who had aroused ill feeling over his methods of dealing with the influenza pandemic and had been strongly opposed by the returned soldiers. Russell, aware of the necessity of securing strong support from women voters, held several women-only campaign meetings devoted to questions of interest to women. Although Dan Sullivan had captured the Reform vote at the previous election, this year it was expected to go unreservedly to Colonel Albert Edward Loach, who would receive a considerable sympathy vote because of his war service. One Avon voter ventured that Annie Herbert would 'command the support of a large number of electors by her straightforward manner, her fluent and lucid oratory' and her 'keen insight into modern social problems'.[65] However, her prospects were slim, aside from possibly polling a large women's and prohibition vote. The real question was, from which of the other three candidates would she take the most votes.

At the close of nominations the media made some mileage of McVicar's insistence on standing in the Wellington East electorate as an Independent Reform candidate. They surmised that although she had an excellent record in local affairs, she had the least chance of winning. She was under constant pressure to withdraw as, it was felt, her candidature compromised the chances of the official Reform candidate, retired drapery manager Forsyth; the two other candidates, Colonel Thomas William McDonald (Liberal) and sitting Labour member Alec Monteith, would likely profit from the splitting of the Reform vote. McVicar told her campaign audience that she had been subjected to a lot of worry on the subject and had felt very hurt by it, but she was determined to continue; as she said: 'If I had consented to stand down it would have had a bad effect on the movement among women to take an active and practical part in politics.'[66]

Melville's decision to stand as an Independent Reform candidate meant her campaign would always be controversial. According to Bill Massey, the political situation in the Roskill electorate was similar to that in several other electorates: there were too many Reform candidates. This, he claimed, was a positive reflection on the popularity of the government. When asked directly why he had not supported Melville, the prime minister replied that he made it a rule to ask electors to choose their own candidates. He professed a great deal of respect for Miss Melville, but said she should not have come into the Roskill electorate without consulting the Reform Party in Auckland. The official Reform candidate, Vivian Potter, had served the government well in the last three years and was a tried and tested candidate and the prime minister hoped the voters in Roskill would return him as their member. But to Melville's mind, Reform Party organisers were out of touch with the 'wave of advancement in the women's movement all over the world' and she accused Potter of being another blind follower of the party.[67] She held that people who were in sympathy with the Reform platform were tired of being dictated to by the leaders and the self-elected guardians of the Reform Party.

The three women candidates all encountered sexism during their campaigns, and McVicar and Melville were also subjected to bullying. Annie Herbert, at her first campaign meeting, countered the claim that a woman's place was in the home; she asserted that women had won their place 'and the door which had been so difficult to open would not be again shut against woman'.[68] At one meeting Melville was asked whether she would be better employed learning to cook and sew instead of trying to get into Parliament, to which she calmly responded, 'It is rather unfortunate for the questioner that he should have asked that question tonight. As it happens, I made the dress I am wearing, and while I do not make any pretensions to style, still it is a dress.'[69]

The results of the general election confirmed that the three-party political system was now a reality. Despite an increase in the overall vote, the Reform Party won 37 of the 80 seats in the House, 10 fewer than in the previous general election. The Liberal Party lost some of its share of the overall vote but increased its number of seats to 22. The dramatic change was for the Labour Party under leader Harry Holland, which won 17 seats – nine more than in the previous election. With no single party with an overall majority in the House, less than a week after the election speculation was rife as to whether a coalition could be formed or whether a fresh election would need to be called.

Compared to the 1919 election, newspaper reports were less generous in their comments on the polling for the women candidates. The *New Zealand Herald* reported that 'The failure of the women candidates was remarkable,' and that 'Mrs McVicar's defeat was most humiliating.'[70] Both Melville and Herbert polled lower than expected, and McVicar achieved only 414 votes. Disappointingly, Melville polled more than 1000 fewer votes than in the 1919 election, although she gained 136 votes more than the Labour candidate. Herbert polled 1407 votes, 324 fewer than her nearest rival, but 3055 fewer than the returned incumbent Dan Sullivan. A commentator in the *Press* attributed the failure of the women candidates to 'a deep conviction on the part of the mass of electors, not that "women's place is in her home" … but that the work of Parliament can be done better by men than by women'. The writer went on to say that while the time may come when women would share the duties of a legislator, 'that time is not yet', but that in the meanwhile, 'there is a large field of usefulness outside Parliament in which they can exercise their womanly abilities to the great benefit of those whom they serve.'[71] From the point of view of the Auckland Branch of the NCW, the lesson to be taken from the election was that women had not yet 'learned the value of cohesion and of loyalty to their sex'.[72]

When Parliament met in February 1923, in a mood described as 'fractious, very sensitive and deliberately provocative', both Thomas Wilford as leader of the Liberal Party and Harry Holland as leader of the Labour Party, each vying for recognition as the real Opposition, moved a motion of no confidence in the government. Most of the Liberal caucus left the Chamber before the division on Holland's motion; those who stayed voted with Reform, and the motion was spectacularly defeated by 40 votes to 18. Labour then voted with the Liberals on Wilford's motion, which meant the Reform Government narrowly survived the Liberal motion of no confidence by a margin of three votes. However, with no secure majority in the House, the Reform Government was unable to introduce any controversial legislation, and Prime Minister Massey was reported to have conceded, in an unguarded moment, that the session was 'hell most of the time'.[73]

Melville felt keenly the failure of her candidacy in the 1922 general election and she aired her frustration in her president's report to the NCW's annual conference the following year. She exhorted members to take a broader view of issues and to appreciate that they were part of a worldwide organisation and needed to take their citizenship responsibilities more seriously. Women in other countries had looked to New Zealand as a mecca for women, but New Zealand was lagging behind most of the 36 other countries affiliated to the International Council of Women. She urged those present to go beyond petitions and letters, to work towards having a branch in every township in the country in order to 'make the National Council a tremendous instrument for getting what it wants' so that instead of passing the same resolutions year after year 'we would get them on the Statute book and in action'. They needed to convince the government they were united and determined in their demands and, above all, they needed a woman to represent them in Parliament.[74]

To this end the Auckland delegate, Miss Jackson, moved what was to prove a controversial resolution: that the constitution of the National Council of Women be altered to enable it to support, but not to initiate, the candidature of suitable women for election to Parliament. Members opposing the notion reminded those present that a fundamental basis of the council worldwide was that it did not take part in either politics or religion, and spoke in favour of members doing what they could individually but not as a council. Others thought that if the council supported a woman candidate only as representing women's interests, 'there was nothing party about it'. Speaking from personal experience, Melville said women candidates did not need to represent a party and, as far as the council's purposes were concerned, 'A Liberal woman, or a Reform woman, or a Labour woman ... was immensely better than a Liberal man, or a Reform man or a Labour man'. She added that there was no suggestion that the council should take part in political propaganda, but women ought to have a seat in Parliament. The motion was carried with nine voting for and eight against, as was a motion by Melville that the conference make representation to the head of each political party, urging them to include some women in their list of candidates for each election.[75]

In April 1924 Melville went on an extended trip to England, America and Canada during which she networked with various members of the national councils of women, feminist leaders and women lawyers, and attended several conferences. A highlight of her trip was hearing British feminist Margery Corbett Ashby at the International Federation of University

Women conference in Christiania (now Oslo) in Norway. Ashby was one of 17 women candidates who had contested the postwar election after the passing of the Parliament (Qualification of Women) Act 1918 which granted women over the age of 21 the right to stand for election as a member of the House of Commons. In her capacity as a member of the Auckland Library Committee, Melville also attended a conference of municipal librarians. While holidaying in Scotland she was the invited guest of the countess of Aberdeen, the president of the International Council of Women, at her home, and, before departing for Europe, she was a guest at a party hosted by Conservative member of the House of Commons, Lady Astor, for leaders of the feminist movement. Her time in England coincided with a general election and she had the opportunity to assist with Lady Astor's election campaign. When she returned to New Zealand at the end of January 1925, she shared her insights at the Auckland Lyceum Club and as part of the Grafton Library winter series on the women's movement overseas and on the role of women's clubs – illustrated with specially prepared lantern slides.[76]

1925 general election: 'We are not wanting to introduce anything revolutionary'

In May 1925 after a brief illness Bill Massey died in office. He was succeeded by Gordon Coates who, on return from serving in the war, had been promoted to a Cabinet position and groomed to be Massey's successor. Coates brought a new image to the Reform Government. Aged 47, a 'tall, lithe man, erect and soldierly in figure', not associated with any distinct political philosophy or faction, and known for his 'genial progressivism', he was destined to become popular with Parliament, the press and the people.[77]

The Reform and Liberal parties both regarded Labour as subversive and revolutionary, and the New Zealand Welfare League and the New Zealand Reform League were particularly active in their attempts to convince the public that the Labour Party was indicative of a dangerous revolutionary force at work in the country. There was growing concern within government that an increased number of candidates standing under various political platforms would advantage the Labour Party at the upcoming general election. To counter this threat of vote splitting at the general election,

Independent member for Nelson, Harry Atmore, led a move to unite the Reform and Liberal parties under the name of a National Party in opposition to the growing influence of socialism and the Labour Party. Discussions around this 'fusion' of the two parties were conducted 'with the greatest earnestness, harmony, and good-will'[78] and Liberal Party leader Thomas Wilford indicated he would not seek office if the amalgamation went ahead. Coates clarified that the purpose of the two parties merging would be 'to present a more united front against that section of the people who actively espouse extreme Socialistic and Communist ideals' rather than 'only for the purpose of fighting Labour', as there were many workers who supported the government.[79]

In July 1925, during the first week of the fourth session of Parliament, Atmore signalled his intention to propose an amendment to the Address in Reply 'that it is imperatively necessary in the best interests of the Dominion that a strong and stable National Government should be formed during the present session in order to provide a comprehensive policy of reconstruction and economic and social betterment'.[80] But before he had an opportunity to formally move the amendment, Coates stated that precedent and custom dictated that any amendment to the Address in Reply to the governor-general's speech would have to be treated as a motion of no confidence – precisely what Atmore had attempted to avoid. Atmore accused the government of 'weak subterfuge' in saying it was simply following custom, as it was not incumbent on the government to treat the amendment as a motion of no confidence.[81] He insisted that the need for a national government had been before the people for several years: the late prime minister Massey had raised it shortly after the previous election, the leader of the Opposition had publicly stated he believed it was a necessity, individual Reform candidates had raised it during their election campaigns, and it was on record in *Hansard* that the Reform Party unanimously passed a resolution in favour of a National Party comprised of Liberal and Reform members. But despite a long, detailed and impassioned speech by Atmore, followed by considerable debate and Coates insisting that there was no mandate from the people, his amendment was defeated.

Coates had successfully argued that fusion of Reform and Liberal would be futile as the Liberal Party was well in decline. Others insisted that rather than being dead, Liberalism was 'merely disorganised' and its political exponents were diffused in both the Reform and Liberal camps.[82] Indicative of attempts to reposition themselves in a changing political climate, the majority of Liberal candidates contested the 1925 general election under the name Nationalists.

While the Labour Party focused on party policy and attacking the record of the Reform Government, the Reform Party under the organisation of Albert (Bert) Davy embarked on a carefully stage-managed presidential-style campaign that focused on the leadership and personality of Gordon Coates alongside an anti-'Red Menace' message. Davy, who was described as a 'clever organiser ... who introduced meticulous checking of rolls and thorough canvassing of electorates and ... high pressure sales tactics to sell his wares',[83] issued candidates and their campaign committees with material briefing them on how to run their campaigns. Advertisements promoted Coates as a man of action in whom the people could be confident. Women were specifically targeted in the campaign, along with strong appeals to patriotism.

Despite the volatile political climate the Reform Party selected Ellen Melville as an official candidate for the Labour seat of Grey Lynn, which had been held by Fred Bartram since the 1919 general election. She was the only woman to contest a seat at the 1925 general election. Melville adopted a friendly informality in her address to a meeting of her women supporters; instead of presenting policies she spoke on matters of special interest to women voters. She emphasised the urgent need for women's viewpoints to be part of legislative deliberations, and that there was not a single law that did not affect women, either individually or through their husbands and children. She pointed out that there was a greater proportion of women voters than men in the Grey Lynn electorate and that, with support from women voters, she could win the seat. She repeated her long-held view that with women in many countries now in Parliament, New Zealand was 'limping sadly in the rear' so far as women's progress was concerned. She advised patience: even if a woman was elected to Parliament, 'We are not likely to get all we want at once.' Male politicians would need to be educated and it would likely be 'a slow process of convincing them that we are not wanting to introduce anything revolutionary, but simply to do our best for the well-being of the whole country'.[84] She touched on a few policy matters: she expressed her support for the Bible in Schools Bill that had been presented in the last parliamentary session, and assured those present that she was a prohibitionist, 'and if anyone tries to tell you the brewers are "running" me, you needn't believe it!' She made a spirited attack on Labour's proposed nationalisation of land. The reporter for the *New Zealand Herald* noted that 'The feminine touch was again pleasantly in evidence at the conclusion of the meeting' when the wife of the deputy mayor suddenly appeared from behind a screen and invited the ladies present to stay for a cup of tea.[85]

It proved to be a divisive campaign. The government's openly hostile representation of Labour Party policies led to accusations of dirty politics and Labour supporters mounted a campaign of disrupting the meetings of Reform candidates. Melville was not immune to these tactics and held her ground when a small but noisy section of Labour supporters made their presence known at one of her early campaign meetings. At a packed St George's Hall in Kingsland from which many were turned away, she delivered a scathing attack on the professed aims of the Labour Party. Her suggestion that the platform adopted at the Labour Party conference earlier in the year, when there was not such a close eye on the election, was a truer indication of the intentions of the Labour Party, evoked a storm of dissent. The constant interjections from Labour supporters were such that the chairman of the meeting felt it necessary to step in to intervene, but Melville, showing her mettle, said she would deal with them herself; she recognised them as having been at her earlier meeting in Grey Lynn. It had not escaped her notice that Labour Party leader Harry Holland had touted his support for the removal of all political disabilities of women. Her response to this was: 'If the Labour Party was genuine in its attitude toward women it would put up some women candidates. They cannot tell me that they have not got women in the movement in Auckland equal at least to the men they are supporting.'[86]

The 'election rowdyism' shown by Labour supporters at one meeting prompted some Grey Lynn residents to write to the press. One pointed out that the 'ignorant obstructionists' were not residents of Grey Lynn but had come out from the city on the tramcar.[87] Another suggested the men who were going around disturbing political meetings should confine themselves to their own party. This person had been at the meeting and had found it impossible to hear the candidate's address, although she offered her 'loyal respect and congratulations to the lady candidate for the noble, womanly way in which she met the disturbance and for the firmness of character with which she handled one particular brawny Scotsman'.[88] The sitting Labour member for Grey Lynn, Fred Bartram, and the deputy leader of the Labour Party, Michael Savage, appealed to Labour supporters for order at meetings and, like the editor of the *Auckland Star*, acknowledged that Miss Melville had not been received with the fairness that was the due of every candidate.[89]

The calls for restrained behaviour from political opponents seem to have had some effect. At a meeting at the Jubilee Hall several days later it was obvious from occasional gentle remarks during the meeting and from the tenor of the subsequent questions that Melville's views were not shared by a considerable section of the audience but there were no objectionable remarks or interruptions throughout, even though she continued to denounce the Labour Party as extremists. She was not an advocate for proportional representation, and she exposed the lack of logic in the Labour Party's proposal of proportional representation which would see 37 women in Parliament; if Labour were serious about the policy, she said, they should act on their principles and have that proportion of women among their candidates.[90]

Melville's marital status was raised explicitly and implicitly during the campaign. Bartram, the Labour candidate for Grey Lynn, was asked whether he thought it was fair to send an unmarried woman all the way down to Parliament, especially for the late-night sittings. To his credit, he replied that he had nothing to say on the matter as the lady concerned was old enough to decide for herself. But in another campaign speech he was quoted as saying in confidential tones: 'I am not a mother – no, I'm not! But I would be if I were a woman,' and adding that he was the father of four mothers and the grandfather of a lot of grandchildren.[91]

The truce in dirty politics in the Grey Lynn electorate proved to be shortlived: Bartram alleged he had been slandered by a canvasser who said she was working for Miss Melville. According to Bartram, the woman had called on his daughter and had repeated a rumour that he had been seen intoxicated at Parliament and, on another occasion, at Point Chevalier. He refuted the claim and strongly condemned such attempts to malign his character. When the Labour candidate for Auckland East, John A. Lee, confirmed that he had heard the same reports in his electorate, Bartram replied in his own defence that in his present condition, after his war service, even if he had the inclination for alcohol he would not have the digestion. Labour supporters were urged to take note of the names of anyone heard spreading such slander, with a view to court proceedings.[92]

Melville conducted meetings for women on several occasions throughout her campaign. At one of these Mark Cohen, a member of the Legislative Council and a strong supporter of equal rights for women who had travelled up from Dunedin to assist Melville in her campaign, addressed the audience. He paid tribute to Melville for her work on the Auckland City Council and in various women's organisations, then he reviewed the progress of the women's movement since the granting of the franchise, countering claims that women in New Zealand had done little to advance the feminist movement beyond a few measures passed for the benefit of children. His speech set the tone for Melville's rally call for women to rise to their duties and responsibilities as citizens. In line with the government's campaign tactics, Melville's focus was largely on denouncing the Labour Party's programme as being utterly impracticable and impossible to achieve, mainly because of the party's refusal to borrow or to engage in other revenue-gathering measures.

Early calls on the outcome of the Grey Lynn electorate were that even though Melville was waging a resolute and sustained attack on the Labour stronghold, Bartram should be able to win again comfortably. As the campaign progressed, her abilities as a campaigner were acknowledged. One editor wrote, 'Miss Melville stands as a woman candidate, and within limits as a woman's candidate. Yet she has met the opposition on all points with as much readiness as any candidate could, has shown a complete grasp of general political issues, and has faced noisy factious opposition without flinching. Grey Lynn has an unequalled opportunity, by voting for Miss Melville in preference to her opponent, of showing that it considers the Government candidate the better man of the two.'[93]

As the initial election results came in on the evening of 4 November 1925, Ellen Melville held the lead; but this was soon overturned. Labour held the Grey Lynn seat, but their majority was more than halved: Bartram polled 6061 votes while Melville trailed by only 765 votes, with a total of 5296. The election was hailed as a magnificent victory for the government, which secured 55 seats – increasing their majority from the previous election by 18 seats. But Melville claimed a victory for the women of New Zealand by polling the most votes of any woman candidate to date.

1926 by-election for Auckland Suburbs: 'Fossil prejudice and party intrigue'

Ellen Melville did not have to wait another three years before returning to the hustings. Soon after the 1925 general election Sir James Parr resigned his Eden seat when he was appointed high commissioner in London, necessitating a by-election. Eden was a government seat that Parr had retained in the previous general election with a comfortable majority of over 2300 votes. Interest in the by-election was high: while the government had an outright majority of 30 seats, with Labour holding 12 seats and Liberal holding 11, the point at issue was which of these two parties could claim to be the official Opposition.

Names of possible candidates for the Reform Party were put forward, and with eight aspirants identified, including two current mayors, Melville's first hurdle was to gain selection. It would prove to be a controversial and divisive process with far-reaching consequences for her personally and for the feminist movement. Businessman and former mayor of Auckland Sir James Gunson was prepared to stand but would only contest the by-election as the official government candidate. Melville had received a very large and representative petition from men and women asking her to stand and she made it plain from the start that she was very keen to contest the by-election.

The selection committee consisted of 127 delegates elected by the various district branches of the Reform League. The process for selection involved the committee meeting and hearing the would-be candidates before a ballot was taken. The voting would not be accepted as final until one candidate received an absolute majority of more than half the votes. To avoid vote-splitting, before going to the ballot candidates would be required to pledge not to stand as Independents if they were not selected as the official Reform candidate. Although Melville had now stood for Parliament on three occasions, twice for Grey Lynn and once for Roskill, both of which adjoined the southern boundaries of the Eden electorate, the Eden electorate was largely rural and there was concern that this might militate against her chances of selection. One staunch Reform voter wrote to the *New Zealand Herald* to say that while he was not opposed to women contesting city seats, he did not think women were suitable for country electorates 'where activity and capacity to get about among the electors on the land, and a sympathetic and an understanding mind in relation to land problems are necessary qualifications'. This writer believed there were 'many matters which are essentially a man's job, affecting the individual farmer which are beyond the feminine mind to comprehend from the practical standpoint unless trained or brought up with the proper environment'.[94]

Ellen Melville had strong support from the Grey Lynn branch of the party, who unanimously passed a resolution wishing her every success and promising their assistance to the Eden branch in every way possible to secure her successful election. However, after a meeting lasting four and a quarter hours, the Reform Party selected Sir James Gunson as their official candidate. But it was what happened before and during this meeting, rather than the decision made by the selection committee, that was to prove controversial.

Acting as spokesperson for four of the unsuccessful candidates, Melville raised concerns with the office of the *Auckland Star* about the methods followed in conducting the selection meeting. The candidates had each received a telegram instructing them to attend the meeting at the Kozie Theatre in Mount Albert on the evening of 8 March. When they arrived at the theatre they were conducted upstairs and admitted to the dress circle room under instruction not to leave except under guard. Their names were drawn from a hat to determine the order in which they would address the selection committee. Interestingly, Gunson was not present in the room, and it later transpired he was standing outside next to his motorcar and within hearing of the other candidates' speeches. When they inquired about his whereabouts, the party organiser Bert Davy informed them that Gunson had not been seen for the past fortnight and he did not even know if he was in Auckland. Gunson was fifth on the order of speakers and Melville was seventh. After drawing the names, Davy left the room and locked the door; Melville commented at the time that the mayor of Mount Albert (Leonard Rhodes) was locked up in a room in his own borough like a common criminal. Before the names had been put into the hat, the mayor of Avondale (William Tait) had told Davy that he wished to withdraw his nomination, but he was not permitted to leave the room.[95]

After some considerable time the first speaker was summoned and the room was again locked, and this was repeated as each candidate was escorted to and from the meeting room. As Melville said, 'You never saw seven madder people than we were – except that we laughed at ourselves for being so foolish as to allow ourselves to be treated so.'[96] There was an interval of about quarter of an hour after the fourth speaker, during which time they presumed Gunson was addressing the meeting. At this point, the 'imprisoned' candidates signed a written protest against the preferential treatment accorded to him. The next candidate presented this protest when it was his turn to address the selection committee. As the last speaker was returned to the room, the candidates prevented the door being locked on them and filed out as a body, led by Melville, to deliver their protest to the gathered delegates. They were promptly escorted back while the ballot was being taken.

After another hour and a half Melville and one of the other candidates, Mr Oldfield, were again asked to appear before the selection committee. They were joined by Gunson. The chairman of the committee announced that Gunson had received the required majority and was therefore the selected candidate and that Melville was second and Oldfield was third. Melville immediately expressed her regret at the way the proceedings had been conducted and said that in the light of those proceedings she did not consider herself bound by any undertaking she had given to the Reform Party organisation. Davy accused the unsuccessful candidates of being 'disgruntled' and 'not sports'.[97] Melville and Oldfield held their ground but, after continued accusations from Davy, they left the meeting.

A telegram signed by each of the unsuccessful candidates was sent to Prime Minister Coates the following evening, claiming serious irregularities in connection with the proceedings and informing him they would not be bound by the pledges they had signed. The telegram made clear that their chief criticism was that while they had effectively been treated as prisoners, Gunson had been given preferential treatment, was able to hear the speeches of the other candidates and had been in private communication with the organiser throughout the evening. They received no reply from the prime minister.

As soon as the telegram had been sent to the prime minister, Melville confirmed her intention to contest the Eden seat 'in the interests of true Reform', and added that she was acting on 'urgent representations from every portion of the Eden electorate, together with offers of assistance from many loyal supporters of the Reform party'.[98] The following morning most of the unsuccessful candidates met in Melville's law office to discuss the situation. Opinions were divided as to their best course of action. Some thought the matter had been compromised by sending the telegram to the prime minister and that they should be true to their party, even though mistakes may have been made. There was some concern that the telegram had been published in the newspapers without the explicit consent of all the signatories, and one of the candidates said he was 'amazed at the gross breach of faith that has been committed by those responsible for the publication of the protest'.[99] He accepted Gunson's claims that it was quite unintentional that he was apart from the other candidates during the selection committee meeting and that he had not heard the others' speeches and had no advantage over them. Unsurprisingly, Davy spoke out harshly: he said he deeply deplored the actions taken by those who had made public the business of a party conference; their protest was 'ridiculous in the extreme',[100] and the charges levelled against him had no foundation in fact. He disputed that they had been 'imprisoned', and claimed that the door to the meeting room had been locked only to prevent the public from intruding at the meeting; the candidates could have gone outside into the street with Gunson at any time, if they had so desired. He was adamant that the fair democratic method of selection had been strictly observed and that the unsuccessful candidates were bound to honour their written pledges. Since the selection committee had made its decision, meetings of various branches of the Reform League had met and motions had been carried affirming the decisions of the delegates.

The whole affair stimulated increased interest in the Eden by-election and there was a sudden influx of applications for enrolment at the office of the registrar of electors. The public backlash was swift and intense. As the various claims and counter-claims played out in the newspapers, there were mixed opinions as to the legitimacy of the grievances. Melville was singled out for particularly harsh criticism. One writer referred to her as having dominated the women's movement in Auckland for about 10 years during which time she 'has invariably held herself forth to the public as a leading representative woman in all that pertains thereto ... but her present action in repudiating a solemn pledge for any reason whatsoever, except actual dishonesty, will prove the greatest set-back to women's public and political advancement in New Zealand'.[101] The writer called on Melville 'in the interests and for the honour of the women's movement in New Zealand' to remain loyal to her pledge and settle any personal grievance with her party in private.[102] The letter generated some comment by other members of the public, one of whom suggested that if Miss Melville's alleged repudiation of a solemn pledge was indeed a setback to women's public advancement in New Zealand, what could be said of the six male candidates, including two mayors? Was not the repudiation of those men six times as bad as that of Ellen Melville? This writer believed that the question for women electors of Eden was not whether Melville's alleged actions would be a setback to the women's movement, but to 'the true value the Reform Party puts on a woman Member of Parliament'.[103] Another writer cautioned Miss Melville that the strong polling she achieved in the recent general election was largely due to her having the backing of the Reform Party as well as the confidence of electors in the present prime minister. This support would now transfer to the official Reform candidate and, according to this voter, 'Miss Melville will find without it her chances worthless, and that she will receive the support of only a very few thoughtless followers who will be content to throw their valuable votes away.'[104]

Public opinion was strong that Ellen Melville was playing into the hands of enemies of the Reform Party who would naturally be delighted to see her contest the seat and split the Reform vote, allowing the Labour candidate a chance of victory, and there were calls for her to withdraw her candidacy. Some members of the public were quite hostile: one accused her of being 'a pawn in the game to help a lame dog over a stile', and stated that '"Eden" does not want another "Eve", the one written of in Biblical history did enough damage, anyway'.[105] But Melville had her supporters, too: she said she had 'splendid support, and have received expressions of sympathy and encouragement from many quarters,'[106] and that, despite rumours to the contrary, she was committed to going to the poll.

Amid all the public debate, Melville headed to Wellington at the request of the prime minister for an interview. The date of the by-election had still not been fixed. She declined to disclose what took place in this personal interview, stating only that she was determined to contest the by-election as an Independent Reform candidate. The day after their meeting Coates announced he was pleased to endorse the nomination of Gunson as the government candidate at the by-election.

Editorials on the whole affair were mixed. The *Evening Post* acknowledged that Miss Melville would be a worthy first representative of her sex in the New Zealand Parliament but questioned whether she had forfeited the right to seek that honour with her actions.[107] The editor of the *Auckland Star* received a large amount of correspondence in support and in judgement of her actions. In Wellington there was widespread feeling that Melville had been badly treated by her political party, while those with a finger on the political pulse in Auckland considered Gunson's chances of election to the vacant seat would have been not nearly as rosy as Melville's if she had had the government backing.

With rumours circulating, on the advice of her election committee Melville decided to hold a public meeting in the electorate. Before the meeting, however, a deputation of leaders in the women's movement in Auckland and delegates from the Eden electorate met with her. Ethel Kidd, member of the NCW and widow of former Liberal politician Alfred Kidd, introduced the deputation: she said they were there to represent the opinions of the majority of members of various women's organisations, and that '[we] deplore your decision to stand as an Independent candidate having regard to your pledge not to stand in opposition to the selected candidate'. The deputation urged her to reconsider her decision to stand, and assured her they were not concerned with the party aspect 'except in so far as it prejudices the prospects of representation of the interests of women and children directly by a woman in Parliament by losing us the confidence of the present Government, and of all thinking men and women'.[108] Many among the deputation had supported her candidature in the past and were quite willing to work for her again in the future. Their request was that she stand down in the interest of the party because of the danger of vote splitting, but their main concern was that she had broken her word by turning back on her pledge.

Melville was direct in her response: she had not the least intention of withdrawing her candidature. She believed she had not, in fact, given any pledge; what she had given was an undertaking. It was a contract between two parties and, when broken by one side, was not binding on the other. The Reform Party had not kept faith with her. She had shifted in her position; she now accepted that while everything that had transpired in the delegates' room on the evening of the selection was in order, she alleged there were grave irregularities in the lead-up to that date and she intended to make those irregularities public at her approaching meeting. Her refusal to share the names of those who had sent letters in support of her continued contestation of the Eden seat caused some offence to members of the deputation, and many of the women left the meeting when she invited several of the men present to address them. The members of the deputation met afterwards and agreed that if Miss Melville persisted in her present attitude, they could not be associated with her in any way in the future.

It was apparent there were hostilities on both sides. Melville told a reporter from the *Auckland Star*: 'I know that this is just another move in the campaign. As the deputation was withdrawing I said "Well, ladies, I just want to tell you that you have killed the woman movement in Auckland by your action today! And you have not advanced the candidature of your friend!"'[109] The reporter commented, 'For studied impertinence and rank ingratitude the action of the ladies deputation which waited upon Miss Ellen Melville yesterday, asking her to withdraw from the Eden election contest is hard to excel,' and asked, 'Can one imagine a meeting of men convened for such a purpose coming to such a conclusion? Surely any woman has a right to do what her conscience dictates in such a matter without being sent to Coventry for it. Miss Melville believes that she did not get fair treatment from a party which has "a square deal" for its motto, and there are many who agree with her.' The reporter pointed out that however strongly her opponents disagreed with her position, they had to admit that for many years Miss Melville had been 'at the head and front of the fighting force of the feminist movement in Auckland'. Many women who were prominent in the feminist movement refused to have anything to do with the matter and there was a strong feeling against the actions of the women in the deputation in breaking the understanding that the deputation was private by giving full details to the press.[110]

Not surprisingly, the public meeting called by Melville was crowded and her bitterness at her treatment by the Reform Party was evident. She told those gathered that her name had been used by the Reform Party across the Dominion to show they were sympathetic to the aspirations of women and that it was the only party to support a woman candidate at the previous election. This had been a good propaganda move, given they knew there was no chance that she would secure the Grey Lynn seat. She had been under no delusions about that at the time, but she had been prepared to carry the Reform banner. In her view, if she was good enough to carry it in a losing fight, she should be able to carry it in a winning one. She had been assured by 'a gentleman high in the Reform organisation'[111] just prior to the 1925 general election that if she did not win the Grey Lynn seat, she would be given a safe seat next time. When asked, she refused to name the individual other than to repeat it was a gentleman who was very high in the Reform Party. The Eden by-election was the first opportunity for carrying out that promise but she now felt tricked and deceived by people in the Reform Party. As soon as there had been a prospect of a vacancy in Eden, she had an interview with the prime minister and told him she would not stand aside in favour of 'a certain exalted person' (Gunson). Gordon Coates had been firm that there would have to be a selection ballot and that she would have a fair run. She questioned whether this would be the case if a ballot of delegates was taken but received assurance that she would have a fair run. Having first refused to stand aside, under pressure from the Party organiser she had relented and foolishly signed the pledge. As soon as she had done so, the Reform organisation had taken much less interest in her as a potential candidate. As a lawyer, she had taken the precaution of inserting a proviso and assuring the party organiser that 'if there is any funny business, I won't be bound'. The pledge read:

> *I, Ellen Melville, beg to offer myself as a candidate in the interests of the Reform Party at the forthcoming by-election in Eden having been requisitioned by a large number of electors to accept nomination. I am willing that my name should be placed before the selection committee of the Eden Branch, on condition that I am given the opportunity of addressing the committee before the selection takes place. I am agreeable to leave the matter in the hands of the committee for decision, and to accept such decision providing the selection is carried out in accordance with the constitution and rules of the Reform League, and, subject to this proviso, I will, if not selected, not be a candidate.*[112]

Melville informed those gathered at the public meeting that there had been irregularities with the subsequent meetings to elect delegates to the selection committee. The meetings were never called for that purpose – the advertisements stated only that there was urgent and important business to consider. She claimed that the meetings were 'packed' and that when it came to electing delegates, well-known Reformers were thrown out and unknown persons were elected to the selection committee. Melville mentioned other irregularities: 'plumping', where a member of the selection committee voted for only one candidate even though they were entitled to vote for two or more, was prohibited, and those who voted for less than the full quota of delegates had their papers rejected. The treatment she and the other candidates had received at the selection committee proved to be the last straw. Being locked up with the other candidates enabled them to compare notes and they came to the realisation they had been tricked by the party in the interests of a candidate who had never been associated with Reform let alone stood on a Reform platform or spoken on behalf of the party. Melville said her intention in speaking out now was to keep the party democratic and to let the people rule rather than a small group of 'interested' people. In referring to the recent women's delegation, she said it was despicable on the part of the Reform organisation to use the aspirations of women for political ends.[113] At a subsequent public meeting a few days later in Avondale she provided further details of irregularities associated with the by-election selection committee – namely, that the men who had presided at the district meeting held to appoint delegates to the selection committee had been required to make sworn statements to the effect that the proceedings were regular and were conducted in a proper and impartial manner. These sworn statements were subsequently published in the *New Zealand Herald*.[114]

With the date of the by-election finally set for 15 April, Melville took out several advertisements in the *Auckland Star* announcing her opening campaign address, countering rumours that she was contemplating withdrawing from the by-election, and thanking the large number of citizens in Auckland and throughout the Dominion who had sent letters, telegrams and messages of sympathy and encouragement in her fight in the interests of true Reform in the Eden electorate.[115] But the dirty tactics were not over. As she entered her campaign meeting, she was handed a leaflet in support of the candidature of Sir James Gunson. The leaflet was a reprint of the prime minister's letter endorsing Gunson as the government candidate. She expressed surprise as it was not considered fair play to distribute printed matter at other people's meetings. At her meeting she declared that the paid organiser for the Reform Party (Bert Davy) was going around the electorate attempting to discredit her. He had not met with her face-to-face and his statements had not been made at public meetings; instead he was targeting small meetings of women. At a recent meeting of women in Avondale he had claimed that Melville had been offered 150 pounds a year for three years and then a safe seat if she would retire from the contest. He named the seat and added that she had been highly unreasonable in refusing to retire. The prime minister later stated that he knew nothing of this arrangement, and that the Reform Party deplored any such practices.

But Melville proved she could give as good as she got. She proceeded to ridicule Gunson for bringing out a large contingent of city people in motorcars with four constables in tow to his Henderson meeting, which she described as 'a kindergarten lesson in the rudiments of the Reform policy' and 'a laboured exposition of Sir James's newly acquired political creed'.[116] As the day for the by-election approached there were renewed calls from members of the public for the two Reform candidates to meet and, in the interests of the party, to decide for one to retire and support the other. Melville's response was to emphasise that she had been a true Reformer her whole life whereas Gunson had aligned with the Reform Party only in the previous month. There were obvious signs that the Reform Party hierarchy sought to curtail the threat she posed to their retaining the seat. The party secretary, Ernest James, wrote to the press to complain of Melville's persistence in misrepresenting the selection committee process and publicly accused her of exceeding the bounds of political decency in the charges she had brought against all and sundry of conspiring against her and failing to give her a fair deal.

Undeterred, Melville continued her criticisms of Gunson's credentials as a Reform candidate and stressed her credentials as a true representative of Reform. She had twice contested seats in a Labour stronghold, had given loyal service in adversity, and her politics had been good enough for Grey Lynn five months earlier. She reinforced her message on women's rights: she said it was time the women of New Zealand had representation in

Parliament, and she added, 'Do you think I would have my name bandied about if it were not for the strong conviction that it is necessary that women should have representation in Parliament? Some people think that women in Parliament is the fad of a few faddists. It is no such thing.'[117] She stressed the importance of the women's movement and said the issue at the by-election was not between Reform and Labour but between the women's movement and the Reform Party which, she claimed, did not want to see women in Parliament. She complained about the attitude of the press in general toward her candidature and suggested that the approaching visit of the prime minister to the electorate was an effort to dissuade voters from supporting her. On his tour of the electorate, Prime Minister Gordon Coates, admitted that Melville had been a good representative of the Reform Party in the past and he hoped she would remain a good friend to the party in the future: 'Nothing would give the executive of the party greater pleasure than to endorse her candidature in an election for which the delegates of the party's organisation select her.' It was simply that on this occasion the delegates had selected another candidate and he was sure 'the women do not want a woman candidate to be chosen otherwise than on her merits'.[118]

While the politics of the Reform campaign had largely overshadowed Melville's policy platform, she had also spoken on matters of interest to women, such as the maternal mortality rate, domestic assistance for mothers and the need for women to be involved in the field of film censorship. There had been criticism of her making much of her claim as a woman, but to the editor of the *New Zealand Herald* at least, this was irrelevant, 'since no party in the Dominion opposes the entry of her sex to participation in politics'. However, he did question the wisdom of sending to Parliament someone with a burning personal grievance against the party they were purportedly supporting, particularly as Melville was now something of a liability to the Reform Party after having asserted her private claim against their wider interests.[119]

In the usual predictions of outcome on the day before the by-election, the editor of the *Auckland Star* referred to the 'diverting squabble in the Reform ranks' but gave Melville her due for showing tenacity in the face of certain defeat. He admitted that she had been subjected to 'a good deal of opprobium [sic]' for splitting the party vote and there was no question she had been treated 'shabbily'.[120] She had taken a prominent part in civic affairs over a number of years and had been an able advocate of the rights of her sex, and as a political campaigner she had shown marked ability. Under normal circumstances she would naturally anticipate that she would command a solid women's vote, however, the circumstances of this by-election had proven to be far from normal and the extent to which women would give her their vote was uncertain. Aware of this, ardent feminist and journalist Jessie Mackay wrote to the editor of the *Auckland Star* from her home in Christchurch to urge Eden voters to choose Ellen Melville because she was an experienced candidate of proven civic worth and experience – and, in the process, to wipe away a seven-year-old reproach from New Zealand. Mackay assured voters that 'The woman law-maker is not a fantastic experiment: she is proved to be a twentieth-century necessity in the many countries which have outstripped us – Britain, America, Canada, Rhodesia, Germany, Finland, Austria, Norway, Australia and Czecho-Slovakia.' She urged the women electors of Eden to take this opportunity to not perpetuate 'old limitations', and called on them on behalf of all 'enlightened, patriotic women of New Zealand' to 'rightly demand a voice of more direct and intimate representation than the best of men members can give'. It was not only Miss Melville who was going to the polls, she said, 'it is the embodied principle of women for the full service of humanity'.[121] The editor of the *Auckland Star* agreed with Mackay's sentiments but took a realistic stance: when women were not prepared to rally around someone as suitable a candidate as Miss Melville, 'those who are earnestly working to establish political and economic equality for women must despair'. He felt confident that she was assured of a sympathetic vote, 'but the schism in the particular vote that she has a right to expect disastrously militates against her prospects'.[122]

As the government had feared, Labour won the seat from Reform with a majority of 426 votes. Melville polled 2197 votes compared to Gunson's 4163 votes. The media were consistent in the view that Melville's decision to contest the seat as an Independent Reform candidate cost the government the seat. The *New Zealand Herald* reported that she had 'betrayed the cause she affected to espouse' and it was 'a discreditable anti-climax to the valour which she has heretofore displayed against Socialist–Labour propaganda'. By allowing personal ambition to count for more than party loyalty she had robbed the party of the seat.[123]

In a campaign marked by bitterness, both the Labour and Reform parties claimed that Melville had attracted sympathy votes that would otherwise have gone to their respective candidates. The *Press* viewed the outcome as indicative of women's chances in future elections: it claimed that while one voter in three may have listened to 'her tale of trickery and hardship', two out of three had not.[124] In a similar vein, the *Evening Post* commented that Melville had ruined her prospects in the Reform Party.[125] She was criticised for being neither repentant nor discouraged; and one writer said that her attitude throughout suggested she had never appreciated the gravity of her conduct and that 'her judgement of the situation has been purely feminine'.[126]

Others wrote to the newspapers in support of her actions. One said it was right that her fate was decided by the electors of Eden and not by 'a caucus usurping the functions of the constituency'.[127] Another suggested that if her actions resulted in some real reform through the introduction of proportional representation, she would deserve the thanks of all democrats. A letter signed 'Justice' drew attention to the fact that the charge made by Miss Melville that she had been bribed by the Reform Party to withdraw from the by-election had not been answered and that such a charge, if proved, was a serious criminal offence,[128] and 'Square Deal' claimed that Melville's complaints around the candidate selection process were not peculiar to Eden and that every conference held to select Reform candidates at the last general election was subject to 'the same miserable "round the corner" wire-pulling that she complains of'.[129]

A week after the by-election, Ernest James sent a detailed letter to the editor of the *Evening Post* laying out the official Reform Party version of the facts of the candidate selection process. The officious tone of the letter and the closing comment that Miss Melville's actions had resulted in a seat held by the Reform Party for 39 years being handed over to 'a Labour Socialist' made it plain that, despite the prime minister's hope that Melville would in future continue to support the party, there was little goodwill towards her from party officials.[130] But the ill feeling in Auckland Reform circles engendered by her charge that Davy had offered her money and a safe seat at the next election if she withdrew her candidacy in the by-election was also directed at Davy, and exacerbated strained relations between him and Coates. In June the following year Davy resigned as Reform Party organiser and accepted a similar position in a breakaway United New Zealand Party, recruited from dissatisfied supporters of the Reform Party and the National Party (formerly Liberal Party), and led by Sir Joseph Ward.

Not everyone had lost sight of the fact that the by-election outcome had denied the opportunity to break the barrier of women being elected to Parliament. In the words of one member of the public, 'no amount of bluster or reference to side issues can alter the fact, with its result that New Zealand still stands with the few nations marking time in the old way, instead of taking her place in the onward march with the many, and the electorate of Eden, instead of being reformed, is deformed'.[131]

The fallout was evident the following year at the NCW annual conference. No reference was made in the president's address to the need to have women representatives in Parliament. Moreover, on the recommendation of the Auckland and Hamilton branches, a remit was passed to delete from the constitution the words 'The National Council of Women may support but not initiate the candidature of suitable women appointed by the council for Parliament.'[132] On the final day of the conference, however, a remit was passed urging the government to pass legislation to make the Legislative Council an elected body, thereby providing for women to be eligible to sit in the Upper House.

1928 general election: A group of gallant women

In what has been described as 'a dull session', the main political event of 1928 was the formation of the United New Zealand Party (known as the United Party).[133] Brought into being by disgruntled ex-organiser of the Reform Party Bert Davy, who had taken 'a lot of "political rejects" and young men with ambitions, but no ideas, crushed them together, and called them a party',[134] and dismissed by various Reform Party members as a 'fifth wheel in the political coach',[135] the impression was that the United Party was nothing more than 'a slightly confused harking back to the pre-war era' embodied in its 73-year-old leader Sir Joseph Ward.[136]

The 1928 general election was contested against a backdrop of increasing economic uncertainty and a more obvious widening of the gap between rich and poor in New Zealand. The Reform Party was facing internal division. Farmers were demanding cheaper credit while businessmen were demanding less government interference in marketing and tariffs. This was particularly evident in Auckland, now by far the largest of the four main centres. As the election approached, there was open talk in Reform circles of the formation of political factions and separate parties.

In contrast, the Labour Party was unified and growing in confidence. At its annual conference the previous year the party made a renewed commitment to the core principles of socialism with the greater object of the economic emancipation of man, woman and child. For Labour the challenge of the general election was, in the words of the national president Robert (Bob) Semple, 'to get these principles understood by our people, to remedy false impressions, to create an atmosphere of confidence, trust, goodwill and fraternalism'.[137]

The Reform election manifesto was based on the government's record over the previous three years and emphasised 'a steady persistence with the present policy, which has been designed in the interests of all classes'.[138] The feature of the United Party election campaign was leader Sir Joseph Ward's misreading of his opening campaign speech, in which he announced the party's intention to borrow 70 million pounds in the first year of office for the use of the people; the actual intention was to make arrangements to borrow seven million pounds annually over the course of eight to 10 years, in order to lend money to settlers and homebuilders to advance the prosperity of the Dominion. Regardless of the correction, the Reform Party attacked the United Party throughout the campaign for its extravagant and unworkable proposals.

All three parties were on the lookout for women candidates and there were early indications that several women would oblige by standing for selection. In June it was announced that Elizabeth McCombs, wife of Jim McCombs who held the Lyttelton seat for Labour, had been selected as the Labour candidate for the Kaiapoi seat. Following an approach by an influential deputation of Reform supporters in August,[139] Emily Maguire, wife of the medical superintendent of Auckland Hospital Charles Maguire, decided to contest the Auckland East seat in the interests of the Reform Party against the sitting Labour member John A. Lee. Ellen Melville was the first of three Reform candidates to announce their candidature for the Roskill seat and early signals were that an elimination ballot would be needed. Elizabeth Taylor, dominion president of the WCTU and widow of former radical Independent politician Tommy Taylor, was confirmed as the official United Party candidate for the Christchurch North seat. However, while she was representing New Zealand as a delegate at the first Pan-Pacific Women's Conference in Honolulu in August there were moves to transfer the candidacy of Ernest Andrews, who was standing for the United Party in the Christchurch South seat, to the Christchurch North seat. One of the reasons given for this was that all three present candidates for the Christchurch North seat were supporters of prohibition and, if Andrews stood as a moderate on the licensing question for the seat, he would likely gain a good deal of support. Taylor acceded to a request to step down in favour of Andrews, citing as her reasons that her time was fully occupied among the women and young people of the Dominion in her capacity as president of the WCTU. Three days before nominations closed Louisa Paterson lodged her nomination as an Independent candidate for the Grey Lynn seat and, on the final day of nominations, Margaret Young lodged her nomination as an Independent Labour candidate for the Wellington Central seat. Young's candidature was to prove one of the most conspicuous and talked-of events in the election campaign.

As with the women candidates who stood in earlier elections, the calibre of the four new women who were contesting the 1928 general election was impressive. Born in 1873 in Kaiapoi, Elizabeth Reid McCombs (née Henderson) had developed an intense interest on social questions and socialism from an early age. As a young adult she followed her sisters Christina and Stella on the committee of the Progressive Liberal Association which had as one of its aims the removal of women's civil and political disabilities. Her first public role was as secretary to the Canterbury Children's Aid Society, which was involved in the welfare of neglected and destitute children. She was prominent in the WCTU, and she and her husband Jim were members of the Christchurch Socialist Church and the Canterbury Fabian Society. In 1921 she became the second woman to be elected to the Christchurch City Council and in 1925 was appointed to the Electricity Committee, where she was able to 'promote the domestic feminism she had advanced in the WCTU'.[140]

Emily Maguire had been involved in many patriotic organisations during World War One, including the Auckland Women's Patriotic League, the ladies' auxiliary of the YMCA and the Navy League. Her work for the

Patriotic League was recognised by a service medal and in 1919 she was appointed a Member of the British Empire. She was a member and ex-president of the Auckland Civic League founded by Melville in 1914, and had served on the Auckland City Council from December 1918 until 1923 at the time when Gunson was mayor. Maguire had a reputation as a very capable public speaker and platform debater and was active in speaking on women's issues – particularly to groups of mothers on maternal and child welfare – as one of the founders of the Myers Free Kindergarten, of which she was president.

Few biographical details are known of Margaret Young or Louisa Paterson. By her own report Young had travelled extensively and had lived in America for several years and worked in a wide variety of occupations. She was married to Tom Young, a socialist committed to reformist politics who had been the general secretary of the New Zealand Seamen's Union for 25 years until he was expelled from that position in 1927 by the dominant communist faction of the union. Paterson was well known in Auckland for her social welfare activities and for having the distinction of being the first woman to contest a seat on a borough council in the Auckland Province. In May 1926 she was nominated for a vacant seat on the Mount Albert Borough Council and she tried again unsuccessfully for the seat the following year. During her campaign for the Grey Lynn electorate in 1928 she described herself as the pioneer woman in the Labour movement and as someone who was earnest, sincere and dedicated to the cause of working-class women. She was a woman of principle, prepared to speak her mind even if that could result in a prison sentence and, if returned, she would endeavour to get better conditions for working women. Her strong Christian faith was evident in her campaigning; she believed she was meant to stand and claimed that a divine power was behind her.[141]

Maguire, by her own admission, had taken a good deal of persuading before she agreed to contest the Auckland East seat. Addressing a meeting of about 200 Reform supporters in August, she explained that her commitment to the women's movement and her appreciation of the Reform Party platform had prompted her to take this step into national politics. She described the women's movement in New Zealand as being 'a little backward' in not yet having a woman in Parliament, and suggested it was time 'to wake up and realise our principles' as women had 'shirked their responsibilities long enough'.¹⁴² A resolution was passed at this meeting that the prime minister should be approached to appoint Maguire as the official candidate. This met with opposition from some of the men present, two of whom stated they first desired to hear her speak on vital questions of government. The following week she received an official endorsement of her candidature for the Auckland East seat in the Reform Party interest in a letter from Prime Minister Coates.

Given the events of the 1926 Eden by-election, it was always going to be a challenge for Ellen Melville to gain the endorsement of the Reform Party as the official candidate for the Roskill seat. This was not helped by accusations made in Parliament by the Labour member for Auckland East, John A. Lee, that the Reform Party was attempting to rid itself of encumbrances and that many individuals who imagined they would be desirable candidates were an embarrassment to Reform. A charismatic decorated ex-soldier with a criminal record, Lee was an ambitious, populist politician with an eye for capturing the headlines. As an example of Reform's tactics, he quoted from Melville's account in the *New Zealand Herald* of how the party had attempted to get her out of the way during the Eden by-election. He drew attention to the fact that the member of the Reform executive who had been accused of making inducements to Melville had never publicly denied the statement and was still a member of the Reform executive. He cited other examples of appointments to the Upper House and of individuals being sent on commissions in order not to be an encumbrance to the party. To Lee, these actions were evidence of disintegration of the Reform Party and the prime minister's inability to maintain discipline within the party.¹⁴³

Melville was one of three seeking nomination as the official Reform candidate for the Roskill seat. Acting on behalf of the prime minister, member of the Legislative Council Vernon Reed travelled to Auckland to arbitrate on the respective claims of the three candidates for the nomination – Melville, mayor of Mount Eden Ernest Potter, and member of the Mount Eden Borough Council Robert Morison. By mutual consent the three candidates had agreed to accept Reed's choice of candidate. He chose Melville, and in announcing her selection as the official Reform candidate, her credentials in business, local politics and women's affairs were highlighted. Coates gave her his hearty congratulations and said he looked forward in confidence to a successful result, and he championed the fact that the three prospective candidates had joined to find a solution in the interests of the Reform Party as a striking example of their desire for unity in the ranks of the party.

Immediately Melville's candidature was announced, complaints were made about the process of her selection. One Roskill elector expressed disgust with her being thrust upon the electors as the official candidate in a manner that circumvented the usual process of selection by delegates.[144] Another referred to the selection process as 'high-handed' and, while they stated that the Reform Party had no right to interfere until the electors had made their choice at a properly appointed meeting of delegates, they came out in judgement of Melville having adopted a similar attitude as at the last election, 'caring little if the Reform vote was split, so long as she was a candidate'.[145] Roskill resident Harold Schmidt considered it an affront to the electors that two potential Reform candidates had stood down at the request of a few political enthusiasts; he noted that Miss Melville was not even a resident of the Roskill electorate and, as a member of the city council, had not opposed measures by the council that had resulted in a great deal of inconvenience to local residents. Taking it upon himself to represent the views of most women electors, Schmidt asserted that many electors of both sexes believed that parliamentary life was unsuitable for a woman by virtue of late hours and strenuous responsibilities and that most women electors believed that a man could be depended on to represent them more than could a woman. He added that 'Another big section of womanhood have the pleasure of knowing that their men practically devote all their lives to gladden the hearts of their womenfolk, and that the men are the best champions of their cause. This big section of electors are not likely to vote for a woman candidate, no matter with what party she affiliates herself.'[146]

Within days a prominent supporter of the Reform Party claimed that most Reform electors of Roskill were dissatisfied with the way Melville had been selected as the Reform candidate – they had expected Ernest Potter to gain selection, and apparently 6000 Roskill electors were prepared to sign a petition asking him to stand as an Independent Reform candidate. A petition to the prime minister was circulating with a request that the constitutional rules of the Reform Party be followed in deciding who would be the government candidate for the electorate and asking for a ballot to be taken. If this was refused, public meetings would be called in the electorate to protest the method of selection adopted. When Melville was approached she repeated that all three candidates had agreed to abide by Reed's decision, and she emphasised that when she submitted her name and agreed to the conditions of selection, she had consulted members of her committee, which had representation from every part of the electorate, and they had approved her action.

Ten days after Melville's selection, a meeting of 40 of her friends and supporters at St George's Hall in Mount Albert passed two resolutions: the first affirmed the members' loyalty to the Reform Party and confidence in the prime minister, and the second expressed approval of the selection of Miss Melville as the official Reform candidate. A working committee was set up to assist with her campaign. On the same evening, disgruntled local Harold Schmidt convened a meeting to garner opinion from ratepayers and electors regarding transport problems with a view to selecting a general election candidate irrespective of party who would make the repeal of the Motor-Omnibus Act[147] his primary object if elected. George Munns, the United Party candidate for Roskill, undertook to do this, but another resolution was passed to call on Ernest Potter to stand as an Independent Reform candidate. Potter had been involved with the local bodies that were fighting for the establishment of a metropolitan transport board, whereas Melville, as a member of the Auckland City Council, had been opposed to the urban transport policy. This was to become a major issue in the election campaign for the Auckland seats.

Louisa Paterson's decision to stand as an Independent Labour candidate for the Grey Lynn seat was in response to a petition containing 300 signatures asking her to do so. At a meeting of the United Party candidate, John Fletcher, she asked him why the United Party had failed to put up a woman candidate, to which he replied that no ladies had offered. He explained that before a decision was made on who would stand as the candidate, Paterson had expressed an interest but that the selection committee believed he would have a better chance of getting elected. That was when Paterson announced her intention to stand against him on an Independent Labour platform.[148] She said she was standing to represent the interests of women, particularly working-class women, and emphasised that Mrs Maguire and Miss Melville did not understand the lives and needs of working-class women as she did. She conducted her campaign meetings in outside venues, most likely because she could not afford to hire venues.

Margaret Young's decision to contest the Wellington Central seat came as a surprise to the Labour Party who were anticipating a straight-out contest between the sitting member Peter Fraser and the Reform candidate Dunbar Sloane. Even her husband Tom was not aware of her intention to stand and, when he read of it in the evening newspaper, immediately declared his loyalty to the official Labour candidate. Margaret Young had decided to stand because she firmly believed there was a place in the New Zealand Parliament for women members: 'In my opinion the viewpoint of womanhood and motherhood is a desirable one to have expressed, and its expression must be of assistance in meeting the needs of the women of our country.' She described herself as 'heart and soul a worker for the workman and his wife' and said that, if elected, she promised to devote her entire energies to 'improving the lot of those who perhaps have not had the same chance as others have had'.[149]

Elizabeth McCombs, from the opening of her campaign, established herself as not only a women's candidate but someone with experience and knowledge of the workings of Parliament. She knew many of the sitting and past members, had a solid grasp of party politics and the political history of the Dominion, and was prepared to challenge the outdated wisdom of her male peers. She had spent a great deal of time in the parliamentary gallery over the nine years her husband had been a member of the House of Representatives, and was not at all intimidated by the prospect of taking a seat and a share in parliamentary processes. She drew attention to women's slow progress on the political front and referred to the members of the Legislative Council as 'old dears', and she insisted that it should not be within the power of any non-elective body to veto the decisions of the people's representatives and that it was fitting that, when Labour was in power, it would abolish the Upper House. She was interested in what she referred to as 'the machinery of Government', but even more interested in what she wanted Parliament to do.[150]

McCombs presented thorough and detailed critiques of the failures of the Reform Government's policies at her campaign meetings. Immigration policies had thrown thousands of breadwinners out of work, with disastrous results on their home life. Reckless purchasing of land for soldier settlement had resulted in a land boom and raised interest rates, which had led to thousands being driven off the land and thousands more remaining on the land and eking out a bare subsistence. She said she sympathised with the farmer, but pointed out that farmers' wives were the hardest-worked workers in the Dominion and deserved better conditions for themselves and their children. In her view there was something very wrong when those who did more than their share of the world's work were denied the ordinary comforts of life. She was particularly critical of the special appeal the Reform Party had made to women voters at the previous election, when it had asked them if they were prepared to risk the security of their home life, their husband's employment and the security of their own and their family's future. McCombs questioned how that implied promise of security had been fulfilled when thousands had lost their jobs and their homes. She spoke out on the government's immigration policy, which amounted to 'a campaign of gross misrepresentation' whereby thousands of immigrants had been induced to come to New Zealand but almost immediately upon arrival had no choice but to apply to the hospital boards for charitable aid, and she drew attention to the government's broken promises of increased pensions. In short, the Reform Government's policies could only continue to lead to relief depots, soup kitchens and record bankruptcies in rural areas.[151]

Maguire, once her candidature had been confirmed, lost no time in kicking off her election campaign. The Auckland East electorate encompassed Waiheke Island and several neighbouring islands in the Hauraki Gulf. In early October she started an electioneering tour of Waiheke Island with the intention of meeting as many residents as possible to acquaint them with her political views and to listen to their local needs and problems. Her intention to represent women's interests in Parliament was a central feature of her campaign. From the start she demonstrated that she would not be deterred by the conservative view that she should be at home looking after her husband. When she was constantly interrupted by a woman who was outspoken in her disapproval of women entering Parliament and insisted that woman's place was in her home, Maguire replied that there were three periods in a woman's life: the first 20 years was for a woman's own development and training, the second 20 years was for her business or home, and the third 20 years was for her pleasure and service to her country. Now that she was in the third period of her life, she was just as strong and just as well equipped to represent the electorate in Parliament as any man and, she said, 'I trust this electorate will favour having a woman to represent it. Without boasting, I know I can do the job.'¹⁵² There were several changes she would want to make when she did take her seat in Parliament: she objected to members falling asleep during debates and she expected to be treated with dignity and honour. Making a direct appeal for women's votes, she pointed out that if the 1000 women in the electorate who did not exercise their votes in the last election all cast their vote for her, she would 'sail in'.¹⁵³

Maguire spoke of women's important contribution to Parliament in the field of social services, and suggested that a woman who was a successful housekeeper could assist in the national housekeeping, and she frequently referred to the Reform Government's desire to have women in Parliament. Women did not want to dominate Parliament, she insisted, but they ought to have a modest representation. Her feminism was tempered by her conservative politics. For example, in upholding the government's record on employment policies, she implied that women in employment – particularly single women – was at the expense of men's full employment. She believed the unemployed should be divided into two classes – the unemployed and the unemployables – and that the latter should be put in farm colonies where, under guidance, they could be taught useful and productive occupations. In line with the Reform platform she supported roading improvements throughout the country, particularly in rural areas; she was opposed to a state bank and nationalisation of medical services, and advocated for a national insurance to which the state, employers and employees should contribute. She believed that charitable aid should be a national rather than a local responsibility. Personally, she did not support teaching the Bible in schools, and she was not in favour of discontinuing military training; but she was in favour of equal pay for women and men. If elected, she promised that her behaviour would be exemplary and that she would pave the way for other women to follow. She endorsed fellow Reform candidate Ellen Melville: 'We are the right type of women for Parliament, Miss Melville and I, as we're accustomed to public life. When on the council I knew when to speak and when to keep quiet, and so I would in Parliament.'¹⁵⁴

Amid ongoing controversy over her selection, Melville advertised the opening meeting of her campaign under the banner of 'Official Reform Candidate'. Before an audience of 400 she announced: 'I am not a blind follower of the Government, and I don't think the Government is perfect.' She spoke of women's citizenship rights and said that the fact that she was standing in the new electorate of Roskill meant the course was clear to elect a woman to Parliament 'without unseating a sitting male member'. Her address focused on the government platform in the areas of land and unemployment, but – as with all her campaign meetings – she criticised her Labour and United Party opponents. She contrasted the current established system of individual ownership and control by the citizens with a minimum of interference with Labour's focus which proposed a system of national ownership, and she decried the United Party as being 'united for destruction, barren of leadership and without a constructive policy'.[155] Melville faced a constant barrage of heckling, interruptions and questions throughout and the chair, the mayor of Mount Albert, frequently had to ask the audience for fair play.

Melville presided over a meeting for the women of Auckland at which Millicent Preston Stanley, a former member of the New South Wales Parliament, spoke on her experiences as a woman member of parliament. Stanley had been president of the New South Wales Feminist Club for eight years, and was in New Zealand on a speaking tour in support of prohibition. Advertising for the event quoted William Hughes, former prime minister of the Australian Commonwealth: 'If I were leading a party, I would ask no better or more effective supporter than Miss Stanley,' and the *New Zealand Herald* recorded that, 'As the one woman in the New South Wales Parliament, Miss Stanley battled consistently for the mothers, the children, national health, prison reform, and vocational guidance for youth.'[156] Stanley paid tribute to the group of gallant women who were standing for Parliament and admitted that during her time in the NSW Parliament she had quickly learned the truth of the old adage that things were not as they seemed. She painted a sobering picture of the ways Parliament could practically disenfranchise members of the Opposition. She said she had been banned by the Labour Party and silently undermined by her own, and added that the one subject on which all male members had agreed was that they did not want women in the House. Many outside Parliament were unaware of the ways in which members of the House could be blocked and this led people to conclude that a woman member was less active and took less interest in measures brought before the House. She talked about the ingenious methods used to suppress her efforts to introduce a Maternal and Infant Welfare Bill, and spoke of the control that big money interests had over the male members. In her view, most of the men in Parliament were marionettes, but that women's strings would not be so easily pulled. As the only woman in Parliament she had been deluged with letters and interviews from women, to a far greater extent than her male counterparts. She suggested that a large electorate was better for a woman because with a greater number of people, public opinion was not so easily manipulated.

A Reform reception held in honour of the wife of the prime minister, Marjorie Coates, during the election campaign provided an opportunity for Melville and Maguire to showcase the extent to which women were involved in politics. The event was presided over by well-known women's advocate Hilda Northcroft, who was the dominion president of the International Federation of University Women and former president of the Auckland branch of the NCW, and Melville and Maguire gave speeches, as well as Mrs Coates and the prime minister.

Louisa Paterson's address at her campaign opening was so entertaining that the large open-air audience was reluctant to disperse. She announced that she stood 'four-square for food, clothing and shelter for the people' and a woman's policy of 'making for the uplift of humanity', and stated that she wanted nothing to do with roads or bridges 'and that sort of thing'. Her address was interspersed with comic relief and she engaged in the banter with good humour although she apparently showed some 'asperity' when a man in the crowd asked her why the official Labour candidate Fred Bartram was not a fit and proper person to represent the electorate. She refused to be drawn into personalities but criticised the Labour Party for not putting up women candidates. It was reported that 'fireworks flew' when she was accused of reporting a man to the city council for giving council workers tea during working hours; because of this the men were subsequently forbidden to smoke and drink in working time. She was greeted with laughter and applause when she later admitted that she had been the one to give the workers a cup of tea. The meeting lasted two and a half hours and she was cheerful and smiling throughout.[157] A feature of her campaigning was drawing attention to the gap between the rich and poor. At one meeting she declared that a quarter of the world was dying of pomp, vanity and indigestion, while the rest were dying from starvation.

There were indications from the start that Margaret Young's campaign would be a controversial one. There was a great deal of interest in the fact that her husband was not prepared to vote for her, and that she had decided to stand as an Independent Labour candidate with no backing from any person or party. She explained that her husband had always been a staunch supporter of Labour and was a prime mover in the foundation of the labour movement. She saw it as only natural that she should continue the work he had started. Her decision to stand against the official Labour candidate was because of her dissatisfaction with Holland, Fraser and Semple at the head of the labour movement in New Zealand. In her view these men were communists, 'red feds' and Bolsheviks and she did not think the labour movement had any hope of progressing under their leadership. She intended to reveal to the electors in Wellington Central and to the country as a whole how these men had captured the position they now held, and she promised full disclosure of some of the inner workings of the labour movement in New Zealand at her opening campaign address.[158]

Young received hearty applause the following week when she began her address to an audience of 20–30 women by stating: 'Women have as much right to stand for Parliament as men.' She voiced some strong sentiments in her speech and was constantly challenged by some of those present. Her brief address was followed by 'rapid, insistent, and often loud-voiced questioning'.[159] Speaking candidly, she admitted that things were not altogether pleasant between her and her husband following her decision to contest the Wellington Central seat and that she was essentially working alone to do the best she could for humanity. Her main complaint was that the leaders of the Labour Party were too extreme and anyone who said anything against the party that was not to their liking was branded a traitor. When she was asked how she would vote if a question affecting Labour was raised in the House, she was adamant that she would not support Holland in any way. She was challenged strongly on this point; one woman said it was an astounding assertion for a candidate who was standing under an Independent Labour ticket and yet refusing to vote with Labour on a motion of no confidence. Others suggested she should either join Labour or join another party. But Young was adamant: 'I am fighting for the freedom of women. For the last fifteen years my life has been a misery through these people getting into Parliament. Women will never get what they want while

Fraser, Holland, and Semple are in power. I tell you, they are there for their own ends.'[160] Despite the spirited exchanges, the meeting resulted in the formation of several committees to assist with her campaign – and Young stayed on for some time afterwards talking informally with the women present.

There was overwhelming interest in Young's public meeting held on 5 November. The meeting was advertised to begin at eight o'clock, but by half past six nearly 300 people had congregated outside the New Century Hall in Kent Terrace, and by seven o'clock the building was packed with close to 500 people, and hundreds more outside. The scene was chaotic with loud cheering and hooting, but Young, who had to struggle through the crowds to get to the platform, did not appear nervous or fazed. She was subjected to a running fire of interjections throughout her speech, mostly of a facile and obstructive nature, and at times she could not be heard above the uproar. People tried to enter through the windows, breaking them in their attempts, and at one point a 'double-banger' firework was thrown through an open window, causing pandemonium. Struggling to be heard, Young asserted that the Waihi Strike in 1912[161] had been orchestrated by Holland and Semple to advance their public profiles and that her husband had been punished for his socialist beliefs by being expelled from his position with the Seamen's Union after 25 years of faithful service. She claimed that too much money was being wasted in the labour movement, particularly on tours around the country by the leaders.

Attempting to establish her credentials as a women's candidate, Young said, 'I know the needs of women far more than any man can ever know them ... Women have as much right to be represented and have their needs attended to as anyone else in the world. It may be new in this country, but it won't be new very long, not if the women stick together.'[162] But some were not convinced. One woman asked what she had done for the women of Wellington that qualified her to come forward and claim the right to represent them in Parliament: had she ever worked on a hospital board or on a school committee? Another asked if she understood anything of the policies she had mentioned in her speech. Despite constant interruptions she managed to make some policy statements: she believed in everybody owning their own house, increasing the old age pension, improving services for the blind, free schooling for all children, extending and increasing widows' pensions and improved provision of public restrooms for women.[163] Under pressure from a heckler Young said she did not want her vote – and then she made the extraordinary statement, 'I do not want any of your votes.'[164] 'I think there should be some women in Parliament,' she told them. 'When I get in you won't look upon it as such a joke. I am in earnest, and I am going to head the poll for Wellington Central.'[165]

In what was unfortunate timing, the day after her public meeting Young was the defendant in a civil claim brought against her in the Magistrates Court by the Singer Sewing Machine Company, which claimed she owed the company the sum of eight pounds and 10 shillings on a sewing machine she had bought on hire purchase. Her payments had been irregular, and she was in arrears. The case was complicated by the fact that she had returned her initial purchase and bought another machine for a different price and had subsequently alleged misrepresentation on the part of the company.[166]

Bob Semple vehemently denied Young's accusation that the Waihi strike had been engineered by him and Holland. He suggested the claim had been made solely to damage him personally and the Labour Party generally, and that those who were backing Mrs Young had 'deliberately faked this statement with a view of misleading the general public'.[167] That same day Young countered an accusation made against her by a prominent person whose name she threatened to publish if they did not withdraw their statement. Accused of having taken money from the Seamen's Union during the 1913 waterfront strike[168] – in which her husband and other union leaders were arrested for sedition, along with Holland, Fraser and Semple – she replied that even though she was offered half her husband's salary, she had not accepted any money as there were women and children in greater need, and she added, 'Strikes are dreadful things. They don't hurt the men as much as the women and children. If a few women got into Parliament there wouldn't be so many strikes.'[169]

Three burly police officers were employed to enforce the 'ladies only' rule to the few men who attempted to attend Young's meeting of women residents in Te Aro several days later. It was reported that 'there was no lack of rowdyism, and pandemonium reigned' during the meeting of about 100 women, which eventually dissolved into disorder. Heckled with cries of 'sewing machines', Young said she could not understand the hostile demonstration against her. At one point a woman rushed to the platform waving a newspaper accusing her of telling lies about Semple and Holland's involvement in the Waihi strike. Young responded by explaining her stance as an Independent Labour candidate: 'Although I will give general support to the Labour Party platform, I reserve the right to exercise my judgement on each and every one of its planks, just as I claim the right to exercise my judgement on the planks of the platform of each other political party, but you can depend that on those planks that will improve the well-being of the mass of the people, my hearty cooperation and support will at all times be given, and I will support those measures that are in the interests of New Zealand, and of the British Empire.'[170]

Largely because of the controversial nature of her campaign, Young made political capital – literally – from the large audiences she attracted. In what was believed to be new ground for a political meeting, she charged admission. After speaking to an audience of close to 3000 people at the Town Hall in Wellington she called on the mayor to advise him she was donating half of the receipts to Wellington charities to be nominated by him.

Emily Maguire also met with hostility at some of her campaign meetings, and at one meeting members moved a vote of no confidence in her as a candidate and in the Reform Government. At another meeting where there was a large contingent of Labour supporters, she stated, 'This is the first occasion on which I have felt my disability as a woman, and I would like to camouflage my womanhood for a few weeks to get into Parliament. Women have worked in the past to assist men to Parliament and I cannot see why men should think it infra dig to vote for a woman.'[171]

Melville's meetings were often interrupted by heckling and interjections. At one point, frustrated at what was obviously an organised opposition, she said she doubted the individual lived in her electorate and even if they did she did not want the votes of people who presented the type of mind that deliberately attempted to disrupt her meetings. Like Maguire, she met with several motions of no confidence in her as a candidate and in the Reform Government. In the final days of the election campaign when the prime minister was completing a whirlwind tour of electorates, he encouraged voters in the Roskill electorate to vote for Melville: 'I commend to you our candidate. Elect her and give us that little touch that will make for perfection, particularly in dealing with humane legislation in which the feminine point of view is so very valuable. We hope to have at least two women returned to Parliament, and I can say this for Miss Melville that she has a grasp of affairs equal to that of any man in the country.'[172]

Of the five women candidates contesting the 1928 general election, only McCombs was given any consistent backing by commentators to be in the running.[173] Early in the campaign a political commentator suggested that 'the Government missed a great opportunity in not selecting a stronger candidate' for the Roskill seat. This commentator claimed Melville was not very popular, largely because she was a member of the Auckland City Council which had not had a successful run of late in civic administration. However, he claimed that as her opponents were 'weak ... she may become the first woman candidate to enter Parliament'.[174] But a week out from polling day commentators started making more informed predictions. The editor of the *Waihi Daily Telegraph* considered it highly doubtful that any of the lady candidates in Auckland would be returned. In his view, Miss Melville had given a reasoned defence of the government's policy and Mrs Maguire had shown herself to be a cultured and travelled lady, but Mrs Paterson could not be taken at all seriously: 'She makes a blind, unreasoned appeal to women to return her on the ground that because women have had the franchise for 35 years they should be represented in Parliament.'[175]

The outcome of the 1928 general election was a stunning reversal of the Reform Government's success in the previous election, and resulted in a change of government. On final count the Reform Party held only 28 seats, well short of the required majority of 41. The United Party with 27 seats formed a government led by Sir Joseph Ward with the support of Labour's 19 seats. Among the women candidates, Paterson lived up to the commentators' predictions by gaining a mere 72 votes, while Young fared comparatively better with 843 votes. While Young had no impact on the electorate outcome as the incumbent Peter Fraser increased his majority by nearly 1500 votes, Paterson's votes in the Grey Lynn electorate may have contributed to Labour losing the seat to United by 64 votes. Maguire polled a respectable 2274 seats, and this contributed to the incumbent John A. Lee losing to the United candidate by 37 seats. Although Melville polled significantly lower than when she contested the Roskill seat in the previous general election, her 3345 votes were only 56 fewer than the runner-up – though 2130 fewer than the successful United candidate. The most creditable performance was McCombs who, while she came third in a very closely contested electorate, was only 140 votes behind the runner-up and 236 votes behind the successful United candidate – and 1795 votes more than that polled by the previous Labour candidate in the seat.

Invited to speak of her experiences in the general election campaign to the League of Penwomen, Maguire said that unless the attitude of women in New Zealand altered there would not be a woman in the House of Representatives. She thought her stand against prohibition and the Bible-in-schools movement may have lost her women's votes, but the real problem was apathy. Critical of the many women's associations in Auckland that prided themselves on not being political, she bemoaned the fact that women of influence who ought to be behind the women's movement looked on it as somehow lowering the standard of womanhood. Women needed to cooperate with one another, regardless of party affiliation, and unite in a political movement to raise the status of their sex and to give them a better idea of politics; only then would there be any real hope of women gaining a seat in the New Zealand Parliament. At the final meeting for the year of the Auckland branch of the NCW, a member suggested that if women had wholeheartedly supported the women candidates they would have been elected. But another member countered this by suggesting that if the women candidates had not allied themselves to political parties they would have received more support from women voters.

Maguire's reflections on why women candidates were not sufficiently supported at the polls prompted a letter to the newspaper from 'Independent Woman' about how members of the NCW and its affiliate members were cast in an unfair negative light. The writer felt that the NCW was 'a fine body of thinking women composed of every shade of political outlook … from true-blue Tory to the widest Labour views', and, at pains to point out that party politics would split these societies and hinder their usefulness, she noted that Ellen Melville and Emily Maguire were first and foremost party women and this had undoubtedly played a major part in their poor showing at the polls. Describing them as 'the mouthpieces of a discredited Government in power and not of the women in the districts which they strove to represent', the writer stated that women would continue to be apathetic in politics until a genuine 'women's champion' appeared. 'They know that a woman who enters politics as a party woman, and not as an independent at the request of a large body of women of all shades of political opinion, to fight solely for things and ideals in which women are deeply interested, will fail.'[176]

Several others took up this line of discussion. 'Male Liberal' pointed out that women candidates must always expect to carry the barriers of party conviction: 'It is of no use a woman standing as a party candidate and expecting to get the votes of all women, for with many party comes before personality.' This writer was a Roskill voter who believed strongly that there should be women in Parliament, but believed even more strongly that the Reform Government needed to be voted out of power. He suggested that a woman must either stand for a 'safe' seat, knowing there would always be many others contesting a 'safe' seat, or 'she must be a woman of outstanding personality and achievement standing as an Independent'.[177] 'Super-Independent Woman' believed the lesson for women was to be fair to one another before they attempted to interfere with politics. She questioned why women did not protest when one of them was unjustly treated, and noted there had been many such cases in Auckland.[178] The advice of these writers did not escape those women who had unsuccessfully contested the recent general election.

1931 general election: A women's candidate

Caution proved to be the keynote of policy under the United Government. In a term of office noted for its inactivity, the leadership of ailing Prime Minister Ward was proving an embarrassment to the government. Growing unemployment, increased pressure on the government's unemployment schemes in forestry, irrigation, road and railway projects, and reports of men collapsing from starvation as they waited in queues for assistance were met with the government's concealment of the true unemployment statistics. This political vacuum was accentuated when, from March 1930, Cabinet stopped meeting. The following month, after an eight-month absence in the House because of ill health, Ward died. George Forbes became prime minister and embarked on a programme of financial retrenchment. In the interim, the United Party had lost several seats in by-elections and Reform's share of the votes had increased. By late February 1931 unemployment had reached 27,000 of the total population of just over 1.5 million people.

With widely differing views on how to respond to the Great Depression, the political alliance between the United Government and Labour strained to the point of collapse and the United Party continued to govern with the support of the Reform Party to avert the prospect of an early election.

Only two women contested the 1931 general election. Early in 1931 there had been talk of the possibility that McCombs might stand as a Labour candidate for the Christchurch mayoralty, but by the Labour conference in April it was confirmed she would contest the Christchurch North seat.

In late July 1931 a deputation of women who backed Melville to stand for the Auckland East seat in the upcoming general election waited for members of the Reform Party's executive to request their endorsement of her candidature. To their surprise, this was refused on three grounds: nominations for the Auckland East seat had apparently closed 13 months earlier, a candidate had already been accepted, and the executive of the Reform Party had decided they did not want any female candidates. Notably, Hilda Northcote was one voice on the Reform Party executive who, while she was theoretically in favour of women candidates, did not think a woman had any chance of winning the Auckland East seat. Undeterred, the deputation decided to put Melville forward as a women's candidate and not affiliated to any political party. Aware that the Reform Party had recently approached Sir George Richardson to accept nomination for the Auckland East seat, and not wishing to oppose him if he was committed to stand, the deputation sent a representative to ask if he was intending to contest the seat. When he confirmed that he had no interest in doing so, the committee approached Melville and asked her to stand as a women's candidate.

With the promise of strong support Melville agreed, and on 31 July 1931 it was announced she had consented to stand for the Auckland East seat as a women's candidate and not in the interests of any party. Speaking to a gathering of over 60 women supporters several weeks later, Melville said that with the growing economic stress and the measures passed to deal with that, women were taking a closer interest in politics, realising their duty as citizens and responding to the call for national service, just as they had done during the war. Reforms that all thinking women had set their hearts on could be furthered when they had their own representative in Parliament, just as had happened when women had been elected into the House of Commons. She expressed her support for the formation of a national government comprised of all parties who were prepared to put the interests of the country before party politics. All the women present at the meeting pledged their support for her as a women's candidate and they formed a committee to work for her election. A new stage in women's political organisation had begun.

As a women's candidate, every speaking engagement with women's groups provided an opportunity for Melville to demonstrate her commitment to furthering women's issues in Parliament. Whether it was a talk to the Overseas League on 'Women as empire builders', speaking on the roles women had played in the League of Nations at a meeting of the Auckland Branch of the League of Nations Union, addressing the Auckland Hospital Auxiliary, the Women's Progress Club or the Old Thames Girls' Association on 'Women's share in the making of a nation', Melville drew attention to women's past record of political activity and the need for increased opportunities at all levels of political decision-making. Importantly, her involvement in the newly formed Auckland Women's Unemployment Committee brought her in touch with the grim realities facing unemployed women and with a range of women's employment unions. The committee requested reports on the extent of unemployment among women, and early advice on the intentions of the government Unemployment Board in relation to the unemployment of women. To complement the information on the committee's register of unemployed women and girls they approached the Women Teachers' and Trained Nurses' associations, and the Tailoresses', Shop Assistants' and Hotel and Restaurant Workers' unions to get an indication of numbers of women who may not have formally registered as unemployed.

In September the Reform Party reluctantly agreed to form a coalition government with United to blunt Labour's advantage by ensuring there was not a split in the anti-Labour vote. The terms of the coalition were clear: the coalition Cabinet would have only 10 members, five from each side, which meant at least eight United Cabinet ministers had to be stood down. Furthermore, at the upcoming election, in electorates where there was a sitting member of Parliament of either party he was not to be opposed, so as to maintain a united front against Labour. This had implications for the governing parties who had already selected many candidates; and the *New Zealand Herald* reported that 'There is a feeling particularly in the Auckland district, that some of the prospective anti-Labour candidates seeking Parliamentary honours are of a better calibre than some of those who secured seats, somewhat fortuitously, at the last general election.'[179] Under pressure from business interests, on 23 October it was announced there would be an early election, but it was not until 11 November that the date for the election was announced as 2 December.[180]

In response to the uncertain political situation and the fact that there was now a coalition government, in early November Melville met with her supporters to review whether she would continue to seek the Auckland East seat. Speakers at the meeting expressed disappointment that the coalition government had made no provision for women candidates, particularly given that 14 women had been elected to government in Britain. Melville believed it was now more urgent than ever to have a woman representative to safeguard the interests of wage-earning women who were required to pay an unemployment levy even though they were not eligible for employment relief, as well as to progress the appointment of women police. She was aware that many people in New Zealand still seemed to think that women in Parliament was something revolutionary whereas in many countries it was now commonplace. Women may have been apathetic about asserting their right for a role in government when the country was prosperous, but adversity had awakened a keen interest in what women often referred to as 'the national housekeeping' now that the country was in economic depression. A resolution to the effect that Miss Melville should contest the seat was carried unanimously at the meeting.

The formal opening of Ellen Melville's election campaign on 16 November attracted about 200 people, mainly women. The sense of occasion was evident as she declared that never in New Zealand's history had a women's candidate representing the women of the Dominion solicited the votes of the people. She explained that women were prepared to get women into Parliament, irrespective of party, and for this reason, she had again agreed to stand for election. They now effectively had formed 'a little coalition of our own to obtain representation in the House'[181] on the understanding that once women had gained a footing they would return to their political parties, because women were needed in all parties. Above all, women representatives were needed to speak for women workers, the aged and the helpless. Deserted wives needed a voice, and radical law changes were needed for their protection. There was work to be done for girls who had been 'betrayed', too. Melville stressed that she would be able to represent men as well as women in Parliament; after all, men for many years had represented women as well as men and nobody thought there was anything strange about that. She declared that the right system was one where men and women represented the whole community.

Outlining her political platform, Melville said she favoured thrift and economy in public and private life, more land settlement, opening up of undeveloped land, encouraging local manufacturing, and the establishment of new industries. She was critical of the government's record on unemployment: hundreds of thousands of pounds had been wasted, she said, in unprofitable work for which neither the men employed nor the country itself was better off. Solutions such as opening up the land and developing local industries should be applied, as a subsidy to industry would make more sense than paying relief wages for useless work. She believed the Unemployment Board should devote a greater proportion of its funds to the relief of unemployment among women and girls, particularly as girls working in factories had to pay the wages tax and were effectively getting nothing for that. This was not a fair way to treat women workers who were being overlooked because they had no representative to put their case before Parliament.

During her campaign Melville was a strong advocate for training girls in domestic work to give them a definite status by awarding grades and certificates, and for domestics to be placed on a similar footing to nurses. In her view a domestic's work was just as important as that of a nurse. She also advocated reduction in the duties paid on wheat, a reduction in the number of members of Parliament, the appointment of women police, and two-member constituencies. She believed in a coalition government for New Zealand but thought it preferable to have an ordinary election and then form a national government, which should include a woman member. She confirmed she would not vote on a no-confidence motion against a coalition government if it meant giving the Labour Party power.

As the election campaign got into full swing, Melville faced the now familiar barrage of interjections at her meetings. With four general elections and one by-election under her belt, her experience on the campaign trail came to the fore and she used hecklers' comments to show her mettle. There was general resentment that the coalition government had decided to return sitting members as coalition candidates at the election; many saw this as a negation of democracy. Melville was outspoken on this matter as it affected her directly: not only did it deny that the people were the best judges of their own political loyalties, but the candidate selected by the coalition authorities for the Auckland East seat was, to her knowledge, not even connected with public life in the electorate.

Elizabeth McCombs' campaign slogan was 'Vote the First Woman to the New Zealand Parliament'. Opening her campaign, she presented a sustained critique of recent government policies such as the threat to abolish compulsory arbitration – a move she described as 'the greatest menace to democracy'. She spoke against the unfulfilled promises of the Reform Government and the coalition government's 'gift' to the wealthiest landowners in the country through its repeal of the graduated land tax. She challenged the reduced rates of relief pay to the unemployed, the government's removal of educational facilities, and proposed restrictions on the number of children who would receive secondary education.[182] Her campaign attracted considerable interest and there was talk of a split vote working in her favour.

In the end, neither of the women candidates was to break the barrier to women's entry into Parliament. Of the five candidates contesting the Auckland East seat, Melville polled in fourth place with a disappointing 1002 votes. McCombs had better success, polling in second place in the Christchurch North seat with 3450 votes, but still 2077 votes behind the successful candidate.

In the post-election post-mortems, feminist journalist Miriam Soljak noted that while New Zealand was growing accustomed to criticism of its backwardness in having no women members of Parliament, 'it still disturbs our equanimity, because ... there is no reason why we should not have a dozen women in Parliament'. In her opinion it was not that there was any great degree of 'sex-antagonism' or that male voters were lacking in chivalry or good sportsmanship. There was 'a plethora of women's organisations all supporting female representation' and it could be assumed they would give as much support to a woman as to a man if the individual candidate met with their approval. She offered several reasons why the daughters and granddaughters of those who came here as pioneers and who had proved themselves to be 'as hardworking as adaptable, and as courageous as their men' had not yet taken a place among the country's legislators: first, 'an inability or unwillingness to give electors what they want'; second, 'lack of contact with the great mass of electors'; third, 'an over-stressed feminism which antagonises nearly all male and some female voters'; and last, 'failure to reach to the high standard demanded in a woman candidate'.[183] Soljak was insistent: 'Until the average elector can see a female candidate as a candidate only and not as a woman doing something unusual ... it is essential that one who asks for votes must prove the need of sending her to Parliament'. She suggested that while a female aspirant for a parliamentary seat should be able to deal competently with all matters of the state, she should give special attention to matters of particular relevance and interest to women, such as anomalies in the marriage laws and widows' pensions. Of McCombs, Soljak commented that although she had the advantage of party support as well as 'a facility gained by temperament and training in securing the confidence of the mass of electors', like Melville, 'she failed to stress the importance of giving relief to women in matters that affect them most'. Soljak insisted:

> *While unemployed women and girls live neglected and unaided, while married women teachers are being wrongly dismissed, while children and adolescents are at the mercy of faulty legislation, while the law regarding women's nationality needs amending, and the general retrogressive state of women legally and economically calls for immediate improvement there is ample material for a woman candidate to work on and by efficient handing to secure an advantage over any but the super candidate of the dominant sex.*[184]

Undeterred by their standing in the polls, both Melville and McCombs would seek parliamentary honours again,[185] but for McCombs, when the next opportunity to do so arose it was bittersweet.

*

Between 1919 and 1933 there were five general elections and 21 by-elections. Why did so few women contest these early elections and why were they not successful? It was often stated during this period that if the majority of women voters in any electorate where a woman stood as a candidate had strongly desired to see a woman in Parliament, their combined votes could have seen the woman candidate elected. This view was premised on the problematic – and false – assumption that when faced with a choice between a male candidate and a female candidate, women would choose the latter. Another problematic assumption was that only women would vote for women candidates. Women's lack of success in these early elections is attributable to many factors, including that, for many women voters, being a woman candidate was not sufficient cause to guarantee their vote.[186]

While we cannot know the extent to which any voter, male or female, voted for the candidate or the party, Melville's experiences are emblematic of women's struggle to gain parliamentary honours. The archetypal 'new woman', New Zealand-born Ellen Melville was a well-educated professional of independent means with her own private law business, recognised for her experience and capability in civic affairs and described as 'a womanly woman' with personal and professional integrity. She stood for election on every possible occasion during this period, contesting all five general elections and one by-election. She was deeply committed to the Reform Party and, on all fronts, should have been the first woman to take a seat in the New Zealand Parliament. Instead, when she and her colleagues personally experienced serious improprieties in the party selection process, she stood up and publicly challenged the party political hierarchy. Her actions and her refusal to toe the line led to her being scapegoated by the Reform Party and the newspaper media, and maligned by her feminist sisters who accused her of bringing the women's movement into disrepute. Even when she subsequently stood 'as a straight-out women's candidate'[187] she was unsuccessful. Melville's experiences bear testimony to the extent of the entrenched conservatism and bias against women's full participation in the political sphere.

CHAPTER 6

Our first lady member, 1933 to 1935

The National Council of Women hereby urges that women work with heart and soul to put women into Parliament. — MOTION, National Council of Women annual conference, March 1933[1]

'I owe it to him'

Elizabeth McCombs' husband Jim had often joked with his friends that he would never be defeated in his electorate because history had shown that the member for Lyttelton held their seat until they passed away. On 2 August 1933 his words came true when he became the third successive member for Lyttelton to pass away in office. A week earlier he had suffered a mild stroke but had rallied; however, the following Wednesday morning he suffered a heart attack and died in bed at his home in Clifton, Sumner. Condolences flowed to Elizabeth, her son Terence and daughter Patricia. Amid tributes from the governor-general, the prime minister, politicians of all persuasions, Labour Party stalwarts, trade unions and women's organisations, the newspapers announced that a by-election was imminent. Two days later, eulogies at the public memorial at St John's Anglican Church in Woolston and at the private graveside service at Waimairi Cemetery were intertwined with quiet discussions about a successor for the Lyttelton seat.

Foremost in the minds of the Labour Party hierarchy was Jim McCombs' narrow majority of only 32 votes in the previous election. Anxious to retain the seat, Harry Holland, leader of the Labour Party, wrote to the Party's assistant secretary on 6 August: 'If the seat is lost, it will be lost not by the party, but by the candidate.'[2] Holland personally believed that Elizabeth

McCombs was the best candidate to contest the seat, but he was concerned that general prejudice against female candidates would disadvantage her and the Labour Party. Jim McCombs' good friend, trade union organiser and member for Avon Dan Sullivan, asked Elizabeth on behalf of the Labour Representation Committee if she would be prepared to stand for the seat. She responded in a letter, 'It was my husband's greatest wish that one day as a member of Parliament I might have a wider opportunity of serving the community, and on each of the two occasions when I was selected as a candidate he not only urged me to accept but gave me whole-hearted encouragement and support throughout the campaigns. Remembering this I feel that I owe it to him to reply in the affirmative to the request you conveyed to me from the executive of the Labour Representation Committee.'[3]

There was a large attendance with representatives from all the districts in the Lyttelton electorate at the private meeting of the North Canterbury Labour Representation Committee at the Trades Hall on the evening of 9 August. Discussion was 'full and frank' and resulted in the names of four Labour party members being put forward as suitable candidates.[4] When Elizabeth McCombs' letter to Dan Sullivan was read to those assembled, the other three candidates withdrew, and her nomination was unanimously accepted. The national executive, however, were less supportive and only reluctantly agreed to support her nomination.

With the date for the by-election fixed at 13 September, by the close of nominations on 28 August there were three candidates. The Coalition candidate Frederick William Freeman was Elizabeth McCombs' most serious rival. Having lost to Jim McCombs in the 1931 contest by only 32 votes, Freeman had the support and resources of the Reform Party and the United Party that comprised the coalition government behind him. Also in the running was Christchurch-born civil engineer and surveyor Edward Leslie Hills, who had a strong trade union background and, standing under an Independent Labour banner, posed the threat of splitting the socialist vote. Hills' platform was for greater independence of thought and action in Parliament. Having only recently severed his connection with the Labour movement, he publicly attacked the Labour Party, accusing it of being devious in its methods and denying thousands of workers a say because they were unemployed and their unions could not pay affiliation fees.

Despite money for Labour's campaign being in very short supply, the party determined to wage an intensive campaign, 'attempting to fight a champagne electorate on a beer income',[5] under the direction of party president Frederick Langstone. Elizabeth McCombs was seated on the stage at the formal opening of the party campaign at the Excelsior Hall in Lyttelton on 21 August. She did not speak; it had been agreed that given her recent bereavement her public appearances and speaking engagements would be limited and senior Labour politicians would be brought in to address some of the campaign meetings. Leader of the Opposition Holland paid a glowing tribute to the late Jim McCombs and told the audience of about 250 that the Labour Party was honoured to have Mrs McCombs as its candidate. Holland declared his confidence that Mrs McCombs, whom he described as 'among the ablest of the women in public life in New Zealand', would make history as the first woman to sit in the Parliament of the Dominion.[6] Appealing directly to female voters, he said it would have been a 'graceful gesture' and a compliment to the women of New Zealand if the government had not opposed Mrs McCombs, particularly as the government's existence was not at stake, with 50 seats in the House to Labour's 23.[7] Now it was up to the women of the electorate to make it possible for the first woman to sit in the House of Representatives in New Zealand. He was sure that not only would Labour hold the seat, they would secure an increased majority.

Holland's address was an opportunity to put forward Labour's policies and plan for the nation. He talked at length about unemployment, and condemned the government for imposing taxation on unemployed women and boys and for not being upfront about the scale of unemployment among adult men. His speech canvassed the Labour manifesto: industrial rehabilitation, comprehensive public works schemes, engaging workers in economic undertakings that mattered, banishing relief wages in favour of fair recompense, increasing the purchasing power of the people, large-scale land settlement, guaranteed prices for primary producers, safeguarding and developing secondary industries, and nationalisation of the banking system.

There was some public support for Holland's view that the government should not contest the by-election. Early in the campaign one writer to the newspaper stated they were not voting for Labour, but they were voting for Mrs McCombs as they believed she should occupy the remaining portion of her late husband's elected term of office.[8] Another anonymous supporter suggested the other candidates should, as a matter of respect, withdraw from the campaign and let Mrs McCombs represent the Lyttelton electorate for at least two and a half years. Noting that she currently held several positions, including chairwoman of the City Council Electricity Committee and a member of the Hospital and Tramway boards, and that all these services were freely given, this supporter drew attention to the fact that although Elizabeth McCombs had not succeeded in her earlier stands for Kaiapoi and Christchurch North, she had shown that she would be a good Labour member. They added, 'She deserves the sympathy of every elector, and Lyttelton might show appreciation of her work', and assured readers, 'There are many who think this would be a good thing.'[9] But being a female candidate and recently bereaved was not sufficient to convince another reader who, 'amazed and shocked' by this 'improper' suggestion, wrote, 'One must deal kindly with a woman candidate, but that does not justify her politics, and it is time for a new deal in this electorate. I have every sympathy with the lady in the loss of her husband, but I have no sympathy with her political aspirations, nor with the party she seeks to serve … According to "Practical Sympathy's" logic, the widow of every Parliamentarian should be re-elected in his place. Absurd! The lives and welfare of a million and a half people are bound in the politics of this country. Let them be governed by sound reason and common sense.'[10]

It was openly acknowledged that McCombs would likely receive a strong sympathy vote but, equally, she would be able to command a considerable personal following, having been for many years 'a dominating figure in the civic life of the City of Christchurch' with 'a strong personality without being overbearing'.[11] There were large numbers of unemployed in Lyttelton and this boded well in Labour's favour. There was evidence of a swing in public opinion against the policies of the coalition government; but there were still those who firmly believed there was no reason whatsoever to elect women to Parliament. Writing to the editor of the *Press* under the name 'Homo', one man confessed to not caring about the political significance of the upcoming by-election, but said that 'the time is not ripe, irrespective of any precedent in England, to elect any woman to Parliament in the Dominion'. He was prepared to concede that McCombs deserved parliamentary honours in preference to any woman who had so far contested an election in New Zealand; however, in his view, there was no more reason for women to 'squeal about the handicap of sex ... than a black fellow should curse a white fellow' as these were simply 'an accident of birth'. Claiming he had no prejudice, he said he saw no reason for women to be in Parliament when already 'Half our window displays are set apart for women. Our buses, trams, and picture entertainments are two-thirds occupied by them, and on any sunny afternoon so are our main shopping streets.'[12]

'Homo's' view was not shared by the crowded audience that spilled out into the street to greet Elizabeth McCombs with prolonged applause on the opening of her election campaign at the Oddfellows Hall in Lyttelton on the evening of 25 August. Unbeknown to those assembled, she had been suffering a migraine all day and had struggled over the preparation of her speech and by the time she rose to the platform her knees were like jelly. Her experience as a public speaker helped her through and, to her delight, friendly interjections punctuated her 'stimulating address' on electoral reform, education and unemployment.[13] Commenting on the worldwide advancement of women to positions of responsibility within governments, she urged the introduction of proportional representation as a necessary means of electoral reform to give women direct representation in Parliament. She called for a general referendum law by which 10 percent of the population would have the right to demand a plebiscite vote on any proposed legislation as well as the right to initiate legislation.

McCombs spoke at length on the harm done, particularly to the sons and daughters of working men, by the reduction of spending on education. If elected, she would vote for restoring educational facilities. On the burning issue of unemployment she provoked laughter with her observation, 'When I think of the Government and unemployment, I remember that there are ten Ministers of the Crown and every one of them has twelve thousand million brain cells – all unemployed.'[14] But her message was very serious. She spoke of the 'downright injustice' of the government taxing women and girls, and the indifference shown to women and girls who were unemployed, as being 'nothing short of a scandal'; and she claimed that the government's callous treatment of unemployed women had aroused the indignation of all thinking women, including those who had voted for the two parties that comprised the present government. Likewise, it was 'little short of madness' on the part of the government to stop investing in necessary public works, thereby depriving large numbers of men from productive employment and putting them on unnecessary and unproductive work schemes, just as it was ill advised for the government to assist certain wealthy classes in the community.[15]

McCombs insisted that the true extent of unemployment was hidden as the official statistics did not include women and boys out of work, and many men and women were working part-time and half-time, often at relief rates of pay. A new outlook was needed – as had been the case when the country last underwent a prolonged economic depression in the 1880s and early 1890s; that had resulted in the election of the first Liberal government under Ballance, followed by Seddon. Labour, she insisted, had the most constructive plan for bringing the country back to prosperity: real work for real wages instead of charity. She pointed out that as the government already had a strong majority in the House, a vote for the coalition candidate would be construed as an endorsement for all the government's actions over the previous two years. Hearty cheers and calls for speeches from the Labour members of Parliament present greeted the end of her address and she was given a vote of thanks and a vote of confidence.

In her previous election campaigns, her husband had been at her side. Three weeks after his passing she confided in a letter to a friend how important it was for her that her son and daughter were with her: 'If anything could have consoled me for his absence on Friday night it was their wholehearted delight in my success with the crowd. They were so excited that afterwards I could not get them to bed and next day no work was done for discussing the meeting. For their sakes I pray that I am returned.'[16]

A few days later she was greeted with 'three cheers for Mrs McCombs' and a bouquet from the women of Woolston at a crowded meeting in the local school hall. With more than 450 in attendance, many had to listen to her address over a speaker system from another room. McCombs explained her allegiance to the Labour Party by saying that she had been involved in public affairs long enough to know that the only way to get things done was to belong to a party, and that 'the Labour party was the only party setting itself to make more people happy, and happy in a better way'.[17] The meeting closed with a rendition of 'For She's a Jolly Good Fellow' and a unanimous vote of thanks. Her meeting at the Masonic Hall in Cashmere two days later was more subdued. She spoke for 80 minutes and received questions from an audience of more than 150 electors, 10 of whom voted against a vote of thanks and confidence. At other meetings she spoke on issues of interest to women, such as the need to raise the age of marriage from 12 for girls and 14 for boys, and to introduce equal rights of guardianship.

For the most part McCombs' campaign meetings were chaired by well-known male public figures and politicians, but there were a few exceptions: a meeting at Okains Bay was chaired by Miss Robinson, president of the local women's institute, and women proposed and seconded the vote of thanks and confidence at a meeting at West Lyttelton. Throughout the campaign she received messages of support from women's groups such as the NCW, the WCTU and the New Zealand Federation of University Women. She was careful not to make political mileage of her late husband's passing, but she did mention him on several occasions. At a meeting in Heathcote she promised, 'If elected I will endeavour to carry out my duties in the same spirit that actuated your late member,'[18] and in Redcliffs she told her audience it was her late husband's desire that she should sit in Parliament: 'He always wished that I should extend my sphere of activity in that way, and we had hoped that we might sit in Parliament and work for the country together.'[19]

McCombs' reference to the need for direct representation of women in Parliament caught the attention of the editor of the *Evening Post*. He questioned what she meant by this: should there be separate constituencies for women along the lines of the current separate representation of Māori and Europeans in Parliament, or should women be entitled to half the membership of the House, and would this suggestion have the approval of women? He queried how women would group themselves if they had separate representation: 'Would they be members of existing parties, or would they remain within their own Castle Adamant with their own Prime Minister and Cabinet?' Taking his speculation to the extreme, he cautioned men to be careful about ridiculing these notions and suggested that even if separate representation on the basis of sex would deprive them of half the seats, that would be better than having only a room and some seats in the gallery set apart for members' husbands and sons, as was currently the case for members' wives and daughters.[20]

As the by-election campaign progressed, the differences between the candidates began to emerge. Frederick Freeman's campaign rested squarely on the coalition government's record and on Labour's policies being inadequate for the country's present needs. Apart from reporting that Freeman held an afternoon meeting for women in the conservative stronghold of Akaroa, before a public evening meeting, the newspapers were silent on his views on whether women should be elected representatives in the House. His rival Edward Hills was unequivocal on the matter. At a meeting in Heathcote presided over by two police officers, he was asked if he believed that women should enter Parliament. His response aroused considerable opposition from women and men in the audience: 'I believe the same as Hitler believes, that woman's place is in the home.'[21] His further explanation that he believed the difficulties of the country were too great for women to grapple with led to fiery challenges from some of those present. To claim some moral high ground, Hills said that where others might sidestep the question, he believed even those women who did not agree with him would respect him for his frank expression of his opinions. As the challenges continued, Hills became more entrenched in his position: he declared he was not in the least concerned about the effect this pronouncement might have on his votes, and claimed he was being made a victim of an old electioneering game whereby if a candidate did not give the answer required they would be punished at the polls.

McCombs' view was that women in New Zealand had earned the right to sit in Parliament, and she thought it entirely appropriate that the first woman sent to Parliament should come from Canterbury, because of the central role women in that region had played in the suffrage campaign three decades earlier. Two days out from the by-election, 'Tory Englishwoman' thought it 'necessary and advisable to clear up some of the vagueness in the minds of women electors regarding their candidate'.[22] She had chosen these words deliberately, 'for Mrs McCombs is first, and should be foremost, the women's candidate'. This supporter proffered four reasons for her assertion. First, Elizabeth McCombs' family had been instrumental in getting New Zealand women the franchise. Second, her career and upbringing demonstrated she had always been at the forefront of women's questions and was never afraid to speak up for women. Third, as a housewife she was accustomed to the basic principle of keeping expenditure within the limits of her purse and, through the hard facts and thousand-and-one tasks that fell to her each day, had an invaluable grasp of what was important when considering the economic problems faced by the government. And fourth, McCombs' training as a mother meant she could do great service to her country 'by bringing to bear on political questions minds intent on learning the facts and deciding on them without fear or favour'. Rallying women voters, 'Tory Englishwoman' ended her letter, 'Women have passed through the illusion of feminism to the reality of equal citizenship status; even the women of New Zealand, who after having the vote for more than 30 years, have yet no women in Parliament. The electors of Lyttelton have now the opportunity of removing this blot from the fair name of New Zealand. What better time than the present? What better woman than Elizabeth McCombs?'[23]

As election campaigns went it was a relatively clean contest, although there was public criticism of the behaviour of Labour supporters towards both rival candidates. Hills was often heckled and interrupted and there were reports of the hall being picketed at one of his meetings. At another campaign meeting that was declared 'black' and boycotted by Labour supporters, police and newspaper reporters outnumbered the meagre audience. Frustrated and angered by these actions, Hills expressed his surprise and disgust that the Labour Party had adopted unsporting attitudes and tactics. And the 'disgraceful conduct' of some Labour supporters at some of Freeman's meetings led one voter to conclude that Mrs McCombs' failure to speak out against such behaviour was indicative of her 'complete unfitness for the responsibilities of public office'.[24]

The Lyttelton electorate was as diverse politically as it was geographically. Lyttelton, Woolston, Heathcote and Opawa were strong Labour districts, but Cashmere, Sumner, Akaroa and the dairy farming and pastoral districts across Banks Peninsula were equally strong 'Tory' constituencies, and other areas were evenly split in their political preferences. The timing of the by-election two years into the coalition government's ministry, along with the electorate being evenly balanced in its political opinions, meant the by-election would provide a good measure of public opinion on the government's policies. With 13,721 registered on the rolls (1096 more than at the 1931 general election), a heavy voter turnout was anticipated.

A red-letter day

Despite the wet weather, polling proceeded smoothly throughout the day and was largely without incident, apart from a minor disruption when several Labour supporters assisting in the by-election had their names taken by police for breaching the Electoral Act 1927 by wearing badges with a photograph of McCombs on the front and the phrase 'Vote for Mrs McCombs' on the back.[25] In anticipation of large crowds gathering, within only minutes of the polls closing at seven o'clock the results were posted on a large display board specially erected over the main doors of the Press office in Christchurch, as well as being broadcast over loudspeakers in Cathedral Square. In Lyttelton the results were posted on the windows of the Press office on Oxford Street where a loudspeaker had been installed on the veranda. The returns from the Chatham Islands were sent by wireless and arrived 22 minutes after the polls closed; and in under an hour and a half, apart from 483 absentee, postal and seamen's votes, the results were known: McCombs 6080, Freeman 3480, Hills 263. McCombs' majority of 2600 votes was larger than any majority her late husband had achieved in his 20 years in Parliament; she had outpolled him in all but one polling place, with her greatest majorities in Woolston, Lyttelton and Heathcote, and she had outpolled her nearest rival in 16 of the 28 polling places.

Flush with the news of her victory, McCombs made her way with Labour leader Harry Holland, member for Christchurch South Ted Howard and prominent social worker and fellow member of the Hospital Board Teresa Green to the balcony of Warner's Hotel in Cathedral Square to address the crowd of 2000 gathered below. Much to the consternation of those assembled, the lift stopped and jammed for about three minutes just below the first floor. When it eventually restarted it descended faster than usual, coming to a stop with the heads of the passengers just visible above the level of the ground floor. Deciding on the safer option, the group took the stairs up to the balcony and were greeted with long cheering from the crowd, many of whom had been waiting in the wind, rain and biting cold for more than an hour. Using a loudspeaker, McCombs announced, 'This is one of the proudest as well as one of the saddest days of my life. I owe my position today first to my sister, who taught me the principles of Radical politics, and then to my husband, who encouraged and helped me through the whole of our married life together.'²⁶ Acknowledging it was a red-letter day for the women of New Zealand, she said she was glad to know that the first woman elected to the Parliament of New Zealand was a member of the Labour Party, because it had always stood for equal rights of citizenship for men and women. She endorsed the view that the result showed clearly that electors were not prepared to endorse the policies of the present government which were daily bringing fresh difficulties to business and farming communities and to the working classes, and that they did not agree with the government's decision to lengthen its term of office for an additional year.

After thanking all those who had voted for her and all who had worked for her, McCombs passed the loudspeaker to Freeman, who was given a noisy reception but managed to say a few words before calling for three cheers for Mrs McCombs. By then the jubilant crowds were calling for Holland to speak and completely drowned out Hills, who congratulated himself for having made political history and for a wonderful performance at the polls. As Holland took the loudspeaker, he received a tremendous ovation. He claimed the day was a victory for Labour, for women, and for the unemployed, and a smashing defeat for the coalition. Renewed cheering accompanied the announcement of the result, with further speeches from five other Labour MPs. Interviewed immediately after the crowd had dispersed McCombs said, 'I am the proudest woman in New Zealand tonight, but when the excitement of this wonderful day is over I shall be the humblest. I do hope that the women of New Zealand will realise that where they are concerned, and where the welfare of all men, women, and children is concerned, I shall be their representative first. I hope that where there are people who suffer, or are in trouble at any time, they will forget that I am a member of the Labour party, and remember that I am a woman.'²⁷ The group proceeded to a packed Returned Soldiers' Association hall in Lyttelton. By the time McCombs reached her car to return home to Sumner, ropes had been fastened to it and a crowd of admirers pulled the vehicle around the main streets of the port.

On news of the result, Acting Prime Minister Coates sent an ungracious telephone message to the Press office: 'The contest is over, and the winning candidate is to be congratulated both on her handsome win and on being the first woman to gain Parliamentary honours in New Zealand. The electors of Lyttelton have preferred the illusionary and airy promises of the Labour party and its speakers, involving violent inflationary measures irrespective of their consequences rather than the policy of paying our way and aiming insistently for a budgetary balance within a reasonable period. I desire to congratulate Mr Freeman upon the excellent fight he has put up. He has done all that could be expected of any candidate.'[28]

McCombs' success was heralded in the newspapers with headlines such as 'Member at Last: Dominion takes the plunge'[29] and 'The First Woman Member: Mrs McCombs deserves the honour.'[30] Her win was a victory for all women and an event of historic significance: 'Not Lyttelton only, nor Christchurch, nor Canterbury but all New Zealand will watch Mrs McCombs' parliamentary career with a genuine hope that she may find it full of opportunity to serve according to her truest wisdom.'[31] There were many public tributes to her personal attributes and capabilities, and the editor of the *Press* asserted that her opponents and supporters alike would agree that 'no other woman has prepared herself for this long-delayed triumph by so thorough a discipline of study and public service.'[32] The editor of the *Stratford Evening Post*, who had followed her campaign assiduously, declared, 'A pioneer in every sense of the word, it is fitting that Mrs Elizabeth Reid McCombs takes her place as the first woman in the House of Representatives. No woman in the Dominion has a greater right to this honour, whether the measure be applied to service or native ability, and New Zealand women will have no cause to be ashamed of the fact that Mrs McCombs is their first direct representative in the Government of the country which led the way in granting the female franchise.'[33]

Congratulatory telegrams flooded in from women and women's organisations throughout New Zealand. Ellen Melville, as president of the Auckland branch of the NCW, said 'it was fortunate that the first woman elected to Parliament should be one of such undoubted capacity and experience in public work, and one who would be able to convince the public that women were as well suited as men for Parliamentary work.'[34] Blanche Carnachan, former dominion president of the council and a past member of the Auckland Unemployed Women's Emergency Committee, was delighted; McCombs, she said, 'was the right kind of woman to be elected': 'It had now been proved that her worth had been recognised not only by women (who had long known it), but by men.'[35] Hilda Northcroft, who was active in the Reform Party's women's auxiliaries, commented that it was appropriate that Canterbury, 'which was a pioneer in all women's movements', should send the first woman to Parliament.[36] One message was conspicuous by its absence: the mayor of Auckland declared the motion lost on a technicality for the Auckland City Council to forward to Mrs McCombs its congratulations on her being the first woman to gain parliamentary honours in New Zealand.[37]

In the post-election analysis, newspaper commentators interpreted McCombs' emphatic majority as a complete lack of confidence in – and a warning to – the coalition government. There were mixed views on the extent to which she had received a sympathy vote, but most people recognised that any sympathy vote would have been offset by the general prejudice against electing a woman to the Parliament, and was not sufficient to explain such a substantial majority. Likewise, her success could not be attributed solely to a strong Labour vote, as her majority suggested she had received support from previously non-Labour voters in the electorate. Labour's message during the campaign had been that a vote for McCombs would not change the composition of Parliament, and this effectively gave voters permission to cast their politics aside and respond to personal sympathy for the candidate, or to cast a vote against the coalition government rather than for either McCombs or the Labour Party. As one commentator put it, 'The win can be put down to two things – Mrs McCombs' ability, and dissatisfaction with the Government'.[38]

The issue of whether the government should have contested the by-election resurfaced. In congratulating McCombs on her success, the United Party member for Eden, Arthur Stallworthy, said the actions of the government in contesting the seat were deeply resented by women's organisations throughout New Zealand and that it was a 'grave blunder' on the government's part to give the impression they wished to deny women direct representation in government. The result showed that this tactic had backfired, with women turning to the Labour Party to achieve their goal. Stallworthy suggested it would have been 'infinitely better for those honourable gentlemen to have figuratively laid their cloaks over the muddy path of party politics, and given a welcoming hand to this forerunner of other ladies who will come into politics'.[39] But as another member commented, 'there is a greater satisfaction in entering the House after a decisive victory over a formidable opponent than in being allowed to sit here as the result of a walk-over'.[40]

Immediately following news of McCombs' success, some writers to the newspapers turned their attention to the 'interesting complications' her election posed for procedures in Parliament. The vice-regal speech read at the opening of each session of Parliament for nearly 80 years began with the words: 'Honourable gentlemen of the Legislative Council and gentlemen of the House of Representatives' – and this would need to be changed. Would McCombs, as a matter of courtesy, be invited to take her late husband's seat in the front row of the Opposition bench or would they readjust the seating plan to leave a back-bench vacancy for the new member? As had been the case when Lady Astor first entered the British House of Commons, there was a great deal of speculation as to whether Mrs McCombs would wear a hat in the House: the rules of the House provided that any member may wear a hat while seated but must remain uncovered when speaking. With Parliament due to meet in one week's time, it would not be long before these questions were answered.

A lady in the House

On the morning of 21 September 1933, Elizabeth McCombs travelled from Christchurch to Wellington, where she was met with a constant stream of callers and congratulatory messages. She was photographed with a group of her colleagues in the Labour whip's rooms, and then had some time to prepare for the afternoon's formal proceedings in the room allotted to her by the speaker in the old section of Parliament House. Dull showery weather did not dampen the expectation of the large crowds that assembled in Parliament Grounds to witness the pomp and ceremony of the arrival of the vice-regal party for the opening of the twenty-fourth Parliament of New Zealand. Governor-General Lord Bledisloe inspected the guard of honour before proceeding to the Legislative Council Chamber to deliver the Speech from the Throne.

When the House of Representatives assembled, McCombs and the prime minister's wife Emma Forbes were presented with a bouquet of crimson flowers by the speaker of the Legislative Council, Sir Walter Carncross. Dressed in a tailored heather-brown costume and without a hat,⁴¹ McCombs 'created a splendid impression, comporting herself with dignity and charm, and displaying no sign of nervousness, nor of excessive assurance'.⁴² She was greeted with a round of spontaneous applause which she acknowledged with a smile and a bow before taking the seat formerly occupied by her husband in the front Opposition benches, which had been adorned with beautiful bouquets of tulips. Prime Minister Forbes immediately crossed the floor, warmly took her hand to express his congratulations, and welcomed her to the Assembly. He was followed by Leader of the Reform Party Gordon Coates and other members of Cabinet, who formed a line to shake her hand. She then joined in the procession to the Legislative Council where Lord Bledisloe opened his speech with the traditional greeting, 'Honourable gentlemen of the Legislative Council and members of the House of Representatives'.⁴³

After the governor-general's speech, the clerk of writs formally announced the outcome of the Lyttelton by-election and, amid warm applause from the crowded galleries and corridors, McCombs was escorted to the foot of the Speaker's Chair by Labour whips Edwin Howard and Dan Sullivan, where she took the oath of allegiance by affirmation⁴⁴ and was sworn in by Sir Charles Stratham in front of her 79 male colleagues. Later, when the House rose, she was the centre of attraction with members from all sides wishing her well. That evening she was entertained at a social in her honour at the Trades Union Hall, where she delighted those present with the news that she had received messages of congratulations from every part of New Zealand, including one from 'the uttermost backblocks' that read, 'The angels in Heaven rejoice, and the foundations of Hell quiver', to which she added, 'That is the spirit we want throughout New Zealand, and I believe we are going to get it.'⁴⁵ Reflecting later on the momentous occasion, she said,

> *It is difficult to form a clear impression of Parliament from the inside on such an occasion. One cannot, of course, help being impressed by the solemnity of the opening prayer, and the formalities of the Lower House, prior to the ceremony of the entrance of the Black Rod bearing the summons from the Governor-General.*
>
> *The friendly congratulations of members of the House, including the Prime Minister and all other Ministers, took away any sense of aloof-*

ness that might otherwise have embarrassed one; and in taking part in the procession of members to the Legislative Chamber, I felt that I walked not as one woman, but as the representative of many women throughout New Zealand.

There is dignity, colour and historic charm in the ceremonial of the Upper House, surrounding the presentation by His Excellency the Governor-General of the Speech from the Throne. Sitting in the quiet of the chamber, with my fellow members of Parliament about me, pride in the wonderful honour that has been conferred upon me was tempered by a sense of the responsibility that is now mine.

Following upon the return of members to the Lower Chamber, the swearing-in ceremony took place. This was brief and dignified. Mr Speaker read the declaration of the poll, his deep, resonant tones imparting an air of great importance to the occasion. After this the affirmation was made, and the signature attached to the necessary document. Then the House settled down to business, which to me was very like local body business on a larger scale. With the presentation of petitions and of questions, I began to feel more at home.

The whole occasion has had for me a glamour and a deep interest that I shall not soon forget, and that will colour all my future days in Parliament – days when my desk will not be heaped with flowers, and when perhaps I shall not be so cordially received by my fellow members.[46]

She later revealed she had received some interesting gifts to mark the occasion: a cure for colds, some verses, and an art union ticket in her name – which she found amusing given her stance against lotteries and art unions.

It is difficult to imagine what Elizabeth McCombs must have felt and thought as she sat in her husband's former seat in the House a few days later when the prime minister rose to formally move a tribute, 'That this House records its high sense of the faithful services rendered to New Zealand by the late Mr James McCombs, a Member of the House of Representatives, and respectfully tenders to his widow the assurance of its sincere sympathy in her bereavement.'[47] The next speaker, Harry Holland, made the poignant observation of Jim McCombs:

If it is true that the spirit lives when the body has moulded into dust – if to-day from some Elysian field, Olympic height, or eternal Holy City he looks down upon what is happening here – it will be with a supreme joy that his most ardent wish will have been fulfilled. It is fitting that she who was his helpmate in life and to whom he owed so much of his success should come to represent in this honourable House the people he loved and served. Fitting, too, that she should occupy the place he filled with such outstanding capacity and distinction.[48]

Jim McCombs' friend and colleague Dan Sullivan spoke of him as 'easily one of the bravest men who ever held a seat in this House' and 'one of the most lovable men we have ever had in Parliament'.[49] One by one his colleagues stood up and attested to his ability and integrity and, above all, to his having been a man of principle.

Later that evening Elizabeth McCombs attended a 'strictly non-political' reception at the Pioneer Club in Wellington with representatives from more than 50 women's organisations to celebrate the advent of women into Parliament.[50] Among the speakers were Annie McVicar, who said that Mrs McCombs had served her apprenticeship 'well and gracefully, and had earned the respect of every woman in New Zealand who knew anything about public work'; Mary Richmond, the first woman to sit on a public body in New Zealand; and Margaret (Maggie) Magill, the first woman president of the New Zealand Educational Institute, who spoke of the honour all women felt in her achievement, as well as the need for women of New Zealand to be realistic in their expectations of her as 'progress might necessarily be slow'.[51] Elizabeth McCombs told the women present that she had received over a thousand letters congratulating her on her achievement, from women of every shade of political opinion and every religious denomination. She was presented with flowers from the WCTU and from the Pioneer Club and the evening was marked by songs and recitations.

The following day the Address in Reply debate resumed in the House, followed by Holland as leader of the Opposition moving the traditional motion of no confidence in the government and presenting the Opposition's critique of government policies. In accordance with tradition, McCombs, as the only new member of Parliament, seconded the motion; she rose to speak for the first time with the simple sentence, 'I second the amendment',[52] while reserving her right to speak later. That opportunity was to come on the evening of 28 September, but an unexpected turn of events almost upset the arrangement whereby she would have pride of place in the evening's list of speakers. The Independent member for Wellington Suburbs proposed a second amendment to the motion of no confidence, calling for a reversal of the government's high exchange policy which, in his view, was having disastrous effects on the business community. Another member seconded this motion which, had it proceeded to a division, would – to the embarrassment of the Labour Party – have resulted in Holland's amendment being removed from the Order Paper. The surprise tactical manoeuvre led to a confused delay in proceedings, heated exchanges, and accusations from the Leader of the Opposition that regardless of whether this had been staged by the government or was due to lack of knowledge of the procedure of the House, it was playing the government's game. After consultation with the whips and party leaders, the speaker ruled that the official programme would continue, and the new member could present her maiden speech.

Spectators in the gallery joined in the hearty applause that greeted McCombs as she took the floor but, given the significance of the occasion, the speaker excused this breach of parliamentary rules. A special parliamentary reporter described the scene:

> It would have been a severe ordeal for any new member to rise to begin a maiden speech in such an agitated atmosphere and it is to the credit of Mrs McCombs that she acquitted herself most creditably.
>
> Beneath the gaze of the crowded galleries – many ladies had to be accommodated in the overflow gallery – and in the presence of a remarkably high attendance of 68 members of the House Mrs McCombs, a slight brown-costumed figure, was called on by Mr Speaker. If she had any qualms of nervousness she concealed them admirably and within a few minutes she was speaking with the unhurried precision of an old campaigner.[53]

The reporter noted that Mrs McCombs proved a joy to the Hansard recorders as she spoke clearly, slowly and concisely, flavouring her speech with mots justes and humorous anecdotes.

In her maiden speech, McCombs began by expressing her sincere thanks for the kind reception she had been accorded by members of the House.

She acknowledged that they had established a very good working basis. She then issued a challenge to her parliamentary colleagues: she would be failing in her duty, she told them, if she did not take the first opportunity presented to bring the prime minister and members of the government the message that the great majority of electors in the Lyttelton electorate had expressed great dissatisfaction with the administration of the government.[54]

Reiterating many of the issues raised in her election addresses, she canvassed matters of unemployment, education and community services and cited many actual cases of individuals and families who were disadvantaged by the government's policies. There was 'keen competition' for the honour of granting her extension of time,[55] and she went on to mention reforms that women's societies had been advocating for many years; she commended the government for introducing a bill to raise the age of marriage, but stressed the urgent need for women police, particularly in the large cities, to protect women, children and young people of both sexes. In her closing comments she quoted an old saying, 'Satan finds some mischief still for idle hands to do', and said she hoped honourable members on the government benches would 'lay that to their hearts'.[56] This brought a smile from the prime minister's face and a quiet assertion, 'We will,'[57] which prompted a Labour member to comment, 'You've softened him' – as she sat down to another round of applause.[58]

Members from both sides of the House complimented her on her speech and the sincerity with which it was delivered. The member for Christchurch South Ted Howard said no one could have listened to her speak on unemployment 'without being impressed with the cool, calm way in which she laid bare the troubles of her sex'.[59] After congratulating her on being the first woman to sit in the House the member from Patea said that having had the pleasure of listening to maiden speeches by women members in the British Parliament, 'for matter and the way in which it was delivered the speech of our first lady member in New Zealand compared very favourably with any of them. It was a womanly speech, and I think we all admire a womanly woman.'[60] Political reporters compared her maiden speech favourably to those of her male counterparts. The parliamentary reporter for the *Press* noted that 'Every sentence she started she also finished, and that is a distinction that belongs not to all members of the House,'[61] and another described her speech as 'a reasoned address, characterised by fluency and a neat marshalling of facts, and relieved by subtle thrusts'.[62] They also noted that she had a larger vocabulary than the average male member.[63]

One member of the government who was not there to congratulate her after her maiden speech was Gordon Coates, leader of the Reform Party; he had listened to her for only about 10 minutes before leaving the Chamber.

Large shoes to fill

The parliamentary reporter for the *Press* expressed confidence that Elizabeth McCombs would be as valuable to the Labour Party as her husband had been. Her value would be of a different kind, though, as she brought a fresh outlook and represented new interests: 'she can deal with the sentimental side of unemployment and poverty, and deal with it impressively, where a man would fail'.[64] Her first speech had been impressive and had even provoked a Cabinet minister to give his undertaking that issues she had raised would be carefully examined. With high expectations on both sides of the House for her to make a difference, her speech had left no doubt that she was committed to bringing a strong and insistent voice to the debating chamber on social issues in general and on matters that directly affected women and families.

Over the years many male politicians had been optimistic that women members of Parliament would have a focus and influence on legislation around social issues. In the debates just prior to the passing of the Women's Parliamentary Rights Act 1919, Labour member for Wellington Central Peter Fraser had suggested that the agendas of women members would focus on issues such as how the resources of the country could be developed and distributed in ways that ensured that every man, woman and child would be sufficiently provided for, so that every individual had the opportunity to be the best they could be; how to ensure children were not born in hovels; how to ensure that widows and orphans would be economically secure; and how to ensure that everyone, no matter where they lived, would have proper access to education and health services. He would no doubt have been heartened by the clear signals McCombs gave of her political priorities.

Elizabeth McCombs was aware that her late husband had left very large shoes to fill. With reminders of his legacy at every turn, she lost no time in demonstrating she was up for the challenge. On the day after her election she had sent a telegraph to the acting minister of education requesting that his department remit the fee of 10 shillings for the children of relief workers and others in similar circumstances to sit the Proficiency Examination which, if they passed it, would entitle them to at least two years' free secondary schooling under the Free Place system,[65] and that late entries for the examination be accepted. On the day she was sworn in she placed two questions on the Order Paper, one relating to the unemployment of young men, women and girls, and the other to the raising of the age of marriage. And on the day she presented her maiden speech she tabled a question on the law in respect of New Zealand women retaining their nationality when they married aliens.

Alongside her parliamentary and local government responsibilities, McCombs maintained a very busy public profile and was in constant demand as a speaker at various community events. Whether it was opening the annual sale of work by the Women's Working Party of the Terrace Congregational Church in Wellington, or events in her own electorate such as opening the Redcliffs Croquet Club season, the garden party in aid of the YMCA Ladies' Queen Carnival in Mount Pleasant, the Sumner–Redcliffs Rowing Club, or the bring-and-buy fair at the Opawa School, she made herself available and always had something specific to the occasion to share. Businesses tried to cash in on her popularity: an advertisement for agricultural equipment appeared in the *Press* that read, 'MRS McCOMBS'S MAJORITY. More than 2000 majority was the vote for the Dominion's First Lady MP, but that is nothing to the majority of farmers who prefer Boothmac Haymaking Machinery, Pumps and Pumping Appliances'.[66]

Understandably there was a great deal of interest in her personal career, especially her experiences in Parliament. At a meeting of the Lyceum Club in Wellington she spoke freely of the difficulties she encountered as a woman in public life, but her message was positive and encouraging: 'the key to success ... was hard work and persistence in effort, with, if possible, a special study of some particular subject'. Her choice of subject was electricity because 'by cheapening electrical equipment in the home she could ease the burden of other women'.[67] At the business girls' reception hosted by the YWCA Business and Professional Women's Round Table Club in Wellington she spoke of the respect she had for all business and professional women, and admitted that one thing she personally lacked was business training. She told the young women present that she had always respected efficiency and thoroughness and that she had found businesswomen to be efficient housewives because they had trained minds. She commended the club for developing women who were good citizens and well equipped to take part in public affairs.[68]

In her public appearances, her respect and care for working people was always foremost. A typical example was when she attended the ceremony to turn the first sod at the Soldiers' Settlement Scheme at Sandilands on the New Brighton tramway route in Christchurch. She told those present that during the war years she had sat in the gallery of the House of Representatives and listened to the promises made by members of Parliament. She stressed that all who had served their country were changed by the experience, and often it took years for the scars to be revealed. On the topic of the Settlement Scheme, which was to provide 91 semi-detached cottages for returned soldiers who had become prematurely aged through their war experiences, she urged that the work should be carried out under trades union conditions and rates of wages. She gave assurance she would do whatever was in her power to help the scheme; and, true to her word, the following month she raised these issues in the debate on the government's financial statements.

There were many Labour Party events, too, such as the mass demonstration at the Wellington Town Hall, organised shortly after she was elected, to protest against the government's financial policies. At a social and dance organised in her honour by the Lyttelton branch of the Labour Party, the president, J. Sargentina, said he hoped it would not be long before Mrs McCombs would become the first woman Cabinet minister in the southern hemisphere. Their gift of a bright red leather travelling case with her initials stamped in gold was well chosen, as she regularly travelled by ferry steamer between Lyttelton and Wellington. Presenting her with the gift, Mr Sargentina joked that just as Florence Nightingale was known around the world as the lady with the lamp, she might be known as the lady with the red bag. McCombs was delighted with the gift; she said she had 'never had anything so swell in my life' and that people would have no trouble working out what political party she supported.[69]

McCombs confided to her Labour Party colleagues in Lyttelton that she enjoyed her life in Wellington but that she felt like a third person looking on at herself working.⁷⁰ Several weeks after she took her seat in Parliament, when she was asked at the Taranaki Federation of Women's Institutes half-yearly meeting in Patea how it felt to be the first woman in Parliament, her response was telling: 'I do not feel that I am "A" woman, but that I represent ALL women.' The meeting was the largest gathering of women ever held in Patea and the dominion president of the federation, Mrs Kelso, said that Mrs McCombs' election had demonstrated that women had finally realised they did not have to imitate anyone in how they voted. Mrs Kelso commented on McCombs' decision to enter politics as a Labour Party candidate, and expressed her belief that if women had their way, they would want to go into Parliament independently and tackle the broad issues. She assured those present that while Mrs McCombs would need to vote with her party, women could be reassured that she would always stand on her principles.⁷¹ Journalist Jessie Mackay, in her retrospective article on the status of women in 1933, confirmed McCombs' wider constituency: 'Her lifelong service to women and humanity uplifts her sweeping victory from the welter of partisanship; though very faithful to her party, she unquestionably takes New Zealand for her electorate; wherever women need to be spoken for, they are her constituents.'⁷²

In Parliament, McCombs was keen to sit on house committees that her husband Jim had sat on, and within a few weeks she was appointed a member of the Committee to Examine Public Accounts and the Local Bills Committee. A defining feature of her contributions to the debates in Parliament was the way she consistently drew on her own experiences as a social worker to bring a community perspective to her speeches. She made it clear she was representing the views of a wide range of women beyond those in her constituency, and she held her fellow MPs accountable for the positions they took in debates on social issues. When the Invalid Pensions Bill was introduced, for example, she informed her colleagues that the bill made provision for the relief of 'the most unfortunate and the most pathetic of the applicants for charity and for relief that come before our public bodies', and she added that the members of charitable institutions and of hospital board benevolent committees 'look with some interest and anxiety towards this House to see what is to be the effect of the appeals that are made in connection with this measure'.⁷³ To emphasise her point, she cited actual cases that had come before the hospital boards where sickness was the cause of destitution. 'I can imagine no worse position,' she said, 'than that of a woman in whose home the breadwinner is an invalid, who, to save her sense of dignity, to save her self-respect, goes out to work so as to support her sick husband and a number of little children by her pitiful earnings; and who, in addition to doing that, has to undertake the care of the children, the care of the home, and the nursing of the husband.' In a direct challenge to her parliamentary colleagues she added, 'If any honourable member thinks that the burden of that woman is not too great, well, I would like him to stand up and let us see him.'[74]

McCombs constantly reminded MPs of their accountability to women constituents. When the Marriage Amendment Bill, which would raise the minimum age of marriage to 16 for both sexes, was introduced in October 1933, she informed members of the House that the bill had been instigated by the NCW and that 'there is not a dissentient voice among the women's societies with regard to this question of the raising of the marriage age', and she put her fellow MPs on notice that 'the women of the Dominion are determined that they will not rest until this measure is passed through both Houses of this Parliament'. She welcomed the bill as 'a very distinct step forward in the reform of our social laws', and said that the absence of law in New Zealand on this matter was a blot and a disgrace on the country.[75] She spoke out on the need for the state to make provision for the children of deserted wives, and she spoke poignantly of the difficulties for men and women in asking for charity and of seeing strong men break down when they were driven to this.

Throughout her term, McCombs made regular use of urgent questions to hold the government and individual members accountable. Following through on employment issues she had signalled in her maiden speech, she asked the minister of employment if he would take steps to exclude women workers from the levy for relief workers because they had received practically no assistance from the fund. She spoke of 'the indignation of the people at the Government's incapacity and ineptitude in handling the unemployment problem'. She challenged all members of the government, but particularly members of Cabinet, to try to picture to themselves what it must be like for a man or a woman who has had a decent home and been living in the respect of the community, whose children attended school on an equal footing with every other child in the school, to now find themselves with bailiffs at the door and being driven from pillar to post in order to have a roof over their heads. She asked them to imagine the position of a woman who had been able to maintain her self-respect up to the point when her husband lost his job, now having to line up and beg at the door of the relief depot 'for a few cast-off pieces of clothing, or a couple of shillings worth of groceries'.[76] She went so far as to accuse the government of being 'a composite dictatorship',[77] claiming it had betrayed the people and had thrown out practically every democratic ideal, and she criticised the government's intention to impose duties on New Zealand manufacturers: the government, she said, was deliberately setting out 'to make human sacrifices to propitiate the gods', with workers, women and children as the sacrifice.[78]

McCombs' Christian socialism and her belief in the responsibility of the government to provide for individuals and communities in need was evident in many of the causes she spoke out on in Parliament. Whether it was the exorbitant interest rates charged for hire purchase, the proposal to reduce the customs and excise duties on beer, flagrant breaches of the sale of liquor after hours laws, or any proposed measures that compromised the democratic rights of the people, she was a consistent voice for the people. As she had promised in her maiden speech, she was committed to holding the government to account. She frequently interjected in debates; she claimed the government was not in full possession of the facts of the matter at hand, and recounted examples of the detrimental effects of government policies on real people. At one point she even suggested the minister of finance should consider going away to reflect on his sins and not return to Parliament.

Her commitment to be a representative for all women was unflinching. Following up on an issue constantly raised by the NCW, she questioned the minister of police on his intention to introduce a measure to provide for the appointment of women police, and on the issue of pay equity she asked the minister why police matrons who had responsibilities equal to those of any man in a similar position were paid at a lower rate than the lowest paid constable. When a petition protesting unfair treatment of women teachers was presented to Parliament, she spoke of the extraordinary action on the part of the government in subjecting women teachers to additional taxation, and stated that women in the teaching profession suffered the indignity of being treated as though they were of less value to the community than men. This was wrong: women did equal work to men, worked more efficiently than men, were paid at a lower rate, and suffered in both status and salary.[79]

Another issue that had been discussed in the NCW over many years was the need for recognition of women's independent nationality. This had come to wider public attention after the 1925 general election when the vote count for the Lyttelton seat (held by Jim McCombs) was tied, and the disqualification of the votes of four New Zealand-born women married to foreigners was debated in the press. The opportunity to make gains in this area arose in late 1934 when the British Nationality and Status of Aliens (in New Zealand) Amendment Bill was in committee in the House. Under the existing legislation, a New Zealand woman who married a foreigner took on the nationality of her husband. In committee, the minister of internal affairs added a new clause giving women in New Zealand married to aliens the power to declare their own nationality. McCombs thanked the minister for having met the wishes of women's organisations, and at the same time she stressed the principle that marriage should not be a grounds for penalising women. When another member expressed doubt about the wisdom of this move, McCombs accused him of 'living out of his time' and likened him to the poet who 'thought that a woman was born in a cage and that to leap from perch to perch was joy enough for any bird'.[80] She raised the matter of the working conditions of girls employed in abattoirs and freezing works and the lack of women inspectors.

At the local level McCombs was a dedicated electorate MP. She drew attention to the inadequate conditions and lack of training for girls at the borstal at Point Halswell Prison, and criticised the government's lack of action in assisting girls on their discharge. She raised issues such as the children of Woolston School being deprived of the services of the school dental clinic because their parents were unable to pay the fees, the urgent need for a radio installation at the Chatham Islands, and the desperate circumstances of single unemployed men in Lyttelton who were without work and sustenance, and she called on the government to provide urgent assistance. When the Defence Committee declined petitions from some of her local constituents for war pensions, she accused the government of no longer demonstrating sympathy towards those who had suffered during and after the war. She expressed disappointment that the Woolston Tanneries' request for an investigation by the government into its operations during the war years, with a view to having 25,000 pounds of overpaid income tax refunded, had been declined by the Public Petitions Committee. Unlike other tanneries that had profited by inflation during the war, the Woolston Tanneries had been controlled by the government and had suffered from a lack of profits during the war and deflation after the war. In McCombs' view this was yet another example of the government being unsympathetic to those who had provided a service to the government during the war.

Her reception in the House was certainly not all plain sailing. In her first month of office the accuracy of some of her statements on the government's unemployment schemes was questioned, and she was criticised by the member for Rangitikei, Alexander Stuart, for comments he considered to be insulting to farmers' wives. Although he could not remember the exact words McCombs had used, as representative of a farming constituency he said he could not accept her claim that farmers' wives were not looking after their employees adequately by keeping them properly housed and fed. He took umbrage at her suggestion that women from the cities be employed as inspectors in farming districts. He added, 'I regret that I have had to be the first to stand up and criticise the honourable member in this House, but so far as I am concerned, if the honourable member makes such statements, she will have to take her gruelling along with other honourable members in this House.'[81] McCombs responded by calling a point of order saying her comments had been misrepresented, and proceeded to carefully clarify what she had actually said. The press covered the incident in detail with headlines such as 'Mrs McCombs Rebuked' and 'Mrs McCombs Criticised'[82]. On another occasion criticisms she made in the House that the government was doing nothing to prepare and assist girls for their discharge from the borstal at Point Halswell Prison were challenged both within the House and in a letter to the editor of the *Evening Post* by the chairman of the Women's Borstal Association as being misinformed and calculated to do harm. Her response was the model of professionalism: in a letter to the editor she explained that the account printed in the newspaper of her speech in Parliament was very superficial and omitted any reference to the high compliment she had paid to the work of the ladies' committee and the refusal of the government to provide facilities for occupational training.

There were occasions when her efforts to influence proceedings in the

House were rebuffed. One attempt to amend a clause in a bill in committee was overturned by the chair, who said her proposed amendment did not make sense. When McCombs stood on her right as a member to propose the amendment again the chair again refused, saying the amendment would be 'absurd'. With no alternative she claimed a division on the clause as it stood but was defeated by 52 votes to four.[83] On another occasion her efforts to use a report from the Public Petitions Committee to try to further the aim of getting the government to appoint women police was rejected by a Labour colleague. In this case it was likely her relative lack of understanding of the protocols around acting on the recommendations in reports from the Public Petitions Committee that led to her suggestion being dismissed. But she was not averse to using her relative ignorance of parliamentary procedure to further her agendas, as was evident when she questioned what was really behind the Gaming Bill. She prefaced her statement with, 'I, as a new member of the House and one not well versed in the intricacies of the Standing Orders and the methods by which the business of the country is proceeded with, would like to be enlightened.' She then asked why 'the whole business of the country' was being held up because of the interests of the gaming lobby and 'just what standing these people have who are able to control matters in this House to such an extent'. When called to order she complained, 'We are being held up on every possible occasion by the Standing Orders of the House. They hem us in on every side.'[84]

Any dispensation made for her because of her sex was balanced by the respect she earned through her tenacity, good humour and eloquence in the debating chamber. When the Stock Remedies Bill was introduced by the government in July 1934, for example, McCombs was one of several Labour members who complained that the government was wilfully wasting time when there were urgent matters such as unemployment to address. As she started to recount a case of extreme hardship, the chairman of committees interrupted her to say that unless it was a very brief illustration she would have to be ruled out of order. Her response was greeted with laughter: 'I'll be very brief, sir. Women are seldom out of order. I ask you to bear with me. It now appears that pigs and cattle are more important in the eyes of the House than human beings ... I just thought I should like to let the House know, and the women of this country know, that I am still learning strange things here. Today marks a forward step in my Parliamentary education.'[85]

'The hours of work are long and the work is continuous'

Detractors of women being admitted to Parliament had claimed that women would not have the physical stamina to cope with the demanding hours and all-night sittings of the House. Initially, at least, McCombs was to prove them wrong. When she was interviewed after leaving the House at six o'clock in the morning after taking part in her first all-night sitting, she said, 'I quite enjoyed it. It did not tire me and I don't think I am showing any signs of weariness.'[86] Throughout the 15-hour sitting, during which she had left the Chamber for an interval of only one hour, she had maintained a lively interest in the debate and had not found it as onerous as long meetings on the Christchurch City Council. She found the discussion on national questions led to a wider and calmer view, and this was a welcome compensation from the heavier responsibilities of representing her electorate. As the parliamentary session was coming to a close just before Christmas in 1933, it was her exhausted male colleagues who were falling asleep on their benches at 10.30 in the morning. Members were under pressure to pass the government's Finance Bill, and the days had been long and exhausting. When McCombs remarked that members were not in a fit condition to deal with such important legislation she was met with a chorus of disapproval. Despite having only 13 weeks' parliamentary experience, she was undeterred and took the government to task for a clause hidden away in a seemingly inoffensive measure that dealt with earthquake insurance that was of great importance to the working classes. In an impassioned speech she accused the government of assisting their friends at the expense of the workers by denying workers their right to compensation, giving them no right to defend their interests, and giving their representatives in Parliament very little opportunity to gather evidence or to consult with their constituents on the matter. She could not believe that any government, no matter how bad, could wish to inflict such an injustice.

Reflecting on her first full year in the House McCombs was optimistic: 'Twelve months' experience of Parliament at work has increased my faith in the democratic principles of the Labour Party, and in the parliamentary institution. Those who paint pictures of Parliament as a kind of political bear-garden can have very little idea of the real work that is done or of the way in which it is done. The earnestness and sincerity of members of all parties have impressed me.'[87] She described the work of Parliament as much like the work she had performed for many years in local body politics: while questions were 'thrashed out in debate on the floor of the House' most of the essential work was done in committee and it was there that the administrative abilities of members came to light. She saw there was room for efficiencies such as carrying out more of the administrative work in committees of the House. The demands on individual members were onerous and she admitted that while Parliament was sitting the hours were long and the work was continuous: 'One is facing problems all day long, and even one's letters often contain as many problems as there are letters.'[88] She described Parliament as 'something like a school, in which all members are at the same time teachers and scholars. Everyone is anxious to teach, but all are not willing to learn'.[89] As a member of the Opposition, she said, 'Naturally I disagree with the views of the majority, and feel that their efforts are ill-directed, but that cannot detract from my recognition of their sincerity. After all I feel that we are here to try to convert them to more rational views.'[90] She concluded, 'I have greatly enjoyed my first year in Parliament and it has been a privilege to have shared work with my colleagues in one of the most difficult and most interesting periods in the history of our country. Every courtesy has been extended to me in the House.'[91]

As the reporter who interviewed her commented, she was by no means physically robust and had stood up to the tiring routine of parliamentary work with determination but, having suffered 'indifferent health' all her life, it had not taken long for the strain of her work commitments to take a toll.[92] At the end of her first session in Parliament in December 1933 she admitted to being too weary to even go on a holiday; instead she attended to her rock garden on her hillside home in Sumner and spent a few shillings on detective stories that she read one after another. Although some 'ungallant critics' had predicted that once she was in Parliament little would be heard from her, she had taken part in the general discussions to a considerably greater extent than most other new members and was one of the most consistent Labour speakers.[93] Unlike others, she had never breached parliamentary protocol by reading her speeches, and while she had consistently followed the party line on issues, she had shown herself to be an independent thinker and had held her ground, even on the occasion where she had proposed an amendment that was not supported by her fellow Labour members.

From practically her first day in Parliament McCombs would arrive to her desk piled high with letters from people throughout New Zealand making requests of her time and services. That she read and responded to every letter was testament to the conscientious way she discharged all her parliamentary duties, be it sitting on committees, preparing and delivering speeches or meeting with deputations. As time passed, though, it was impossible to ignore the fact that the demands were taking a toll on her physical health. Colleagues, officers and attendants in the House assisted her when possible, knowing she often worked in her room in the Parliamentary Buildings long after it was believed she had retired for the evening. Her time outside Parliament was equally as heavily committed to activities in her Lyttelton electorate with the usual rounds of opening fêtes and flower shows, addressing local organisations and speaking at various women's organisations, including the annual conference of the NCW. By mid-1934 it was evident that the pressure of her commitments was too great, and something had to give. In addition to the weekly commute between her home in Sumner and Wellington when the House was in session, she had continued to serve on the Christchurch City Council, often presiding over meetings and attending functions when the mayor was unavailable. She was also chair of the Electricity Committee and a member of the Hospital Board, working on its Benevolence Committee, and a member of the Tramways Board and the Domains Board, and in November 1933 she had been re-elected president of the Sumner branch of the WCTU. With another parliamentary session about to begin, in June 1934 she resigned from the North Canterbury Hospital Board after 12 years of service. The following month she was granted four days' leave of absence from the House due to illness.

In August 1934 McCombs signalled her intention to introduce a bill to make it compulsory for courts to be closed during the hearing of domestic cases involving husbands, wives and children. The current law granted magistrates discretionary power to order the public to leave the court if they considered it was not in the public interest for those not connected with the case to be present. This discretion was not frequently exercised, and McCombs wanted it to be compulsory to exclude 'all such persons as are there merely out of curiosity or because they are morbid-minded'.[94] Ideally, special tribunes would deal with domestic cases along the lines of the domestic courts that operated in British Columbia and some of the American states, and her Destitute Persons Amendment Bill to close existing courts when dealing with these cases was a preliminary step toward that objective. If passed, the legislation would allow only parties to the action such as police officers and other such persons as the magistrate may admit to be present for domestic cases, and would prohibit publication of reports of these cases unless specifically permitted by the magistrate. Some members of the public took exception to the proposed legislation. A woman wrote to the editor of the *Evening Post* to express her disappointment that 'our first lady member would take this retrogressive step'; she thought that, while such cases were regrettable, they should not be hushed up, and she hailed 'a free and open Press' as a 'priceless possession'.[95] The Destitute Persons Amendment Bill was introduced in Parliament but did not proceed beyond its first reading.

In September 1934 McCombs was inadvertently the focus of a controversy that played out in the pages of the newspapers when 10 leading Arawa Māori left the House when she rose to speak. The delegation, comprised of members of Ngāti Whakaue, had been invited to take a seat in the public gallery after presenting a petition to the Native Affairs Committee. Newspapers reported conflicting accounts of the incident. The secretary of Te Akarana Maori Association explained that the incident occurred because Māori held very definite beliefs as to the place of women in social life, a place divorced from politics and public speaking. He stated that 'it was felt that by entering the province of the men, women must perforce neglect something in their own' and that 'the influence of women in anything was felt to be effeminising'; and he stressed that Māori still agreed with the Pākehā adage that 'the woman's place is in the home'.[96] Commenting on this, prominent Wellington businessman, patron and officeholder of many local clubs and organisations, and brother of the first Bishop of Aotearoa, H.D. Bennett (Te Arawa), confirmed that Māori and, more particularly, Arawa from the Rotorua district 'did not allow their womenfolk to enter an arena reserved for men', but added that 'it was quite a different matter if, as reported, a number of men from a tribe, after having entered Parliament House, presumably by invitation, there showed any feeling on the question'. In his view, an apology was due to Mrs McCombs 'as well as to countless women of both races who give their services in a common endeavour to lift humanity'. Bennett stated he was in a position to speak on behalf of a large section of the Arawa people and that, on their behalf, 'he entirely dissociated himself from the senseless action of the few Maoris concerned'. He sought to make due apology to the House, 'as a slur could not be confined to the lady member for Lyttelton'.[97] But the Minister of Native Affairs Sir Āpirana Ngata disputed Mr Bennett's version and the need for any apologies, and said he believed 'far too much has been made of the incident'. In Ngata's account, the Arawa Māori present had heard most of Mrs McCombs' speech and had left for other reasons, even though one Arawa kaumātua did express impatience at any woman being permitted to address Parliament. This, Ngata added, was understandable because in most tribes women were not expected to speak.[98]

With multiple versions of the incident being reported, a member of the Arawa group concerned entered the media fray to settle the facts of the matter. Reverend H.W. Munro was reported to have said, 'The story is quite fantastic and someone must have been using his imagination. There was no concerted movement of the Arawas present to leave the gallery, and nothing was further from our thoughts than discourtesy to Mrs McCombs. It is true that it is not the Arawa custom for women to speak on the marae, but we do not expect our customs to be observed on the marae of other people and would not be so discourteous as to take the action reported merely because our customs are not so observed.'[99] Munro's explanation of the incident was perfectly straightforward: having been invited to take a seat in the public gallery, the Ngāti Whakaue delegation listened to the debate for some time but, finding it not very interesting, they gradually left. He concluded that 'the whole story was a figment of the imagination of some person who had not taken the trouble to ascertain the facts'.[100]

McCombs' health problems returned in the new year. When Parliament resumed in mid-February she attended for the first week but was suffering from influenza. She was granted another period of leave due to ill health and was on extended leave from her position on the Christchurch City Council, having signalled her intention to not seek re-election. It was reported at the time that her doctor had advised her to withdraw from active public life for at least three months. Labour Party leader Michael Savage told the party conference on 23 April, 'there appears to be no doubt that her illness to a large extent resulted from the long hours and heavy strain involved in the execution of her Parliamentary duties. We join in wishing Mrs McCombs a very speedy recovery, and in assuring her of a hearty "welcome home", not only from her colleagues, but from all members of Parliament, when she again takes her seat in the House.'[101]

Elizabeth McCombs did not return to the House. In the early hours of 7 June 1935, at the age of 61, she passed away in hospital in Wellington. The newspapers reported that throughout her time in Parliament her admirers and supporters had watched anxiously as this indomitable woman became more fragile with each public appearance: 'the gallant spirit that had carried her so far in her brilliant career was undaunted, but many saw that her strength was being overtaxed – that she was sacrificing herself on the altar of service to her fellows'.[102] Flags were flown at half-mast across the country and tributes filled the pages of the nation's newspapers.

Of the tributes that flowed, none was more poignant than that of Dan Sullivan, then mayor of Christchurch and sitting member for the Avon electorate. He had been sitting talking with her in hospital just a few evenings earlier; her body was emaciated and frail, but her spirit was strong, and her mind was clear. Although he had been informed by the doctors that she would not live long, she had expressed confidence that she would rally and that she was not done yet. Shocked to have lost such a well-respected bench-mate, so soon after the death of his dear friend and comrade Jim McCombs, Sullivan paid tribute to her dedication and responsiveness to her constituents. So, too, did Elizabeth Taylor, widow of Tommy Taylor, who had known Elizabeth McCombs since she was a young girl involved in the WCTU when McCombs was secretary of the Children's Aid Society, and had worked alongside her in the Progressive Liberal Association. Taylor said she had always worked for the underdog and was always dependable. She spoke of how fortunate the women of New Zealand were that their first representative in Parliament was a woman of such calibre. She believed there were women capable of carrying on the work in keeping with McCombs' ideals, women who would 'seek power not through personal ambition or the love of power itself, but to strive for the placing of home life and the welfare of their children on a securer basis'.[103]

Elizabeth McCombs' death was a great loss to the Labour Party. The president of the Lyttelton branch described her passing as not merely a loss but 'a calamity which will affect the whole community'. Michael Savage said,

'Her passing has created a gap in the ranks of the Labour party that will be hard to fill. She was not only the first woman to occupy a seat in the Parliament of New Zealand, but also, by her outstanding ability, both in the House and out, she made a very effective reply to those who maintained that women are not the equals of men, either in local or national government.'[104] Ted Howard was a colleague who was particularly well placed to comment on her achievements in the political arena, and his tribute was raw and honest and heartfelt:

> *Elizabeth McCombs was a loyal, lovable, and motherly woman. The women of New Zealand could not have had a better type as a pioneer. Her home was all that the word home means ... As a candidate she was ideal. She told her own story in her own way, but she was a splendid candidate from an organiser's point of view. Never late, never too early, but almost to the tick she stepped on to the platform cool, calm, and prepared. In Parliament she was the same. 'Fitted in,' are the best words to describe her – nothing petty, no pushing into the limelight, just ready when you wanted her. As one of the whips, I can say she was one of the best of the team.*[105]

On the morning of 10 June 1935, hundreds of people filed through the doors of the council chambers to pay their respects to her body lying in state. Cold weather and heavy rain did not deter the thousands who lined the route of the funeral procession to the Waimairi Cemetery. Cars in the official party lined up in front of the council chambers and in Gloucester Street, stretching along Manchester Street to the north and into Armagh Street. Three hundred trade unionists assembled in Latimer Square and were marshalled into ranks of four to take up their position in front of the hearse, along with employees of the Tramways Board, trade union leaders and members of the Woolston and Lyttelton branches of the Labour Party. It took more than 15 minutes for the last of the cars in the official cortège 'representative of all classes and creeds' to depart.[106] As they reached Christchurch Public Hospital the walking entourage drew to the side of the road and the motor procession continued along Riccarton Avenue to Riccarton Road and Straven Road, with pockets of public gathered along the entire route along Fendalton Road, Burnside Road and Grahams Road to the cemetery, where scores of cars were parked. Ted Howard's tribute said it all: 'She lived a splendid life and she died as she lived, facing the sun. She gave her life to the people – the people who loved her.'[107]

Elizabeth Reid McCombs was very clear that the achievement of becoming the first woman to sit as a member in the New Zealand Parliament was not a personal achievement but one of and for the women of New Zealand who had worked toward this goal for many decades. Likewise, she had a strong commitment to being a woman's – and every woman's – representative in Parliament. Her words at a reception held in her honour in her home city of Christchurch in November 1933 encapsulate the spirit of her all too brief parliamentary career: she was reported to have said, 'It was wonderful to be a representative of all classes and all shades of opinion', and that 'as a woman member of Parliament she would not only represent the women but the community, for in every department of public work women were no more important than men, but were equally as important as men, and the children's interests were more important than all'.[108]

*

Several factors contributed to Elizabeth McCombs being the first woman to take a seat in the New Zealand House of Representatives. New Zealand was still in the throes of the Great Depression and unemployment was in the tens of thousands. The policies of the sitting government had been very harsh, and people were suffering. The by-election for the Lyttelton seat was necessitated by the sudden death in office of Jim McCombs, the sitting member who had held the seat for Labour for 20 years. As his widow, Elizabeth McCombs undoubtedly attracted a sympathy vote but, besides the fact that there had never been a woman elected to Parliament in the country's history, there were many other influences working against her. There was still a mountain of general prejudice against women candidates and, although the seat had been held by Labour for 20 years it was by no means a safe seat; Jim McCombs' majority in the previous election had been only 32 votes and his runner-up Frederick Freeman had stood again as the coalition candidate in the by-election. There was also the issue of vote splitting, when a disgruntled Edward Hills stood as an Independent Labour candidate.

There were many factors in Elizabeth McCombs' favour. Granted she attracted a sympathy vote, but she also attracted the anti-government vote, the votes of electors who lacked confidence in government policies and of those who wanted to send a warning to the government to be on guard for the next general election. The coalition government had a substantial majority, which meant a vote for Labour would not change the government. Effectively, this gave voters permission to vote for the person and not be tied to party loyalties. Voting politics aside, Elizabeth McCombs had a solid reputation in her own right through her many years of civic service in Christchurch and, in the words of member of the Legislative Council Mark Cohen, she was 'a lady with pronounced political proclivities … who can hold her own with her male colleagues'.[109]

CONCLUSION

The 'ungallantly long hesitation'

And all this cock-a-doodling by masculine women and feminine men is because of the very regrettable but absolutely unimportant fact that a woman has been sent to Parliament from Lyttelton. What good or harm will that do? I hope it will be remembered in New Zealand history as an occasion on which an electorate in a burst of sentimentalism or a fit of absent-mindedness forgot itself and sent a woman to Parliament – a performance which the rest of the Dominion accepted as an object lesson of what should not be done by any sensible, self-respecting electorate. Mrs McCombs is the first woman in Parliament. I hope she will have the distinction of being the last and only one. — 'LORD OF CREATION', LETTER TO THE EDITOR, *PRESS*, 13 October 1933

I do not think it is at all likely, if this measure goes on the statute-book, that we shall have for years to come many lady members. When we do have them they will be few and far between. — WILLIAM PEMBER REEVES, MHR, 11 July 1894[1]

An object lesson

With the barrier of women achieving a seat in the House finally broken, there was renewed hope for success in women's parliamentary representation at the next general election. Postponed for a year in the hope of improvement in the economy,[2] the 1935 general election campaign was marked by strident opposition to the economic policies adopted by the coalition government in response to the Great Depression. Since the 1931 general election, the fall in export prices meant the coalition government had been operating on less than half its normal revenue: public works expenditure had been slashed, old age and war pensions had been reduced, family allowances had been abolished, and tens of thousands of a population of only one and a half million were unemployed. For those who were in paid work the situation was grim, too: minimum wage rates had been abolished, relief rates had been reduced, even public service wages had been cut by more than 10 percent. In a charged political climate, the Unemployed Workers Union membership had risen, and the Communist Party had increased its activity through very active women's committees. Although the recovery of export prices had led to unemployment numbers beginning to decrease by 1935, the momentum for political change that had been galvanised by the large-scale riots of unemployed three years earlier was evident throughout the election campaign. The stage appeared to be set for the acceptance of the need for women's voices in setting the nation back on the track of economic and social recovery.

Bolstered by the precedent set by the late Elizabeth McCombs, five women candidates contested the 1935 general election.[3] Elizabeth Knox Gilmer, seventh daughter of the late premier, Richard Seddon, had been approached by several organisations and political parties to seek nomination as a candidate for the Wellington North seat.[4] Rehutai Maihi's name[5] had been put forward by a local chieftainess Pepi Henare at a meeting at Utakura in the Hokianga as a possible Labour selection for the Northern Maori electorate.[6] Helen Black, wife of Robert Black, former mayor of Dunedin, was asked by the local executive of the Democrat Party[7] to contest the Dunedin Central seat. Elsie Andrews, president of the NCW and former president of the New Zealand Women Teachers' Association, announced her intention to contest the New Plymouth seat as an Independent candidate,[8] and Connie Rawcliffe stood as a candidate for the Communist Party in the Wellington East electorate.

Of the five women who stood, Gilmer's campaign attracted the greatest media coverage and she amassed the largest audiences at her rallies. As the campaign progressed political capital was made of her paternal political pedigree. Demonstrating her credentials to women voters, Gilmer said it would be in the national interest for there to be a few determined and sincere women in Parliament, and she stressed, as McCombs had always done, that women could balance the budget with the best of them. There was nothing, she insisted, that came before Parliament that did not concern the women of the country: 'In their households they are directly affected by public finance, by unemployment, and, indeed, by everything relating to public welfare.'[9] Gilmer came a creditable runner-up in the electorate, achieving 4225 votes – only 794 votes behind the successful candidate, and 979 votes ahead of the third candidate.

Considering she was the first Māori woman to seek election to the New Zealand Parliament, the newspapers gave scant coverage to Rehutai Maihi's election campaign. Maihi descended from a granddaughter of the Ngāpuhi chief Hongi Hika on her father's side and from Patuone, elder brother of chief Tāmati Waka Nene on her mother's side.[10] Her whakapapa to Ngāpuhi leaders meant she was permitted to speak on some marae as she travelled from one end of her constituency to the other during her election campaign. Her main interests were in the welfare of Māori women and children. She strongly advocated for the establishment of technical schools for Māori at which the boys would receive instruction in agriculture and useful trades and the girls in domestic science. She stressed the need for an advanced general education to enable Māori young people to take an intelligent interest in local and national affairs. With the vote against the sitting member split between six opposing candidates all actively campaigning for the Northern Māori electorate, Rehutai Maihi was fifth runner-up with a total of 162 votes.[11]

At the formal opening of her election campaign Helen Black stressed her credentials as a women's candidate. She believed that true democracy required representation of both sexes in government, that women did not desire to run the country but only asked for some representation, and that men tended to see things from a material standpoint whereas women were more concerned with the human element, which was sometimes of far greater importance.[12] For the most part she campaigned on the policy lines announced by the Democrat Party, but she also emphasised issues of particular relevance to women and children, such as the need to research the causes of ill health, in particular malnutrition, and for the government to support the milk in schools programmes. Like the other women candidates, she made a direct appeal to women voters, but her chances of success would always be compromised by the general view that the Democrat platform promised too much and was undeliverable. This was to be the only election the Democrat Party contested and although the party won a sizeable proportion of the overall vote, they won no seats. Black polled 1073 of the 11,666 votes cast in the electorate.

Connie Rawcliffe's campaign on behalf of the Communist Party for the Wellington East seat began just three weeks before the election but she received a reasonable amount of media coverage of her campaign meetings. Her audiences were generally very attentive and enquiring. Unlike the other women candidates, newspaper reports of her campaign focused exclusively on the policies of the Communist Party rather than on her personal attributes as a candidate. She did not seek to justify her candidacy to the voting public and her key message was true to party lines with her campaign speeches sounding like introductory lectures in classic Marxist and communist theory. As one of only four candidates standing across the country for the Communist Party, she was never considered to pose a threat of vote splitting in the Wellington East electorate, and she gained only 70 of the 15,528 votes cast in the electorate.

Elsie Andrews received the least media attention of all the women candidates. In her campaigning she emphasised women's abilities as 'natural economists'; she referred to women as 'the practical financiers of the State' and promoted the idea that there should be a practical woman in every government department to oversee the expenditure.[13] Of the five candidates contesting the seat, she was second runner-up with a poll of 786 votes from a total of 12,389 votes cast in the electorate.

The retrospectives that followed the election were largely silent on why none of these women candidates had been successful. Disappointing as the outcome was for women, the general election was very significant: unlike the five elections held before Elizabeth McCombs' election to Parliament in 1933, the media was focused on the likelihood of election of New Zealand's first Labour Government and was not consumed by the prospect of a woman being elected to the House. Except for Gilmer, of whom it was admitted that had there been a system of preferential voting in place she would probably have won the seat, all the women who contested the 1935 general election did so in seats for which there was virtually no prospect of them winning. It was worth noting, too, that of the five women who finally stood, none represented the two main contenders in the election, namely the Labour Party and the United–Reform Coalition. There may now have been a level of acceptance that women could be elected to Parliament, but it would seem there was still a considerable way to go before the male-dominated political party apparatus and the voters were prepared to genuinely back women candidates.

Important advances had been made, though. More women had considered nomination than at previous elections, even if fewer were nominated and fewer still were selected as candidates;[14] women's involvement in various parts of the campaign process was becoming more accepted; and, in what was believed to be unprecedented in New Zealand politics, two women took to the stage during the opening campaign meeting for a male candidate.[15] Progress may have been slow, but it was progress nonetheless.

Few and far between

Between 1935 and 1969, there were 12 general elections and 40 by-elections. Seventy-four women stood as candidates in those 12 general elections; only four were elected. Of the seven women who stood in the 40 by-elections, five were successful. By the time the Women's Parliamentary Rights Act 1919 had been on the statute books for 50 years, only 11 women had been elected to Parliament. Despite this continued 'ungallantly long hesitation to show "my lady" to a seat', there were incremental gains made over those 50 years that deserve attention.[16] After decades of politicians promoting the Legislative Council as more suited to women's political aspirations, in 1941 women finally achieved the right to be appointed to the council. It was another five years before the first two women took their seats in the Upper House. Only five women sat in the Upper House, of whom three were appointed as part of the so-called 'suicide squad' to vote for the abolition of the council; their stories are yet to be told. In 1949 Iriaka Rātana became the first Māori woman elected to Parliament. Her selection as the Labour candidate for the Western Maori district after the death of the sitting member, her husband Matiu Rātana, had been controversial on several counts. Her nomination was strongly opposed by Princess Te Puea Herangi and other leaders at a 1500-strong hui who objected to a woman 'aspiring to captain the Tainui canoe',[17] while members of the Labour Party expressed concern that, as the mother of a large family, her domestic commitments would compromise her ability to represent a large and scattered constituency. Iriaka Rātana won the election with a majority of over 6300 votes, and the month after she took her seat she became the first member of Parliament to give birth while in office. She successfully represented the Western Maori electorate for 20 years until she retired in 1969. There were other important milestones in that first half-century, including Labour member for Christchurch East Mabel Howard having the honour in 1943 of being the first woman to second the Address in Reply and, four years later, becoming the first woman Cabinet minister, as minister of health and minister in charge of child welfare.

The history of women taking a seat in Parliament has been at least neglected, if not a somewhat embarrassing and hushed footnote[18] in the shadow of New Zealand's proud status as the first country in the world to grant women the vote. The myth persists that 'New Zealand women were apparently content ... not to have the right to sit in Parliament [and] made little or no effort to take the logical step of qualifying themselves for election to Parliament'.[19] Inasmuch as the history of showing 'my lady' to a seat reflects the entrenched conservatism of male politicians, it bears testimony to a history of women's persistence, perseverance, tenacity and resilience.

GLOSSARY OF POLITICAL TERMS

Address in Reply: the formal response of the House of Representatives to the Speech from the Throne. Traditionally, two new members of Parliament from the Government side move and second the Address-in-Reply as their maiden speech. Prior to 1990 this was an annual event.

Address in Reply debate: the opening debate for the parliamentary session that immediately follows the Address-in-Reply, in which the Government advances its policies and the Opposition criticises them. It was traditional for the Opposition to introduce motions testing the confidence in the Government.

bill: the process of passing a bill into law required three readings in each of the two Houses of Parliament. In its first reading, a bill was introduced to the House with a brief summary of its provisions. The second reading usually involved substantial debate to reach agreement on the principles of the legislation. At this point some bills would be referred to select committees before being considered clause by clause in the committee of the whole House. Following any amendments, the bill would move to its third reading. Following a bill's passage through the House it was referred to the Legislative Council for consideration. If amended by the Legislative Council the bill would be returned to the House for passing before being sent to the governor/governor-general for assent. Most bills originated in the Lower House.

Chamber/Debating Chamber: an alternative name for the House of Representatives where the main parliamentary debates took place.

conference: If there was disagreement on a bill between the Lower and Upper Houses, a conference, overseen by managers, would be called to identify the points of disagreement.

division: voting by dividing the House; members would be summoned to the Chamber by the ringing of division bells; party whips would announce the total numbers when a division was called; on matters of conscience members would file into the lobbies to record their votes.

filibustering: the practice of bringing parliamentary business to a standstill by using Standing Orders and speeches to create delays; also known as stonewalling.

***Hansard*:** the official transcript of debates in the New Zealand Parliament, also known as *New Zealand Parliamentary Debates*, kept continuously since 9 July 1867. Speeches made in the House of Representatives and the Legislative Council between 1867 and the commencement of Parliament in 1854 were compiled in 1885 from earlier newspaper reports, and this compilation forms part of the New Zealand Hansard record.

House of Representatives: comprised of elected members of Parliament; known as 'the House' or the Lower House.

Legislative Council: modelled on the British House of Lords, this appointed body was designed to prevent laws being passed too quickly; also known as the Upper House, it was abolished in 1951.

Lower House: alternative name for the House of Representatives from between 1854 and 1951, the period during which New Zealand had a bicameral system of government with the legislature made up of two Houses. See also Upper House.

Order Paper: sets out the proposed agenda for Parliament for any given day.

pairs: an agreement of convenience between members on different sides of the House whereby if one member was absent the other would refrain from voting. With the advent of the mixed member proportional (MMP) electoral system, pairing was replaced by proxy voting.

Parliament: from 1854 to 1951 the New Zealand Parliament consisted of the governor, the (called the governor-general from 1917), the elected House of Representatives, and the appointed Legislative Council.

plebiscite: the direct vote of all members of an electorate on an important public question, sometimes referred to as an advisory referendum because, unlike a referendum in which voting is compulsory and binding on the government, it does not require the government to act upon the issue; often used interchangeably with 'referendum' which is the phrasing that describes what the vote is about.

Glossary of political terms

prorogue: to discontinue a session of Parliament without dissolving it.

second ballot system: a form of proportional representation, also known as the absolute majority system. The Second Ballot Act 1908 provided for a second ballot to be taken between the top two candidates in cases where there was not an outright majority of fifty percent of all votes cast in the electorate achieved by the top candidate.

session: the period during which Parliament was convened; until 1984 sessions usually started in the middle of the year as many politicians were farmers, and lasted several months to allow politicians to return home in time for Christmas. The House usually sat for three days a week, from early afternoon, and sometimes finished in the early hours of the morning. By the late 1930s all-night sittings had largely disappeared.

slaughter of the innocents: the practice of sacrificing less important bills towards the end of sessions.

Speech from the Throne: a speech delivered by the governor-general on the second day of a new Parliament to outline the Government's policies and legislative programme; prior to 1990 this was an annual event.

Standing Orders: the rules of procedure for Parliament and its committees.

tellers: members tasked with ticking off names from division lists.

Upper House: alternative name from between 1854 and 1951 for the Legislative Council. See also Lower House.

whips: members of the Government and Opposition tasked with special responsibilities such as monitoring the order paper, organising speakers for debates, maintaining discipline, ensuring that a quorum (and majority) would be maintained, granting leave, etc. to ensure the smooth running of the House.

TIMELINE OF SIGNIFICANT POLITICAL EVENTS, 1835 TO 1935

1835 Declaration of Independence: asserted independence of New Zealand with all sovereign power and authority resting with the hereditary chiefs and tribes.
1840 Treaty of Waitangi signed.
(May) Hobson proclaimed British sovereignty over all New Zealand; New Zealand became a dependency of New South Wales.
1841 New Zealand became a separate Crown colony.
1852 New Zealand Constitution Act, passed by British Parliament, established a system of representative government based on provincial councils and a General Assembly comprised of an appointed Legislative Council and an elected House of Representatives.
1853 First election for the House of Representatives (37 members).
1854 (May) First Parliament met in Auckland.
1856 Colonial Laws Validity Act passed by UK Parliament to clarify which UK laws applied in self-governing colonies.
(April) 'Responsible' government began in New Zealand; Cabinet Government under Premier Henry Sewell, continued until 1890.
(May) William Fox became premier.
(June) Edward Stafford became premier.
1861 (July) William Fox became premier.
1862 (August) Alfred Domett became premier.
1863 (October) Frederick Whitaker became premier.
1864 Ladies Gallery established; later a Speaker's Ladies Gallery was added for the wives of ministers and for important female visitors authorised by the Speaker.
(November) Frederick Weld became premier.
1865 Parliament moved to Wellington.
(October) Edward Stafford became premier.
1867 Four Māori electorates created as a temporary measure; universal suffrage for Māori males aged over 21; made permanent in 1876; 74 MPs in the House.
1868 First Māori elections held.
1869 (June) William Fox became premier.

'An Appeal to the Men of New Zealand' published by Fémmina (Mary Ann Müller)

1870 Secret ballot implemented for parliamentary elections.

1872 (September) Edward Stafford became premier.
(October) George Waterhouse became premier.

1873 (March) William Fox became premier.
(April) Julius Vogel became premier.

1875 (July) Daniel Pollen became premier.

1876 (February) Julius Vogel became premier.
(September) Harry Atkinson became premier.
Abolition of the provinces, leaving central government as the single legislative authority.
Māori electorates made permanent.
Municipal Corporations Act, entitled women who owned property and were ratepayers to vote and stand in local body elections.

1877 (October) George Grey became premier.

1879 Universal suffrage introduced for all males aged over 21.
Parliamentary term reduced from five to three years.
(October) John Hall became premier.

1881 First general election with universal male suffrage.

1882 (April) Frederick Whitaker became premier.

1883 (September) Harry Atkinson became premier.

1884 (August) Robert Stout became premier.

1885 Women's Christian Temperance Union formed; first national women's organisation in New Zealand.

1887 (October) Harry Atkinson became premier.

1891 (January) Election of Liberal Government under Premier John Ballance; continued until 1912.

1893 (May) Richard Seddon became premier.
(September) Universal suffrage introduced for all women aged over 21.
(November) Elizabeth Yates became first woman mayor in the British Empire.

1896 National Council of Women of New Zealand formed.
'The Charter of the Independence of Women' (Removal of Women's Disabilities Bill, 1896) presented by George Russell to House of Representatives.

1902 Number of MPs increased to 80.

1906 (June) William Hall-Jones became prime minister.
(August) Joseph Ward became prime minister.

Timeline of significant political events, 1835 to 1935

1907 New Zealand acquired Dominion status.
1908 New Zealand population reached one million.
1910 Contagious Diseases Act 1969 repealed.
1912 (March) Thomas Mackenzie became prime minister.
(July) Election of Reform Government under Prime Minister William Massey; continued until 1928.
1913 Ellen Melville, first woman to be elected to the Auckland City Council.
1915 (August) National Ministry formed as wartime coalition government with William Massey as prime minister and Liberal leader Joseph Ward as unofficial co-leader; continued until September 1919.
1917 Title of governor changed to governor-general.
1919 (September) William Massey became prime minister.
(September) Women's Parliamentary Rights Act, women eligible to be members of the House of Representatives.
(October) Rosetta Baume, first woman to announce her intention to contest a parliamentary seat.
1925 (14 May) Francis Bell became prime minister.
(30 May) Gordon Coates became prime minister.
1926 Quinice Cowles, first woman employed in the Parliamentary Library.
1928 (December) Election of United Government under Prime Minister Joseph Ward; continued until 1931.
1930 (May) George Forbes became prime minister.
1931 (September) Election of United–Reform Coalition Government under Prime Minister George Forbes; continued until 1935.
1933 (September) Elizabeth McCombs, first woman elected to Parliament.
1935 Rehutai Maihi, first Māori woman to contest a parliamentary election.
(December) Election of First Labour Government under Prime Minister Michael Joseph Savage; continued until 1949.

APPENDIX
WOMEN MEMBERS OF THE NEW ZEALAND HOUSE OF REPRESENTATIVES 1933 TO 2019

1. Elizabeth Reid **McCombs** (1933, Labour)
2. Catherine Campbell Sword **Stewart** (1938, Labour)
3. Mary Manson **Dreaver** (1941, Labour)
4. Mary Victoria Cracroft **Grigg** (1942, National)
5. Mabel Bowden **Howard** (1943, Labour)
6. Grace Hilda Cuthberta **Ross** (1945, National)
7. Iriaka Matiu **Ratana** (1949, Labour)
8. Ethel Emma **McMillan** (1953, Labour)
9. Esme Irene **Tombleson** (1960, National)
10. Rona Miriel **Stevenson** (1963, National)
11. Tini Whetu Marama **Tirikatene-Sullivan** (1967, Labour)
12. Mary Dorothy **Batchelor** (1972, Labour)
13. Dorothy Catherine **Jelicich** (1972, Labour)
14. Colleen Elizabeth **Dewe** (1975, National)
15. Marilyn Joy **Waring** (1975, National)
16. Margaret Ann **Hercus** (1978, Labour)
17. Helen Elizabeth **Clark** (1981, Labour)
18. Ruth Margaret **Richardson** (1981, National)
19. Margaret Kerslake **Shields** (1981, Labour)
20. Frances Helen **Wilde** (1981, Labour)
21. Margaret Elizabeth **Austin** (1984, Labour)
22. Lowson Anne **Fraser** (1984, Labour)
23. Judith Mary **Keall** (1984, Labour)
24. Annette Faye **King** (1984, Labour)
25. Katherine Victoria **O'Regan** (1984, National)
26. Sonja Margaret Loveday **Davies** (1987, Labour)
27. Jennifer Norah **Kirk** (1987, Labour)
28. Jennifer Mary **Shipley** (1987, National)
29. Patricia Elizabeth **Tennet** (1987, Labour)
30. Lianne Audrey **Dalziel** (1990, Labour)
31. Christine Elizabeth **Fletcher** (1990, National)

32. Marie Bernarde **Hasler** (1990, National)
33. Gail Helen **McIntosh** (1990, National)
34. Marilyn Joy **McLauchlan** (1990, National)
35. Margaret **Moir** (1990, National)
36. Judith Ngaire **Tizard** (1990, Labour)
37. Ruth Suzanne **Dyson** (1993, Labour)
38. Pauline Mona **Gardiner** (1993, National; United NZ)
39. Sandra Rose Tehakamatua **Lee** (1993, Alliance)
40. Janet Elsdon **Mackey** (1993, Labour)
41. Marjorie Jill **Pettis** (1993, Labour)
42. Suzanne Mary **Sinclair** (1993, Labour)
43. Jacqueline Jill **White** (1993, Labour)
44. Dianne Fae **Yates** (1993, Labour)
45. Donna Lynn **Awatere Huata** (1996, ACT; Independent)
46. Ann Lynette **Batten** (1996, NZ First; Independent, Mauri Pacific)
47. Jenny **Bloxham** (1996, NZ First)
48. Phillida Elizabeth **Bunkle** (1996, Alliance)
49. Pamela **Corkery** (1996, Alliance)
50. Jeanette Mary **Fitzsimons** (1996, Alliance; Green)
51. Elizabeth Audrey **Gordon** (1996, Alliance)
52. Laila Jane **Harré** (1996, Alliance)
53. Marian Leslie **Hobbs** (1996, Labour)
54. Manu Alamein **Kopu** (1996, Alliance; Independent; Mana Wahine)
55. Robyn Jane **McDonald** (1996, NZ First)
56. Nanaia Cybele **Mahuta** (1996, Labour)
57. Deborah Louise **Morris** (1996, NZ First; Independent)
58. Muriel **Newman** (1996, ACT)
59. Patricia **Schnauer** (1996, ACT)
60. Georgina Manunui **Te Heuheu** (1996, National)
61. Tariana Woon **Turia** (1996, Labour; Independent; Maori)
62. Belinda Jane **Vernon** (1996, National)
63. Pansy Yu Fong **Wong** (1996, National)
64. Annabel Margaret **Young** (1997, National)
65. Helen Patricia **Duncan** (1998, Labour)
66. Georgina **Beyer** (1999, Labour)
67. Susan **Bradford** (1999, Green)
68. Stephanie Anne **Chadwick** (1999, Labour)
69. Margaret Ann **Hartley** (1999, Labour)
70. Susan Jane **Kedgley** (1999, Green)
71. Luamanuvao Winifred Alexandra **Laban** (1999, Labour)

Appendix

72. Katherine **Rich** (1999, National)
73. Lynda Marie **Scott** (1999, National)
74. Anne Merrilyn **Tolley** (1999, National)
75. Mary Penelope **Webster** (1999, ACT)
76. Margaret Anne **Wilson** (1999, Labour)
77. Deborah Leslie **Coddington** (2002, ACT)
78. Judith Anne **Collins** (2002, National)
79. Sandra Anne **Goudie** (2002, National)
80. Barbara Lynne **Pillay** (2002, Labour)
81. Heather Jean **Roy** (2002, ACT)
82. Barbara Joy **Stewart** (2002, NZ First)
83. Metiria Leanne Agnes Stanton **Turei** (2002, Green)
84. Judith Anne **Turner** (2002, United Future NZ)
85. Moana Lynore **Mackey** (2003, Labour)
86. Lesley Frances **Soper** (2005, Labour)
87. Paula Lee **Bennett** (2005, National)
88. Jacqueline Diane **Blue** (2005, National)
89. Jacqueline Isobel **Dean** (2005, National)
90. Darien Elizabeth **Fenton** (2005, Labour)
91. Joanne Gay **Goodhew** (2005, National)
92. Suzanne Mary **Moroney** (2005, Labour)
93. Maryan **Street** (2005, Labour)
94. Nicola Joanne **Wagner** (2005, National)
95. Catherine Joan **Wilkinson** (2005, National)
96. Katrina May **Shanks** (2007, National)
97. Louisa Harerua **Wall** (2008, Labour)
98. Amy Juliet **Adams** (2008, National)
99. Jacinda Kate Laurell **Ardern** (2008, Labour)
100. Carol Ann **Beaumont** (2008, Labour)
101. Clare Elizabeth **Curran** (2008, Labour)
102. Catherine **Delahunty** (2008, Green)
103. Rahui Reid **Katene** (2008, Maori)
104. Nicola Laura **Kaye** (2008, National)
105. Melissa Ji-Yun **Lee** (2008, National)
106. Patricia Hekia **Parata** (2008, National)
107. Carmel Jean **Sepuloni** (2008, Labour)
108. Louise Claire **Upston** (2008, National)
109. Hilary Jane **Calvert** (2010, ACT)
110. Margaret Mary **Barry** (2011, National)
111. Julie Anne **Genter** (2011, Green)

112. Heather Janet **Logie** (2011, Green)
113. Le`aufa`amulia Asenati **Lole-Taylor** (2011, NZ First)
114. Tracey Anne **Martin** (2011, NZ First)
115. Mojo Celeste **Mathers** (2011, Green)
116. Denise Maree **Roche** (2011, Green)
117. Eugenie Meryl **Sage** (2011, Green)
118. Holly Ruth Haines **Walker** (2011, Green)
119. Megan Cherie **Woods** (2011, Labour)
120. Claudette **Hauiti** (2013, National)
121. Melissa Heni Mekameka **Whaitiri** (2013, Labour)
122. Munokoa Poto **Williams** (2013, Labour)
123. Sarah Maree **Dowie** (2014, National)
124. Marama Kahu **Fox** (2014, Maori)
125. Joanne Kowhai **Hayes** (2014, National)
126. Barbara Joan **Kuriger** (2014, National)
127. Kushmiita Parmjeet Kaur **Parmar** (2014, National)
128. Jennifer Teresia **Salesa** (2014, Labour)
129. Ria Daphne Iris **Bond** (2015, NZ First)
130. Marama Mere-Ana **Davidson** (2015, Green)
131. Maureen Helena **Pugh** (2015, National)
132. Kiritapu Lindsay **Allan** (2017, Labour)
133. Virginia Ruby **Andersen** (2017, Labour)
134. Elizabeth Dorothy **Craig** (2017, Labour)
135. Golriz **Ghahraman** (2017, Green)
136. Harete Makere **Hipango** (2017, National)
137. Anahila Lose **Kanongata'a-Suisuiki** (2017, Labour)
138. Denise Adrienne **Lee** (2017, National)
139. Maria Josina Elizabeth **Lubeck** (2017, Labour)
140. Jo-Anne Marie **Luxton** (2017, Labour)
141. Jennifer Lyn **Marcroft** (2017, NZ First)
142. Willow-Jean **Prime** (2017, Labour)
143. Priyanca **Radhakrishnan** (2017, Labour)
144. Deborah Faye **Russell** (2017, Labour)
145. Erica Louise **Stanford** (2017, National)
146. Chlöe Charlotte **Swarbrick** (2017, Green)
147. Janette Rose **Tinetti** (2017, Labour)
148. Angela Maree **Warren-Clark** (2017, Labour)
149. Nicola Valentine **Willis** (2018, National)

WHEN THE LADIES GET THEIR RIGHTS
(FOR THE *OBSERVER*)

You ask me why I'm ageing, why I'm looking thin and queer,
Why I don't enjoy my baccy and my pint or two of beer,
Why I have to nurse the babies and to cook the family grub,
And do all the family washing for the missus at the tub?
I'm a slave of tyrant woman, and she works me like a hoss,
For when she got the franchise woman got to be the boss;
Since a chap named Tommy Taylor passed a little Bill of his
For the purpose of removing women's disabilities.

Such a harmless little Bill it was when first he brought it in,
You wouldn't a thought it covered so much devilment and sin;
He worked upon our feelings like a deep, designing cuss,
To elevate the women to equality with us.
He said he only wanted to remove the social checks
That tyrant man imposed upon the freedom of the sex;
'The weaker sex' he called 'em, they're 'the stronger sex' since then,
He removed those disabilities and shoved 'em on the men.

But it gave me quite a facer when I saw my lovely spouse
Announced that she was standing for election to the House;
She stumped the country over and she canvassed far and near,
Boozed up the 'orny-handed with unstinted pints of beer,
And when she was defeated 'twas a very bitter pill
To mortgage all the furniture to pay her little bill,
I thought this degradation would have brought some sense of shame,
But she swears at next elections she will get there all the same.

Then my eldest daughter, Sally, in a military rig,
Surmounted by a helmet several sizes much too big,
With her back hair hanging downward and a-blowing to and fro,
And a gun upon her shoulder, went a-doing sentry-go.
When I said it was indecent, and would drive me to despair,
She pulled her false moustachios with a military air,
And says she 'It's women's duty to repel our enemies
Since you've passed that Act removing women's disabilities.'

From Suffrage to a Seat in the House

I met my cousin Mary, and it gave me quite a shock,
She was dressed in fancy bloomers, strolling up and down the block.
She was puffing at a meershaum as she walked along the street,
And she said she'd only just come out 'to give the boys a treat.'
She frequents public-houses, at the bars she takes a drink,
And pours a big long-sleever down her throat without a wink;
And when she's flush of money she throws Yankee grab for fizz,
For Taylor's Act abolished women's disabilities.

My sister Angelina, who was always rather fast,
Has slipped aboard a vessel as a hand before the mast;
She says it's awful jolly to go sailing on the sea,
And the height of her ambition is to pass for an A.B.
She's versed in all the phrases of the nautical lingo,
Can chew a quid and spin a yarn that girls ought not to know
We men have got to shut our eyes to little things like these
Since we passed that Act removing women's disabilities.

At the very next election, out there came a perfect mob
Of pushing female candidates intent upon the job,
And so cleverly they managed us male voters to cajole,
That fifty female members got elected at the poll.
The paper said the presence of those female candidates
Would tend to raise the dignity and the tone of the debates.
There would be no more obstruction, they would settle down to biz,
Those lovely female members, free from disabilities.

But one day a point of order Mrs Brown got up to raise,
That Mrs Jones made use of an unparliamentary phrase,
By remarking Mrs Brown was very far from being a saint,
And alleging her complexion showed a trifle too much paint;
Mrs Jones insinuated Mrs Brown had told a lie,
And a state of party feeling was soon running very high;
For they sailed into each other quite regardless of the chair,
And the floor was littered over with false teeth and tufts of hair.

But they always voted solid in a systematic plan
On any legislation that affected tyrant man;
They interdicted smoking, and deprived us of our beer,
And stuck a tax on bachelors of a hundred pounds a year;
They sacked the civil servants from all billets small and great,
And declared that only females should hold offices of State,

And they said that men no longer should enjoy monopolies,
They were all reserved for women freed from disabilities.

If a man makes any money by his hand or by his brains,
He must hand it to the missus – 'tis the law that so ordains
He must ante up his earnings, for in law it is a crime
If he doesn't part the dollars and look pleasant all the time;
He may groan beneath the burden, but he can't escape the facts,
He's a lunatic responsible no longer for his acts;
He is quite *non-compos mentis*, simply helpless as he is,
Till he gets an Act removing all his disabilities.

'Automathes', *Observer*, 13 August 1898, p. 18.

NOTES

INTRODUCTION
Showing 'my lady' to a seat

1. Matanga, 'My lady in politics: Votes and seats', *New Zealand Herald*, 16 September 1933, p. 1 (Supplement).
2. Elizabeth McCombs, *NZPD*, vol. 236 (28 September 1933), p. 156.
3. James Wallis, *NZPD*, vol. 28 (8 August 1878), p. 135.
4. During the nineteenth century the term 'women's disabilities' referred to the ways in which women were subjected to civic and political discrimination.
5. See Kate Hunter, 'Women's mobilization for war (New Zealand)' in: 1914-1918-online, International Encyclopedia of the First World War, eds Ute Daniel, Peter Gatrell, Oliver Janz, Heather Jones, Jennifer Keene, Alan Kramer & Bill Nasson (Freie Universität Berlin).
6. Editorial, *Press*, 18 November 1919, p. 6.
7. 'Women in Parliament', *New Zealand Herald*, 31 October 1928, p. 1.
8. 'Cradle-rockers face the polls', *NZ Truth*, 1 November 1928, p. 21.
9. Edna Graham Macky, 'National consciousness: New Zealand women awake', *New Zealand Herald*, 17 November 1928, p. 6 (Supplement).
10. 'New Zealand politics: Apathy of women', *New Zealand Herald*, 24 November 1928, p. 22.

CHAPTER 1
Passionate philosophical parliamentary debates, 1852 to 1893

1. Sir John Finlay, *NZPD*, vol. 184 (26 September 1919), p. 974.
2. These comments are attributed to premiers James FitzGerald and Harry Atkinson, as cited in Keith Sinclair, *A History of New Zealand*, 4th rev. edn (Auckland: Penguin, 1991), p. 112.
3. Sinclair, *A History of New Zealand*, p. 112.
4. Hugh Carleton, *NZPD*, vol. 7 (22 June 1870), p. 57.
5. David Pinkerton, *NZPD*, vol. 73 (24 August 1891), p. 502.
6. Edward Stafford, *NZPD*, vol. 7 (22 June 1870), p. 64.
7. In the nineteenth century a married couple was, in legal terms, a single entity under the control of the husband. This meant a wife's money and property, regardless of whether it was acquired before or after the marriage, was legally her husband's. The Married Women's Property Protection Act 1870 extended protection orders for married women's property in cases of cruelty, open adultery, habitual drunkenness or habitual failure to provide maintenance for a wife and children. It was not until the Married Women's Property Act 1884 that married women had a separate legal existence enabling them to own property,

make contracts in their own right, and sue or be sued.
8. 'Death of Dr J. Wallis', *New Zealand Herald*, 27 May 1912, p. 5.
9. Dr James Wallis, *NZPD*, vol. 25 (12 September 1877), pp. 445, 446.
10. William Travers, *NZPD*, vol. 25 (19 September 1877), p. 561.
11. Colonel George Whitmore, *NZPD*, vol. 25 (26 September 1877), p. 650.
12. Fémmina, 'An Appeal to the Men of New Zealand', (Nelson: J. Hounsell, 1869), p. 3.
13. Ibid., p. 5.
14. Ibid., p. 7.
15. Ibid., p. 5.
16. Keith Jackson & Alan McRobie, *Historical and Political Dictionary of New Zealand*, 2nd edn (Rangiora: MC Enterprises, 2008), p. 39.
17. See Neill Atkinson, *Adventures in Democracy: A history of the vote in New Zealand* (Dunedin: Otago University Press, 2003).
18. Jackson & McRobie, *Historical and Political Dictionary*, p. 40.
19. Patricia Grimshaw, *Women's Suffrage in New Zealand*, 2nd edn (Auckland: Auckland University Press, 1987), p. 46.
20. Henry Fish, *NZPD*, vol. 73 (24 August 1891), p. 519.
21. Grimshaw, *Women's Suffrage in New Zealand*, p. 16.
22. Dr James Wallis, *NZPD*, vol. 28 (7 August 1878), p. 102.
23. Dr James Wallis, *NZPD*, vol. 28 (8 August 1878), p. 137.
24. Ibid., p. 131.
25. Ibid., p. 132.
26. Ibid., p. 133.
27. The Electoral Bill 1878 introduced on behalf of the government by Attorney-General Robert Stout included provision for all ratepayers to have the electoral franchise. The Parliamentary Representation Bill 1878 introduced by Frederick Whitaker granted the electoral franchise to adult male residents.
28. Robert Stout, *NZPD*, vol. 28 (8 August 1878), p. 137.
29. Henry Feldwick, *NZPD*, vol. 28 (15 August 1878), p. 289.
30. Vogel's letter to Mary Ann Colclough is cited the article 'Mother's vote: Has it altered the trend of legislation?', *New Zealand Free Lance*, 11 November 1936, p. 23. The article is attributed to Mary Ann Colclough's daughter, journalist Mary Wilson, and is contained in the scrapbook 'From English, Australian and New Zealand papers by Mrs Hannon Wilson' (private family collection).
31. See Sir Julius Vogel, *Anno Domini 2000; or, Woman's Destiny* (London: Hutchinson, 1889).
32. Sir Julius Vogel, *NZPD*, vol. 57 (12 May 1887), p. 231.
33. W. Sidney Smith, *Outlines of the Women's Franchise Movement in New Zealand* (Christchurch: Whitcombe & Tombs, 1905), p. 38.
34. Ibid., pp. 39–40.
35. President's Address, Recommendations for 1889, No. 4, *Report of the National WCTU of New Zealand, Fourth Annual Meeting*, Wellington, 27 February 1889, p. 33.

Notes for Chapter 1

36. Hall's amendment read: 'In the paragraph "'Person' does not include female," to strike out the words "does not include," and substitute the word "includes".' Sir John Hall, *NZPD*, vol. 73 (14 August 1891), p. 309.
37. 'Suffrage notes', *The Prohibitionist* (November 1892), p. 8.
38. Ibid.
39. William Gisborne, *NZPD*, vol. 28 (13 August 1878), p. 200.
40. Eugene O'Conor, *NZPD*, vol. 73 (24 August 1891), p. 534.
41. James Carroll, *NZPD*, vol. 73 (24 August 1891), p. 546.
42. Sir Julius Vogel, *NZPD*, vol. 57 (12 May 1887), p. 230.
43. Alfred Saunders, *NZPD*, vol. 28 (13 August 1878), p. 204.
44. William Cutten, *NZPD*, vol. 28 (20 August 1878), p. 338.
45. Ibid., p. 339.
46. William Fox, *NZPD*, vol. 28 (20 August 1878), p. 347.
47. Henry Manders, *NZPD*, vol. 28 (20 August 1878), p. 348.
48. Albert Pitt, *NZPD*, vol. 33 (31 October 1879), p. 32.
49. John Sheehan, *NZPD*, vol. 28 (20 August 1878), p. 341.
50. Wī Pere, *NZPD*, vol. 57 (12 May 1887), pp. 240–41.
51. William Murray, *NZPD*, vol. 33 (31 October 1879), p. 35.
52. William Buckland, *NZPD*, vol. 57 (12 May 1887), p. 236.
53. Richard Seddon, *NZPD*, vol. 33 (31 October 1879), p. 39.
54. James Thomson, *NZPD*, vol. 33 (14 November 1879), p. 273.
55. Frederick Moss, *NZPD*, vol. 57 (12 May 1887), p. 232.
56. Alfred Saunders, *NZPD*, vol. 68 (5 August 1890), p. 398.
57. Thomas Tanner, *NZPD*, vol. 68 (5 August 1890), p. 399.
58. Edwin Blake, *NZPD*, vol. 68 (5 August 1890) p. 400.
59. Henry Fish, *NZPD*, vol. 68 (5 August 1890), p. 402.
60. Henry Fish, *NZPD*, vol. 73 (24 August 1891), p. 513. In November 2017, the Speaker Trevor Mallard nursed three-month-old Heeni while her mother Willow-Jean Prime debated the bill to extend paid parental leave.
61. Richard Oliver, *NZPD*, vol. 33 (14 November 1879), p. 277.
62. Female Suffrage Bill 1890 (No. 114-1), cl. 2.
63. Sir John Hall, *NZPD*, vol. 68 (5 August 1890), p. 391.
64. Alfred Saunders, *NZPD*, vol. 68 (5 August 1890), p. 398.
65. James Carroll, *NZPD*, vol. 73 (24 August 1891), p. 546. In response, Sir John Hall clarified that, 'This Bill makes no distinction whatever with regard to race. Where the law at present gives the vote to a Maori man, this Bill would give a vote to a Maori woman' (ibid., p. 550).
66. Fémmina, 'An Appeal to the Men of New Zealand', p. 7.
67. Ibid., p. 8.
68. Ibid., pp. 11–12.
69. See letter dated 5 October 1893 from Mary Müller to Mrs Sheppard, Kate W. Sheppard Correspondence 1893, Canterbury Museum Library.
70. Polly Plum, 'What have women to do with politics?', *Daily Southern Cross*, 4 August 1869, p. 5.

71. Polly Plum, *Weekly News*, 26 February 1870, p. 21.
72. 'Local and General Intelligence', *Tuapeka Times*, 28 July 1880, p. 2.
73. Henry Fish, *NZPD*, vol. 68 (5 August 1890), p. 401.
74. 'Women's Christian Temperance Union', *Star*, 7 February 1891, p. 2.
75. See Report of the National WCTU of New Zealand, Fifth Annual Meeting, Dunedin, 1890, White ribbon [microform], Massey b1770936, Massey University Library.
76. *Clutha Leader*, 23 January 1891, p. 5.
77. The other amendments proposed by Fish were that, if passed, the operation of the Act would be delayed until 1 January 1894, and that the Act would not come into operation until a poll had been taken of the men and women in the colony aged 21 and over and that a majority of both sexes were in favour of conferring the franchise on females. If these amendments were not carried, Fish intended to propose another – that the franchise be extended only to women over the age of 35.
78. Sir John Hall, *NZPD*, vol. 73 (24 August 1891), p. 501.
79. James Carroll, *NZPD*, vol. 73 (24 August 1891), p. 546.
80. James Mackintosh, *NZPD*, vol. 73 (24 August 1891), p. 528.
81. Richard Taylor, *NZPD*, vol. 73 (24 August 1891), p. 529.
82. Ibid., p. 529.
83. Section 3, Female Suffrage Bill 1891 (No. 59-2).
84. Smith, *Outlines of the Women's Franchise Movement*, p. 66.
85. See *NZPD*, vol. 74 (9 September 1891), p. 406.
86. Lady Harberton co-founded the Rational Dress Society in London in 1881.
87. James Fulton, *NZPD*, vol. 74 (9 September 1891), p. 408.
88. Henry Miller, *NZPD*, vol. 74 (9 September 1891), p. 416.
89. Patrick Buckley, *NZPD*, vol. 74 (10 September 1891), p. 466.
90. John Ballance, *NZPD*, vol. 75 (1 July 1892), p. 151.
91. Ibid.
92. George Hutchison, *NZPD*, vol. 75 (5 July 1892), p. 232.
93. Meri Mangakahia (1893), 'So that women may receive the vote', reprinted in Charlotte Macdonald (ed.), *The Vote, the Pill and the Demon Drink: A history of feminist writing in New Zealand, 1869–1993* (Wellington: Bridget Williams Books, 1993), p. 42.
94. See John Grigg, *NZPD*, vol. 81 (31 August 1893), p. 508.
95. Richard Seddon, *NZPD*, vol. 82 (19 September 1893), p. 380.
96. Approximately 80% of the total adult female population had been registered on the electoral rolls by the closing date of enrolment, and around 85% of those enrolled voted.
97. 'Women's franchise: Public meeting in the state school room', *Feilding Star*, 28 September 1893, p. 2.
98. Male Voter, 'Sphere of women's usefulness', *Evening Star*, 30 September 1893, p. 1 (Supplement).
99. Ibid.

100. 'Women's franchise', *Evening Star*, 30 September 1893, p. 4.
101. Of the 109,461 women who had enrolled (representing about 84% of the adult female population), 90,290 women cast votes on the day. In addition, women accounted for about 4000 of the 11,269 Māori votes cast. For further information on women's voting in the 1893 general election, see nzhistory.govt.nz/page/women-vote-first-general-election
102. Elizabeth Yates was indifferent to the suffrage campaign in large part because of her anti-prohibition stance. As a member of a local literary society, she became a delegate to the Auckland Union Parliament, a debating group organised along parliamentary lines that discussed issues of national importance. See Judith Devaliant's biography, *Elizabeth Yates: The first lady mayor in the British Empire* (Auckland: Exisle Publishing, 1996).
103. Henry Feldwick, *NZPD*, vol. 28 (15 August 1878), p. 289.
104. Ballance's view was, at least in part, self-serving as he believed it would take more time to educate women to support the Liberal Government's reform agenda and thereby secure their votes.

CHAPTER 2
The logical conclusion to female franchise, 1894 to 1896

1. James Carroll, *NZPD*, vol. 73 (24 August 1891), pp. 545–46.
2. Unlike modern-day political parties which are characterised by organisation from outside Parliament, the Liberal Party at this time was a looser grouping of men who generally subscribed to a comprehensive programme when they were in Parliament. 'By contrast, the Reform Party and the Labour Party were organised outside parliament to establish in parliament effective vehicles for the political opinion of sectional interests which felt they were not adequately represented by the Liberal Party': J.C. Clarke, 'The New Zealand Liberal Party and Government, 1895–1906', MA thesis, University of Auckland, 1962, p. 24.
3. 'Plural voting' was a voting system that operated from 1853, in which men who owned property of a certain value could vote in every district in which they qualified. This was abolished under the Representation Act Amendment Act 1889, which allowed for plural registration (wherein property owners could enrol in every electorate in which they qualified) but enacted the principle of 'one man, one vote' with the exception of Māori property owners, who could vote in both Māori and European electorates. Plural registration and plural voting were abolished in 1893.
4. David Hamer, *The New Zealand Liberals: The years of power, 1891–1912* (Auckland: Auckland University Press, 1988), p. 13.
5. Premier John Ballance died in office on 27 April 1893 and was replaced by Richard John Seddon.
6. Hamer, *The New Zealand Liberals*, p. 112.
7. Ibid., ch. 4.
8. See Fides et Justitia, letter to the editor, *Evening Post*, 13 June 1894, p. 3.

9. The letter was subsequently published in the newspaper; see E.E. Hill & E. Hume, letter to Dr Newman dated 21 June 1894, 'The political rights of women', *Evening Post*, 23 July 1894, p. 2.
10. Ibid.
11. Letter from E. Hume to Kate Sheppard, 28 July 1894, Kate W. Sheppard Correspondence, 176/53, Box 2, Folder 6, Item 248.
12. 'Political Notes', *Star*, 7 July 1894, p. 6.
13. Ibid.
14. Dr Alfred Newman, *NZPD*, vol. 83 (11 July 1894), p. 404.
15. Ibid.
16. Captain William Russell, *NZPD*, vol. 83 (11 July 1894), p. 405.
17. Felix McGuire, *NZPD*, vol. 83 (11 July 1894), p. 408.
18. William Reeves, *NZPD*, vol. 83 (11 July 1894), p. 408.
19. Captain William Russell, *NZPD*, vol. 83 (11 July 1894), p. 406.
20. Ibid., p. 406.
21. Ibid.
22. Hone Heke, *NZPD*, vol. 83 (11 July 1894), p. 407. Two months later, he introduced the Native Rights Bill, which sought to establish a constitution for Māori through a Declaration of Independence, protection of their rights under the Treaty of Waitangi, and a separate parliament subject only to the governor, which was empowered to legislate for and between Māori particularly in respect of lands and personal property. Although it had the support of many tribes, the Native Rights Bill did not pass into law but did have some influence on the Maori Councils Act 1900.
23. William Massey, *NZPD*, vol. 83 (11 July 1894), p. 410.
24. Alfred Saunders, *NZPD*, vol. 83 (11 July 1894), p. 411.
25. Ibid. Mr Roderick McKenzie also suggested a third house specially set apart for the ladies (see *NZPD*, vol. 83, p. 569).
26. Dr Alfred Newman, *NZPD*, vol. 83 (11 July 1894), p. 412.
27. Ibid.
28. Mr Speaker (Sir George O'Rorke), *NZPD*, vol. 83 (11 July 1894), p. 412.
29. Alexander Hogg, *NZPD*, vol. 83 (18 July 1894), p. 568.
30. Clarke, 'The New Zealand Liberal Party and Government', p. 30.
31. There was no Riverton electorate; this is a typographical error in *Hansard*, referring to the newly elected member George Russell, who held the new electorate seat for Riccarton.
32. Alexander Hogg, *NZPD*, vol. 83 (18 July 1894), p. 568.
33. George Russell, *NZPD*, vol. 83 (18 July 1894), p. 570.
34. 'Political Intelligence', *Otago Daily Times*, 19 July 1894, p. 3.
35. 'Parliamentary Gossip', *Auckland Star*, 19 July 1894, p. 2.
36. 'Disabilities of Women', *Poverty Bay Herald*, 19 July 1894, p. 3.
37. 'Editorial: Women in Parliament', *New Zealand Times*, 19 July 1894, p. 2.
38. S.R. Hendre, letter to the editor, *Auckland Star*, 24 July 1894, p. 2.
39. Women's Political Rights Bill 1894, cl. 2.

40. Local bills are bills promoted by a local authority and affect only that locality. See David McGee, *Parliamentary Practice in New Zealand*, 4th edn (Auckland: Oratia Books, 2017), pp. 359–61.
41. 'Parliamentary Gossip', *Auckland Star*, 20 July 1894, p. 3.
42. George Russell, *NZPD*, vol. 83 (19 July 1894), p. 602.
43. Ibid., p. 603.
44. Ibid.
45. Ibid.
46. Ibid.
47. 'Editorial: Women in Parliament', *New Zealand Times*, 19 July 1894, p. 2.
48. Ibid.
49. *AJHR*, 1894, Session I, I-01, Reports of the Public Petitions A to L Committee, Petition 731, p. 16.
50. 'Hugging our chains', *The Prohibitionist*, July 1895, p. 8.
51. American educator, temperance reformer and women's suffragist Frances Willard served as national president of the American WCTU from 1879 until her death in 1898.
52. *The Prohibitionist*, July 1895, p. 8.
53. Ibid.
54. 'Dunedin Women's Franchise League', *The Prohibitionist*, September 1894, p. 8.; 'Women's Franchise League', *Evening Star*, 23 August 1894, p. 1.
55. 'Daybreak', *New Zealand Times*, 9 February 1895, p. 2.
56. 'About women', *Evening Star*, 2 March 1895, p. 2 (Supplement).
57. 'Maori women's rights', *Otago Daily Times*, 7 January 1895, p. 4.
58. The resolutions passed were: 'That we have nothing further to do with the Native Land Court; that we cease selling lands; that there be no further renting of lands; that no further surveys be gone into; that should any man, woman, or child break the above regulations they shall be fined whatever the committee think fit; that the parchment which is to be signed by all Natives of both islands is to be completed within this year, and that the amount paid by each person who signs the parchment is to be £1, according to the rules laid down in 1892, and such an amount is to be paid this year'. See 'Native Women's Parliament', *Otago Daily Times*, 15 January 1895, p. 2.
59. 'The Maori Women's Parliament', *Hawke's Bay Herald*, 14 January 1895, p. 4.
60. Priscilla Peahen, letter to the editor, *Nelson Evening Mail*, 17 January 1895, p. 2.
61. *Journals and Appendix to the Journals of the Legislative Council*, Session 1895, no. 3.
62. *Journals of the House of Representatives*, Session 1895, no. 70.
63. Ibid., no. 139.
64. Ibid., no. 138.
65. Ibid., no. 132.
66. Ibid., no. 227.
67. Ibid., no. 79.
68. 'Political Notes', *Otago Daily Times*, 3 July 1895, p. 2.

69. Dr Alfred Newman, *NZPD*, vol. 87 (17 July 1895), p. 632.
70. Walter Carncross, *NZPD*, vol. 87 (17 July 1895), p. 633.
71. Ibid., p. 632.
72. Thomas Mackenzie, *NZPD*, vol. 87 (17 July 1895), p. 633.
73. William Maslin, *NZPD*, vol. 87 (17 July 1895), p. 635.
74. John Graham, *NZPD*, vol. 87 (17 July) p. 637; John McLachlan, *NZPD*, vol. 87 (17 July 1895), p. 636.
75. Thomas Mackenzie, *NZPD*, vol. 87 (17 July 1895), p. 633.
76. Robert Thompson, *NZPD*, vol. 87 (17 July 1895), p. 634.
77. Roderick McKenzie, *NZPD*, vol. 87 (17 July 1895), p. 641.
78. John Duthie, *NZPD*, vol. 87 (17 July 1895), p. 634.
79. William Maslin, *NZPD*, vol. 87 (17 July 1895), p. 635.
80. William Tanner, *NZPD*, vol. 87 (17 July 1895), p. 639.
81. Janice C. Mogford, 'Yates, Elizabeth', *Dictionary of New Zealand Biography*, Te Ara – the Encyclopedia of New Zealand: https://teara.govt.nz/en/biographies/2y1/yates-elizabeth
82. Dr Alfred Newman, *NZPD*, vol. 87 (17 July 1895), p. 641.
83. William Tanner, *NZPD*, vol. 87 (17 July 1895), p. 638.
84. Ibid., pp. 638, 639.
85. William Collins, *NZPD*, vol. 87 (17 July 1895), p. 639.
86. Major William Steward, *NZPD*, vol. 87 (17 July 1895), p. 633.
87. Ibid., pp. 633–34.
88. See George Smith, *NZPD*, vol. 87 (17 July 1895), p. 638; William Tanner, *NZPD*, vol. 87 (17 July 1895), p. 639.
89. William Hall-Jones, *NZPD*, vol. 87 (17 July 1895), p. 635.
90. John Graham, *NZPD*, vol. 87 (17 July 1895), p. 637.
91. William Collins, *NZPD*, vol. 87 (17 July 1895), p. 640.
92. Dr Alfred Newman, *NZPD*, vol. 87 (17 July 1895), p. 641.
93. See *Evening Post*, 23 April 1893, p. 2.
94. See advertisement, *Taranaki Herald*, 2 July 1895, p. 2.
95. 'Entertainment in St Mary's School', *Taranaki Herald*, 12 July 1895, p. 2.
96. 'Entertainment at St Mary's School', *Taranaki Herald*, 15 July 1895, p. 2.
97. Removal of Women's Disabilities Bill 1895.
98. 'Women's Franchise League', *Evening Star*, 27 July 1895, p. 4 (Supplement). The Female Law Practitioners Bill 1895 had a first reading on 12 July 1895 but was discharged without debate on 2 October 1895.
99. 'Notes of the Week', *Otago Daily Times*, 5 October 1895, p. 4.
100. Louise Blake to Mrs Sheppard, 21 January 1896, Kate W. Sheppard Correspondence 1896, 176/53, Box 2, Folder 8, Item 295.
101. 'Canterbury Women's Institute', *Star*, 11 February 1896, p. 4.
102. Ibid.
103. Constitution and Conference Minutes, MS-Papers-1371-106 National Council of Women of New Zealand Records, Minutes of the first meeting.
104. 'Sweating industries' referred to factories and workshops – particularly the

clothing industry, which employed mainly women and girls – that subjected manual workers to poor working conditions, long hours and very low rates of pay.
105. J.M.C., 'The Women's Convention', *Press*, 23 April 1896, p. 6.
106. *Bruce Herald*, 23 June 1896, p. 2.
107. George Russell, *NZPD*, vol. 92 (25 June 1896) p. 337.
108. Ibid., p. 338.
109. Ibid.
110. Ibid.
111. James Allen, *NZPD*, vol. 92 (25 June 1896), p. 338.
112. George Hutchison, *NZPD*, vol. 92 (25 June 1896), p. 340.
113. George Russell, *NZPD*, vol. 92 (25 June 1896), p. 342.
114. 'Political Notes', *Lyttelton Times*, 27 June 1896, p. 5.; 'Political Notes', *Lyttelton Times*, 30 June 1896, p. 5.
115. R.T. Shannon, 'The fall of Reeves, 1893–1896', in Robert Chapman & Keith Sinclair (eds), *Studies in a Small Democracy: Essays in honour of Willis Airey*, (Auckland: University of Auckland, 1963), pp. 127–52 (140).
116. 'Parliamentary Notes', *Hastings Standard*, 3 July 1896, p. 3.
117. 'Political Notes', *Lyttelton Times*, 11 July 1896, p. 5.
118. John McLachlan, *NZPD*, vol. 93 (8 July 1896), p. 51.
119. Thomas Mackenzie, *NZPD*, vol. 93 (8 July 1896), p. 52.
120. Ibid.
121. Richard Seddon, *NZPD*, vol. 93 (8 July 1896), p. 53.
122. Ibid.
123. Ibid.
124. Ibid., pp. 53, 54.
125. George Russell, *NZPD*, vol. 93 (8 July 1896), p. 54.
126. William Earnshaw, *NZPD*, vol. 93 (8 July 1896), p. 57.
127. Dr Alfred Newman, *NZPD*, vol. 93 (8 July 1896), p. 60.
128. See letter and editorial comment, Elector, 'Mr Flatman at Temuka and Geraldine', *Temuka Leader*, 1 December 1896, p. 3. The editor subsequently decided to publish the second letter; see An Elector, 'Mr Flatman on female rights', *Temuka Leader*, 3 December 1896, p. 3.
129. Charles Mill, *NZPD*, vol. 93 (8 July 1896), p. 55.

CHAPTER 3
Serving their political apprenticeship, 1897 to 1910

1. Alexander Hogg, *NZPD*, vol. 102 (29 July 1898), p. 151.
2. David Hamer, *The New Zealand Liberals: The years of power, 1891–1912* (Auckland: Auckland University Press, 1988), p. 208.
3. 'A memorable day in the city', *New Zealand Times*, 5 December 1896, p. 2.
4. Kate Sheppard, 'Presidential Address', *White Ribbon* (April 1897), cited in Margaret Lovell-Smith, *The Woman Question: Writing by the women who won the vote* (Auckland: New Women's Press, 1992), p. 209.

5. Ibid., p. 208.
6. See Roberta Nicholls, 'Daldy, Amey 1829?–1920' in *The Suffragists* (Wellington: Bridget Williams Books/Dictionary of New Zealand Biography, 1993).
7. Amey Daldy, 'The disabilities of women', *White Ribbon* (April 1897), cited in Lovell-Smith, *The Woman Question*, p. 195.
8. Ibid., p. 196.
9. Patrick O'Regan, *NZPD*, vol. 83 (18 July 1894), p. 570.
10. Letter to Mrs K.W. Sheppard from P.J. O'Regan, dated September 25, 1897, Kate W. Sheppard Correspondence, 176/53, Box 2, Folder 9, Item 300.
11. 'Women's disabilities', *White Ribbon*, vol. 4, no. 38 (August 1898), p. 7.
12. See telegram to Mrs Sheppard from R.J. Seddon dated September 29, 1897, Kate W. Sheppard Correspondence, 176/53, Box 2, Folder 9, Item 301.
13. 'Removal of women's disabilities', *White Ribbon*, vol. 3, no. 28 (October 1897), p. 10.
14. Telegram to Mrs K.W. Sheppard from R.J. Seddon, dated October 11, 1897, Kate W. Sheppard Correspondence, 176/53, Box 2, Folder 9, Item 303.
15. Letter to Mrs Sheppard from T.E. Taylor dated October 1, 1897, Kate W. Sheppard Correspondence, 176/53, Box 2, Folder 9, Item 302.
16. Letter to Mrs Sheppard from T.E. Taylor, dated October 15, 1897, Kate W. Sheppard Correspondence, 176/53, Box 2, Folder 9, Item 304.
17. Letter to Mrs Sheppard from J. Hall, dated February 16, 1898, Kate Sheppard Correspondence 1898–99, 176/53, Box 2, Folder 10, Item 306.
18. 'National Council of Women', *White Ribbon*, vol. 3, no. 35 (May 1898), pp. 1, 2.
19. Ibid., p. 1.
20. Ibid., p. 3.
21. Letter to Mrs Sheppard from Mary Müller, dated August 18, 1898, Kate Sheppard Correspondence 1898–99, 176/53, Box 2, Folder 10, Item 310.
22. 'Political Gossip', *Evening Star*, 4 July 1898, p. 2.
23. Hamer, *The New Zealand Liberals*, p. 211.
24. Removal of Women's Disabilities Bill 1898, cl. 2.
25. Thomas Taylor, *NZPD*, vol. 102 (29 July 1898), p. 146.
26. Ibid.
27. Ibid., p. 147.
28. Ibid., p. 148.
29. William Tanner, *NZPD*, vol. 102 (29 July 1898), p. 150.
30. Alexander Hogg, *NZPD*, vol. 102 (29 July 1898), p. 151.
31. Beatrice Webb, *Visit to New Zealand in 1898: Beatrice Webb's diary with entries by Sidney Webb* (Wellington: Price & Milburn, 1959), p. 34.
32. *International Council of Women Report of Transactions of The Second Quinquennial Meeting held in London July 1899* (London: T. Fisher Unwin, 1900), p. 127.
33. 'Political Notes', *Otago Daily Times*, 20 August 1898, p. 4.
34. G.W. Russell, 'Removal of Women's Disabilities Bill', *Star*, 2 August 1898, p. 4.
35. Michael Gilfedder, *NZPD*, vol. 106 (19 July 1899), p. 675.

Notes for Chapter 3

36. The general election was held on 6 December 1899 for the European electorates and on 19 December for the Māori electorates.
37. 'Parliamentary Echoes', *Hastings Standard*, 16 October 1899, p. 3.
38. Ibid.
39. 'The new party', *Lyttelton Times*, 2 July 1896, p. 2.
40. J.C. Clarke, 'The New Zealand Liberal Party and Government, 1895–1906', MA thesis, University of Auckland, 1962, p. 51.
41. George Russell, *NZPD*, vol. 88 (9 August 1895), p. 604.
42. George Russell, *NZPD*, vol. 111 (28 June 1900), p. 148.
43. Hamer, *The New Zealand Liberals*, p. 197.
44. Hamer (p. 197) described Edward Smith as wearing 'frock-coat, wide waistcoat, large buttonhole, and, when out of doors, a tam-o'-shanter.'
45. Edward Smith, *NZPD*, vol. 111 (28 June 1900), p. 149.
46. George Fisher, *NZPD*, vol. 111 (28 June 1900), pp. 150, 151.
47. Ibid., p. 150.
48. Ibid., p. 151.
49. 'Women in office', *Auckland Star*, 5 July 1900, p. 4.
50. 'Removal of Women's Disabilities', *Evening Star*, 5 July 1900, p. 5. For a full account of this exchange, see 'Women's disabilities', *New Zealand Herald*, 5 July 1900, p. 6.
51. Hamer, *The New Zealand Liberals*, p. 197.
52. Scotter, cited in Hamer (1988), pp. 197–98.
53. 'Removal of Women's Disabilities', *Evening Star*, 5 July 1900, p. 5.
54. 'The Gossip's Diary', *Hastings Standard*, 7 July 1900, p. 2.
55. 'The Session', *Temuka Leader*, 12 July 1900, p. 2.
56. 'Parliamentary Notes', *Evening Star*, 5 July 1900, p. 2.
57. Ibid.
58. Ibid.
59. 'A Woman', letter to the editor, *Press*, 6 February 1901, p. 4.
60. This is presumed to be the American women's rights periodical founded by Lucy Stone and her husband Henry Blackwell in 1870, by this time under the editorship of their daughter Alice Stone Blackwell. The weekly newspaper was 'devoted to the interests of woman, to her educational, industrial, legal and political equality, and especially to her right of suffrage' and was distributed to 39 countries, including New Zealand. Agnes E. Ryan, *The Torch Bearer: A look forward and back at the* Woman's Journal, *the organ of the woman's movement*. (Boston: Woman's Journal & Suffrage News, 1916) p. 59.
61. 'The indifference of women', *White Ribbon*, vol. 6, no. 70 (March 1901), p. 10.
62. Ibid.
63. Untitled, *Wanganui Herald*, 19 March 1902, p. 3.
64. 'Progress in politics', *Lyttelton Times*, 21 March 1902, p. 4.
65. M.H. Sievwright, 'Removal of the disabilities of women', *Hawera and Normanby Star*, 7 March 1902, p. 4.
66. Ibid.

67. Ibid.
68. 'President's Address', National Council of Women of New Zealand Annual Meeting, 6 May 1902, reprinted in *Hawke's Bay Herald*, 7 May 1902, p. 3.
69. Ibid.
70. On 22 August 1902, three petitions for the removal of women's civil and political disabilities were presented to the Upper House and one to the Lower House.
71. Margaret Sievwright, 'Economic independence of married women', paper read before the National Council of Women of New Zealand, cited in 'National Council of Women', *Hawke's Bay Herald*, 12 May 1902, p. 4.
72. Ibid.
73. Mrs H. Hill, 'Men's rights and women's claims', paper read before National Council of Women of New Zealand, 11 May 1902, cited in 'National Council of Women', *Hawke's Bay Herald*, 12 May 1902, p. 4.
74. Mrs K.W. Sheppard, 'Reform in government', paper read before the National Council of Women of New Zealand, 9 May 1902, Kate W. Sheppard Ephemera, 176/53, Box 3, Folder 21, Item 481, p. 2.
75. Ibid., p. 3.
76. See *JAJLC* 1902, No. 9; *JHR* 1902, no. 350.
77. George Russell, *NZPD*, vol. 122 (9 September 1902), pp. 203–04.
78. Mrs Emily Nicol, 'Women's suffrage: A woman's view of its results', *New Zealand Times*, 19 September 1902, p. 2.
79. 'Women's suffrage', *Hastings Standard*, 20 September 1902, p. 2.
80. See Mercutio, 'Local Gossip', *New Zealand Herald*, 17 June 1899, p. 9.
81. A. Daldy, 'Rev. J. Parker and the National Council of Women', *New Zealand Herald*, 28 June 1899, p. 7.
82. Emily Nicol, letter to the editor, *New Zealand Herald*, 29 June 1899, p. 7.
83. See 'Canterbury Women's Institute', *Lyttelton Times*, 12 November 1902, p. 9.
84. Hamer, *The New Zealand Liberals*, p. 233.
85. Several prohibitionist candidates stood in multiple electorates; the Rev. Frank Isitt was nominated as the prohibitionist candidate in 10 separate electorates, and came second in eight.
86. Hamer, *The New Zealand Liberals*, p. 233.
87. The Representation Act 1900 increased the number of seats in the House of Representatives from 70 to 76.
88. Petition Nos. 275, 365, 364 and 525, Reports of Public Petitions A to L Committee, I-1, *Appendix to the Journals of the House of Representatives of New Zealand*, Session 1903.
89. Petition No. 3, Schedule of Petitions Presented to the Legislative Council, *JAJLC*, Session 1903.
90. 'Women's disabilities', *White Ribbon*, vol. 8, no. 96 (May 1903), p. 2.
91. Ibid.
92. Ibid.
93. Ibid.
94. 'Women's Temperance Convention', *New Zealand Herald*, 14 March 1903, p. 6.

Notes for Chapter 3

95. 'Women and politics', *Southland Times*, 20 March 1903, p. 2.
96. 'The emancipation of women', *Lyttelton Times*, 14 March 1903, p. 6.
97. From 1894 when the Local Option Poll was introduced, the WCTU invested considerable resources to achieve the three-fifths majority required to introduce prohibition in local liquor licensing districts. The 'no licence' campaign became synonymous with public perceptions of the work of the WCTU.
98. 'The women's franchise', *Manawatu Evening Standard and Pohangina Gazette*, 1 August 1903, p. 4.
99. 'Removal of the civil disabilities of women: Interview with the Premier', *White Ribbon*, vol. 9, no. 99, August 1903, p. 8.
100. See 'A women's deputation', *New Zealand Herald*, 3 August 1903, p. 5.
101. 'The shrieking sisterhood', *Mataura Ensign*, 4 August 1903, p. 2.
102. 'Women's disabilities', *Hastings Standard*, 10 August 1903, p. 2.
103. 'Women's National Council', *Feilding Star*, 11 August 1903, p. 4.
104. 'Women's disabilities', *Hastings Standard*, 10 August 1903, p. 2.
105. 'Removal of the civil disabilities of women, p. 9.
106. Richard Seddon, *NZPD*, vol. 124 (5 August 1903), p. 273.
107. Alfred Fraser, *NZPD*, vol. 124 (5 August 1903), p. 278.
108. 'The National Council of Women', *Taranaki Daily News*, 7 September 1903, p. 2.
109. Letter from Margaret Sievwright to Amey Daldy, 1903, cited in Betty Holt, *Women in Council: A history of the National Council of Women of New Zealand from 1896 to 1979* (Wellington: National Council of Women of New Zealand, 1980), p. 45.
110. See 'Passing Events', *New Zealand Mail*, 16 September 1903, p. 46.
111. See 'Our progressive sisters', *Free Lance*, 19 September 1903, p. 8.
112. Letter from Margaret Sievwright to Amey Daldy, 1903, cited in Holt, *Women in Council*, p. 45.
113. Richard Seddon, *NZPD*, vol. 127 (2 November 1903), p. 261.
114. 'W.C.T.U.', *Wanganui Chronicle*, 22 March 1905, p. 5.
115. Lovell-Smith, *The Woman Question*, p. 216: Margaret Lovell-Smith, 'Smith, Lucey Masey 1861–1936' in *The Suffragists*, p. 135.
116. Lucy Smith, 'Wanted – A Woman's Party', *White Ribbon*, vol. 10, no. 114 (November 1904), p. 7.
117. 'Local and General News', *New Zealand Herald*, 27 April 1905, p. 4. For precedents of the Young New Zealand Party, see 'Wellington Notes', *Lyttelton Times*, 5 May 1905, p. 3.
118. Electoral Bill 1905 (79-1), cl. 99, subs. 5: 'Every nomination paper of a woman as a candidate shall be absolutely void and of no effect, and shall be rejected by the Returning Officer without question.'
119. 'Women in Parliament', *White Ribbon*, vol. 11, no. 124 (September 1905), p. 6.
120. Ibid., pp. 6–7.
121. 'Sessional Notes', *New Zealand Times*, 25 August 1905, p. 7.
122. See *NZPD*, vol. 134 (24 August 1905), pp. 82–83.
123. 'An injustice to women', *Lyttelton Times*, 26 August 1905, p. 4.

124. 'A forgetful generation', *Lyttelton Times*, 20 September 1905, p. 6.
125. K.W. Sheppard, letter to the editor, *Lyttelton Times*, 21 September 1905, p. 3.
126. 'An ungrateful generation', *Lyttelton Times*, 21 September 1905, p. 6.
127. See 'The Electoral Bill', *Lyttelton Times*, 29 September 1905, p. 4.
128. See 'Women's Christian Temperance Union', *Lyttelton Times*, 2 December 1905, p. 9.
129. 'Women's political disabilities', *New Zealand Mail*, 7 March 1906, p. 41.
130. 'National Council of Women', *Lyttelton Times*, 30 April 1906, p. 10.
131. The term 'prime minister' became the official title from 1906. William Hall-Jones, who was acting premier at the time Seddon died, was subsequently invited by the governor Lord Plunket to form a ministry and became the first designated prime minister. On the return of Joseph Ward from a conference in Rome, Hall-Jones offered his resignation after six and a half weeks in office.
132. 'Disabilities of women', *Press*, 15 October 1906, p. 8.
133. 'Women's disabilities', *Lyttelton Times*, 28 March 1907, p. 6.
134. 'Women's disabilities', *Star*, 27 June 1907, p. 4.
135. 'Women and the vote', *Timaru Herald*, 12 February 1907, p. 4.
136. See 'The enfranchisement of women', *Lyttelton Times*, 6 September 1907, p. 6.
137. Wilford's amendment provided that 'any person may be nominated or capable of being elected who is entitled to vote under the provisions of section six of the Electoral Act, 1893': Thomas Wilford, *NZPD*, vol. 140 (7 August 1907), p. 113.
138. Thomas Wilford, *NZPD*, vol. 184 (26 September 1919), p. 976.
139. See 'Respect', 'Women in Parliament', *Dominion*, 16 November 1911, p. 4.
140. Sir Joseph Ward, *NZPD*, vol. 140 (14 August 1907), p. 230.
141. Ibid.
142. 'Not good for man to be alone', *White Ribbon*, vol. 14, no. 147 (August 1907), p. 7.
143. Ibid.
144. 'Women in Parliament', *White Ribbon*, vol. 14, no. 154 (March 1908), p. 7.
145. 'The Premier in Palmerston', *Evening Post*, 20 October 1908, p. 6.
146. 'Women's Christian Temperance Union', *Poverty Bay Herald*, 9 May 1911, p. 7.
147. 'Women's Christian Temperance Union', *Press*, 18 September 1909, p. 12.
148. 'Canterbury Women's Institute President's Report', *Lyttelton Times*, 13 March 1908, p. 3.
149. 'Women's rights', *Lyttelton Times*, 16 March 1908, p. 6.
150. See 'Woman's world', *Press*, 22 August 1908, p. 7.
151. 'Where are the disabilities?' *Observer*, 13 March 1909, p. 16; 'They say', *Observer*, 27 March 1909, p. 7.
152. 'Women's welcome', *New Zealand Times*, 5 October 1909, p. 8.
153. 'The suffragette agitation', *West Coast Times*, 10 February 1910, p. 2.
154. A.E.T., 'A women's parliament', *Evening Star*, 5 March 1910, p. 5.
155. 'Parliamentary Debating Society', *Wairarapa Daily Times*, 28 June 1910, p. 5.

CHAPTER 4
The full privilege of citizenship, 1911 to 1919

1. 'Women's sphere', *Wairarapa Age*, 3 July 1911, p. 4.
2. The adoption of this system was influenced in part by the growth of independent Labour politics in Australia and Britain and was viewed by the Liberal Government as a cautionary measure to prevent loss as a result of split votes of Liberal seats. The provisions of this system applied only to the 76 European electorates and not to the four Māori electorates, and were abolished in 1913 because it did not work equitably under the party system.
3. Four seats from the Government changed to the Opposition, two Opposition seats changed to the Government, the Opposition lost one seat to Labour and one seat changed from one Liberal candidate to another. See David Hamer, *The New Zealand Liberals: The years of power, 1891–1912* (Auckland: Auckland University Press, 1988), pp. 310–12.
4. Ibid., p. 330.
5. See, for example, 'Notes of the Day', *Dominion*, 9 December 1911, p. 4.
6. 'Views of the leaders', *New Zealand Herald*, 9 December 1911, p. 8.
7. Ibid.
8. Justitia, Letter to the editor, *Lyttelton Times*, 11 December 1911, p. 7.
9. 'Every vote on Thursday', *Dominion*, 12 December 1911, p. 9.
10. 'Ministry's precarious tenure', *Evening Post*, 15 December 1911, p. 7.
11. Hamer, *The New Zealand Liberals*, p. 352.
12. For detailed discussions of the post-1911 election period and the formation of the Reform Government, see Elizabeth Ward, '"For light and liberty": The origins and early development of the Reform Party, 1887–1915', PhD thesis, Massey University, 2018, pp. 166–83, and Michael Bassett, *Three Party Politics in New Zealand 1911–1931* (Auckland: Historical Publications, 1982), pp. 3–14.
13. See Keith Jackson & Alan McRobie, *Historical Political Dictionary of New Zealand*, 2nd edn (Rangiora: MC Enterprises, 2008), pp. 40, 211–12.
14. See Ward, '"For light and liberty"', Chapter 7.
15. Ibid., p. 219.
16. 'W.C.T.U. Convention', *Taranaki Herald*, 29 March 1911, p. 2.
17. 'Women's Christian Temperance Union', *Poverty Bay Herald*, 9 May 1911, p. 7.
18. 'Editorial: Women's sphere', *Wairarapa Age*, 3 July 1911, p. 4.
19. Ibid.
20. See 'Women's sphere', *Otago Daily Times*, 19 March 1912, p. 2.
21. 'The responsibilities of women as citizens', *White Ribbon*, vol. 18, no. 214 (April 1913), p. 2.
22. In 1897, Dunedin-born Ethel Benjamin became the first New Zealand woman admitted to the bar.
23. 'New women's society', *New Zealand Herald*, 25 March 1914, p. 7.
24. See 'Auckland Civic League successful half year', *New Zealand Herald*, 7 October 1914, p. 9.

25. 'Memorable scene', *New Zealand Herald*, 6 August 1914, p. 9.
26. 'Housewife' was the name given to a cloth sewing kit dating back to the mid-eighteenth century. Those used in the armed forces were usually a roll of flannel holding needle and thread.
27. 'Women and the War', *Dominion*, 7 August 1914, p. 2.
28. See 'The Budget and the Opposition', *Dominion*, 7 August 1914, p. 4.
29. William Massey, *NZPD*, vol. 169 (4 August 1914), p. 381.
30. George Witty, *NZPD*, vol. 171 (22 October 1914), p. 277.
31. See 'Legislative Council Bill', *NZPD*, vol. 171 (23 October 1914), p. 311.
32. John Barr, *NZPD*, vol. 171 (2 November 1914), p. 686.
33. Henry Wigram, *NZPD*, vol. 171 (2 November 1914), p. 689.
34. John Barr, *NZPD*, vol. 171 (2 November 1914), p. 687.
35. John Paul, *NZPD*, vol. 171 (2 November 1914), p. 688.
36. William Beehan, *NZPD*, vol. 171 (2 November 1914), p. 688.
37. William Massey, *NZPD*, vol. 171 (2 November 1914), p. 692.
38. Sir Joseph Ward, *NZPD*, vol. 171 (2 November 1914), p. 692.
39. George Russell, *NZPD*, vol. 171 (2 November 1914), p. 694.
40. Alfred Newman, *NZPD*, vol. 171 (2 November 1914), p. 695.
41. Patrick Webb, *NZPD*, vol. 169 (29 July 1914), pp. 268–69.
42. See James McCombs, *NZPD*, vol. 171 (22 October 1914), pp. 268, 268–69.
43. Ibid., p. 280.
44. James McCombs, *NZPD*, vol. 171 (3 November 1914), p. 799.
45. John E. Martin, *The House: New Zealand's House of Representatives, 1854–2004* (Palmerston North: Dunmore Publishing, 2004), p. 148.
46. I am indebted to Jim McAloon's 'Governments, parliaments and parties (New Zealand)' in the online International Encyclopedia of the First World War for this overview of the New Zealand political arrangement during World War One.
47. 'Women's International League', *Maoriland Worker*, 2 August 1916, p. 3.
48. Barbara Brookes, *A History of New Zealand Women* (Wellington: Bridget Williams Books, 2016), p. 146.
49. Ibid., p. 176.
50. 'The Hospital Ship: Funds for equipment', *New Zealand Herald*, 24 May 1915, p. 4.
51. See, for example, 'Majority of women's suffrage: A symposium', originally published in the *Evening Star*, 19 September 1914 and subsequently published as a 15-page pamphlet.
52. 'Franchise Day', *White Ribbon*, vol. 21, no. 243 (September 1915), p. 9.
53. See Raewyn Dalziel, 'Political organisations', in Anne Else (ed.), *Women Together: A history of women's organisations in New Zealand/Ngā rōpū wāhine o te motu* (Wellington: Historical Branch, Department of Internal Affairs, 1993).
54. Melanie Nolan, 'Snow, Sarah Ellen Oliver', *Dictionary of New Zealand Biography*, first published in 1998. Te Ara – the Encyclopedia of New Zealand: https://teara.govt.nz/en/biographies/4s35/snow-sarah-ellen-oliver
55. 'Public meeting', *White Ribbon*, vol. 22, no. 263 (May 1917), p. 5.
56. Charles Statham, *NZPD*, vol. 178 (19 July 1917), p. 593.

Notes for Chapter 4

57. See www.bl.uk/votes-for-women/articles/womens-suffrage-timeline
58. In 1918 suffrage was granted to women in Britain over the age of 30; it was not until the Representation of the People Act 1928 that women over the age of 21 received the franchise in Britain.
59. See 'Women's franchise', *NZPD*, vol. 183 (26 November 1918), p. 396.
60. James McCombs, *NZPD*, vol. 183 (5 December 1918), pp. 843, 844.
61. Ibid., p. 844.
62. Alfred Newman, *NZPD*, vol. 183 (5 December 1918), p. 845.
63. John Payne, *NZPD*, vol. 183 (5 December 1918), p. 846.
64. Sir Francis Bell, *NZPD*, vol. 183 (6 December 1918), p. 850.
65. Sir William Hall-Jones, *NZPD*, vol. 183 (6 December 1918), p. 850, 851.
66. John Paul, *NZPD*, vol. 183 (6 December 1918), pp. 852, 853.
67. William Earnshaw, *NZPD*, vol. 183 (6 December 1918), p. 853.
68. 'Women in Parliament', *Evening Post*, 7 December 1918, p. 8.
69. See 'Women and politics', *Otago Daily Times*, 9 December 1918, p. 2.
70. William Massey, *NZPD*, vol. 183 (7 December 1918), p. 924.
71. Sir Joseph Ward, *NZPD*, vol. 183 (7 December 1918), p. 925.
72. James McCombs, *NZPD*, vol. 183 (7 December 1918), p. 926.
73. Kate Hunter, 'Women's mobilization for war (New Zealand)', in 1914-1918-online, *International Encyclopedia of the First World War*.
74. 'The Women's Movement in New Zealand', *Maoriland Worker*, 15 November 1916, p. 7.
75. Ibid.
76. Dorothy Page, *The National Council of Women: A centennial history* (Auckland: Auckland University Press, 1996), p. 56.
77. Letter from Kate W. Sheppard to Sir William Hall-Jones, 4 February 1919, Hall-Jones, William (Sir), 1851–1936 Papers, MS-Papers-5755-68, ATL.
78. 'Women in Parliament', *Auckland Star*, 7 August 1919, p. 10.
79. Women's Parliamentary Rights Bill 1919 (60-1), cl. 2.
80. Kate Sheppard, 'President's Address', National Council of Women of New Zealand Conference, 9 September 1919, p. 2, MS-Papers-1371-107, ATL.
81. Ibid., p. 7.
82. Ibid., p. 12.
83. 'Women and citizenship', *Dominion*, 9 September 1919, p. 2.
84. Ibid., p. 4.
85. See editorial, 'The emancipation of women', *Dominion*, 9 September 1919, p. 4.
86. William Massey, *NZPD*, vol. 184 (26 September 1919), p. 964.
87. Ibid.
88. Sir Joseph Ward, *NZPD*, vol. 184 (26 September 1919), p. 964.
89. Ibid., p. 965.
90. Ibid.
91. Kate Sheppard, 'President's Address', National Council of Women of New Zealand Conference, 9 September 1919, p. 1, MS-Papers-1371-107, ATL.
92. Ibid., pp. 3, 5.

93. Henry Holland, *NZPD*, vol. 184 (26 September 1919), p. 967.
94. Peter Fraser, *NZPD*, vol. 184 (26 September 1919), p. 976.
95. Vigor Brown, *NZPD*, vol. 184 (26 September 1919), p. 977.
96. Although she was in Holloway prison at the time for suspected involvement in entering into treasonable communication with the German enemy, the Countess Markievicz was elected with a majority of more than 4000 votes as a Sinn Féin member for the Dublin St Patrick's Ward. She refused to acknowledge the British government and did not take her seat.
97. Robert Wright, *NZPD*, vol. 184 (26 September 1919), p. 970.
98. Ibid., pp. 970, 971.
99. Christopher Parr, *NZPD*, vol. 184 (26 September 1919), p. 968.
100. Robert Wright, *NZPD*, vol. 184 (26 September 1919), pp. 969–70.
101. Peter Fraser, *NZPD*, vol. 184 (26 September 1919), p. 974.
102. Alfred Newman, *NZPD*, vol. 184 (26 September 1919), p. 972.
103. Thomas MacGibbon, *NZPD*, vol. 184 (2 October 1919), p. 1103.
104. John MacGregor, *NZPD*, vol. 184 (2 October 1919), p. 1103.
105. Sir Francis Bell, *NZPD*, vol. 184 (2 October 1919), p. 1104.
106. Women's Parliamentary Rights Bill 1919 (60-3), Legislative Council, 3 October 1919. Emphasis and striking out are in the original text.
107. John Paul, *NZPD*, vol. 185 (3 October 1919), p. 2.
108. William Earnshaw, *NZPD*, vol. 185 (3 October 1919), p. 4.
109. Te Heuheu Tukino, *NZPD*, vol. 185 (3 October 1919), p. 6.
110. William Massey, *NZPD*, vol. 185 (6 October 1919), p. 79.
111. George Jones, *NZPD*, vol. 185 (7 October 1919), p. 101.
112. James McCombs, *NZPD*, vol. 185 (9 October 1919), pp. 208, 209.
113. Ibid., p. 210.
114. Sir John Finlay, *NZPD*, vol. 185 (9 October 1919), p. 211.
115. Richard McCallum, *NZPD*, vol. 185 (9 October 1919), p. 212.
116. Sir Joseph Ward, *NZPD*, vol. 185 (9 October 1919), p. 212.
117. Thomas Wilford, *NZPD*, vol. 185 (9 October 1919), p. 213.
118. Henry Holland, *NZPD*, vol. 185 (9 October 1919), pp. 213, 214.
119. Peter Fraser, *NZPD*, vol. 185 (9 October 1919), p. 218.
120. William Massey, *NZPD*, vol. 185 (17 October 1919), p. 499.
121. Women's Parliamentary Rights (No. 2) Bill, 1919, cl. 2.
122. Sir Francis Bell, *NZPD*, vol. 185 (23 October 1919), p. 756.
123. Henry Michel, *NZPD*, vol. 185 (23 October 1919), p. 758.
124. One woman was elected but was later disqualified from taking a seat in the British House of Commons.
125. George Jones, *NZPD*, vol. 185 (23 October 1919), p. 761.
126. 'The council and women', *New Zealand Times*, 28 October 1919, p. 4.
127. Ibid.
128. 'Women's parliamentary rights', *Evening Star*, 1 November 1919, p. 9.
129. Kate Sheppard, 'President's Address', p. 1.

CHAPTER 5
Petticoated candidates, 1919 to 1933

1. Mr Wilford, *NZPD*, vol. 184 (26 September 1919), p. 977; Mr Wright, *NZPD*, vol. 184 (26 September 1919), p. 970.
2. Sandra Coney, 'Ellen Melville, 1882–1946', in Charlotte Macdonald, Merimeri Penfold & Bridget Williams (eds), *The Book of New Zealand Women: Ko kui ma te kaupapa* (Wellington: Bridget Williams Books, 1991), p. 442.
3. Harry Holland won the by-election for the Grey electorate after incumbent Paddy Webb was imprisoned for two years for refusing to be conscripted for military service.
4. 'Political', *Stratford Evening Post*, 1 October 1919, p. 5.
5. The Women's National Reserve was launched in August 1915 as a reserve of womanpower for the war effort: women registered for either general employment or employment in specific fields such as farming, domestic work, factory work, professional and clerical work, and work in shops.
6. V. Kuitert, 'Ellen Melville 1882–1946', MA research essay, University of Auckland, 1986, p. 121.
7. Suzanne Starky, 'Garmson, Aileen Anna Maria', first published in *Dictionary of New Zealand Biography*, vol. 2, 1993; Te Ara – the Encyclopedia of New Zealand: https://teara.govt.nz/eb/biographies/2g1/garmson-aileen-anna-maria
8. At her final election campaign meeting Cooke stated she had been closely associated with the people and politics of New Zealand for over 40 years; she had arrived in New Zealand when she was 17 with only five pounds in her pocket; see 'Thames seat', *Thames Star*, 16 December 1919, p. 1.
9. 'The Parnell contest', *New Zealand Herald*, 20 November 1919, p. 10. One of the cases Baume took to the Arbitration Court was on behalf of adult women upholsterers who, despite having served four years' apprenticeship, were receiving less than a living wage of 19 shillings and sixpence a week. See 'Contest for Parnell: Address by Mrs Baume', *New Zealand Herald*, 2 December 1919, p. 8.
10. See 'Mrs Baume and Labour', *Auckland Star*, 28 November 1919, p. 18.
11. 'All Sorts of People', *Free Lance*, 29 October 1919, p. 4.
12. A 'Progressive Reform' group of vaguely left political tendencies developed among back benches during 1918–19 when Massey was in Europe.
13. 'Local Gossip', *New Zealand Herald*, 15 November 1919, p. 1 (Supplement).
14. 'Grey Lynn seat', *New Zealand Herald*, 27 November 1919, p. 8.
15. 'Mrs Lindsay Cooke', *Thames Star*, 7 November 1919, p. 3.
16. For details of the Returned Soldiers platform, see 'The Soldiers' Party', *Hawkes Bay Tribune*, 24 July 1919, p. 2.
17. The Women's Citizen's Association was formed in August 1918 'to unite women, to stimulate their interest in civic life, and to foster a sense of civic responsibility with regard to their use of the vote'; 'Women's Citizens' Association Annual Meeting', *Evening Star*, 5 November 1919, p. 8.
18. See, 'Political Notes', *Press*, 25 November 1919, p. 7.

19. 'The Parnell contest', *New Zealand Herald*, 20 November 1919, p. 10.
20. 'Lady legislators', *Free Lance*, 3 December 1919, p. 10.
21. See 'Grey Lynn electorate: Speech by Miss Melville', *New Zealand Herald*, 26 November 1919, p. 10.
22. 'A woman candidate', *Waikato Times*, 19 November 1919, p. 7.
23. 'Political campaign: The Thames seat', *Auckland Star*, 19 November 1919, p. 3. Minister of Labour William Pember Reeves was largely responsible for the Industrial Conciliation and Arbitration Act, 1894, which recognised trade unions and individual employers or industrial unions of employers as responsible parties in the negotiation of wages and other employment conditions. The Act made New Zealand the first country in the world to outlaw strikes and introduce compulsory arbitration.
24. See Ruby Watson, letter to the editor, *Thames Star*, 20 November 1919, p. 1.
25. 'Local and General', *Waihi Daily Telegraph*, 21 November 1919, p. 2.
26. 'Untitled', *Press*, 25 November 1919, p. 6.
27. 'Election Notices', *Thames Star*, 24 November 1919, p. 1.
28. See 'Protestants organise', *Wanganui Herald*, 18 July 1917, p. 8; John Brennan, 'The Protestant Political Association', *Auckland Star*, 10 August 1918, p. 9.
29. See Stephen Barnett, *Those Were the Days: A nostalgic look at the 1920s from the pages of the* Weekly News (Auckland: Moa Publications, 1988), p. 24.
30. 'Grey Lynn electorate: Speech by Miss Melville', p. 10.
31. 'Election speeches: Miss Melville's debut', *Auckland Star*, 26 November 1919, p. 9.
32. 'Grey Lynn electorate: Speech by Miss Melville', p. 10.
33. Ibid.
34. See 'Grey Lynn seat: Women's viewpoint', *New Zealand Herald*, 27 November 1919, p. 8.
35. 'Political pebbles', *Observer*, 6 December 1919, p. 26.
36. 'Grey Lynn electorate: Address by Miss Melville', *New Zealand Herald*, 6 December 1919, p. 12.
37. 'All Sorts of People', *Free Lance*, 3 December 1919, p. 4.
38. 'The Premier on tour', *Clutha Leader*, 2 December 1919, p. 5.
39. See advertisements, *Thames Star*, 14 November 1919, p. 1, col. 5.
40. Advertisements, *Thames Star*, 11 December 1919, p. 1, col. 6.
41. 'Labour aims', *Dominion*, 29 December 1919, p. 4.
42. 'The defeat of Sir Joseph Ward', *Press*, 18 December 1919, p. 6.
43. 'The game of forfeits', *Feilding Star*, 20 December 1919, p. 2.
44. 'Editorial: Women candidates at the election', *Press*, 23 December 1919, p. 8.
45. Ibid.
46. Letter from K.W. Sheppard to Lady Aberdeen from Christchurch, 31 March 1920, MS-Papers-3969-1, ATL.
47. See, for example, her talk to senior clubs of the YWCA, reported in 'Woman's World', *Auckland Star*, 2 September 1921, p. 8.
48. See Dorothy Page, *The National Council of Women: A centennial history* (Auckland: Auckland University Press, 1996), pp. 63, 67.

49. Minutes of annual meetings and conferences, 29 September 1921, pp. 6–7, MS-Papers-1371-126, ATL.
50. Board of Health, Report on Venereal Diseases in New Zealand, 1922 (*AJHR*, 1922, Session I, H-31a). For a detailed discussion of the positions of various women's organisations on this issue, see Philip J. Fleming, '"Shadow over New Zealand": The response to venereal disease in New Zealand 1910–1945', PhD thesis, Massey University, 1989, pp. 50–61.
51. Kate Sheppard, 'President's Address', National Council of Women of New Zealand Conference, 9 September 1919, p. 10, MS-Papers-1371-107, ATL.
52. See Fleming, '"Shadow over New Zealand"', pp. 69–70.
53. Board of Health, Report on Venereal Diseases in New Zealand, 1922, p. 14.
54. Ibid., p. 22.
55. Ibid., p. 2. Subsequent to this report, in 1924 a committee of inquiry was held into 'Mental defectives and sexual offenders'.
56. See 'Early poll wanted', *Auckland Star*, 8 August 1922, p. 5.
57. 'Test questions to candidates', *Press*, 9 November 1922, p. 14. The concluding remarks in the Report of the Committee of Inquiry into Venereal Diseases referred to the worrying proportions of 'mental and physical defectives reproducing their kind'. These concerns gave rise to a second official inquiry in 1924 into 'Mental defectives and sexual offenders in New Zealand'.
58. 'The Avon seat', *Auckland Star*, 8 August 1922, p. 5. At the first AGM of the Social Welfare Guild it was reported that alongside the everyday work of the guild, a Young Person's Guild had also been established, hundreds of families had received food parcels at Christmas, assistance had been provided to some families to shift to the country where they had found work, and a library had been established at a home for elderly men in Ashburton. See, 'Social Welfare Guild', *Press*, 3 June 1922, p. 2.
59. 'Mrs Herbert's campaign for Avon', *Press*, 23 November 1922, p. 9.
60. Advertisements, *Press*, 4 December 1922, col. 2, p. 14.
61. 'The General Election', *Press*, 14 November 1922, p. 9.
62. 'Mrs Herbert's campaign for Avon', p. 9.
63. 'A woman candidate', *Press*, 10 November 1922, p. 16.
64. 'Avon seat', *Nelson Evening Mail*, 16 October 1922, p. 5.
65. Avon Elector, letter to the editor, *Press*, 25 November 1922, p. 11.
66. 'Wellington woman candidate', *Press*, 30 November 1922, p. 10.
67. *NZ Truth*, 4 November 1922, p. 6.
68. 'The General Election', *Press*, 14 November 1922, p. 9.
69. 'Miss Melville silences an interjector', *Press*, 23 November 1922, p. 9.
70. 'Failure of women candidates', *New Zealand Herald*, 9 December 1922, p. 10.
71. 'Women candidates', *Press*, 11 December 1922, p. 6.
72. Annual Report, Auckland Branch of the National Council of Women, extract reprinted in 'Council of Women', *New Zealand Herald*, 30 May 1923, p. 14.
73. Michael Bassett, *Three Party Politics in New Zealand 1911–1931* (Auckland: Historical Publications, 1982), pp. 32, 33.

74. President's Address, Fourth Annual Conference, 17 September 1923, p. 23, MS-Papers-1371-126, ATL.
75. Minutes, Fourth Annual Conference, 17 September 1923, p. 38, MS-Papers-1371-126, ATL.
76. Lantern slides were images printed on glass slides, projected through a 'magic lantern' with a light source.
77. Michael Bassett, 'Coates, Joseph Gordon', *Dictionary of New Zealand Biography*, first published 1996. Te Ara – the Encyclopedia of New Zealand: https://teara.govt.nz/en/biographies/3c24/coates-joseph-gordon
78. 'Fusion prospects', *Evening Star*, 22 June 1925, p. 6.
79. 'Political situation', *Otago Daily Times*, 6 June 1925, p. 12.
80. 'Member for Nelson', *Nelson Evening Mail*, 1 July 1925, p. 5; for the full text of the amendment, see Harry Atmore, *NZPD*, vol. 206 (10 July 1925), p. 404.
81. Harry Atmore, *NZPD*, vol. 206 (10 July 1925), p. 402.
82. 'Wanted – A National Party', *Nelson Evening Mail*, 16 May 1925, p. 6.
83. R.G. Habershon, 'A study in politics, 1928–31', MA thesis, University of Auckland, 1958, p. 6.
84. 'Miss Melville's campaign', *New Zealand Herald*, 9 October 1925, p. 11.
85. Ibid.
86. 'Unsuccessful attack', *New Zealand Herald*, 15 October 1925, p. 14.
87. 'Election rowdyism', *New Zealand Herald*, 22 October 1925, p. 7.
88. Ellen Green, letter to the editor, *New Zealand Herald*, 22 October 1925, p. 7.
89. See 'Election meetings', *Auckland Star*, 23 October 1925, p. 6.
90. 'Woman's rights', *Auckland Star*, 24 October 1925, p. 14.
91. 'Campaign notes', *Evening Post*, 26 October 1925, p. 9.
92. See 'Alleged slanders', *New Zealand Herald*, 27 October 1925, p. 12.
93. 'Auckland electorates', *New Zealand Herald*, 2 November 1925, p. 10.
94. 'Staunch Reformer', letter to the editor, *New Zealand Herald*, 27 February 1926, p. 12.
95. 'Reform's methods', *Auckland Star*, 4 March 1926, p. 6.
96. Ibid.
97. Ibid.
98. 'By-election in Eden', *New Zealand Herald*, 5 March 1926, p. 10.
99. Ibid.
100. Ibid.
101. Woman Citizen, letter to the editor, *New Zealand Herald*, 6 March 1926, p. 9.
102. Ibid.
103. Equality, letter to the editor, *New Zealand Herald*, 9 March 1926, p. 7.
104. Reform Always, letter to the editor, *New Zealand Herald*, 9 March 1926, p. 7.
105. Anti-Petticoat and Labour, letter to the editor, *Auckland Star*, 12 March 1926, p. 12.
106. 'Miss Melville determined', *Auckland Star*, 8 March 1926, p. 5.
107. 'Topics of the day', *Evening Post*, 11 March 1926, p. 8.
108. 'Miss Melville firm', *New Zealand Herald*, 19 March 1926, p. 12.

Notes for Chapter 5

109. 'Just another move', *Auckland Star*, 19 March 1926, p. 5.
110. 'Miss Melville's lady friends', *Auckland Star*, 19 March 1926, p. 6.
111. 'Eden by-election: Miss Melville's plaint', *New Zealand Herald*, 20 March 1926, p. 12.
112. Ibid.
113. Ibid.
114. 'Declarations by chairmen', *New Zealand Herald*, 24 March 1926, p. 15.
115. See Advertisements, *Auckland Star*, 26 March 1926, p. 14, col. 3.
116. 'Contest for Eden', *New Zealand Herald*, 30 March 1926, p. 14.
117. 'The rights of women', *New Zealand Herald*, 12 April 1926, p. 12.
118. '"A clean-cut issue": Mr Coates and the electors', *New Zealand Herald*, 14 April 1926, p. 16.
119. 'The Eden contest', *New Zealand Herald*, 14 April 1926, p. 12.
120. 'Editorial: A representative for Eden', p. 6.
121. Jessie Mackay, letter to the editor, *Auckland Star*, 14 April 1926, p. 17.
122. 'Editorial: A representative for Eden', *Auckland Star*, 14 April 1926, p. 6.
123. 'The Eden by-election', *New Zealand Herald*, 16 April 1926, p. 10.
124. 'The Eden by-election', *Press*, 16 April 1926, p. 8.
125. 'Eden's verdict', *Evening Post*, 16 April 1926, p. 6.
126. Roskill Elector, letter to the editor, *New Zealand Herald*, 20 April 1926, p. 7.
127. C.H.N., letter to the editor, *Auckland Star*, 17 April 1926, p. 16.
128. Justice, letter to the editor, *Evening Post*, 17 April 1926, p. 8.
129. Square Deal, letter to the editor, *New Zealand Herald*, 19 April 1926, p. 7.
130. Ernest A. James, letter to the editor, *Evening Post*, 22 April 1926, p. 10.
131. Pro Bono Publico, letter to the editor, *New Zealand Herald*, 20 April 1926, p. 7.
132. See report of first day of the conference, *New Zealand Herald*, 2 March 1927, p. 14.
133. R.M. Chapman, 'The significance of the 1928 General Election: A study of certain trends in New Zealand politics during the nineteen-twenties', MA thesis, University of New Zealand, 1948, p. 43.
134. 'The United Party', *Press*, 3 November 1928, p. 17.
135. 'Election notes', *Otago Daily Times*, 7 November 1928, p. 10. This description of the United Party was first made several months earlier; see 'Notes and Comments', *Patea Mail*, 27 August 1928, p. 2.
136. Chapman, 'The significance of the 1928 General Election', p. 49.
137. Robert Semple, cited in Bruce Brown, *The Rise of New Zealand Labour: A history of the New Zealand Labour Party 1916–1940* (Wellington: Milburn, 1962), pp. 89–90.
138. 'Election campaign', *New Zealand Herald*, 16 October 1928, p. 13.
139. The deputation that met with Emily Maguire in her own home included the president of the Auckland Branch of the New Zealand Political Reform League, the chairman and the president of the Auckland East branch of the League, the organiser, and member of the Auckland Hospital Board Ethel Kidd who had led

the delegation to Ellen Melville in the Eden by-election to insist she retract her candidature.
140. Jean Garner, 'McCombs, Elizabeth Reid', *Dictionary of New Zealand Biography*, first published 1998. Te Ara – the Encyclopedia of New Zealand: https://teara.govt.nz/en/biographies/4m3/mccombs-elizabeth-reid
141. See 'Divine power', *Auckland Star*, 10 November 1928, p. 14.
142. 'Auckland East contest: Mrs Maguire's candidature', *New Zealand Herald*, 14 August 1928, p. 8.
143. See John A. Lee, *NZPD*, vol. 218 (15 August 1928), pp. 161, 263–64.
144. See Elector, letter to the editor, *New Zealand Herald*, 31 August 1928, p. 14.
145. John Patterson, letter to the editor, *New Zealand Herald*, 1 September 1928, p. 14.
146. Harold Schmidt, letter to the editor, *New Zealand Herald*, 1 September 1928, p. 14.
147. Increased competition for trams and buses operated by local authorities with the rapid rise of privately owned bus companies led to the Motor-Omnibus Act 1926, which enabled local authorities to restrict entry to the passenger transport industry. The question of whether the cost of administration of the regulations under the Act should be borne by central government or local councils was a matter of contention.
148. 'A new candidate', *New Zealand Herald*, 23 October 1928, p. 11.
149. See 'Leaders assailed', *New Zealand Herald*, 1 November 1928, p. 15. On reading of Young's candidature in the *Evening Post*, Peter Fraser wrote to her husband to assure him he did not think Young had anything to do with his wife's candidature against the Labour Party, but Fraser requested written assurance that this was the case so he could assure their many mutual friends of the fact, and he added, 'In any case, I would be sorry if anything occurred to estrange you from the Labour Party, and would like to feel that our friendship will remain unbroken, in spite of this complication'; 'Mr Fraser's letter', *Evening Post*, 6 November 1928, p. 10.
150. 'Kaiapoi: The Labour candidate', *Press*, 20 October 1928, p. 16.
151. Ibid.
152. 'Women in politics', *New Zealand Herald*, 17 October 1928, p. 15.
153. Ibid.
154. 'Women in Parliament', *Auckland Star*, 10 November 1928, p. 14.
155. See '"No Blind Follower"', *Auckland Star*, 17 October 1928, p. 11.
156. 'Meetings', *New Zealand Herald*, 24 October 1928, p. 22.
157. 'Woman on soap box', *New Zealand Herald*, 2 November 1928, p. 13.
158. See 'Leaders assailed', *New Zealand Herald*, 1 November 1928, p. 15.
159. 'General Election: Mrs Young's reasons', *Evening Post*, 3 November 1928, p. 10.
160. Ibid.
161. In May 1912 the militant Waihi Trade Union of Workers went on strike in protest at the formation of a breakaway union for engine drivers. The militancy of the strike was exacerbated by the election of Massey's conservative Reform Party in July and his determination to crush the 'Red Feds' who were backing the

Notes for Chapter 5

strike. The strike was notable for the death of Fred Evans, one of the strikers, on 12 November.
162. 'Lively scenes: Mrs Young's meeting', *Evening Post*, 6 November 1928, p. 10.
163. The provision of restrooms in country towns was a specific objective of the Women's Division of the Farmers' Union.
164. 'More heckling', *Evening Post*, 9 November 1928, p. 11.
165. 'Lively scenes: Mrs Young's meeting', p. 10.
166. See 'Mrs Young in court', *Evening Post*, 6 November 1928, p. 11.
167. 'The Waihi Strike. Mr Semple's denial', *Evening Post*, 7 November 1928, p. 12.
168. In October 1913 a dispute between the Wellington shipwrights and the Union Steam Ship Company over travelling time, wages and conditions led to a waterfront strike. At the time the Wellington watersiders were one of the largest and most militant unions in the Federation of Labour. Within a week watersiders around the country had joined the strike in sympathy. The strike leaders, Holland, Fraser and Semple were all arrested for using inflammatory language.
169. '"Strikes are dreadful"', *Evening Post*, 7 November 1928, p. 12.
170. 'More heckling', *Evening Post*, 9 November 1928, p. 11.
171. 'Interrupted address', *New Zealand Herald*, 24 October 1928, p. 14.
172. 'Ready to carry on', *New Zealand Herald*, 13 November 1928, p. 15.
173. 'Canterbury seats: Prospects reviewed', *Evening Post*, 31 October 1928, p. 14.
174. 'Auckland seats', *Press*, 22 October 1928, p. 11.
175. 'The women candidates', *Waihi Daily Telegraph*, 10 November 1928, p. 2.
176. Independent Woman, letter to the editor, *Auckland Star*, 26 November 1928, p. 6.
177. Male Liberal, letter to the editor, *Auckland Star*, 27 November 1928, p. 6.
178. Super-Independent Woman, letter to the editor, *Auckland Star*, 29 November 1928, p. 6.
179. 'Choosing candidates', *New Zealand Herald*, 24 October 1931, p. 10.
180. The date for the election for the Māori seats was 1 December 1931.
181. 'Women's candidate', *New Zealand Herald*, 17 November 1931, p. 11.
182. 'Christchurch North', *Press*, 21 November 1931, p. 19.
183. M.B. Soljak, 'Not admitted. Women and Parliament: The New Zealand attitude', *Auckland Star*, 10 December 1931, p. 27.
184. Ibid.
185. Ellen Melville unsuccessfully contested the nomination for the National Party candidate for the Remuera seat in 1941 (although the election was postponed due to the war), and unsuccessfully contested the Grey Lynn seat in the 1943 general election for the National Party.
186. For a critical discussion of the campaign promises of women parliamentary candidates between 1919 and 1969, see Sandra Wallace, 'Members for Everywoman? The campaign promises of women parliamentary candidates', *New Zealand Journal of History*, vol. 27, no. 2, 2006, 187–98.
187. 'Two women aspirants', *Northern Advocate*, 4 December 1931, p. 6.

CHAPTER 6
Our first lady member, 1933 to 1935

1. Report of 10th Annual Conference, Wellington, March 1933, p. 109, MS-Papers-1371-126, ATL.
2. Cited in David Gee, *My Dear Girl: A biography of Elizabeth McCombs, New Zealand's first woman member of Parliament, and her husband, James McCombs, member of Parliament for Lyttelton for twenty years* (Christchurch: Treehouse, 1993), p. 113.
3. 'Lyttelton seat', *Press*, 10 August 1933, p. 8.
4. Mr J.K. Archer, Mr P.C. Webb, and Mr J. Mathison were also proposed.
5. Cited in Gee, *My Dear Girl*, p. 114.
6. 'Mr Holland outlines Labour Party's plan', *Stratford Evening Post*, 22 August 1933, p. 6.
7. 'Labour Party's policy', *Press*, 22 August 1933, p. 10.
8. See Sumner Ratepayer, letter to the editor, *Press*, 21 August 1933, p. 6.
9. Practical Sympathy, letter to the editor, *Press*, 19 August 1933, p. 19.
10. Matter of Fact, letter to the editor, *Press*, 21 August 1933, p. 6.
11. 'Labour's chances at Lyttelton', *Stratford Evening Post*, 26 August 1933, p. 4.
12. Homo, letter to the editor, *Press*, 23 August 1933, p. 6.
13. 'Hearty Cheers', *Auckland Star*, 26 August 1933, p. 17.
14. 'Mrs McCombs outspoken', *Auckland Star*, 28 August 1933, p. 9.
15. Ibid.
16. Cited in Gee, *My Dear Girl*, p. 116.
17. 'A warm welcome: Mrs McCombs at Woolston', *Press*, 29 August 1933, p. 10. At another campaign rally McCombs said, 'I am a member of the Labour Party because it is the only party which seems to offer solutions for the problems in which I am interested'; see 'Mrs McCombs at Redcliffs', *Press*, 7 September 1933, p. 10.
18. 'Meeting at Heathcote', *Press*, 4 September 1933, p. 10.
19. 'Women and Parliament: Two candidates' views', *Auckland Star*, 7 September 1933, p. 13.
20. 'Women in Parliament', *Evening Post*, 5 September 1933, p. 6.
21. 'Woman's place: Mr Hills's political views', *Press*, 7 September 1933, p. 10.
22. Tory Englishwoman, letter to the editor, *Press*, 11 September 1933, p. 7.
23. Ibid.
24. F.S., letter to the editor, *Press*, 12 September 1933, p. 15.
25. Offences listed under the Electoral Act 1927 included a person liable for a fine not exceeding 20 pounds who at an election interferes with any elector with the intention of influencing their vote. When this incident was discussed in the House some weeks later, the Labour member for Christchurch South complained that the police action against those wearing the badges was offensive, in breach of procedures outlined in the Electoral Act, and indicative of the way the actions of heads of the police force in Christchurch were motivated by party politics: see *NZPD*, vol. 237 (8 November 1933), p. 99.

Notes for Chapter 6

26. '"Proud and sad"', *Auckland Star*, 14 September 1933, p. 9.
27. Ibid.
28. 'Mr Coates's comment', *Press*, 14 September 1933, p. 10.
29. *New Zealand Herald*, 14 September 1933, p. 3.
30. *Stratford Evening Post*, 14 September 1933, p. 5.
31. 'The Lyttelton result', *Press*, 14 September 1933, p. 8.
32. Ibid.
33. 'The first woman member: Mrs McCombs deserves the honour', *Stratford Evening Post*, 14 September 1933, p. 5.
34. '"Undoubted capacity"', *Evening Post*, 14 September 1933, p. 12.
35. Ibid.
36. Ibid.
37. As the Standing Orders required three weeks' notice for any resolution, councillor Rosser requested permission to move without notice that the Auckland City Council forward its congratulation to Mrs McCombs. Councillor Donaldson moved (seconded by Councillor Ellen Melville), that Rosser be given permission to move the motion. The mayor called for a show of hands and although 15 votes for and only six voted against, the mayor declared the motion lost as the Standing Orders required that such action be agreed by not less than three quarters of the members present; see 'Permission denied', *New Zealand Herald*, 15 September 1933, p. 12.
38. 'The lesson at Lyttelton', *Stratford Evening Post*, 14 September 1933, p. 4.
39. Arthur Stallworthy, *NZPD*, vol. 236 (5 October 1933), p. 323.
40. James Hargest, *NZPD*, vol. 236 (4 October 1933), p. 273.
41. In an interview earlier that day McCombs had explained she had never worn a hat during her many attendances at local body meetings and had every intention of continuing that convenient practice in the Chamber.
42. 'Enter Madame: Mrs McCombs' day. Opening of Parliament. Universal welcome', *Auckland Star*, 22 September 1933, p. 3.
43. Lord Bledisloe, *NZPD*, vol. 236 (21 September 1933), p. 1.
44. The oath of allegiance by affirmation omits any reference to God.
45. 'Mrs McCombs speaks. Rejoicing in Heaven', *Evening Post*, 22 September 1933, p. 11.
46. 'Her first day: Entering House. Mrs McCombs' impressions', *Auckland Star*, 22 September 1933, p. 5.
47. George Forbes, *NZPD*, vol. 236 (26 September 1933), p. 43.
48. Harry Holland, *NZPD*, vol. 236 (26 September 1933), p. 46.
49. Daniel Sullivan, *NZPD*, vol. 236 (26 September 1933), p. 46.
50. 'Reception to Mrs McCombs, MP', *Evening Post*, 22 September 1933, p. 11.
51. 'First Women MP', *Evening Post*, 27 September 1933, p. 13.
52. Elizabeth McCombs, *NZPD*, vol. 236 (27 September 1933), p. 96.
53. 'Maiden speech: Mrs McCombs' success. Excellent impression', *New Zealand Herald*, 29 September 1933, p. 11.
54. Elizabeth McCombs, *NZPD*, vol. 236 (28 September 1933), p. 156.

55. 'Maiden speech: Mrs McCombs' success', p. 11.
56. Elizabeth McCombs, *NZPD*, vol. 236 (28 September 1933), p. 161.
57. Mr Forbes, *NZPD*, vol. 236 (28 September 1933), p. 161.
58. 'Maiden speech: Mrs McCombs' success', p. 11.
59. Edwin (Ted) Howard, *NZPD*, vol. 236 (28 September 1933), p. 169.
60. Harold Dickie, *NZPD*, vol. 236 (28 September 1933), pp. 201–02.
61. 'First speech in House', *Press*, 29 September 1933, p. 12.
62. 'Mrs E.R. McCombs: Her first speech', *Evening Post*, 29 September 1933, p. 7.
63. 'Day in Parliament', *Auckland Star*, 29 September 1933, p. 8.
64. 'Work for the Cabinet', *Press*, 2 October 1933, p. 12.
65. The Free Place system was introduced by the Liberal Government in 1903 as a means of extending access to secondary education to all socioeconomic classes.
66. Advertisements, *Press*, 3 October 1933, p. 8.
67. 'Welcome to Mrs McCombs, MP', *Evening Post*, 7 October 1933, p. 18.
68. 'Mrs McCombs guest', *Evening Post*, 26 October 1933, p. 15.
69. 'A red suitcase', *Evening Post*, 24 October 1933, p. 11.
70. 'A complimentary social', *Press*, 23 October 1933, p. 10.
71. 'Women's Institutes', *Patea Mail*, 9 October 1933, p. 4.
72. Jessie Mackay, 'Women in 1933: A retrospective', *Auckland Star*, 30 December 1933, p. 11.
73. Elizabeth McCombs, *NZPD*, vol. 236 (4 October 1933), p. 256.
74. Elizabeth McCombs, *NZPD*, vol. 238 (5 July 1934), p. 179.
75. Elizabeth McCombs, *NZPD*, vol. 236 (6 October 1933), pp. 364, 366.
76. Elizabeth McCombs, *NZPD*, vol. 238 (20 July 1934), pp. 604, 605.
77. Elizabeth McCombs, *NZPD*, vol. 238 (14 July 1934), p. 631.
78. Elizabeth McCombs, *NZPD*, vol. 238 (17 July 1934), p. 468.
79. Elizabeth McCombs, *NZPD*, vol. 240 (18 September 1934), p. 4.
80. 'Wife's status: Marriage to alien', *Auckland Star*, 4 October 1934, p. 11.
81. Alexander Stuart, *NZPD*, vol. 236 (26 October 1933), p. 751.
82. *New Zealand Herald*, 27 October 1933, p. 11; *Press*, 27 October 1933, p. 12.
83. The exchange was not recorded in *Hansard* but was reported by a special parliamentary reporter; see '"Does not make sense": Mrs McCombs' amendment', *New Zealand Herald*, 13 December 1933, p. 13.
84. Elizabeth McCombs, *NZPD*, vol. 240 (11 October 1934), pp. 501, 502.
85. This exchange was in committee and consequently not recorded in *Hansard*; the source is from a special parliamentary reporter, 'Members complain', *New Zealand Herald*, 19 July 1934, p. 15.
86. '"Quite enjoyed it": All-night sitting', *Auckland Star*, 27 October 1933, p. 5.
87. 'A woman's view point', *New Zealand Herald*, 5 September 1934, p. 13.
88. Ibid.
89. Ibid.
90. 'First year in Parliament', *Press*, 5 September 1934, p. 12.
91. 'A woman's view point', p. 13.
92. Jean Garner, 'McCombs, Elizabeth Reid', *Dictionary of New Zealand Biography*,

first published 1998. Te Ara – the Encyclopedia of New Zealand: https://teara.govt.nz/en/biographies/4m3/mccombs-elizabeth-reid
93. 'Lonely Woman Legislator', *Auckland Star*, 27 January 1934, p. 16.
94. Elizabeth McCombs, *NZPD*, vol. 239 (8 August 1934), p. 46.
95. Margaret L. Stafford, letter to the editor, *Evening Post*, 21 July 1934, p. 8.
96. 'Parliament', *Bay of Plenty Times*, 24 September 1934, p. 3.
97. 'Abrupt departure: Natives and Parliament', *Northern Advocate*, 24 September 1934, p. 2.
98. '"Too much made of it": Native Minister's view', *Auckland Star*, 22 September 1934, p. 10.
99. 'Incident in House', *New Zealand Herald*, 25 September 1934, p. 11.
100. Ibid.
101. 'Mrs McCombs, MP: Strain of long hours', *Evening Post*, 23 April 1935, p. 10.
102. 'Career ends', *Auckland Star*, 7 June 1935, p. 8.
103. 'Death of Mrs McCombs', *Press*, 8 June 1935, p. 14.
104. Ibid.
105. Ibid.
106. 'Death of Mrs J. McCombs, MP', *Akaroa Mail and Banks Peninsula Advertiser*, 11 June 1935, p. 2.
107. 'Death of Mrs McCombs', *Press*, 8 June 1935, p. 14.
108. 'Mrs E.R. McCombs: Reception by women's organisations', *Press*, 14 November 1933, p. 2.
109. 'Women councillors', *Northern Advocate*, 3 May 1923, p. 4.

CONCLUSION
The 'ungallantly long hesitation'
1. William Reeves, *NZPD*, vol. 83 (11 July 1894), p. 408.
2. The United–Reform coalition government amended the Electoral Act in 1934 to extend the parliamentary term to four years but after the 1935 general election it was again reduced to three years.
3. A sixth woman, Elizabeth Hotchkin, announced her intention to stand for the Democrat Party following a request by 200 voters in the Hurunui electorate, but withdrew from the contest before the election was held.
4. As part of her manifesto, Elizabeth Gilmer advanced 10 reasons why some women should be in Parliament: 'Nearly half the population are of our sex and Parliament cannot be complete without their direct representation; Women are taxpayers and "taxation without representation" is a glaring injustice; There can be no true democracy without the inclusion of women; It is recognised by all educationists and thinking men that women's mental power of intuition is of great value and should not be neglected; That laws and administration which directly affect women and children should have the full consideration of women in Parliament; That in several countries women have demonstrated their fitness to be on public bodies and in Parliament; That women's presence is more likely to

raise than to lower the tone of Parliament; That educated women of experience have as much concern for financial stability as men; That New Zealand should advance from its backward state; That the attitude of the National and Labour Parties in having no women candidates is a sad reflection when we think of how they look for women's support': 'Women in Parliament: Reasons why', *Evening Post*, 6 November 1935, p. 10.

5. Before her marriage, Rehutai Maihi was known throughout the North as Nell Nathan; after her marriage in 1933 she was known as Mrs Nellie Gilberd. She campaigned under her birth name Rehutai Maihi; see 'Another barrier down: Maori woman in politics', *Northern Advocate*, 11 November 1935, p. 6.

6. See 'Woman mentioned: Northern Maori seat', *Northern Advocate*, 12 April 1935, p. 6.

7. This would be the first general election contested by the recently formed ultra-conservative Democrat Party. However, before the party had even determined its final policy points for the election and published a full list of candidates, there were already signs that this would be the only election it would contest. The entrance of a third party in the parliamentary election campaign risked splitting the vote to the advantage of the Labour Party. Seeking to avoid this possibility, a section of the local executive resigned from the party. The party received 7.8% of the vote and gained no seats.

8. Mrs W.J. Hunter had been announced as a likely candidate for the National Party in the Christchurch East seat but after giving the matter 'earnest consideration' she had decided not to stand; see 'Christchurch East Seat', *Press*, 8 October 1935, p. 12. Likewise, Mrs W. Mackey was announced as the National Government candidate for Christchurch South but withdrew her candidature before the nominations closed; see 'Dominion Gossip', *Waikato Independent*, 26 October 1935, p. 6.

9. 'Women in politics', *Evening Post*, 23 October 1935, p. 10.

10. See 'Northern Maori. Woman candidate', *New Zealand Herald*, 21 November 1935, p. 13.

11. There was a separate election process for the four Māori electorates and voting took place the day before the general election. No rolls were prepared, and voting was done by declaration. Electors were admitted one by one into a room where the deputy returning officer and his assistant sat. The elector gave their name, age, tribe, subtribe, place of residence and whether they were on any European electoral roll. The name of the selected candidate was written on the voting paper and witnessed by the assistant returning officer, and the votes were counted in the usual manner. Rolls were compiled for the Māori electorates from 1949.

12. 'The first shot: Opening of election campaign', *Evening Star*, 24 October 1935, p. 7.

13. 'Election points', *Otago Daily Times*, 12 November 1935, p. 5.

14. See Sandra Wallace, 'Powder-politicians: New Zealand women parliamentary candidates', PhD thesis, University of Otago, 1992, ch. 6.

15. During the election campaign of George Wildish, former mayor of Gisborne contesting the Grey Lynn seat, prominent social worker E.B. Turkington took

the chair and Wildish's wife made a 'fighting address' on behalf of her husband: 'Woman takes the platform', *Otago Daily Times*, 1 November 1935, p. 10.
16. Matanga, 'My lady in politics: Votes and seats', *New Zealand Herald*, 16 September 1933, p. 1 (Supplement).
17. 'Maori women candidates', *New Zealand Herald*, 26 November 1949, p. 8. Princess Te Puea had been invited to stand for the Western Maori electorate in 1946 but had declined the invitation on principle.
18. The notable exception is Sandra Wallace, *Out of the Home and into the House* (Wellington: Department of Justice, 1993).
19. New Zealand Broadcasting Service, 'Today in history: September 13, first woman MP', Ref. 34503, Sound Collection, Ngā Taonga Sound and Vision.

BIBLIOGRAPHY

Primary sources

MISCELLANEOUS MANUSCRIPTS AND COLLECTIONS

Alexander Turnbull Library

International Council of Women: Correspondence relating to National Council of Women of New Zealand, 1896–1926, MS-Papers-3969-1
    Correspondence: Letter from K.W. Sheppard to Lady Aberdeen, 31 March 1920
Legislative Council papers, 1913–1936. Hall-Jones, William (Sir), 1851–1936: Papers, MS-Group-0532
    Letter from Kate Sheppard, 4 February 1919, MS-Papers-5755-68
National Council of Women of New Zealand Records, MS-Group-0225
    Constitution and conference minutes, Minutes of the first meeting, April 1896, MS-Papers-1371-106
    Minutes of annual meetings and conferences, 29 September 1921, MS-Papers-1371-126
    Minutes, Fourth Annual Conference, 17 September 1923, MS-Papers-1371-126
    President's Address (Mrs Kate Sheppard), 1919, MS-Papers-1371-107
    President's Address, Fourth Annual Conference, 17 September 1923, MS-Papers-1371-126
    Reform in Government. Paper read by Mrs Sheppard before the NCW, MS-Papers-1371-106
    Report of Tenth Annual Conference, Wellington, March 1933. MS-Papers-1371-109

Canterbury Museum Library

Kate W. Sheppard Correspondence 1893, Box 1:
    Folder 5, Item 215, Letter from Mary Müller to Mrs Sheppard, 5 October 1893
Kate W. Sheppard Correspondence, 176/53, Box 2:
    Folder 6, Item 248, Letter from E. Hume to Kate Sheppard, 28 July 1894
    Folder 8, Item 295, Letter from Louise Blake to Mrs Sheppard, 21 January 1896
    Folder 9, Item 300, Letter from P.J. O'Regan to Mrs K.W. Sheppard, 25 September 1897
    Folder 9, Item 301, Telegram from R.J. Seddon to Mrs Sheppard, 29 September 1897
    Folder 9, Item 302, Letter from T.E. Taylor to Mrs Sheppard, 1 October 1897
    Folder 9, Item 303, Telegram from R.J. Seddon to Mrs K.W. Sheppard, 11 October 1897
    Folder 9, Item 304, Letter from T.E. Taylor to Mrs Sheppard, 15 October 1897

Folder 10, Item 306, Letter from J. Hall to Mrs Sheppard, 16 February 1898
Folder 10, Item 310, Letter from Mary Müller to Mrs Sheppard, 18 August 1898
Kate W. Sheppard Collection, 176/53 Box 3:
Folder 21, Kate W. Sheppard Ephemera, Item 481, Mrs K.W. Sheppard, 'Reform in Government', paper read before the National Council of Women of New Zealand, 9 May 1902

Massey University Library
Report of the National Women's Christian Temperance Union of New Zealand, Fifth Annual Meeting, Dunedin, 1890, White ribbon [microform], Massey b1770936

Ngā Taonga Sound and Vision
'Today in History: September 13, First woman MP', Sound Collection, New Zealand Broadcasting Service, Ref. 34503

PUBLISHED OFFICIAL PAPERS AND LEGISLATION

Appendices to the Journals of the House of Representatives (AJHR)
Journals and Appendix to the Journals of the Legislative Council
Journals of the House of Representatives
New Zealand Parliamentary Debates (Hansard)
'Venereal Diseases in New Zealand', Report of the Committee of the Board of Health Appointed by the Hon. Minister of Health, 1922
Electoral Bill 1905 (No. 79-1)
Female Suffrage Bill 1890 (No. 114-1)
Female Suffrage Bill 1891 (No. 59-2)
Removal of Women's Disabilities Bill 1895 (No. 82-1)
Removal of Women's Disabilities Bill 1898 (No. 55-1)
Women's Parliamentary Rights Bill 1919 (No. 60-1)
Women's Parliamentary Rights Bill 1919 (No. 60-3)
Women's Parliamentary Rights (No. 2) Bill 1919 (No. 106-1)
Women's Political Rights Bill 1894 (No. 81-1)

CONTEMPORARY NEWSPAPERS AND PERIODICALS

Akaroa Mail and Banks Peninsula Advertiser
Auckland Star
Bay of Plenty Times
Bruce Herald
Clutha Leader (Balclutha)
Daily Southern Cross (Auckland)
Dominion (Wellington)
Evening Post (Wellington)

Bibliography

Evening Star (Auckland)
Feilding Star
Free Lance
Hastings Standard
Hawera and Normanby Star
Hawke's Bay Herald
Hawke's Bay Tribune
Lyttelton Times
Manawatu Evening Standard and Pohangina Gazette
Maoriland Worker
Mataura Ensign
Nelson Evening Mail
New Zealand Herald
New Zealand Mail
New Zealand Times
New Zealand Truth
Northern Advocate
Observer (Auckland)
Otago Daily Times
Patea Mail
Poverty Bay Herald
Press (Christchurch)
Southland Times
Star (Christchurch)
Stratford Evening Post
Taranaki Daily News
Taranaki Herald
Temuka Leader
Thames Star
The Prohibitionist
Timaru Herald
Tuapeka Times
Waihi Daily Telegraph
Waikato Independent
Waikato Times
Wairarapa Age (Wellington)
Wairarapa Daily Times (Wellington)
Wanganui Chronicle
Wanganui Herald
Weekly News (Auckland)
West Coast Times
White Ribbon

CONTEMPORARY BOOKS, PAMPHLETS AND ARTICLES

Fémmina (Mary Ann Müller), 'An Appeal to the Men of New Zealand' (Nelson: J. Hounsell, 1869)

International Council of Women *Report of Transactions of the Second Quinquennial Meeting held in London July 1899* (London: T. Fisher Unwin, 1900)

Mangakahia, Mere, 'So that women may receive the vote', Paremata Maori o Nui Tireni, *Proceedings of the Maori Parliament*, 1893, reprinted in Charlotte Macdonald (ed.), *The Vote, the Pill and the Demon Drink* (Wellington: Bridget Williams Books, 1993)

President's Address, Recommendations for 1889, No. 4. *Report of the National W.C.T.U. of New Zealand, Fourth Annual Meeting* (Wellington: Lyon & Blair, 1889)

Smith, W. Sidney, *Outlines of the Women's Franchise Movement in New Zealand* (Christchurch: Whitcombe & Tombs, 1905)

Vogel, Sir Julius, *Anno Domini 2000: or, woman's destiny* (London: Hutchinson, 1889)

Secondary sources

BOOKS AND ARTICLES

Atkinson, Neill, *Adventures in Democracy: A history of the vote in New Zealand* (Dunedin: Otago University Press, 2003)

Barnett, Stephen, *Those Were the Days: A nostalgic look at the 1920s from the pages of the* Weekly News (Auckland: Moa Publications, 1988)

Bassett, Michael, *Three Party Politics in New Zealand 1911–1931* (Auckland: Historical Publications, 1982)

Brookes, Barbara, *A History of New Zealand Women* (Wellington: Bridget Williams Books, 2016)

Brown, Bruce, *The Rise of New Zealand Labour: A history of the New Zealand Labour Party 1916–1940* (Wellington: Milburn, 1962)

Burdon, R.M., *The New Dominion: A social and political history of New Zealand, 1918–1939* (Wellington: A.H & A.W. Reed, 1965)

Coney, Sandra, 'Ellen Melville, 1882–1946', in Charlotte Macdonald, Merimeri Penfold & Bridget Williams (eds), *The Book of New Zealand Women: Ko kui ma te kaupapa* (Wellington: Bridget Williams Books, 1991)

Dalziel, Raewyn, 'Political organisations', in Anne Else (ed.), *Women Together: A history of women's organisations in New Zealand/Ngā rōpū wāhine o te motu* (Wellington: Historical Branch, Department of Internal Affairs, 1993)

Devaliant, Judith, *Elizabeth Yates: The first Lady Mayor in the British Empire* (Auckland: Exisle Publishing, 1996)

Gee, David, *My Dear Girl: A biography of Elizabeth McCombs, New Zealand's first woman member of Parliament, and her husband, James McCombs, member of Parliament for Lyttelton for twenty years* (Christchurch: Treehouse, 1993)

Bibliography

Grimshaw, Patricia, *Women's Suffrage in New Zealand*, 2nd edn (Auckland: Auckland University Press, 1987)
Hamer, David, *The New Zealand Liberals: The years of power, 1891–1912* (Auckland: Auckland University Press, 1988)
Holt, Betty, *Women in Council: A history of the National Council of Women of New Zealand from 1896 to 1979* (Wellington: National Council of Women of New Zealand, 1980)
Jackson, Keith & Alan McRobie, *Historical Political Dictionary of New Zealand*, 2nd edn (Rangiora: MC Enterprises, 2008)
Lovell-Smith, Margaret, *The Woman Question: Writing by the women who won the vote* (Auckland: New Women's Press, 1992)
——, 'Smith, Lucy Masey 1861–1936', in *The Suffragists: Women who worked for the vote* (Wellington: Bridget Williams Books, 1993), 133–36
Martin, John E., *The House: New Zealand's House of Representatives, 1854–2004* (Palmerston North: Dunmore Publishing, 2004)
McGee, David, *Parliamentary Practice in New Zealand*, 4th edn (Auckland: Oratia Books, 2017)
Nicholls, Roberta, 'Daldy, Amey 1829?–1920' in *The Suffragists* (Wellington: Bridget Williams Books/Dictionary of New Zealand Biography, 1993)
Page, Dorothy, *The National Council of Women: A centennial history* (Auckland: Auckland University Press, 1996)
Ryan, Agnes E., *The Torch Bearer: A look forward and back at the* Woman's Journal, *the organ of the woman's movement* (Boston: Woman's Journal and Suffrage News, 1916)
Shannon, R.T., 'The fall of Reeves, 1893–1896' in *Studies in a Small Democracy: Essays in honour of Willis Airey*, eds Robert Chapman & Keith Sinclair (Auckland: Auckland University Press, 1963)
Sinclair, Keith, *A History of New Zealand*, 4th rev. edn (Auckland: Penguin, 1991).
Wallace, Sandra, *Out of the Home and into the House* (Wellington: Department of Justice, 1993)
——, 'Members for Everywoman? The campaign promises of women parliamentary candidates', *New Zealand Journal of History*, vol. 27, no. 2, 2006, 187–98
Webb, Beatrice, *Visit to New Zealand in 1898: Beatrice Webb's diary with entries by Sidney Webb* (Wellington: Price & Milburn, 1959)
[Wilson, Mary], 'Mother's vote: Has it altered the trend of legislation?' *New Zealand Free Lance*, 11 November 1936, 23

THESES, RESEARCH ESSAYS AND UNPUBLISHED PAPERS

Chapman, R.M., 'The significance of the 1928 General Election: A study of certain trends in New Zealand politics during the nineteen-twenties', MA thesis, University of New Zealand, 1948
Clarke, J.C., 'The New Zealand Liberal Party and Government, 1895–1906', MA Thesis, University of Auckland, 1962

Fleming, Philip J., '"Shadow over New Zealand": The response to venereal disease in New Zealand 1910–1945', PhD thesis, Massey University, 1989

Habershon, R.G., 'A study in politics, 1928–31', MA thesis, University of Auckland, 1958

Kuitert, V.,'Ellen Melville 1882–1946', MA research essay, University of Auckland, 1986

Shannon, R.T., 'The decline and fall of the Liberal Government: A study in an aspect of New Zealand political development, 1908–1914', MA thesis, University of Auckland, 1953

Wallace, Sandra, 'Powder-politicians: New Zealand women parliamentary candidates', PhD thesis, University of Otago, 1992

Ward, Elizabeth, '"For light and liberty": The origins and early development of the Reform Party, 1887–1915', PhD thesis, Massey University, 2018

INTERNET SOURCES

Bassett, Michael, 'Coates, Joseph Gordon', *Dictionary of New Zealand Biography*, first published in 1996. Te Ara – the Encyclopedia of New Zealand: https://teara.govt.nz/en/biographies/3c24/coates-joseph-gordon

Garner, Jean, 'McCombs, Elizabeth Reid', *Dictionary of New Zealand Biography*, first published in 1998. Te Ara – the Encyclopedia of New Zealand: https://teara.govt.nz/en/biographies/4m3/mccombs-elizabeth-reid

https://nzhistory.govt.nz/page/women-vote-first-general-election

Hunter, Kate, 'Women's mobilization for war (New Zealand)', in: 1914–1918-online. International Encyclopedia of the First World War, eds Ute Daniel, Peter Gatrell, Oliver Janz, Heather Jones, Jennifer Keene, Alan Kramer & Bill Nasson (Freie Universität Berlin, Berlin), 2015-11-13. DOI. 10.15463/ie1418.10768

Mogford, Janice C., 'Yates, Elizabeth', *Dictionary of New Zealand Biography*, first published 1993. Te Ara – the Encyclopedia of New Zealand: https://teara.govt.nz/biographies/2y1/yates-elizabeth

McAloon, Jim: 'Governments, parliaments and parties (New Zealand)' in: 1914–1918-online: International Encyclopedia of the First World War, eds Ute Daniel, Peter Gatrell, Oliver Janz, Heather Jones, Jennifer Keene, Alan Kramer & Bill Nasson (Freie Universität Berlin, Berlin), 2015-11-13. DOI: 10.15463/ie1418.10768

New Zealand Parliament: www.Parliament.nz/en/pb/hansard-debates/for-the-record-150-years-of-hansard

Nolan, Melanie, 'Snow, Sarah Ellen Oliver', *Dictionary of New Zealand Biography*, first published 1998. Te Ara – the Encyclopedia of New Zealand: https://teara.govt.nz/en/biographies/4s35/snow-sarah-ellen-oliver

Starky, Suzanne, 'Garmson, Aileen Anna Maria', first published in *Dictionary of New Zealand Biography*, vol. 2, 1993. Te Ara – the Encyclopedia of New Zealand: https://teara.govt.nz/eb/biographies/2g1/garmson-aileen-anna-maria

www.bl.uk/votes-for-women/articles/womens-suffrage-timeline

INDEX

Bold denotes illustrations.
I, II, III, IV etc denote picture section page numbers.

Address in Reply 193
  debate 93, 128–29, 253
Admission of Women to Parliament Bill 1895 62–66
Admission of Women to Parliament Bill 1896 74–78
alcohol *see* liquor/liquor licensing; prohibition
All perfect ladies (cartoon, *Auckland Star*) XI
Allen, James 72
Andrews, Elsie 276, 278
Ashby, Margaret 191–92
Atkinson, Harry 32, 48
Atkinson, Rose 121
Atmore, Harry 193
Auckland City Council 131, 132, 197, 217, 227, 249
Auckland Civic League 132, 141
Auckland Star (newspaper) 56, 91, 178, 196, 199, 203, 204, 206, 208, 209
Auckland Women's Political League 43, 62, 69, 122
Australia, women's political rights/women in politics 63, 75, 80, 106, 114, 116, 121, 155, 173, 221

Ballance, John 22, 37–38, 40, 45, 48, 113, 167, 303n104
Bartram, Fred 196–97
Baume, Rosetta 132, 172–73, 174, 175–76, 178, 180, 181–82, **IV**
Bell, Francis 146, 148, 164
Bennett H.D. 268–69
Black, Helen 276, 277–78
Blake, Louisa 68
Brown, Vigor 156
by-elections
  1911 130
  1913 139
  1914 139–40
  1918 172

1926 198–211, 215
1933 13, 237–50
1935 to 1969 279

Canterbury Women's Institute 69, 101–02, 111
Carncross, Walter 38, 41, 63
Carroll, James 28, 33, 37, 47, 62
cartoons, political **VII, VIII, IX, X, XI**
Charter of the Independence of Women *see* Removal of Women's Disabilities Bill 1896
Coad, Nellie 147–48
coalition governments 140, 145, 172, 231–32, 233, 234, 238, 240, 242, 247, 249, 273, 275
Coates, Gordon 192, 193–94, 200, 203, 205, 208, 215–16, 247–48, 256
Cohen, Mark 60, 197, 273
Colclough, Mary Ann 25, 34–35
colonial government 16
Communist Party 276, 278
Connell, John 35
Conservative Opposition 52, 54, 119
Cooke, Aileen 173–74, 175, 176–77, 181–82, **IV**

Daldy, Amey 62, 69, 81, 101, 115
Davy, Albert 194, 199, 200, 201, 207, 210–11
Daybreak (perodical) 60
Deceased Wife's Sister Marriage Bill 1877 19–20
deputations to Parliament 89, 96, 103–04, 105–08, 115–16, 147–48, 151
Destitute Persons Amendment Bill 267–68
'disabilities of women, The' (Daldy) 81
'disabilities of women, The' (Sheppard) 103
Dominion (newspaper) 134, 153

Earnshaw, William 77, 160
Electoral Act 1893 41–42
Electoral Act 1902 111
Electoral Act 1927 246
Electoral Bill 1878 27, 298n27
Electoral Bill 1892 26–27, 39–40
Electoral Bill 1902 99–100
Electoral Bill 1905 111–12
Evening Post (newspaper) 50, 203, 210, 243, 263, 268
Evening Star (Dunedin newspaper) 42–43, 56, 93–94
Executive Council 16

Feilding Star (newspaper) 107
Feldwick, Henry 24
Female Suffrage Bill 1890 32–33
Female Suffrage Bill 1891 22, 33, 36–37, 38
Finlay, John 15, 162
first woman elected to Parliament 9, 13–14, 246–50
  see also McCombs, Elizabeth
Fish, Henry 22, 31–32, 35, 36–37
Fisher, George 89–90, 90–91
Foljambe, Arthur *see* Governor Liverpool
Forbes, George 229, 251, 252
Fox, William 18
France, women's political rights 154–55
Fraser, Alfred 108
Fraser, Peter 155, 163, 223, 224, 227, 256
Free Lance (newspaper) **VII, IX, X**
Freeman, Frederick 238, 243–44, 246
Fulton, James 38–39

General Assembly 16, 17, 62, 83
  see also House of Representatives, New Zealand; Legislative Council
general elections
  1853 16
  1890 22, 48
  1893 41–42, 43, 48, 57
  1896 79
  1899 88
  1902 102
  1905 114, 119
  1908 119, 125–26
  1911 126, 127–29
  1914 139
  1919 156, 172–84

1922 184–92
1925 13, 192–98
1928 13 211–29
1931 229–35
1935 275, 276–79
1935 to 1969 279
Gillies, Thomas 25
Gilmer, Elizabeth 276–77, 278, 325n4
glossary of political terms 283–85
Governor Liverpool 133, 141
Great Depression 230, 272, 275–76
Gunson, James 198, 199, 200, 201, 203, 205, 207, 209, **XII**

Hall-Jones, William 146–47, 150
Hall, John 25–26, 32–33, 36–37, 38, 39–40, 84, 113, 116
Hastings Standard (newspaper) 101, 107
Hatton, Marion 59
Herbert, Anne 185, 186, 187, 188, 189, 190, **IV**
Hill, H. 98–99
Hills, Edward 238, 244, 245, 246
Hogg, Alexander 55, 79
Holland, Harry 155, 163, 172, 189, 190, 223, 224, 225, 226, 237–38, 239, 247, 252–53
Hospitals and Charitable Aid Boards Election Bill 1901 96–97
House of Representatives, New Zealand 16
  Electoral Bill 26, 27
  first woman to be elected 13–14, 246–50, 272–73
  Legislative Council, rivalry with 93, 161–63, 169
  New Zealand Constitution Act 1852 10
  opposition to women's admission 29, 30, 41, 49, 100
  Parliamentary Disabilities of Women Abolition Bill 51
  petitions 25–26, 35, 36, 50, 62, 99, 103
  Qualification of Electors Act 1879 25
  support for women's admission 62, 71, 113, 154, 159
  women's desire for admission, questioning of 93, 160
  women's right to sit 33, 38, 45, 93, 154, 159–60, 165–66

Index

women members, list of 291–94
see also support/advocacy for women in Parliament *and* opposition to women in Parliament
Howard, Mabel 280
Howard, Ted 255, 271–72

immigration 218, 219
Independent Labour members/candidates 22, 146, 181–82, 213, 217 223, 226, 238, 272
see also Labour Party; *specific individuals*
Independent Liberal members/candidates 51, 52, 55, 74, 77, 78, 89–90, 92, 102, 105, 106, 174, 177, 181
see also Liberal Party; *specific individuals*
Independent Political Labour League 114
Independent Reform candidates 156, 185, 187, 188–89, 203, 209, 216, 217
influenza pandemic 143–44, 168–69
International Council of Women 68–69, 86–87, 115, 182, 192
international women's political rights 154–55, 191
   Australia 63, 75, 80, 106, 114, 116, 121, 155, 173, 221
   France 154–55
   United Kingdom 116, 121, 144, 165, 182, 192
   United States of America 63, 116, 154
Invalid Pensions Bill 259–60

Jones, George 165

Labour Party 127, 129
   1919 general election 172, 181
   1922 general election 189
   1925 general election 192, 194, 195–96
   1926 by-election 198, 202, 208, 209, 210
   1928 general election 212, 217, 218, 223–24
   1933 by-election 13, 237–38, 238–39, 242
   emergence 142–43
   first Māori member of Parliament, view on 279

gift to Elizabeth McCombs 258
Women's Parliamentary Rights Bill 1919 155
Lady Liverpool 133
Lee, John 215, 227
legislation
   Admission of Women to Parliament Bill 1895 62–66
   Admission of Women to Parliament Bill 1896 74–78
   Deceased Wife's Sister Marriage Bill 1877 19–20
   Destitute Persons Amendment Bill 267–68
   Electoral Act 1893 41–42
   Electoral Act 1902 111
   Electoral Act 1927 246
   Electoral Bill 1878 27, 298n27
   Electoral Bill 1892 26–27, 39–40
   Electoral Bill 1902 99–100
   Electoral Bill 1905 111–12
   Female Suffrage Bill 1890 32–33
   Female Suffrage Bill 1891 22, 33, 36–37, 38
   Hospitals and Charitable Aid Boards Election Bill 1901 96–97
   Invalid Pensions Bill 259–60
   Legislative Council Amendment Bill 1918 144–49
   Legislative Council Bill 1914 134–37
   Legislative Council Election Bill 1907 117–18
   Legislature Amendment Bill (No. 2) 1914 137–39
   Marriage Amendment Bill 260
   New Zealand Constitution Act 1852 10, 15, 16, 161
   Parliamentary Disabilities of Women Abolition Bill 1894 50–56, 57, 60
   Removal of Women's Disabilities Bill 1895 67–68
   Removal of Women's Disabilities Bill 1896 71–74
   Removal of Women's Disabilities Bill 1898 85–87
   Removal of Women's Disabilities Bill 1899 87–89
   Removal of Women's Disabilities Bill 1900 89–94

Women's Parliamentary Rights Bill
    1919 150–51, 153, 156–163,
    165–66, 169
Women's Parliamentary Rights (No. 2)
    Bill 1919 164–66
Women's Political Rights Bill 1894 57–
    61
Women's Suffrage Bill 1887 25, 28–30
Women's Suffrage Bill 1890 35
Women's Suffrage Bill 1892 39
Women's Suffrage Bill 1893 41
Legislative Council
    abolition 96, 218, 279
    appointment to, system of 16, 48,
        134–35, 145, 162, 211, 215
    blocking of legislation 20, 39, 45, 71,
        138, 147–48, 158–59
    Deceased Wife's Sister Marriage Bill
        1877 20
    Electoral Bill 1893, passing of 41
    Elizabeth McComb's first day in
        Parliament 251, 252
    Female Suffrage Bill 1891 38–39
    House of Representatives, rivalry
        with 93, 161–63, 169
    Kate Sheppard's description of 99
    New Zealand Constitution Act
        1852 16
    Parliamentary Disabilities of Women
        Abolition Bill 51
    petitions 40, 62, 99, 103
    privileges and infringements to 158,
        159, 161, 163–64, 166
    reform of, need for 117–18, 134–36,
        166
    Removal of Women's Disabilities
        Bill 71
    women's desire to be appointed 38,
        160, 164, 279
    women's right to be appointed 15,
        146–47, 162, 279
    women's appointment to, support
        for 31, 48, 51, 100, 117–18,
        135–36, 144, 145, 150, 157, 159,
        160, 164, 182, 211, 279
    Women's Parliamentary Rights Bill
        1919 151
    see also specific members
Legislative Council Amendment Bill
    1918 144–49

Legislative Council Bill 1914 134–37
Legislative Council Election Bill 1907 117–
    18
Legislature Amendment Bill (No. 2)
    1914 137–39
Liberal Government/Ministry 48–49, 53,
    56, 96, 167
1890 general election 48
1893 general election 41–42, 48
1899 general election 88–89
1905 general election 114
1908 general election 119, 125–26
1911 general election 126
Electoral Bill 1893 41
first 22
Legislative Council Election Bill
    1907 117
Liberal–Labour Federation 102
no confidence vote 128–29
Liberal Party 57, 74, 84, 89, 102, 119,
    125–26, 127, 145, 172, 181, 189,
    192–93, 301n2
    see also National Party
Liberal philosophy 31, 52
Liberal–Labour Federation 102, 119, 126
Liberal–Labour politics 119
Liberalism 49, 84, 87, 89, 193–94
liquor/liquor licensing 19, 35, 102, 178,
    261
    see also prohibition
Lord Bledisloe 250, 251
Lower House see House of
    Representatives, New Zealand
Lunday, Kate 59
Lyttelton Times (newspaper) 104–05, 112,
    113, 121

MacGregor, John 158, 159
Mackay, Jessie 209
Mackenzie, Thomas 75, 129
Mackintosh, James 37
Maguire, Emily 13, 212, 213–14, 214–15,
    219–20, 226, 227, 228, **VI**, **XII**
Maihi, Rehutai 276, 277
Manders, Henry 29
Mangakahia, Meri 40
Māori conscription 140–41
Māori electorates 15, 17
Māori members of Parliament, views
    of 28, 33, 53–54, 160, 165

Index

Maori Parliament (Te Kotahitanga) 40–41, 53
Māori view on women's roles 160, 165, 268–69
Māori women
  activism 10–11, 40–41, 61
  elected to Parliament 279–80
  Parliamentary candidates 276, 277, 279
  Parliamentary Disabilities of Women Abolition Bill 51–52, 53–54
  political rights 40–41, 51–52, 53, 160
Māori women's parliament 11, 61
Marriage Amendment Bill 260
married women's property 19, 22, 23, 33–34, 297n7
Massey, William
  1905 general election 119
  1911 general election 127
  1919 general election 180–81
  1922 general election 188–89
  death 192
  Ellen Melville (1919 general election) 180–81
  leader of the Opposition 126, 128
  leadership style 139
  Legislative Council Amendment Bill 1918 144, 146, 148
  no confidence vote, 1912 129
  women's admission to Parliament, views on 54, 135, 153
  Women's Parliamentary Rights Bill 1919 153, 160
  World War I 133, 134
Matanga 9
McCombs, Elizabeth **V**
  1928 general election 212, 218–19, 228
  1931 election 230, 234, 235
  1933 by-election 13, 237–38, 239–43, 244–45, 246–50, 272–73
  career in Parliament 256–69
  death/funeral 270–72
  first day in Parliament 250–53
  health 266, 267, 269–70
  maiden speech 9, 13–14, 254–56
  physical/mental demands of Parliament 265–67
McCombs, Jim 13, 137–39, 144, 145–46, 148–49, 156, 157, 160, 161, 237, 252–53, 272, **II**

McKenzie, Roderick 64, 92
McLachlan, John 75, 92
McLaren, Eva 68–69
McNab, Robert 96, 105, 115–16
McVicar, Annie 185–86, 187, 188, 189, 190, 253, **VI**
Melville, Ellen 131–32, **III, XII**
  1919 election 172–73, 174–75, 176, 177–78, 179–82
  1922 election 185, 187, 188–89, 190–91
  1925 election 194–98
  1926 by-election 198–99, 200, 201–09
  1928 election 212, 215–17, 220–22, 226–27, 228
  1931 election 230–31, 232–34, 235, 236
  Auckland City Council 131–32, 227
  Auckland Civic League 141
  deputations to Parliament 151
  Elizabeth McCombs, telegram to 248
  Legislative Council Bill 1914 136
  National Council of Women 152, 171
  overseas trip (1924) 191–92
  Women's Christian Temperance Union convention 143
  Women's Parliamentary Rights Bill 1919 166
'Men's rights and women's claims' (Hill) 98–99
Michel, Henry 164–65
Mill, John Stuart 19
Mills, Charles 78
Mrs Baume to Miss Melville (cartoon, *Free Lance*) **X**
Müller, Mary 20–21, 33–34, 85
Municipal Corporations Act 19
Munro, H.W. 269

National Council of Women of New Zealand (NCW) 68–70, 77, 80–81, 86–87, 93
  1922 general election 184–85
  1928 general election 228
  conferences/conventions 13, 80, 81, 84, 95, 96, 97–98, 99, 108–09, 150, 151, 182–83, 190–91, 211, 237
  demise/criticism 96, 100, 101, 102–03 108–09, 114–15

deputations to Parliament 105–06, 115–16
formation 11, 14, 69–70, 150
letter to Joseph Ward 115
petitions 96, 99
reinstatement/revival 150, 171–72, 182
resolutions 191
Sheppard resignation/final address to NCW 151–53, 154, 171
National Party 193, 211
Newman, Alfred 10, 11, 71, 86, 146, 161, 167, I
1899 general election 88
Admission of Women to Parliament Bill 1895 62–64, 65–66, 67
Admission of Women to Parliament Bill 1896 74–75, 76–77
Legislative Council Bill 1914 134, 137
Legislative Council, comment on 158
Parliamentary Disabilities of Women Abolition Bill 1894 50–52, 54, 55–56
Removal of Women's Disabilities Bill 1896 72–73
retirement 185
New Zealand Constitution Act 1852 10, 15, 16, 161
New Zealand Herald (newspaper) 106–07, 181, 190, 195, 206, 208, 209, 221, 231–32
New Zealand Housewives' Union 142
New Zealand Mail (newspaper) 109, 114
New Zealand Parliamentary Debates (Hansard) 14, 45, 50, 56, 91, 193, 254
New Zealand Seamen's Union 214, 224, 225
New Zealand Times (newspaper) 56, 58, 100, 165–66
Ngāpua, Hōne 53–54
Ngāpuhi 53, 277
Ngata, Āpirana 269
Ngāti Whakaue 268, 269
Nicol, Emily 100–01
Northcroft, Hilda 182, 222, 248–49
NZ Truth (newspaper) 13

O'Regan, Patrick 81–82
Observer (magazine) 122, 180
Oliver, Richard 32

opposition to women in Parliament 10, 28–32, 168
1933 by-election 240–41, 275
Admission of Women to Parliament Bill 1895 63–64, 65–66
Admission of Women to Parliament Bill 1896 75, 76–77
Electoral Bill 1893 41
Female Suffrage Bill 1891 33
Fish, Henry 22
Parliamentary Disabilities of Women Abolition Bill 1894 53, 55–56
Removal of Women's Disabilities Bill 1898 86
Removal of Women's Disabilities Bill 1900 90–93
Women's Parliamentary Rights Bill 1919 153–54
Women's Parliamentary Rights (No. 2) Bill 1919 164–65
Women's Political Rights Bill 1894 59
Women's Suffrage Bill 1893 35–36
Otago Daily Times (newspaper) 62–63, 68

Parliament as Dr Newman would like to see it (cartoon, Blomfield) VIII
Parliamentary Disabilities of Women Abolition Bill 1894 50–56, 57, 60
parliamentary privilege(s) 150–59, 161, 162–64, 166, 167
parliamentary protocol 12, 23, 24, 58, 158, 161, 169, 266
Paterson, Louisa 213, 214, 217–18, 222, 227
patriotic organisations, women's involvement 133, 141, 173
Paul, John 131, 147, 159–60
Peahen, Priscilla 61
Peep into the future, A (cartoon, *Free Lance*) IX
petitions 35, 36–37, 50, 94, 105, 111, 119, 123, 140, 168, 174
1922 general election 185–86
1926 by-election 198, 216, 217
Admission of Women to Parliament Bill 1895 62
Electoral Bill 1892 40
Kate Sheppard, by 25–26
Removal of Women's Disabilities Bill 95–96, 97–98, 99, 103

women teachers, unfair treatment of 261
police force, women in 120, 152, 180, 182, 185, 255, 261
Political Reform League 130, 186
Potter, Ernest 215, 216, 217
Press (newspaper) 12, 94, 121–22, 181, 182, 190, 210, 240, 248, 255, 257, 275
Progressive Liberal Association 96, 213, 270
prohibition 83, 84, 102, 108, 177, 178, 195, 213, 221, 228
Prohibitionist, The (magazine) 26–27, 59, 110, 167
proportional representation 152, 196, 210
Protestant Poltical Association 177–78
provincial government system 16, 17, 21
Public Petitions Committee 263, 264

Queen City, The (cartoon, *Free Lance*) VII

Rātana, Iriaka 279–80
Rawcliffe, Connie 276, 278
Reed, Vernon 215, 217
Reeves, William 52, 55, 176, 275
Reform Party/Government 234
    1911 general election 129–30, 134
    1914 general election 139–40
    1918 by-elections 172
    1919 general election 177, 179–80, 181
    1922 general election 185–86, 188–89, 190
    1925 general election 192, 193, 194
    1926 by-election 199–201, 202, 204–05, 207–11
    1928 general election 212, 215–17, 227
    1931 general election 230, 231
    advent 126–27
    candidates, Auckland (1928) XII
    early years in government 139
    Legislative Council Amendment Bill 1919 144
    see also Independent Reform candidates
Removal of Women's Disabilities Bill 1895 67–68
Removal of Women's Disabilities Bill 1896 71–74
Removal of Women's Disabilities Bill 1898 85–87
Removal of Women's Disabilities Bill 1899 87–89
Removal of Women's Disabilities Bill 1900 89–94
Russell, George 10, 11, 62, I
    1922 general election 188
    Admission of Women to Parliament Bill 1896 76–77
    Electoral Bill 1902 99–100
    Hospitals and Charitable Aid Boards Election Bill 1901 97
    Legislative Council Bill 1914 137
    Liberalism 89
    loss of parliamentary seat 79, 88
    National Council of Women of New Zealand 69
    Parliamentary Disabilities of Women Abolition Bill 1894 51, 55–56
    Removal of Women's Disabilities Bill 1895 67–68
    Removal of Women's Disabilities Bill 1896 71–74
    Removal of Women's Disabilities Bill 1898 87
    Removal of Women's Disabilities Bill 1900 89–90, 92
    Women's Political Rights Bill 1894 57–58
Russell, William 52, 53, 92

Sargentina, J. 258
Saunders, Alfred 21, 31, 33, 54, 79, I
Saunders, Samuel 113
Saunders, W. 60
Savage, Michael 196, 269, 270–71
Schmidt, Harold 216, 217
Seddon, Richard
    criticism of 79, 83–84, 87, 98
    death 115
    deputations to Parliament 89, 96, 105–07
    Electoral Act 1893 41
    general election 1899 88
    general election 1902 102
    Kate Sheppard, letter from 83
    Liberal Ministry early years 49
    no-confidence motion 85

Parliamentary Disabilities of Women
  Abolition Bill 1894 55
Referendum Bill 109-10
Removal of Women's Disabilities Bill
  1900 92, 96
women in Parliament, support
  for 76-77
women's suffrage, opposition to 30, 45
Semple, Robert 212, 223-24, 225-26
Sheppard, Kate 11, 43, 84, 85, 169, **II**
  conferences 80, 84, 99, 151
  criticism of women 113
  deputations to Parliament 106,
    107-08
  'disabilities of women, The' 103
  Female Suffrage Bill 1891 38
  National Council of Women 68-69,
    80, 84, 151-53, 154
  petitions 25-26, 38
  'Reform in government' 99
  Removal of Women's Disabilities
    Bill 81-82, 83, 84, 85
  'Some points on the question of
    women's disabilities ...' 121
  venereal disease, views on 183
  Women's Parliamentary Rights Bill
    1919 150-51
  Women's Political Rights Bill 1894 59
Sievright, Margaret 86, 96, 97-98, 105-06,
  109
Sinclair, Keith 17
Smith, Edward 90
Smith, Lucy 110-11, 112
Snow, Sarah 142-43
Soljak, Miriam 234-35
'Some points on the question of women's
  disabilities ...' (Sheppard) 121
Southland Times (newspaper) 104
Stafford, Edward 18
Stallworthy, Arthur 249
Stanley, Millicent 221
Steward, William 66
Stout, Anna 44
Stout, Robert 24, 27, 83
Stratford Evening Post (newspaper) 248
strikes 22, 173, 224, 225-26
Stuart, Alexander 263
Subjection of Women, The (Mill) 19, 34
suffrage, women's 15, 17, 18
  1893 general election 41-42, 43, 48, 57
  achieving 10, 15, 41-42, 47
  Electoral Act 1893 41-42
  Electoral Bill 1893 41
  Female Suffrage Bill 1890 32-33
  Female Suffrage Bill 1891 22, 33,
    36-37, 38
  opposition to 28, 29, 44, 45, 86-87;
    see also opposition to women in
    Parliament
  support for 23-24, 25, 28, 31, 47; *see
    also* support/advocacy for women
    in Parliament
  United Kingdom 75, 121, 144
  United States of America 63, 116, 154
  Women's Suffrage Bill 1887 25, 28-30
  Women's Suffrage Bill 1890 35
  Women's Suffrage Bill 1892 39
  Women's Suffrage Bill 1893 41
  see also international women's political
    rights
Sullivan, Dan 188, 238, 253, 270
support/advocacy for women in
  Parliament 15, 19-20, 23-24, 34, 47,
    113, 167
  Admission of Women to Parliament
    Bill 1895 63-64
  Admission of Women to Parliament
    Bill 1896 75, 76
  Barmaids Abolition Bill 108
  Electoral Amendment Act 1903 105
  Legislative Council Amendment Bill
    1918 145-47
  Legislative Council members 136
  Legislature Amendment Bill (No. 2)
    1914 137-39
  Parliamentary Disabilities of Women
    Abolition Bill 51-52, 54-55
  Removal of Women's Disabilities Bill
    1896 72-73
  Removal of Women's Disabilities Bill
    1898 85-86
  Removal of Women's Disabilities Bill
    1900 90
  Women's Christian Temperance Union
    convention 131
  Women's Parliamentary Rights Bill
    1919 155
  Women's Political Rights Bill 1894 60
  women's suffrage bills 25, 31, 32,
    38-39

Index

Tanner, Thomas 31, 33
Taranaki Daily News (newspaper) 108
Taylor, Elizabeth 212-13
Taylor, Richard 37-38
Taylor, Thomas 79, 83-84, 85-86, 87-88, 112, 114, **II**
Te Arawa 268, 269
Te Heuheu Tukino, Tureiti 160
Te Kotahitanga (Maori Parliament) 40-41, 53
Thames Star (newspaper) 176-77, 181
timeline of political events 287-89
Tomoana, Akenehi 40, 41
trade unions 139, 142, 173, 231, 238, 271
  New Zealand Seamen's Union 214, 224, 225
  see also strikes
Treaty of Waitangi 15, 61

unemployment 22, 220, 229-30, 231, 232, 233, 235, 239, 241-42, 276
United Government 229-30
United Kingdom, women's political rights 116, 121, 156, 165, 182, 192, 314n96
United New Zealand Party 211, 212, 221, 227, 231
United States of America, women's political rights 63, 116, 154
universal suffrage 15, 17, 18
Upper House *see* Legislative Council

venereal disease 183-84
Vogel, Julius 25, 28-29

Waihi Daily Telegraph (newspaper) 177, 227
Waihi Strike 224, 225
Wairarapa Age (newspaper) 125
Wallis, James 9, 19-20, 21, 23-24, 44-45, **I**
Waota, Makera 61
Ward, Joseph
  1908 general election 119, 125, 126
  1911 general election 128
  1919 general election defeat 181
  1928 general election 212
  coalition government, leaving 172
  death 229
  deputations to Parliament 151

Electoral Bill 1905 112
  Legislative Council Amendment Bill 1918 148
  Legislative Council Bill 1914 136
  Legislative Council Election Bill 1907 118
  prime minister, becoming 115
  Reform Party 127
  Women's Parliamentary Rights Bill 1919 151, 153-54, 162
Women's Social and Political League 122
Webb, Beatrice 86-87
Webb, Paddy 137
When The Ladies Get Their Rights (*Observer* magazine) 295-97
White Ribbon (magazine) 82, 94, 95, 103, 107, 110, 112, 118, 131, 142, 167-68
  see also Women's Christian Temperance Union (WCTU)
Whitmore, George 20
Wilford, Thomas 117-18, 171, 190, 193
Witty, George 135
Woman's Journal (magazine) 95, 307n60
Woman's Parliament *see* National Council of Women
Woman's Party, call for 110-11
women in local government 19, 65, 120, 131-32, 136, 143, 173, 174, 186, 213, 214, 217, 227, 240, 267
women members of the New Zealand House of Representatives, list of 291-94
  see also specific individuals
women Parliamentary election candidates 235-36
  1919 general election 172-82
  1922 general election 185-89
  1925 general election 194-97
  1926 by-election 198-210
  1928 general election 212-28
  1931 general election 230-31, 232-35
  1933 by-election 238-45
  1935 general election 276-78
  endorsement by political parties 172
  convincing/empowering women to come forward 172
  first Māori woman 276, 277
  see also specific individuals

343

Women's Christian Temperance Union
  (WCTU) 11, 110, 116–17, 167–68
  1928 general election 212, 213
  conventions/meetings 26, 35–36, 95,
    110, 119–21, 130, 131, 143, 184
  Electoral Bill 1905 111–12
  Franchise Department 14, 25
  Kate Sheppard resignation 43
  Legal and Parliamentary
    Department 111–12
  petitions 62, 94
  resolutions 59, 104, 116–17, 130, 145
  Women's Political Rights Bill 1894 59
  World War I 140
women's desire for parliamentary rights,
  questioning of 18, 33–34, 35–37, 75,
  78, 82, 92, 93–94, 104–05, 148, 153,
  160, 164–65
Women's Franchise League 42, 44, 59–60,
  62, 68, 69, 81
women's independent nationality 257,
  262
Women's International League for Peace
  and Freedom 140, 176
Women's National Reserve 12, 173,
  315n5
Women's Parliamentary Rights (No. 2)
  Bill 1919 164–66

Women's Parliamentary Rights Act
  1919 9, 12, 256
Women's Parliamentary Rights Bill
  1919 150–51, 153, 156–63, 165–66,
  169
Women's Political Club 50
Women's Political Rights Bill 1894 57–61
women's right to stand for Parliament,
  achieving
  passing of bill 165–66
  reasons for delay 166–68
  see also legislation
Women's Social Political League 43–44,
  76, 122, 130
women's suffrage *see* suffrage, women's
Women's Suffrage Bill 1887 25, 28–30
Women's Suffrage Bill 1890 35
Women's Suffrage Bill 1892 39
Women's Suffrage Bill 1893 41
World War I 133–34, 140–41, 143,
  168–69, 263
Wright, Robert 156–57, 171

Yates, Elizabeth 43, 60, 64–65, 301n102
Young Women's Christian Association
  (YWCA) 35, 173, 257–58
Young, Margaret 213, 214, 218, 223–26,
  227, VI